Talcott Parsons Today

Talcott Parsons Today

His Theory and Legacy in Contemporary Sociology

Edited by A. Javier Treviño
Foreword by Neil J. Smelser

ROWMAN & LITTLEFIELD PUBLISHERS, INC.
Lanham • Boulder • New York • Oxford

0306319

ROWMAN & LITTLEFIELD PUBLISHERS, INC.

Published in the United States of America
by Rowman & Littlefield Publishers, Inc.
4720 Boston Way, Lanham, Maryland 20706
www.rowmanlittlefield.com

12 Hid's Copse Road
Cumnor Hill, Oxford OX2 9JJ, England

British Library Cataloguing in Publication Information Available

Library of Congress Cataloging-in-Publication Data

Talcott Parsons today : his theory and legacy in contemporary sociology / edited by A.
Javier Treviño ; foreword by Neil J. Smelser.
    p. cm.
    Includes bibliographical references and index.
    ISBN 0-7425-0957-5 (alk. paper)–ISBN 0-7425-0958-3 (pbk. : alk. paper)
    1. Parsons, Talcott, 1902– 2. Sociology–United States–History. 3. Sociology–United
States–Methodology. I. Treviño, A. Javier, 1958–

HM477.U6 T35 2001
301'.0973–dc21

                                                        2001019742

Printed in the United States of America

♾ ™ The paper used in this publication meets the minimum requirements of American
National Standard for Information Sciences—Permanence of Paper for Printed Library
Materials, ANSI/NISO Z39.48-1992.

For my son
Myles J. Treviño

Contents

0306319

Acknowledgments

Cover Drawing by Bruce C. Wearne

Figures I.1, I.3, 6.1, and 6.2 were produced by Daniel R. Wolf.

Neil J. Smelser kindly gave his permission to reprint figure I.2.

"Parson's Second Project: The Social System. Sources, Development, and Limitations" is reprinted by permission of Transaction Publishers and the author.

Foreword

Neil J. Smelser

It is a pleasure to welcome this extremely valuable collection of contributions to the current understanding of the sociological work of Talcott Parsons. This volume is notable on three counts. First, its appearance coincides with the fiftieth anniversary of the publication of *Toward a General Theory of Action* and *The Social System*, which constitute a most important watershed in Parsons's prolific career. Second, as noticed by Treviño in his admirable, comprehensive introduction, this book appears in the context of a revival of interest in Parsons's theoretical project, both in the United States and Europe. Finally, all the chapters in these pages are remarkable for their quality—excellence of scholarship, insightfulness, sophistication, and faithfulness in appreciating Parsons's sociology.

The title of the work, *Talcott Parsons Today,* is both apt and intriguing. It connotes several possible lines of exploration into his work, all represented in this volume:

- New understanding of historical influences on Parsons's work: Bryan Turner's suggestions that Parsons's sociology reflects an optimistic consensus capitalism in mid-century America; Buxton and Rehorick's assessment of the impact of Weber on the middle phase of Parsons's work (and Parsons's use and adaptation of Weber); Nichols's tracking of the special influence of Parsons's local situation at Harvard on his intellectual strategies as represented in *The Structure of Social Action.*
- Deepening our understanding of Parsons by comparing and contrasting his efforts with the agendas and work of other theorists: Wearne's tracking of the divergences between Parsons and Elias on the problem-historical method and Fuchs on Parsons, Luhmann, and network analysis as social-systems theory.
- New exegesis, elaboration, and extension of Parsonian formulations: Treviño's multileveled representation of Parsons's intellectual career; Barber on the development of Parsons's social system; Gerhardt's explication and systematization of

Parsons on the societal community; Lidz's analysis of language within the generalized media framework; Jonathan Turner's reformulation of structural-functionalism in an ecological framework; and Gould's effort to extract normative principles and guidelines from action theory.

- Applications of Parsonian insights and formulations to historical-empirical situations that have developed in the decades since Parsons's work: Gerhardt's application of the logic of societal community to global developments and Bryan Turner's arguments concerning the limitations of Parsonian insights to the postmodern situation.

All of these readings of *Talcott Parsons Today* are legitimate undertakings, and the fact that all are represented in the pages of this work gives it a special depth, importance, and significance.

Over the years I have given much thought to the continuing relevance, non-relevance, and irrelevance of different aspects of the Parsonian enterprise, though I have recorded few of these reflections. Restimulated by reading the work of Treviño and his colleagues, I would like to conclude this Foreword with a few remarks on this subject.

It appears to me that, both in this volume and in the more general revival of interest, Parsons is considered mainly as a figure in the history of sociological thought (that is, as part of a "legacy" appearing in this volume's subtitle), as a product of his times, as relevant to the understanding of his times (but not ours), or as a person to be "rewritten" in terms of new theoretical developments and empirical knowledge. Gerhardt's chapter appears to be the only positive effort to apply Parsons's formulations—as they were formulated—to contemporary empirical situations and problems.

While acknowledging the importance of all the lines of work represented in this volume, I am also of the conviction that some of Parsons's formulations, *as such*, continue to be directly relevant to framing, understanding, and explaining contemporary phenomena—that is, his work is "of our time" as well as "of his time." This implies, contrary to the suggestion by Bryan Turner, that much of Parsons's work is an expression of a certain phase of capitalism, that some parts of it have general and continuing applicability.

Moreover, my reflections instruct me that two ingredients of Parsonian thinking in particular continue to have relevance for our time. These elements are the pattern-variables and the logic of structural differentiation. Rather than develop a detailed defense of this assertion in the compass of these few pages, let me settle for a few pointed illustrations:

1. Affirmative action constitutes one of the most daring institutional innovations in the United States in the second half of the twentieth century. The phenomenon is notable for its appearance and consolidation in the greatly troubled political decade overlapping the second half of the 1960s and the early 1970s. It is also characterized by a long and embittered history and a partial dismember-

ment after forty years of uneasy institutionalization. I would argue that we cannot understand this complex history without acknowledging that many of its dynamics involved continuing and unresolved tugs-of-war between the poles of universalism-particularism and achievement-ascription.

2. Another monumental development in American and other societies has been the dispersion of the traditional nuclear family into many alternative forms and the resulting revolution in the social structuring of intimacy. We cannot understand these and related changes without invoking the logic of structural differentiation along the instrumental-expressive and affectivity-affective neutrality axes.

3. A third twentieth-century revolution has been the unprecedented advance of globalization, accompanied by apparent threats to the nation-state and diverse reassertions of regionalism and localism as foci of solidarity and identity. We cannot reflect intelligently on these dynamics of globalism without referring to the unprecedented set of economic and political differentiations occasioned by the conquest of multinational, global capitalism, as these have impinged on traditional sources of integration and spawned new ones. The frameworks of universalism–particularism and self-orientation–collectivity orientation bear directly on the understandings and explanation of these changes.

I have argued elsewhere (Smelser, 1990; 2000) that the pattern-variable and structural differentiation formulations are inadequate and therefore unacceptable in some of their particulars. However, if reduced to their essentials, their logic continues to be vital and applicable to our continuing efforts to develop theoretical understandings and empirical explanations of contemporary historical trends.

REFERENCES

Smelser, Neil J. 1991. *Social Paralysis and Social Change: British Working-Class Education in the Nineteenth Century.* Berkeley: University of California Press.

———. 2000. "Introduction" to the republication of *Toward a General Theory of Action*, edited by Talcott Parsons and Edward A. Shils. New Brunswick, N.J.: Transaction Publishers.

Introduction: The Theory and Legacy of Talcott Parsons

A. Javier Treviño

TALCOTT PARSONS TODAY

After a lengthy period of visceral hostility toward, indeed, of outright dismissal of the work of Talcott Parsons, it is today enjoying a revival in the world of sociology (Alexander, 1983; Turner, 1999: 6). Partly as a consequence of the collapse of world communism and the subsequent disenchantment with 1960s-style radicalism (Aronson, 1995), partly as a result of the emergence of the neofunctionalist perspective (Alexander, 1985; 1988; Colomy, 1990), and partly owing to scholars attempting to better understand the theories of Jürgen Habermas and Niklas Luhmann, both of whom were deeply influenced by Parsons (see Luhmann and Habermas, 1971; Habermas, 1981; Luhmann, 1995), as well as of Georg Simmel and Norbert Elias, both of whom have been frequently compared to Parsons (see Levine, 1980; Goudsblom, 1987; Lidz, 1993; Turner, 1999: 6–13; Wearne in this volume), the 1980s and 1990s brought a major resurgence of interest in Parsonian theory and a plethora of books devoted to a reassessment of his work (see Adriaansens, 1980; Bourricaud, 1981; Münch, 1982, 1987; Alexander, 1983; Buxton, 1985; Holton and Turner, 1986; Alexander, 1987; Lackey, 1987; Wearne, 1989; Camic, 1991; Robertson and Turner, 1991; Gerhardt, 1993; Holmwood, 1996; Turner, 1999).

Other indications of a Parsonian revival include the international conference of June 1997, organized by Bernard Barber and Uta Gerhardt, and held at the University of Heidelberg. The conference, which drew Parsonian scholars from all over the world, had as its theme "A Legacy of *Verantwortungsethik*: Talcott Parsons's *Structure of Social Action* after Sixty Years." Out of the conference came a book, *Agenda for Sociology: Classical Sources and Current Uses of Talcott Parsons's Work* (1999), edited by Barber and Gerhardt. More recently, the summer 1998 issue of the journal, *The American Sociologist* was devoted to an analysis of Parsons's work. And, nearly fifty years after its initial publication, Parsons and Shils's *Toward a General Theory of Action* ([1951] 2000) was recently reissued, this time with a new introduction by Neil J. Smelser.

The project for a renewed appreciation, a reevaluation, of Parsons's work will doubtless continue unabated for some time to come. It is to this project that the ten essays in this volume make a contribution. However, before we begin a preliminary introduction of the essays, some biographical and theoretical background must be discussed in order to better understand them. Accordingly, the following lengthy section gives a comprehensive survey of Talcott Parsons's life and work. Readers already acquainted with his analytical framework and its major concepts may wish to skip this next section.

TALCOTT PARSONS: HIS LIFE AND WORK

Talcott Parsons became the leading theorist in American sociology, from the 1940s to the 1960s, largely as a result of having produced a distinctly modern sociological theory. During this time he created the dominant school of thought that made "Parsonian" a standard term in academic sociology. Thus, any survey of the development of sociology since World War II would be wholly inadequate without an account of the principal role Parsons played in the development of contemporary sociological theory. By the late 1950s, Parsons had taken on a "paternalistic role in American sociology" (Hamilton, 1983: 8) as his theories became the most seriously regarded in the discipline. Accordingly, he became the mid-twentieth century's most celebrated academic sociologist of any nationality.

Parsons's postwar writings not only reflect his own prominence as a world figure, but also the ascendancy of American sociology in academic life. No other social theorist had commanded the attention that Parsons received in the sociological community. As such, he inspired three generations of sociologists, many of whom studied with him at Harvard, and who continued to expand and build upon his work. Included among them are Robert K. Merton, Kingsley Davis, Wilbert Moore, Robin Williams, as well as three of the contributors to this volume, Bernard Barber, Victor Lidz, and Mark Gould. It was only toward the end of the 1960s that his theoretical work began to be eclipsed by more radical theories.

Personal Background

Biography

The youngest of five children, Talcott Parsons was born in Colorado Springs, Colorado, on December 13, 1902. His father, Edward Smith Parsons, was a Congregational minister who attended Yale Divinity School, where he was ordained. The elder Parsons was also an English professor who later became president of Marietta College in Ohio. Additionally, Talcott's father was active in the Social Gospel movement, and his mother, Mary A. Ingersol Parsons, was a suffragist who supported various progressive causes. Thus, the young Talcott was born into a Protestant, social reformist, and politically "liberal" family. In 1914 the family moved to New York City, where Talcott attended Horace Mann, the experimental boys' high school operated by Teachers College, Columbia University.

In 1920 he enrolled at Amherst College, which his father and two older brothers had attended. Like many Eastern liberal arts colleges at that time, Amherst had no department of sociology, and no such courses were taught there at the time Parsons was a student. Initially attracted to a career in medicine, he consequently studied a great deal of biology and even spent a summer working at the Oceanographic Institution at Woods Hole, Massachusetts. Although Parsons was later to devote a significant amount of time to a sociological analysis of the medical profession (indeed, he always hoped to complete a major monographic study of medical practice), he was not destined to become a physician. It is important to note, however, that early in his education Parsons was exposed to the major trends in the natural and particularly the biological sciences. This knowledge of biology would, throughout his career, greatly influence his sociological theory.

Upon his graduation from Amherst in 1924 one of Parsons's uncles offered to finance a year's foreign study for him. Seizing this opportunity, Parsons opted to attend the London School of Economics, where he spent the academic year 1924–25 as a nondegree student. It was at the LSE that he had his first in-depth exposure to the social sciences. Indeed, by the end of his year in London Parsons had received the beginnings of a grounding in sociology and enthusiastically absorbed a wide range of other social science influences. Doubtless, this cross-disciplinary introduction influenced Parsons's later attempt to cultivate ties between sociology and the other social behavioral sciences—namely, clinical psychology and cultural anthropology.

Before completing his first year at the LSE Parsons received an exchange fellowship, made available through the auspices of an Amherst philosophy professor, Otto Manthey-Zorn, to study at the University of Heidelberg in Germany. There Parsons took up philosophy as well as sociological and economic theory and soon developed an interest in economics and the sociology of economic life. In sociology, his main teacher and examiner was Alfred Weber, Max Weber's younger brother. In addition, Parsons took a seminar on Max Weber with Karl Mannheim. Another of Parsons's teachers at Heidelberg was Karl Jaspers, with whom he undertook an intensive study on the philosophy of Immanuel Kant. This exposure indelibly marked Parsons, throughout his life, as a neo-Kantian.

At Heidelberg Parsons became intrigued with the question that launched his theoretical program and that was to occupy his intellectual interest for many years: What exactly is the relationship between economics and sociology? Although he had gone to Heidelberg with no intention of taking a degree, he soon began work on a doctorate. After one year at Heidelberg, Parsons returned to the United States and taught for a year in the economics department at Amherst, where he completed his dissertation, "The Concept of Capitalism in Recent German Literature," on the conceptions of capitalism in the work of Karl Marx, Werner Sombert, and Max Weber. He received his Ph.D. from Heidelberg in 1927 and the following year secured a faculty position in the economics department at Harvard University.

During his first couple of years at Harvard Parsons applied himself to the task of making Max Weber better known in the English-speaking world by translating *The Protestant Ethic and the Spirit of Capitalism,* which Weber had published in 1904–05. Parsons's training at Harvard increasingly diverted him from the study of economics proper and toward the study of sociology. As his interests in the noneconomic assumptions of economic theory continued to expand, this led him into a much wider investigation of social theories, and so four years after arriving at Harvard he was transferred to the sociology department. At the time that Parsons began teaching sociology courses there were only two sociologists on staff, Carl C. Zimmerman and the Russian émigré Pitirim A. Sorokin, who was the chairman of the Department.

Sorokin, who had already achieved an established international reputation prior to his arrival at Harvard, became that university's first professor of sociology and his reputation attracted many who came to study sociology there. Parsons and Sorokin, however, were never on good terms and the latter was quite unsympathetic, even hostile, to the former's work. To add fuel to the fire, Sorokin's graduate students, a brilliant cohort that included Robert K. Merton, George C. Homans, Bernard Barber, Robin Williams, Kingsley Davis, and Wilbert Moore, were increasingly attracted away from him and toward the lowly instructor in sociology which Parsons had become in 1931. As Merton states, "although we students came to study with the renowned Sorokin, a subset of us stayed to work with the unknown Parsons" (1980: 69).

Bitterly resenting Parsons's popularity, Sorokin, in 1936, opposed his promotion to assistant professor. It was only the pressure of faculty outside the Sociology Department that helped Parsons attain the post, after spending nine years as an instructor. Apparently enjoying considerable support in the university's power structure, he was promoted to associate professor in 1939, and to full professor in 1944. That year Parsons was asked to take the chairmanship with the promise that he would be able to reorganize the department. In the fall of 1946 he was instrumental in creating the Department of Social Relations, an interdisciplinary endeavor that organizationally unified sociology, anthropology, and psychology, and that, for over two decades, brought together a noted group of sociologists, anthropologists, and psychologists.

By the 1950s Parsons's work was expanding rapidly as he developed his theories at breakneck speed. Between 1946 and 1956 he published some twenty-seven items (Hamilton, 1983: 42–43). But it was *The Social System* and *Toward a General Theory of Action,* both of which appeared in 1951, that assured Parsons a place in the annals of sociological theory and catapulted him to the pinnacle of his profession. With *The Social System* he brought the concepts of "system" and "function" into greater prominence and usage in sociology.

But what was Parsons, the man, about? Bierstedt (1981: 395) provides a rare glimpse into Parsons's complex character as he states that, on the one hand, Parsons, in person and in personal relationships, was extremely modest, unassuming, uncritical of others, reluctant to mention himself in conversation, much less to talk about his accomplishments. On the other hand, Parsons became the opposite in his writings, claiming for himself many "major breakthroughs" in the development not only of his own theory but also of sociological theory more generally. In fact, Parsons equated his own theory with sociological theory itself.

In 1970, the Department of Social Relations was dissolved, thus ending the great interdisciplinary enterprise that Parsons had begun and had cultivated so assiduously. A few years later he retired from Harvard, after having served forty-six years on the faculty. Indeed, except for one year at the University of Pennsylvania, another at Rutgers University, and visiting appointments at Chicago, Columbia, Brown, Berkeley, Cambridge, and Kwansei Gakuin University in Japan, Parsons spent his entire career at Harvard. It is no exaggeration to say that Harvard became the center of American sociology until the mid-1960s largely because of Parsons. On the occasion of his retirement 150 former students, ranging in age from twenty to sixty-three, and in place from Germany to California, came to Cambridge to honor him (Bierstedt, 1981: 392; Fox, 1997: 395). Although Parsons's departure from Harvard marked sociology's turning away from the brand of structural functionalism and systems theory that he had popularized, his output of work nonetheless continued well into his retirement years.

In 1979 Parsons traveled to Germany to take part in the celebrations of the fiftieth anniversary of his being awarded the doctorate at the University of Heidelberg. On the evening of May 8, the day after the celebrations in Heidelberg had ended, Talcott Parsons died of heart failure, in Munich, where he had gone to deliver a series of lectures.

Intellectual Influences

Although his major at Amherst was biology, Parsons took a course with the institutional economist, Walter Hamilton, and subsequently developed an interest in the social sciences. In addition, Parsons's fascination with political economy was sparked by the influence of another Amherst economist, Clarence Ayers (Ayers later went on to become a professor of economics at the University of Texas, where he taught C. Wright Mills during the late 1930s), who taught a course entitled, "The Moral Order" and instructed his students to read the works of William Graham Sumner, Charles Horton Cooley, and Émile Durkheim. No doubt this reading list served to, at least indirectly, introduce Parsons to sociology.

Both Hamilton and Ayers admired the work of social economist Thorstein Veblen, and both inclined Parsons in the direction of the social sciences. Parsons was particularly intrigued by "institutional" economics, which sought to present economic processes in terms of their effects on the wider society. Because the institutional economics practiced by Hamilton and Ayers relied fairly heavily on sociology, Parsons was exposed to certain key theorists in both American and European sociological thought. In summing up his studies at Amherst, Parsons states that he read Sumner, Cooley, and a little Durkheim in addition to a lot of Veblen.

At the London School of Economics the new "functionalist" social anthropology of Bronislaw Malinowski had a significant impact on Parsons. During this time, the mid-1920s, British social anthropology was undergoing a period of exciting theoretical development. Malinowski and his English colleague A. R. Radcliffe-Brown were the chief proponents of a perspective that emphasized the functions of human cultural institutions as mechanisms for directing basic drives and instincts. Malinowski's functional view of cultures as systems of interdependent parts and his emphasis on the universal biopsychological and social needs underlying cultural differences also made lasting impressions on Parsons, who retained them in much altered form in his own structural functionalism.

Shortly after arriving at Harvard, Parsons, as a young instructor, fell under the influence of Joseph Schumpeter, from whom he gained a sense of the meaning of a system. Additionally, from Alfred North Whitehead, the philosopher, Parsons learned more about the nature of systems. Also of importance to Parsons was Whitehead's advocacy of the notion of the "fallacy of misplaced concreteness." Parsons argued that the positivists in sociology fall victim to this fallacy when they attempt to create theories that are exact descriptions of empirical reality. For Parsons, following Whitehead, the aim of science is not to produce a copy of reality, but to generate meaningful interpretations of its order.

Also at Harvard, Parsons was influenced by Frank William Taussig, who emphasized for him the importance of the neoclassical economist Alfred Marshall, whose work marked the culmination of classical economic theory. Marshall's main contribution to economics had been a theory of utility in which economic activity is an expression of certain qualities of character. According to this theory, economic action is not simply based on self-interest, it is also shaped by shared value standards.

From 1930 to 1934 Parsons worked intently on the economics-sociology matrix, the area in which sociological and economic theory overlap. Accordingly, he read widely in economics, especially the work of Marshall and Vilfredo Pareto, who, at that time, had become something of a cult figure in the Boston area. Aside from Parsons, those others numbered among the group at Harvard that formed a seminar on Pareto, later called the "Pareto circle," were Bernard de Voto, then editor of *Harper's Magazine,* Charles P. Curtis, a lawyer, and such academics as Lawrence J. Henderson, the biochemist; Clyde Kluckhohn, the anthropologist; and George C. Homans, the sociologist, whose first book, cowritten with Curtis, *An Introduction to Pareto,* was published in 1934. The Pareto circle, which met regularly between 1932 and 1934, clearly centered around Henderson, whom Parsons greatly admired, professionally and personally. Indeed, Parsons acknowledged that he owed his sensitivity to the notion of system to both Pareto and Henderson.

Another important influence upon Parsons was Émile Durkheim. During his student days Parsons had two cursory encounters with Durkheim's writings. As mentioned previously he was first introduced to Durkheim in the Ayers course taken at Amherst. Later, Parsons again read some Durkheim in Malinowski's lectures at the London School of Economics. However, it was not until his second or third year at Harvard that Parsons, who was now an instructor, began to seriously read Durkheim's sociology (Bierstedt, 1981: 391).

Parsons's engagement with Durkheim's work provided the springboard for his decisive move into the profession of sociology and, at least for a time, away from his interest in economics. It was Durkheim's concern for the cultural and symbolic processes that make up the social context, and his subsequent focus on values, symbols, and ideas, that became the central theme of Parsons's own work. Indeed, he fully embraced Durkheim's idea that society is a moral entity whose essential characteristic is the body of common values and beliefs. Parsons thus began to realize that the regulation of the market, indeed, the regulation of all economic exchange, is produced not through the rational pursuit of self-interest, as the classical economists would have it, but through the creation of a moral order that controls interaction in terms of shared moral values. For Parsons, then, the discovery of Durkheim provided the key to unlocking the economics-sociology connection. In his later writings Parsons took greater account of the Durkheimian notion of an internalized moral order and was therefore more inclined to view action in terms of its patterning by the processes of internalizing values and norms.

Durkheim's remarkable insights notwithstanding, it was Max Weber who had the most persuasive influence on Parsons's intellectual development. Although Weber had died in 1920, his dominating presence was widespread at Heidelberg when Parsons matriculated there as a student. Indeed, Weber himself had been a student and had later lived and worked at Heidelberg a few years prior to Parsons's arrival. It seemed that everyone at the university was familiar with the work of Weber, and the young Parsons's imagination was fired by his first reading of *The Protestant Ethic and the Spirit of Capitalism.*

Although some of Weber's work had been translated during the 1920s, Parsons, early in his career, was instrumental in incorporating Weberian concepts and methodology into American sociology. With the publication of *The Structure of Social Action* in 1937, Parsons continued his effort to move Weber's ideas into the mainstream of American sociology. In that book Parsons maintains that Weber proposed a theory in which religious and cultural values are accorded an independent causal significance in the structure of social action. Parsons saw in Weber a theory of social action that avoided the conceptual pitfalls of idealism while still allotting significance to meaningful social action. Consequently, Parsons viewed Weber as a voluntaristic action theorist.

In sum, then, the bevy of Parsons's intellectual influences was, to say the least, enormous and varied. Considering that his thinking was shaped by such a large number of diverse theorists, theories, and disciplines, it is little wonder that Parsons's oeuvre constitutes not only a general theory for sociology, it is, more accurately, a general theory for the social sciences and indeed, for the human condition.

THE SOCIOHISTORICAL CONTEXT

A true understanding of the evolution of Parsons's theoretical program—from action schema, to structural functionalism, to social systems analysis—can perhaps best be achieved by situating the development of his work within its prewar and postwar historical milieu. To begin with, prior to World War II American sociology had virtually ignored the sort of theoretical development that Parsons found intriguing in the work of Weber, Durkheim, and Pareto. Relatively isolated from the main trends in European sociological thought, American sociology, during the first three decades of the twentieth century, had followed a course that favored the use of practical facts along with the empirical method of induction for the instrumental purpose of re-solving "real" social problems. Simply put, American sociology before the 1940s was far removed from the formal and deductive theoretical bent that had characterized European sociology.

It is widely acknowledged that the University of Chicago was the central arena of American sociology during the 1920s and 1930s (see Faris, 1967; Kurtz, 1984; Bul-mer, 1984; Abbott, 1999). Parsons, however, departed fundamentally from Chicago-style empiricism, and in Continental fashion, emphasized the role of theory in con-stituting the object of sociological research. Thus, Parsons's prewar theory, which emerged in the late 1930s with the publication of *The Structure of Social Action*, ex-plicitly ignored the predominant trends of Chicago—that is, American—sociology.

In Parsons's defense, however, we may say that his career was rather atypical of a prewar American sociologist in two major respects. First, although he had been in-troduced to the sociology of Sumner and Cooley at Amherst, his encounter with American sociology was not a direct one. As previously indicated, his formal and sys-tematic exposure to sociology had taken place, not in the United States but in Eu-rope. Concomitantly, it was in England and later in Germany that he was deeply in-fluenced by a formal and distinctively macro socioeconomic theory that was largely deductive and highly abstract. (Many of the Chicago sociologists had also studied in Europe but their exposure was principally to microsociology. Albion W. Small, G. H. Mead, and Robert Park, for instance, all studied at the University of Berlin, with Park, and possibly Mead, attending lectures delivered by Georg Simmel.) In any event, Par-sons did not come in contact with the largely inductive and more grounded empiri-cal work of the Chicago School until later in his career.

Second, Parsons's socialization as a sociologist was unique given his placement at Harvard, a university virtually untouched by the main forms of prewar sociology. So-ciology's relatively late arrival at Harvard aside (Harvard's Department of Sociology was created thirty-eight years after Chicago's), that university has long been a vibrant intellectual center in the United States. And with the emergence of Parsonian sociol-ogy after World War II academic sociology's center of gravity shifted from Chicago to Cambridge, from the Midwest to the East Coast. Alvin Gouldner (1970: 145) points out that, compared to Midwestern culture, "Eastern Seaboard culture tends to be somewhat less localistic, parochial, isolationist, and less 'down to earth'; it is, corre-spondingly, more 'intellectualistic,' more national, and more international in its ori-entations. In particular, Eastern Seaboard culture has greater sensitivity to happenings in Europe." Relative to the sociological theory produced before the war, Parsons's was quite distinct in form, scope, and substance. In other words, Gouldner seems to con-tend that Parsonian theory is more formal, general, and conceptually analytical, be-cause it was profoundly Continental and greatly influenced by the dignified conven-tionalities of East Coast cosmopolitanism. And it is precisely this admixture of European and American influences that gives Parsons's theory an international cast.

Let us now briefly examine those sociohistorical factors that help explain Parsons's penchant, especially after the war, for repeatedly underscoring two concepts that are peculiar to his sociological theory—the idea of social order and the notion of shared moral values—and for constructing his theoretical paradigm with such overarching, encyclopedic proportions. Gouldner (1970: 142–44) maintains that Parsons's theoretical concern for social order and moral consensus stems largely from the economic affluence of the immediate postwar years. According to Gouldner, a renewed prosperity, and the social-structural fluctuations that were produced by that prosperity, reduced the likelihood that conformity and social stability would result from people's volitional commitment to shared moral values as had been the case in the more tranquil years before the war. Parsons believed that what was needed to maintain stability and conformity during the mercurial late 1940s was the proper socialization of individuals so that they would be sure to make the "legitimate" choices that society required of them.

Gouldner describes the eventual settling down of postwar America and how this process jibed nicely with Parsons's conceptual desire for order, stability, and completeness:

> Social life ebbed back into more clearly defined structures (buildings, offices, and factories) and into more traditional styles of politics: the daily rhythms of social life once again became routine. To see society in terms of firm, clearly defined structures, as Parsons's new theory did, was now not dissonant with the collective experience, the shared personal reality, of daily life. The new structural vision of Parsons's work, like a leaning tower built of concept piled upon concept, corresponded to a period of social recoalescence that retained an abiding, though latent sense of the powerful potentialities of disorder. The Great Depression had glaringly revealed the possibilities of social catastrophe. But with success in war and the return of affluence, Parsons's confidence in the society seemed vindicated, and he mobilized himself for the Herculean labor of tidying up the residual social debris. Driven toward an all-inclusive comprehensiveness by an impulse to fill in all the empty spaces, he began to seek a conceptual place for everything in society and to put everything in some conceptualized place; it was search for intellectual order that manifests a certain frenetic character. (Gouldner, 1970: 142)

Domain Assumptions

Before we undertake an analysis of Parsons's grand theoretical scheme we must first examine his domain assumptions, or those subtheoretical beliefs that inform that scheme. In particular we will consider Parsons's ideas about individuals and society, as well as his conceptual methodology which includes his notions about analytical realism, systematic theory, positivism and idealism, the subjective point of view, structural functionalism, social systems, and the Hobbesian problem of order.

Individuals

Owing to the fact that Parsons's notion of the individual changed as his theoretical program evolved, we may say that, depending on whether he employed his prewar theory of voluntaristic action or his postwar approach that focuses on systems, he generally viewed individuals in three ways. First, early in his work and from a voluntaristic perspective, Parsons saw individuals as active agents who orient their actions toward the attainment of a goal or goals. In striving for a goal, individuals sometimes take a rational, and sometimes a nonrational, course of action. Parsons views individuals as exercising a considerable degree of choice in the ways in which they pursue their interests, but their choices are constrained by a framework of norms and values that they share with other members of their society. Individuals' actions cannot be reduced to their material circumstances and their individual self-interest, but neither can they be seen as totally irrational expressions of free will. Social actions are neither determined nor free, they are "voluntary." In other words, the means and ends of action are always chosen by the actor in relation to cultural norms and values. It is for this reason that Parsons describes his theory as "voluntaristic." The salient point is that Parsons, in *The Structure of Social Action*, viewed individuals as volitional. That is to say that, for him, people's actions, at least within certain limits, are shaped and motivated by their own desires, decisions, and choices.

Second, with the appearance of *The Social System*, where Parsons began to develop his systems approach, his view of the individual shifted from an examination of the *actions* of the actor to an analysis of the environment of *interactions* occurring with a plurality of actors. Here Parsons takes a highly socialized conception of individuals as he considers the reciprocal interchanges, or the complementarity of actions and expectations, between "self," or *ego*, and "other," or *alter*.

Third, beginning with the 1951 publication of his monograph, "Values, Motives, and Systems of Action," until the end of his life, Parsons stopped considering individuals qua individuals and instead examined their *positions* within the various systems of action. Parsons thus began to regard individuals—along with their need-dispositions, roles, and value-orientations—as being situated at the intersection of four elaborately complex and highly integrated systems: the behavioral, the psychological, the social, and the cultural.

Society

Much like his view of individuals, Parsons's view of society also underwent changes in conjunction with the development of his conceptual scheme. At first Parsons conceived of society as a supraindividual entity—a distinct and independent quantity that must be studied and analyzed on its own level, and not just as a composite resulting solely from the actions of the component individuals. In addition to this he later came to regard society as a coherent whole whose coherence stems from the social integration that is generated by a network of common value orientations shared by its members as they enact patterned role expectations. Moreover, for Parsons, society is a system that tends toward stability and order. Consequently, the paramount and ubiquitous Hobbesian question—How is order possible?—is repeatedly addressed throughout his work. Parsons's focus on the social system's relatively stable order compels him to underscore that singularly important feature that ensures its survival: the social system's self-maintenance, or internal equilibrium. As we shall see, Parsons, partly in response to critiques that he had failed to account for social change, later turned his attention away from social stability and toward an explanation of the evolution of societies.

Conceptual Methodology

In general, Parsons does not distinguish between his conceptual methodology and his empirical methodological research (which in the strict sense of the term is severely limited but not wholly absent in his work). For him conceptualism and empiricism are one and the same and cannot be separated because theory is supposed to guide and structure research. In Parsons's view, theories should be able to grasp aspects of the external world, with varying degrees of adequacy. For Parsons, the primary task of all scientists, including sociologists, is to construct theoretical systems that have an empirical reference and can be empirically tested (Scott, 1995: 34). Indeed, in chapter 18 of *The Structure of Social Action*, entitled "Empirically Verified Conclusions," Parsons vehemently insists that his effort to construct a general theoretical scheme has been an empirical one, and that he has written an empirical monograph. According to him, theories are themselves "facts" that can be verified by the method of "empirical observation."

To be sure, one reading of *The Structure of Social Action* is as an original statement of sociological theory, for which the analysis of European theories provides the raw material of concepts and methodologies. This is why Parsons refers to that book as an "empirical" study: the theories of Marshall, Pareto, Weber, and Durkheim are used as empirical materials for the creation of a new theoretical scheme that unifies the disparate elements of an underlying voluntaristic theory of action as it exists in their work.

Analytical Realism

The conceptual methodology that Parsons laid out in *The Structure of Social Action* was the foundation for everything that he subsequently wrote. Through all the shifts in substantive focus that characterized his later writings, the conceptual methodology which he terms *analytical realism* (Parsons, 1937: 730) remained the constant and unifying thread for him. Analytical realism stresses that "facts" are statements about experience in terms of a specific conceptual scheme that provides a meaningful ordering of that experience. In the final chapter of *Structure* Parsons outlines an analytical-realist methodology that attempts to synthesize positivist and idealist concerns. This methodological approach is the most consistent feature of his lifework and its basis was derived from three major intellectual influences: Alfred North Whitehead's critical analysis of materialism in nineteenth-century physics, Weber's critique of historicism, and Pareto's critique of economic positivism. From these three critiques Parsons concludes that the "facts" of science or history are never simply "observations," but rather classifications of objects using language concepts that various trained observers can share. The "objectivity" of science, then, does not depend on the direct observability of certain properties of interest, rather, it relies on building *conceptual schemes* that researchers can reliably use. In other words, for Parsons the facts of social science are theoretical products: they exist only in relation to specific theories about society, not as universal truths. The abstraction and organization that take place in a science depend upon the particular conceptual scheme that is used. A generalized conceptual scheme comprises "a set of interrelated and systematically organized concepts that provide a basis for selecting and organizing phenomena of experience" (Scott, 1995: 34). At the heart of any conceptual scheme are its most essential elements, or its descriptive "frame of reference."

The *frame of reference* is the most general framework of categories in terms of which empirical scientific work "makes sense" (Parsons, 1945: 44). In sociology the frame of reference is that of "actor-situation," a social system involving a plurality of *inter*acting actors in situations that are partly discrete and partly shared in common. The essential elements of the actor-situation frame of reference are "action," "goal," "affective reaction," and "cognitive orientation." What is more, every essential element applicable to a social system must be referable to a "unit." The unit of all social systems is the human individual *as actor,* capable of action, goal attainment, and meaning. Later in his work, "units," for Parsons, became synonymous with structures, subsystems.

Whitehead had shown, in fact, that as physics developed it gave much less emphasis to directly observable properties, and more to properties involving complex inferences from empirical classifications. As did Weber and Whitehead, Parsons stressed that conceptual schemes, at best, provide selective portrayals of objects. Whitehead had labeled the failure to understand this selectivity *the fallacy of misplaced concreteness,* which is mistaking a partial description of objects for their "essence" or entirety. Parsons showed that Weber's critique of historicism and Pareto's of economic positivism illustrated the same point. Like Whitehead and Pareto, he then drew the "emergentist" conclusion that multiple frameworks and theories can be applied to the same objects without contradiction. As a consequence, Parsons argued in favor of multiple theoretical systems that vary in their degree of independence.

In sum, then, the central contention of Parsons's analytical realism is that a science consists of knowledge that is organized into a *theoretical system.* Scientists formulate propositions about empirical phenomena—the phenomena of observation and experience—and these propositions are systematically interrelated with one another in a logically ordered manner. For this reason, scientific theory is always systemic and general in form. Parsons's ontological assumption is that everything in the social universe displays systemic features that must be captured by a parallel ordering of abstract concepts. To be sure, Parsons throughout his life gave primary consideration to abstract concepts, referring to himself as "an incurable theorist."

A Systematic Theory

For Parsons, the most important measure of a science's state of maturity was the state of its systematic theory. In 1945 he explained that sociology was on the verge of emerging into the status of a mature science with the recent development of a well-articulated generalized theoretical system: the structural functional theory of social systems. Thus, in Parsons's view, theory had to constitute itself as a *system*.

Parsons's notion of sociological theory as a system is that it be conceptually precise in its elaboration and that it be able to make logical connections between its analytical elements and the empirical facts with which it deals—in other words, theory should determine the form and content of the questions sociology should ask. Thus, for Parsons (1945) theory was to be a logically closed system. By "logically closed" he means that a theoretical system has a perfectly coherent logical structure and any proposition in the theoretical system can be derived from and can find expression in another proposition in the system. Thus, Parsons not only developed a theory of systems but a system of theory as well. For him, "the concept of a theory of systems is the most strategic tool for working toward the attainment of a system of theory" (1951: 537). What is more, he attempted to develop the methodological and epistemological implications of a "theoretical system" in social science.

Parsons's analytical realism also recognizes the role that general theoretical concepts play in social analysis and so he undertook the formulation of a comprehensive grand theory. As such, Parsons's theory is limited to abstract conceptual schemes and is thus unconcerned with causal propositions. To be sure, his theoretical analysis of social phenomena is cast at such a high level of abstraction that it poses no fundamental questions about any particular society.

Parsons's intention was to construct a general theory, one that would be universal in scope. This theory is known as his "general theory of action," or his "theory of action systems," and his goal is to specify, in the most general way, all the conceptual elements that permit social action of any type to be explained, in the form of abstract propositions that may be derived through a deductive process. Parsons's main objective, then, was the creation of abstract, general theory that can produce, through deductive reasoning, concrete hypotheses about social action. The theory that Parsons elaborated—that is, the sociological theory that he applied to an ever wider set of empirical areas and conceptual problems in his various works—was intended to be so general that it would be capable of analyzing and ultimately explaining all the components of human social action.

Positivism versus Idealism

During the nineteenth century, positivism and idealism were the two dominant Western outlooks on rationality and individualism in the study of society. Parsons defines positivism as "the tendency to imitate the physical sciences and to make physical science the measuring-rod of all things" (1935: 313). Positivism, therefore, sought an approach to social life closely modeled on natural science. Thus, subjective properties—definable by their meanings to various actors or culture groups—were virtually excluded.

By contrast, idealism (especially as developed in Germany) stressed precisely the subjective, symbolic qualities of humans that set them apart from other species.

Theoretically, the distinctive contribution of historicist idealism is its concept of cultural organization as a system of interdependent meanings. Contrary to the physical systems studied by positivist science, the historicists called attention to the "ideal reality" of cultures (Parsons, 1937: 482–83), whose analysis required a method of *Verstehen* (interpretive "understanding" of a unique system of symbolic connections) rather than explanation by causal laws. In his sociological theory Parsons assumes the superiority of idealism to positivism.

The Subjective Point of View

Another conceptual methodology that Parsons adopted early in his career, and one that he maintained and defended at least until the early 1950s, was the notion that the subjective point of view lends itself to scientific study and interpretation. Put another way, his attempt was to construct a theory of the subjective for sociological use.

For Parsons, ends and values are subjective, not objective, categories. Indeed, as we shall see below, subjectivity informs the very core of the voluntaristic theory of action. Consequently, Parsons maintains that the social scientist should be concerned with the content of the minds of the persons whose action he or she is studying (1937: 46). In order to understand the actions of actors the sociologist must adopt the *subjective point of view*, by which he means that the sociologist is concerned with things and events as they appear from the standpoint of the actor, and not as they might appear to anyone else or to any supposed impartial observer. Parsons therefore stresses repeatedly the meaningful nature of social action and its fundamentally subjective character. The situation in which an actor is placed is relevant to sociology only insofar as the actor is aware of it, gives it a definition, and takes its features into account in deciding on a course of action. A corollary of this view, and one that was to have crucial implications for the voluntaristic theory of action and later, the pattern variables, is that "choice" is central to all human action.

Structural Functionalism

In methodological terms, Parsons's approach to action systems in *The Social System* relied on a structural-functional strategy that was greatly extended during the 1950s. Parsons's structural functionalism and his argument for its sociological use were initially presented in several essays during the 1940s (see Parsons, 1942, 1945) and then illustrated extensively in *The Social System* (1951: 19–22).

Structural functionalism was the preeminent sociological perspective in the United States during the 1940s and 1950s. Indeed, it was so popular that Kingsley Davis, in his presidential address to the American Sociological Association in 1959, took the position that functionalism was, in effect, synonymous with sociological analysis. Although Davis acknowledged that there were several variants of functionalism, he describes those traits most frequently cited as characterizing functional analysis in general:

Functionalism is most commonly said to *do* two things: to relate the parts of society to the whole, and to relate one part to another. Almost as common is the specification of *how* it does this relating—namely, by seeing one part as "performing a function for" or "meeting a need or requirement of" the whole society or some part of it. (1959: 758)

Accordingly, structural functionalism sees society as a *system* made up of differentiated and interrelated structures. In applying a systemic analysis to human societies, this conceptual model focuses on (1) the *functional requisites* or "needs" that a social system must satisfy in order to ensure its survival; (2) the *interconnecting structures* (institutions or "subsystems") that satisfy these needs; and (3) the way that all the institutions reorganize to bring the social system back to an ideal state of harmony or *equilibrium*. Thus, "to speak of the *function* of an institution *for* a society or *for* another institution in that society is a way of asking what the institution does within the system to which it is relevant" (Davis, 1959: 772).

In their examination of how social systems maintain and restore equilibrium, functionalists regard shared norms and values as fundamental to society. Accordingly, they tend to emphasize consensus, or the fact that individuals will be morally committed to the existing social structures. For functionalists, voluntary cooperation and general consensus are what holds the social system together. Thus, any conflicts or disruptions that arise must be quickly and efficiently resolved and mitigated so that the social system can preserve order.

In sum, because structural functionalists, including Parsons, take a holistic view of society, they see it as an integrated system made up of distinct *structures* that perform specialized tasks but that also work together to help the system maintain an orderly state of equilibrium by (1) fulfilling the needs of the social system, and (2) subduing disorder in the social system. For Parsons, the term "structure" refers to those determinate arrangements that tend to develop and be maintained according to an empirically constant pattern, such as, for example, the pattern of growth of a young organism (1945: 48).

In the hands of Parsons, structural functionalism serves to identify three phenomena of a social system. First, it specifies the most important *structural units* of a social system. Structural units are fixed combinations of *analytical elements,* or "general attributes of concrete phenomena relevant within the framework of a given descriptive frame of reference" (Parsons, 1937: 34). Analytical elements refer to general, or universal, properties of a system of action and may include, for example, a certain degree of rationality or disinterestedness in the case of an act. The fundamental structural units of social systems are *roles* and *institutions,* both of which have a functional significance for the social system. Parsons sees *functional significance* as involving the analysis of internal relations (1) between the structural units of the system (integration and interdependence) and (2) between the system and its environment (adaptation).

Thus, the second phenomenon that the conceptual model of structural functionalism identifies for Parsons is that of the structural units' relationship to each other and to the systems' external environment. In this case, sociologists must explain how roles and institutions play an important part in integrating the social system and in adapting it to its environment. Additionally, they must make these fundamental points of reference in the analysis of all other processes. Thus, aside from considering a social system's static structural units, a full structural-functional analysis must also examine its dynamic processes. Indeed, Parsons argues that all scientific theories involve the specification of a static and a dynamic element of the systems they are designed to explain. On the one hand, the static element comprises the structure of the system, the units (which Parsons later refers to as "subsystems") that are interrelated in such a way as to provide a pattern for the system as a whole. On the other hand, the crucial dynamic element is the means of linking the "static" structural categories, and is expressed in the concept of *function* whose crucial role is to demonstrate the importance of dynamic factors and processes within the system.

Parsons therefore believes that sociologists must first describe the static structure of a social system, its roles and institutions, and then examine the dynamic processes involved in the development and maintenance of the structure. He locates the processes of social systems in the individual actors' subjective patterns of motivation. Roles, for example, are maintained only insofar as individuals are motivated, through socialization, to meet the normative expectations that define these roles. Thus, structural-functional analysis must explore the processes of socialization through which motivations are developed in individuals, and it must show how these motives are involved in maintaining roles and institutions. In short, all structures and processes (that is, roles and institutions, motivations and socialization), must be examined when utilizing a complete structural-functional analysis of the social system.

Finally, structural functionalism identifies the structural units' ability to satisfy the needs or requisites of the social system as a whole. As previously indicated, Kingsely Davis states that "function" refers to what a structural unit does for another structural unit and for the entirety of the social system. Parsons extends this notion a bit further and thus for him the function of any component (structure or process) within a system is the contribution that it makes toward the maintenance (stable operation) and survival (continuation) of that system. All component parts that make such a contribution have a specific function in developing and preserving the basic patterns of the social system. Parsons holds that the concept of system implies that all its constituent parts contribute in some positive way and that, therefore, all parts in a system have a function. More specifically, the function of a system's component parts is seen as the contribution that it makes to meeting the "needs," "imperatives," or "requisites" of the system. If a system is to persist over time in its current form, Parsons argues, then certain structures must be present and certain processes must take place. If the structures are absent and the processes fail to occur, the system will "die"—disintegrate—or else be transformed into another type of system. Parsons concludes that all systems that persist over time must, by definition, exhibit a functional interdependence among their components. The correct conceptual method for analyzing systems, then, is to identify the system's needs and to show how the constituent structures and processes contribute to the fulfillment of these needs. Because this third identification of structural functionalism is perhaps the most noteworthy in Parsons's conceptual scheme, we shall examine it later in greater detail.

Social Systems

In Parsons's framework of functional analysis, the concept "society" is replaced by that of the "social system." For him a social system is a conceptual methodology that not only can be used to understand and explain actual societies, it also serves to combine certain analytical elements that are underlying features of social life, to wit, the integration of individuals in their interactions with one another.

Given that Parsons was primarily a systems analyst, the notion of *system* became a key component of his theorizing. He contends that his theory of social systems is an integral part of a larger conceptual scheme that he calls the general theory of action. Parsons constructed his new concept of the social system from his understanding of advances in general systems theory. As previously mentioned, he first became interested in the notion of system in his studies of Pareto during the 1930s, and the idea had subsequently been much elaborated by biologists, mathematicians, and, later, computer scientists. In general systems theory, the idea of the organism as a system of functionally related elements was made into a general principle for the analysis of all "organized" processes. Social life, and human actions more generally, are organized phenomena, and Parsons saw them as prime candidates for systems theory. In *Working Papers in the Theory of Action* (1953) he constructed a distinctive statement of the theory of social systems and system of action.

In addition to the theory of social system, the other three parts, or *subsystems,* of Parsons's general theory of action are the theory of the behavioral system, the theory of the personality system, and the theory of the cultural system. While all four subsystems are interdependent, they are also, however, independent. As a consequence, the theory of social systems cannot be "reduced" to a theory of personality, nor, on the other hand, is it encompassed by a theory of culture. But when we focus on the social system, the other three subsystems become part of its environment.

The most general and fundamental property of a system is the interdependence of its own component parts. Parsons contends that it is impossible to interpret any single social pattern except by reference to some larger systemic whole. Thus, the whole system must be conceptually constituted prior to the empirical investigation of any specific part.

Parsons treats a social system as a "functioning entity." As he puts it, every social system is a functioning entity because "it is a system of interdependent structures and processes such that it tends to maintain a relative stability and distinctiveness of pattern and behavior as an entity by contrast with its—social or other—environment, and with it a relative independence from environmental forces" (1942: 552).

He elaborated his ideas on these interdependent structures and processes on the basis of his earlier discussion of "functional significance" in social systems. Parsons argues that roles and institutions could, within the framework of structural functionalism, be analyzed either in terms of their contribution to the system's internal *integration* or in terms of their contribution to the system's *adaptation* to its external environment. In his systems theory, integration and adaptation became two of the basic functional needs of a system. Thus, for Parsons, functional structures and processes may have an internal or an external orientation. Alongside this distinction, Parsons introduces another: he argues that the functional processes of a system may be *instrumental*, concerned with the means or resources that a system requires, or they may be *consummatory*, concerned with the ends or goals toward which the system is moving. Functional processes in any system, then, can be classified into the four categories that result from a cross-classification of these dimensions. As we shall see, these four functional processes—which he labels "adaptation," "goal attainment," "integration," and "latency"—may themselves be formed into distinct, specialized subsystems of the larger social system.

The Hobbesian Problem of Order

We are on safe ground in arguing that all of Parsons's work, from his earliest writing to his last, constitutes an attempt to account satisfactorily for social order. Parsons's main concern was with the "Hobbesian problem of order," which poses the fundamental question, How is social order possible? Briefly stated, Hobbes had maintained that coercion, or the threat of coercion by the political state, led to a stable social order. By contrast, Parsons holds that most of social order is not coercive but normative. That is to say, for Parsons, the basis of a stable social order does not lie with the external force of the state keeping people in line; rather it lies with society's common value system that obligates people to voluntarily constrain their behavior, to cooperate with one another. Social order, stability in social life, Parsons argues, depends not just on power and coercion, but also on a *normative* order.

Major Work

Throughout his long career, Parsons developed an oeuvre contained in some 160 published items. His major work begins with the publication of *The Structure of Social Action* in 1937 and leads through to *The Social System* in 1951 and then to his final major volume, *Action Theory and the Human Condition* in 1978. Between these books are other prominent monographs including *Toward a General Theory of Action* (1951), *Working Papers in the Theory of Action* (1953), *Economy and Society* (1956), *Societies: Evolutionary and Comparative Perspectives* (1966), *The System of Modern Societies* (1971), and *Social Systems and the Evolution of Action Theory* (1977). While this large body of work exhibits many conceptual continuities, as we shall see, it also "jumps" at a number of points to a higher or more complex theoretical level (Hamilton, 1983: 24–25).

By the mid-1950s Parsons's conceptual scheme combining structural functionalism and systems theory, or systems functionalism, came close to being the overarching paradigm in sociology. Other theoretical orientations certainly existed during this time, but their status was secondary to the systems functionalism of which Parsons was the most impressive exponent. Indeed, owing largely to his theoretical and organizational leadership, systems functionalism constituted the most seriously regarded theory in the discipline. Prior to fully developing his systems functionalism, however, Parsons had initially laid its conceptual foundation in the voluntaristic theory of action.

The Voluntaristic Theory of Action

In 1937, just shy of his thirty-fifth birthday, Talcott Parsons published what is perhaps his most influential book, and the one that made his reputation, *The Structure of Social Action*. Hailed as a work of rare genre when it first appeared, this volume is now regarded as a classic in sociological theory. Here Parsons makes his initial attempt at abstracting from the work of four European social theorists—Marshall, Pareto, Durkheim, and Weber—a single conceptual scheme that would, for all time, serve as sociological theory itself. *Structure* was also the first book to introduce Durkheim, Weber, and Pareto for serious and detailed consideration to Englsh-speaking sociologists, and in the absence of any other English work comparable in quality, it became a standard source.

Parsons's principal argument in *Structure* is that while the four theorists emerged from two quite different, indeed contrary traditions (Marshall, Pareto, and Durkheim were working within the positivist tradition, and Weber was working within the idealist tradition), all of them had, independently of each other, converged toward a similar view of action. The "convergence" that Parsons attributed to them depends as much on their links to the positivist and idealist traditions as to trends in their individual writings (Parsons, 1937: 697–719). Thus Marshall, who was deeply committed to British utilitarian economics, found difficulties in its treatment of ends and was compelled to take account of the concrete wants of people in their daily lives. Pareto, who had come into economics from mathematics and physics, strongly attacked positivistic economics for uniformly imposing common ends and rational norms on actors whether they fitted or not. In later work, he developed a sociological scheme that gave a central place to nonlogical sentiments, which could affect the varying emphases given to economic self-interest (e.g., respect for tradition or the desire for group approval). Durkheim, starting from organicist positivism, developed an argument concerning the essentiality of shared norms for social order. Finally, there was the idealist Weber who posited that each culture had to be understood in its own terms by a method of *Verstehen*.

Parsons intends *The Structure of Social Action* to show that there had been a progression toward a voluntaristic theory of action in the work of the two most significant European sociologists—namely, Durkheim and Weber—who resisted the prevailing utilitarian and reductionist views of social phenomena. Thus, Parsons saw Durkheim and Weber as the most prominent exponents of this new voluntaristic theory, both having attempted to reconcile the analysis of rationality and self-interest with that of norms and values. Parsons's basic tenet in *Structure*, which he derived from his own interpretation of Weber, is essentially that sociology is the study of meaningful social action. In this work Parsons employs this tenet in formulating the voluntaristic theory of action.

The voluntaristic theory of action involves the *action frame of reference,* "the indispensable logical framework in which we describe and think about the phenomenon of action" (Parsons, 1937: 733). Fundamental to the action frame of reference are the concepts of "time" and "purpose." Action is defined by the fact that it is organized over time and involves the purposive use of means to achieve ends. It is in this sense that Parsons claims that action comprises means-ends relations that are organized over time (1937: 732–33). Action involves a state of affairs—and an end or goal—that the person wishes to bring into being or to maintain in existence, and so it can be considered as future-oriented, as concerned with the attainment, realization, and achievement of these goals.

Beyond the notions of time and purpose, the action frame of reference also specifies several analytical elements. To begin with, at its core is the smallest conceivable concrete unit of reference, the *unit act.* The unit act is the fundamental concept of all social analysis, the most elementary form of human action, and the building block for larger systems of action. It is the central "knot" of relations without which action would not have any meaning, to actor or observer. The unit act is constituted of a complex of elements from which all social action is composed. This complex of elements consists of four basic properties: (1) an *actor;* (2) an *end,* or a future state of affairs toward which the process of action is oriented; (3) a *situation,* which in turn contains two elements: *means,* manipulable aspects over which the actor has an appreciable degree of control, and *conditions,* unalterables over which the actor does not; and (4) a *normative orientation,* or those norms, values, and beliefs of the social actor that provide the means for ensuring a minimum degree of social order. Normative orientation, explains Parsons, is the "motor" of social action. It is Parsons's consideration of normative orientation that allows him to focus on the actor's subjective meaning and not just his or her observable behavior.

In short, actors in specific situations are oriented to certain norms and exert a certain amount of effort in the manipulation of means over time so as to attain their ends. The voluntaristic theory of action is therefore a systematic theory of social action, a theory of the relationship of means and ends, that identifies the unit acts from which structured patterns of action are built and describes their features in terms of the action frame of reference. In other words, Parsons endeavors to search for the ways of indicating how social action is patterned into a structure of relationships and interactions.

Parsons's voluntaristic theory of social action states that actors are capable of voluntary action in relation to goals that they attempt to achieve through their *choices* among alternative means. He therefore makes it clear that the theory's frame of reference "is subjective in a particular sense. That is, it deals with phenomena, with things and events *as they appear from the point of view of the actor* whose action is being analyzed and considered" (1937: 46). Thus, in considering the subjective point of view, the unit of reference shifts from the unit act to the actor as "ego." What is more, because social life consists of a system of complementary actions and expectations, ego can only be understood in interaction with "alter." Parsons therefore centers his conception of social systems on the interaction between ego and alter.

The social system which ego and alter constitute consists of two (or more) role players engaged in interaction with one another, conforming to or departing from one another's expectations, having some measure of complementarity in their expectations, so that what ego regards as his or her rights are viewed by alter as his or her duties, and vice versa. This complementarity is, in turn, dependent upon a common orientation to a set of moral values that they share. What makes ego and alter a system is not simply that their behavior is mutually influential or interdependent, but that it contains patterns that tend to be maintained. A social system is and will remain in equilibrium to the extent that ego and alter conform with one another's expectations. The equilibrium of the system is seen as, in effect, largely dependent on the conforming behavior of interactants. Insofar as ego does what alter expects, alter will be gratified, which is to say, in conformity with ego's expectations. Thus, when one behaves in conformity with another's expectations, he or she elicits a response from the other that leads him or her to continue doing so without any change. Parsons calls this "the complementarity of role-expectations."

Complementarity means, first, that what ego defines as his right is defined as a duty by alter, and, second, that what alter defines as her duty is viewed by ego as his right. Parsons stresses that the stability and integration of social systems derives largely from the conformity of role partners to one another's expectations. He acknowledges that the stability of a social system requires that there be some "mutuality of gratification" among the system's members. In other words, for Parsons, system stability depends, in part, on the exchange of gratifications, those provided by one party being contingent on those provided by the other.

His central concern, however, is not with gratification but with the *legitimacy* of behavior patterns, that is, with patterns of action and social interaction that are culturally prescribed and institutionalized. When Parsons analyzes social systems he focuses on the way people's behavior conforms to or deviates from the legitimate expectations of others, and on the way it complies with the requirements of those social statuses or identities that are defined as relevant to the particular social system. In brief, we may say that *Structure* is a study of the structures and conditions that limit and define the freedom actors have to act within interactional contexts.

In closing *The Structure of Social Action* Parsons supplies a definition of sociology that served to guide his work over the next forty years: "the science which attempts to develop an analytical theory of social action systems in so far as these systems can be understood in terms of the property of common-value integration" (1937: 768). Even if it is included in *Structure* only to express the interdependence of action elements or the interdependence of concepts within a theoretical schema, the notion of "system" can be seen to play an important role in Parsons's thinking at this early stage in his career. Thus, as was perhaps foreshadowed by the aforementioned definition, Parsons abandoned the means-end schema after the publication of *Structure* but began a lively and enduring interest in unit-act actions, or *action systems*. Indeed, Parsons maintains that the basic properties of the unit act "do not constitute the subject matter of an independent analytical science. They constitute, rather, the common methodological basis of all the sciences of action, for it is really these basic elementary properties of the unit act in their mutual interrelations which constitute the common frame of reference of all the sciences of action" (1937: 769). In a larger sense, Parsons, in *Structure*, considers the various sciences of action—psychology, cultural anthropology, and sociology—and attempts to produce from them the first definitive statement of a general theory of action. We now, therefore, turn to Parsons's discussion of the types of action systems as described in his general theory of action.

The General Theory of Action

Two main factors compelled Parsons to formulate a general theory of action. To begin with, shortly after the publication of *The Structure of Social Action* he realized that the theoretical aims he had proposed in that book could be achieved only by considering action in terms of systems. As previously indicated, Parsons's definition of sociology toward the end of that volume sees it as a science involved in the analysis, not of social action per se, but of social action *systems*. Moreover, largely as a result of the interdisciplinary collaboration that he experienced with the new Department of Social Relations, Parsons, during the mid-1940s, began to integrate insights from a number of social science disciplines, but in particular, psychology, anthropology, and sociology. These two influences—the notion that action is organized as a system and the attempt at interdisciplinary synthesis—resulted in the construction of a general theory of action published in the monograph appropriately titled *Toward a General Theory of Action* (1951). Here Parsons deals with the incorporation of psychological, anthropological, sociological, and, to a limited extent, biological concepts in his analysis of action; an analysis which was renamed *systems theory* in order to better express systems of action in the personality, cultural, and social spheres. (In the late 1950s, Parsons began to earnestly consider the behavioral organism as a way of bridging the gap between personality and its biological base. Later, he was convinced, by Charles Lidz and Victor Lidz, that the behavioral organism could be better formulated in more cognitive terms, drawing on Jean Piaget's psychology, and it was renamed the "behavioral system.")

Toward a General Theory of Action contains contributions by, among others, psychologists Edward Tolman, Gordon Allport, and Henry Murray; anthropologists Clyde Kluckhohn and Richard Sheldon; and sociologist Samuel Stouffer. Parsons and Shils edited the volume and wrote the four chapters that appear as Part 2, "Values, Motives, and Systems of Action." Parsons was convinced that he and Shils had accomplished "a real breakthrough" in these four chapters; claiming somewhat immodestly that they had produced "an important advance toward the construction of a unified theory of social science." (To be sure, theirs is more a theory of social science than a theory of society.) Broadly speaking, *Toward a General Theory of Action* is an attempt by Parsons and his collaborators to state the relations among three types of action systems—personality, cultural, and social systems.

Parsons considered the personality, cultural, and social systems as the three main interpenetrative types of action organization. Put another way, for Parsons, action has its psychological, cultural, and social aspects, and action systems form themselves into personality systems, cultural systems, and social systems. When focusing on systems of action the unit of reference shifts from the unit act of simple means-ends relations to the more complex frame of reference, the "actor-orienting-to-a-situation." In this case the actor may be either an individual or a collectivity, with each viewed as equally real. Whether individual or collective, action is defined as "behavior oriented to the attainment of ends in situations, by means of normatively regulated expenditures of energy" (Parsons and Shils, [1951] 2000: 53). Behavior-as-action, therefore, includes overt activity as well as the decision-making process that leads to a choice. Action is purposeful as actors seek out and define their environmental stimuli in terms of values and motives. Action includes the alternatives actors reject or defer for a later time and the imagined responses by others to their various action choices. In Parsons's view, each of the three main types of action systems—personality, cultural, and social systems—has a distinctive coordinative role in the action process, and therefore has some degree of causal autonomy. Let us briefly take up each of these three systems of action.

Personality systems are the subject matter of psychology and they appear as the organized *need-dispositions* of individual actors. Personalities organize the total set of learned needs, demands, and action choices of individual actors, no two of whom are alike notwithstanding the fact that the actors may speak the same language and share many cultural values and beliefs. Personality systems are concerned with the motives of action, and Parsons identifies three aspects of these motives: (1) a *cognitive* orientation aspect, which concerns how the actor defines the situation in which his or her need-dispositions are actuated; (2) a *cathectic* aspect, which concerns the gratification or deprivation that he or she receives from the situation; and (3) an *evaluative* aspect which concerns the actor's judgment or interpretation of the meaning of the situation.

Cultural systems are the province of anthropology, but Parsons defines "culture" more systematically and narrowly than most anthropologists. For him, culture consists of norms, values, beliefs, and other ideas relating to action that have been objectified in symbolic codes and can be transmitted from one individual, group, or generation to another. While culture originates in interaction and provides symbolic resources through which action can be structured, it is not, strictly speaking, a system of action; rather, it is a system of symbolic patterns. It therefore serves to organize such patterns into configurations which have symbolic as well as behavioral coherence. Cultural systems are conceptualized as the organization of *value-patterns* that provide the foundations for both the normative structure of the social system and the need-dispositions of the personality system. As we shall see below, in Parsons's later work, where he employs the cybernetic analogy, the cultural system achieves a prominent place in action theory on the "control" level for system change or order.

Finally, social action systems consist of a number of unit acts linked together through chains of elementary interactions that are associated with various "emergent structures." Irreducible elements of human life, emergent structures "emerge" from the linked unit acts but disappear from view if a system of action is broken down into its constituent unit acts. Social action systems are therefore the result of the organization of unit acts into systems. An example of emergent structures at the social level are "common values," which include norms, institutions, and especially, roles. To be sure, in Parsons's later work the building blocks of social action systems are no longer unit acts, they are roles. Social systems have an interpersonal focus and organize the divergent and often conflicting action tendencies of individuals into coordinative forms of relations. As such, social action systems are conceived as the organized interaction or *role-expectations* among two or more actors. In more complex cases, social action systems organize groups into larger organizations through hierarchies or representatives.

The first chapter in Parsons and Shils's "Values, Motives, and Systems of Action" deals generally and in detail with the action schema; the second, with personality as a system of action; the third, with culture as a system of value-orientation; and the fourth chapter outlines some of the major features of the social system. In this fourth chapter Parsons introduces the *pattern variables* that tie the personality, cultural, and social systems together in a "strategically crucial" way.

The Pattern Variables

According to Parsons, the ways in which interaction is organized have to do with the choices actors make among a grouping of variable properties of the action system. These properties he calls "pattern variables," and they constitute a set of five dichotomies that may be used to categorize actors' orientation in the personality system, the value patterns of the cultural system, and normative requirements in the social system (Parsons and Shils, 1951: 48, 76–98, 183–89, 203–4; Parsons and Smelser, 1956: 33ff).

The pattern variables, however, are not only a conceptual scheme for the analysis of personality, cultural, and social systems, they are also a series of "dilemmas of action." For Parsons all action involves a choice, conscious or otherwise, on each of the five pattern variables, and no more than these five variables are involved in the structuring of any social action. As Parsons puts it, an actor in any situation is confronted by "a series of major dilemmas of orientation, a series of choices that [he] must make before the situation has a determinate meaning for him" (Parsons and Shils, 1951: 76). The actor must make all five dichotomous choices (Parsons insists that the twin choices in his sets of variables are dichotomies rather than continua) in order for the social situation to have meaning, and thus to provide it with a recognizable pattern.

Although the pattern variables involve a "dilemma" of choice, Parsons does not claim that actors simply choose one or the other pole of each dilemma. While actions, roles, and institutions do, indeed, involve an emphasis on one pole, they will also require some attention to the opposite orientation. Choice in actions and in the structuring of relations involves giving priority to one or the other pole of each dilemma. Thus, each of the five sets of pattern variables is presented as a binary choice that arises in every social situation and which must be resolved by a clear priority selection before the situation can become meaningful and before the actor can act with respect to that situation. More specifically, we may say that each pair of choices refers to aspects of an actor's definition of roles (e.g., parent, teacher, doctor) or relationships (e.g., familial, friendship, professional). The five pattern variables are indicated in table I.1.

The first pattern variable, involving the dilemma of *specificity versus diffuseness*, concerns the range or scope of orientations that an actor has toward a given interaction situation. Diffuseness means that the actor's orientation involves taking into account the totality of the person (alter) or object. Specificity means that the actor's orientation involves restricting expectations and interests to narrow and limited aspects of alter. In this dilemma the general question is: Should the actor's orientations be broad-ranging and diffuse (e.g., the parent's concern with all aspects of her child's life) or, should the actor's orientations be confined to a specific context (e.g., the dentist's concern with the teeth rather than another aspect of her patient's lives)? In sum, specificity versus diffuseness has to do with whether ego seeks a broad range of gratification from alter or maintains a narrower orientation.

The second pattern variable involves the dilemma of *affectivity versus affective neutrality*, and it covers the emotion or lack of it which is appropriate in a given situation. Affectivity refers to the degree of emotional involvement that an actor has in his or her roles and relationships. Actors involved in action that is affectively oriented are impulsive and emotionally engaged, seeking immediate gratification. Affective neutrality, by contrast, refers to action that is considered disciplined and calculative, the actor taking a purely impersonal orientation. We would, for instance, expect a mother's interactions with her child to be highly affective, while the doctor-patient relationship is more likely to be characterized by affective neutrality. This dilemma has to do with whether ego seeks immediate gratification in the situation (e.g., expresses feelings freely) or exercises restraint toward alter.

The third pattern variable, *universalism versus particularism*, is generated by interactions where the type of evaluative standards to be applied are either general and consensual, that is universal, or ones that are quite unique to particular actors involved. Particularism involves orientations that are subjectively biased in terms of the particular, unique significance that the other has for the actor. Universalism, on the other hand, concerns orientations in which actors structure their relationships with one another by purely "cognitive" standards in terms of which account is taken only of the features that the other person shares with all others of the same type. For example, the father may apply universalistic standards of "intelligence" when interacting

Table I.1.   The Five Pattern Variables

Expressive		Instrumental
1. Diffuseness	v.	Specificity
2. Affectivity	v.	Affective Neutrality
3. Particularism	v.	Universalism
4. Ascription (or Quality)	v.	Achievement (or Performance)
5. Self-Orientation	v.	Collectivity-Orientation

with children not known to him, but particularistic standards when dealing with his own child. This dilemma has to do with whether ego defines alter in terms of a special relation they have (friends, kin), or in terms of alter's membership in a broader status class (fellow citizen, male or female, human).

The fourth pattern variable involves *ascription versus achievement* (later *quality versus performance*) and covers the dilemma posed by whether to assess alter in terms of general performance criteria (e.g., educational qualifications, business success, etc.) or in terms of qualities that are ascribed on the basis of heredity or other forms of endowment (e.g., sex, age, race, ethnicity, etc.) that lack a performance standard. Ascription refers to the orientation taken by the actor toward the other person based on that person's ascribed personal qualities. Achievement refers to the orientation taken by the actor toward the other person based on that person's achievements. This dilemma has to do with whether alter is defined by criteria independent of her actions in a situation, or is defined on the basis of his actions and how well he or she performs them.

Finally, the fifth pattern variable of *self-orientation versus collectivity-orientation* covers orientations of action either to individual interests or to group interests or goals. Self-orientation refers to action that pursues interests that are sectional and roles that involve the legitimate pursuit of private interests. Collectivity-orientation refers to action that pursues interests that are communal and roles that involve the pursuit of the common interests of the group or wider society. For example, should the actor on a sinking ship save himself or seek to ensure that others are helped to safety?

The first two pattern variables form a pair, the second two another pair, and because the scheme is one of "symmetrical asymmetry," the fifth is unpaired. In addition, the first two sets—specificity versus diffuseness and affectivity versus affective neutrality—refer to *orientations*, the actor's relationship to the objects in his or her situation; the second two—particularism versus universalism and ascription versus achievement—refer to *modalities*, the meaning that the object has for the actor. Parsons explains that the "orientation set of pattern variables 'views' the relationship of actor to situation from the side of the actor or actors; the modality set views it from the side of the situation as consisting of objects" (Parsons, 1960: 468). Again, the fifth pattern variable—self-orientation versus collectivity-orientation—does not quite fit this level of analysis.

Parsons believes that he can use his pattern-variable scheme to describe all social relationships. Indeed, he argues that his proposed five pattern variables are irreducible and exhaustive as they consider all of the values that define instrumental and expressive actions. In *instrumental action* actors are concerned with attaining particular goals and they adopt a purely cognitive and formal standpoint toward the conditions that are necessary for attaining them. *Expressive action*, on the other hand, involves actions in which immediate gratification is sought, and objects are evaluated solely in these terms and not as means to other ends.

In addition to instrumental and expressive action orientations, the pattern variables also define role relationships. Business relationships and family relationships, for example, are polar opposites, differing in each set of variables. Thus, family relationships are typically characterized by diffuseness, affectivity, particularism, ascription, and collectivity-orientation, while business relationships are frequently characterized by specificity, affective neutrality, universalism, achievement, and self-orientation. Let us briefly consider two types of business relationships in regard to the pattern variables. The doctor-patient relationship is like most business relationships except that it is likely to be collectivity-oriented in that the physician is concerned with her patients' physical well-being, rather than self-oriented in that she is not primarily concerned with making a profit from her patient's ill health. The social worker–client relationship is like the doctor-patient relationship except that it does not rely on specificity but on diffuseness—the social worker must take into account his client's emotional, physical, financial, and social situation.

The theoretical inspiration for the pattern variables is, as Parsons acknowledges, based on Ferdinand Tönnies's famous *Gemeinschaft-Gesellschaft* distinction between types of social organization. It was Parsons's belief that several main contrasts between traditional and modern societies could be refined in more universal and basic action terms. This led to the formulation of his five pattern variables, which he later reduced to four (omitting self-orientation versus collectivity-orientation), and which Parsons believed was a more refined instrument than Tönnies's *Gemeinschaft-Gesellschaft* for characterizing, describing, and classifying social relationships.

Parsons, however, not only uses the pattern variables to classify actions and relationships, he also classifies roles, institutions, and even entire societies (as combinations of roles and institutions). Accordingly, he maintains that there are four main pattern-variable combinations that encompass the great majority of all societies. The four patterns are constituted from a cross-classification of just two of the pattern variables: particularism-universalism and ascription-achievement. Thus, the four societal forms, the four principal types of social structure that Parsons identifies by their dominant values, are: (1) the particularistic-ascription pattern found in Latin American countries; (2) the particularistic-achievement pattern found in traditional China; (3) the universalistic-ascription pattern found in Nazi Germany and Soviet Russia; and (4) the universalistic-achievement pattern found in the United States and in most "industrial" societies (Parsons, 1951: 180ff). Parsons, following Weber, sees the shift in value orientations and social relationships from particularistic-ascription to universalistic-achievement as indicating that social change involves a move in the direction of the rationalization of social life (1951: 487, 501).

The Social System

The Social System (1951) is essentially an expansion, by Parsons alone, of the four chapters comprising the section entitled "Values, Motives, and Systems of Action" in Parsons's and Shils's *Toward a General Theory of Action*. In *The Social System* Parsons defines the single most central concept in all of his sociological theory: social system. According to him, a social system consists of "a plurality of individual actors interacting with each other in a situation which has at least a physical or environmental aspect, actors who are motivated in terms of a tendency to the 'optimization of gratification' and whose relation to their situations, including each other, is defined and mediated in terms of a system of culturally structured and shared symbols" (1951: 5–6).

A social system, as thus defined, is only one aspect of a completely concrete system of social action. The other two closely related systems which we have already discussed are the personality system and the cultural system. Although analytically independent, transformations between these three systems are possible, and the action frame of reference is common to them all. Parsons warns against considering any one of these systems as being more basic than or as having priority over the other two. In any event, a society is then defined as a social system "which meets all the essential functional requisites of long term persistence from within its own resources" (Parsons, 1951: 19). Any social system that does not qualify as a society under this definition is regarded as a partial social system (later, subsystem). The economy, for example, is a partial social system, as are the polity and the family (or as Parsons sometimes says, the household).

The basic unit of all social systems that links the actor as a "psychological" entity to the wider social structure, is the *role* (Parsons, 1945: 61). A role is a complex of normative expectations concerning the behavior of an actor, and all roles involve reciprocal relations: roles cannot be defined in isolation, but only in relation to specific other roles. Roles comprise the normative expectations that define behavior associated with the holding of a particular social position. Those normative "role expectations" that are sufficiently well established to be regarded as legitimate comprise a social institution. "An *institution* will be said to be a complex of institutionalized role integrates [or status-relationships], which is of strategic structural significance in the social system in question" (Parsons, 1951: 39).

Parsons begins his detailed account of social systems with a discussion of social institutions. The institutionalized role relations of a society comprise its *relational institutions* and these constitute "the structural core of the social system" (Parsons, 1951: 52). Where a prevailing group commitment is made to a set of roles, with some awareness that these commitments are widely shared, Parsons refers to the role norms as being institutionalized in that group, and to the organized systems of such roles as an institution. An institution in this sense represents the internalization of cultural norms in the personalities of alters (the role definers), but it is also an interactional emergent referring to inter-alter relations.

Aside from relational institutions, Parsons distinguishes two other types of institutions in terms of their various functional relationships to the structure of the social system. These he terms the "regulative" and the "cultural." *Regulative institutions* are concerned with limiting the pursuit of sectional interests and so with achieving a degree of social or collective integration. They define the appropriate and inappropriate goals and means that may be employed in actions. *Cultural institutions*, on the other hand, do not directly enter into the regulation of social action. They are latent in role relations and in regulative institutions, but are fundamental to their regulatory powers. Cultural institutions ensure the "acceptance" of particular values that may not be directly relevant to an actor's own role relations.

A system of social relations, a society, is a particular complex of normatively patterned roles and institutions that can be regarded as "boundary-maintaining" in relation to its environment. Relative to its environment, a social system is able to maintain certain constancies in the structure of its roles and institutions. Put another way, for Parsons, "societies" are concrete collectivities, actual clusters of roles and institutions that are relatively self-sufficient, have a particular boundary, and persist over time.

The Four-Function Paradigm

The concept of functional imperatives or, as they are alternatively termed, functional requisites—the famous AGIL four-function paradigm—was elaborated in Parsons's close collaboration with Robert F. Bales and Edward Shils, which produced the volume *Working Papers in the Theory of Action* (1953). The four function paradigm, which became the cornerstone of all of Parsons's theoretical developments, posits that, as a system of action, every social system, from the smallest (ego-alter) to the largest (whole societies), must continually confront and solve two sets of functional problems in order to operate effectively and remain viable as a system.

The first set of problems he calls "adaptation" and "goal-attainment." These problems deal with instrumental actions and concern the social system's relations with its external environment, including its physical milieu, the bodily needs of its members, and other social systems with which it must contend. The second pair of functional problems Parsons refers to as "integration" and "latent pattern maintenance/ tension management." They deal with expressive actions and have to do with the social system's internal organization as a human group of socialized persons with cultural commitments in interaction.

Parsons, Shils, and Bales conclude that all action systems generally could be exhaustively analyzed in terms of processes and structures referable to the solution of four functional problems: "adaptation," "goal-attainment," "integration," and "latent pattern-maintenance and tension-management." The paradigm has become known as the AGIL scheme in accordance with the acronym of the first letters of the names for these four functional requisites.

The "A" function, adaptation, is an external environmental problem that refers to the processes through which the social system procures, and subsequently distributes, the resources it requires for its activities. The "G" function, goal-attainment, is likewise an external environmental problem; it refers to the social system's formulation of goals and the motivation and mobilization of resources directed to achieve those goals. The "I" function, integration, is an internal organizational problem concerned with processes that ensure the coordination of the various relations that make up the social system for the purpose of producing an organization that can prevent or withstand major conflictual disruptions that the system may face. Lastly, the "L" function, latent pattern-maintenance/ tension-management, is also an internal organizational problem, and it refers to the processes whereby the social system maintains normative patterns and manages the strains and tensions of actors.

According to Parsons, any action system, if it is to preserve its equilibrium, will meet these, and only these, four functional requisites. Extending his four function scheme to the most general-action level of system analysis, Parsons states that the cultural system, providing as it does the values and norms that motivate action, serves the function of pattern maintenance. The personality system, being the primary means of formulating goals and making decisions, provides the goal-attainment function. The behavioral organism (later, behavioral system), which is the primary source for providing resources drawn from the environment, to other systems, relates most directly to the adaptive function. Finally, the social system (and especially society), which is the locus of organized configurations of status-roles that integrate the patterns of the cultural system and the needs of the personality system, can be seen as performing the chief integrative function for all action systems. In other words, a general action system comprises the four subsystems of culture, personality, the behavioral system, and the social system. Accordingly, the behavioral system is the A subsystem of action, the personality system the G subsystem, the cultural system the L subsystem, and the social system the I subsystem.

In applying the AGIL scheme exclusively to social systems, Parsons notes that although each of the functional requisites has many implications for the social system as a whole, they nonetheless tend to have primary functional significance for its specific subsystems. Thus, the adaptation function, given the roles and institutions on which it depends (the occupations, technologies, markets, and so on), has economic significance and constitutes the "economy." The goal-attainment function, with its structural units of chiefdom, government, or statehood, comprises the "polity." The integrative function, creating as it does a sense of cohesion and solidarity among the members of the social system, forms the "integrative subsystem" of a society. Finally, the latent pattern-maintenance/tension-management function, which, through the process of socialization, serves to maintain the fundamental value-patterns of the social system is focused on the "fiduciary" institutions of cultural motivation: the family, religion, and education. Structurally differentiated social systems, then, are regarded by Parsons as systems of interrelated functional subsystems, which include the economy, polity, the integrative subsystem (later, societal community), and the pattern-maintenance subsystem. The social system's subsystems are themselves constituted of further subsystems with their AGIL functions. As shown in figure I.1, for example, the economic subsystem of adaptation has its own intra- and interrelated constituent AGIL subsystems.

Input-Output Relations and the Generalized Symbolic Media of Interchange

In *Economy and Society,* Parsons and Neil J. Smelser examine the multiple interchanges that occur among the various systems and subsystems of action. In particular they analyze the relationship between the economic subsystem and the rest of society. In so doing, they lay the groundwork for the eventual emphasis on the generalized symbolic media of interchange.

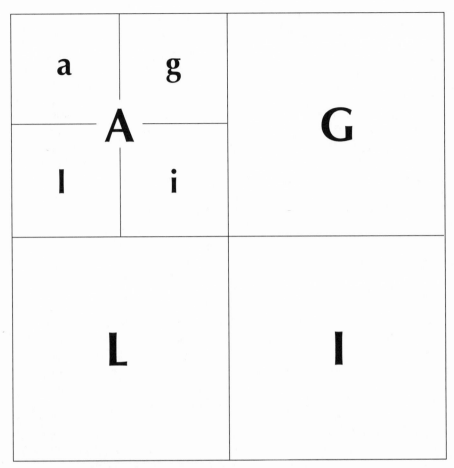

Figure I.1.   Levels of Subsystem Relations

Economy and Society, in which Parsons endeavors to construct a systems theory of modern capitalism, is in some ways a return to the economics-sociology nexus that he had previously considered during the early 1930s. His basic thesis in this volume is that the economy, as a social system, can be fitted into the AGIL schema and, as such, resolve a functional problem for society in its entirety. Given that the economy deals with the production and distribution of goods and services that are functionally necessary to the survival and relative well-being of individuals and collectivities, it "can be regarded first as meeting the *adaptive* exigencies of the society as a whole by means of the production of utility, and second as having goal-attainment, adaptive, integrative, and pattern-maintenance exigencies of its own" (Parsons and Smelser, 1956: 39–40). In relation with other subsystems of society—namely, the polity (goal-attainment), the cultural-motivation subsystem (latency/pattern maintenance), and the integrative subsystem (integration)—the economy fulfills certain types of functional needs.

Parsons analyzes the relations between the four major subsystems in terms of a model of interchanges among them. Because subsystems are not self-sufficient (if they were, they would be freestanding systems rather than subsystems), they must be involved in relations of "functional interdependence," or mutual influence. That is to say, subsystems are viewed as both "cause" and "effect" variables in determining the state of a system as a whole. Parsons argues that the subsystems maintain their connections with one another through processes of interchange in which the resources that are required, the inputs, and the products that are produced, the outputs, of each system are exchanged. Thus, the four differentiated systems of society—the economy, the polity, the integrative system, and the pattern-maintenance system—are connected through "double interchanges" (exchange of inputs and exchange of outputs), and, as shown in figure I.2, the functional interdependencies can be mapped as a pattern of input-output relations between the systems and their constituent subsystems.

According to Parsons, this need for functional interchanges is an essential feature of all societies, and each of the four major social subsystems generates a particular resource that acquires a generalized significance for its interchanges with other subsystems. In societies with a high degree of structural differentiation, in particular those in which the economy and polity have been differentiated from the integrative subsystem (later, societal community), there is a need for more explicit regulation of the interchanges. This regulation occurs, Parsons says, through the use of media of exchange, and the prototype of such a media is *money*.

Money exists as a generalized, symbolic means of exchange; that is to say, it can be used in exchange relations between the economy and the other subsystems of society. Money has several characteristics that allow it to function as a means of exchange. First, it is a measure and store of value, which has general significance in the economy. Second, money is generated within the economy as its own specific means of exchange. Third, it allows the possessors of goods and services to enter into extensive and more enduring exchange relations than are possible on the basis of pure barter. Finally, money encourages an extension of the division of labor, it allows a proper market mechanism to develop, and it permits an effective and efficient allocation of goods and services to occur.

In examining interchanges between the economy and the other subsystems effected through the exchange medium of money, Parsons sees analogous exchange media as emerging in each of the other three subsystems. Thus, using money as his model, Parsons argues that *power* can be seen as a similar symbolic medium of exchange that is generated in the polity. Given that the polity is the subsystem functionally concerned with goal-attainment, it uses power to induce conformity (Parsons, 1963a). What is more, power can be used to regulate interchanges between the polity and other subsystems. Thus, interchanges between differentiated economic and political structures involve transactions that are mediated by the use of both money and power. In sum, money and power represent the generalized media of exchange between the economy and the polity.

Parsons also extends this conceptualization of generalized media to the other two subsystems—the integrative subsystem and the cultural subsystem. The integrative subsystem generates *influence* as a circulating medium, and its interchanges with the

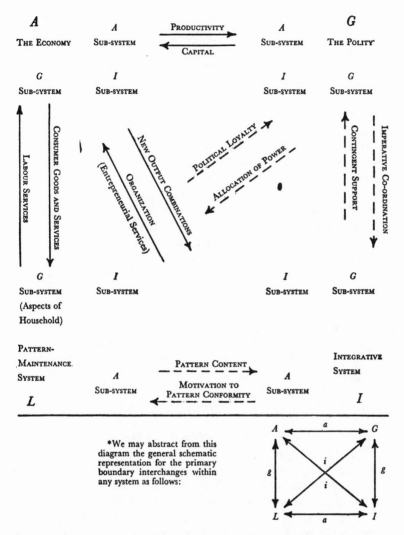

Figure I.2. Boundary Interchanges between the Primary Subsystems of a Society
Source: Reprinted with permission from Talcott Parsons and Neil J. Smelser, *Economy and Society* (New York: Free Press, 1956).

economy and the polity are mediated by influence, and by money or power (Parsons, 1963a, 1963b, 1971: 14). Finally, the cultural subsystem utilizes *value commitments*, or "loyalty" to particular cultural standards (Parsons, 1968). A key point is that all four symbolic media must be combined in any of the four subsystems. Thus, economic interchanges require that adequate investments of power, influence, and value commitments, as well as money, be made.

In sum, Parsons's objective in *Economy and Society* is to specify the nature of the interchanges, or input-output exchanges, of the different symbolic media. This analysis of the generalized symbolic media of interchange was pivotal, and in his later work, money, power, influence, and value commitments appear as the principle media of interchange and are seen as central aspects of the functional interdependence of the four subsystems. (During the mid-1970s, Parsons extended his symbolic media to include intelligence, affect, collective sentiment, and collective representations.)

Shortly after the publication of *Economy and Society,* Parsons, as a result of the generalized media of interchange, directed his work toward a "cybernetically" oriented action theory in which the emphasis is on how a symbolic program of control operates in action systems. In this theoretical development, Parsons returned increasingly to biological analogies and to the major developments in genetics. During the mid-1950s and early 1960s he became interested in the new ideas about cybernetic control in both living and nonliving systems. Thus, during the later phase of his work, there was a pronounced emphasis on biological analogies, cybernetic control, and an interest in processes of social change and evolutionary development. Parsons therefore shifted his attention away from relationships within the four action systems to relationships *between* them, and thus paved the way for an ordering of such systems in terms of a cybernetic hierarchy.

The Cybernetic Hierarchy of Action Systems

By the late 1950s Parsons began to devise a model of relations between action systems on various levels. A major step in this formulation was the introduction of cybernetic concepts into the AGIL scheme, with the object of clarifying the causal relations between the different action systems (Parsons and Smelser, 1956; Parsons, et al., 1961, vol. I: 36–41).

"Cybernetics" refers to the science that deals with information, and thus for Parsons, a system of action is represented in cybernetics as a constant flow of *information* as well as *energy.* Accordingly, he incorporated the concept of information into his general systems theory and viewed the input-output relations of the four action systems as involving informational control and energic conditions.

In addition to the problem of systemic interchanges Parsons was also interested in the interrelations of the four action systems expressed as a type of hierarchy. He argues that those systems with processes that are high in "information" are especially important in controlling the overall development of an action system. By contrast, those systems with processes that are high in "energy" serve to condition this development. Thus, the development of the general action system as a whole is based on the outcome of controlling and conditioning processes that involve both information and energy.

From the perspective of a hierarchy of cybernetic controls and conditions, a system high in information but low in energy (like the cultural system) could, under certain circumstances, control a system with the opposite characteristics (like the social system). This led Parsons to the idea that each of the four action systems represented a step in the hierarchy, with the cultural system representing the pinnacle, given that value-orientations play a specific and crucial role in the production of social order. The cultural system thus produces the values that actually enter into the structuring of action by virtue of their internalization during socialization. At the bottom of the cybernetic hierarchy is the behavioral organism as it articulates the limits on action that are inherent in the external conditions of the physical environment.

In explaining the cybernetic hierarchy of action systems from top to bottom and back again, Parsons sees the cultural system as supplying value-orientations as information to the social system, which organizes them into norms controlling actors' role-playing, which supply the informational control over motivation and individual decision-making processes of the personality system, which in its turn provides an informational control over physicochemical and organic processes in the behavioral organism. In reverse, the behavioral organism supplies energy to the personality system, which in turn supplies energy to the social system, which in organizing status-roles provides the cultural system's energic conditions. Figure I.3 illustrates these cybernetic relations.

Social Evolution and Societal Community

In the mid-1960s, Parsons began to connect the insights derived from the cybernetic hierarchy to the question of social evolution. This was a logical extension given that while the functional interchanges of informational controls and energic conditions typically maintain some measure of stability, they may occasionally produce disruptions and strains in the social system. If these disruptions and strains are particularly great, they may compel the system to change its structure in order to survive.

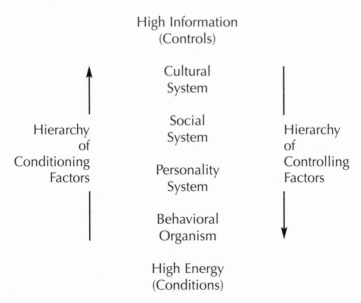

High Information
(Controls)

Cultural
System

Social
System

Personality
System

Behavioral
Organism

High Energy
(Conditions)

Hierarchy
of
Conditioning
Factors

Hierarchy
of
Controlling
Factors

Figure I.3. The Hierarchy of Cybernetic Controls and Conditions

Parsons therefore developed an explicit evolutionary theory of social change that he applied to the comparative analysis of societies. His evolutionary approach, which is most fully and clearly articulated in two slim paperbacks, *Societies: Evolutionary and Comparative Perspectives* (1966) and *The System of Modern Societies* (1971), attempted to apply the cybernetic systems theory in explaining the progression from premodern to modern societies (see 1966: 28–29).

Given the relatively short length of *Societies,* Parsons's explanation of the processes of social evolution is necessarily general. He broadly defines evolution as a process of increasing adaptive capacity of societies to their environments. Thus, by constantly adapting to their changing environments societies undergo structural transformations that, in turn, enhance their general capacity to adapt. Because Parsons focuses on structural differentiation that enhances functional adaptation, he advances the notion that as a society's specialized subsystems become progressively differentiated, this then allows their more flexible mobilization for more varied purposes. Furthermore, if the adaptation is to be successful, the operations of the various subsystems must be coordinated with one another thereby requiring new integrative structures. Achieving integration, Parsons argues, will normally involve a move toward the inclusion and coordination of the differentiated subsystems into the normative structure of the society. Thus, according to Parsons, the process of evolution in social systems occurs principally through structural differentiation.

Parsons outlines what he sees as the four developmental principles of the process of evolutionary change. These are: (1) *differentiation,* or the formation of new subsystems; (2) *adaptive upgrading,* or the increased specialization of a new subsystem; (3) *inclusion,* or the integration of a new subsystem into the rest of society so that its operations are coordinated with the operations of other specialized subsystems, and (4) *value-generalization,* an adaptive process internal to society whereby values are sufficiently general in scope so that they legitimize the new subsystem (Parsons, 1971: 26). Parsons then divides the evolution of societies into three stages: the *primitive,* the *intermediate,*and the *modern.*

Parsons's analysis of evolution begins with the earliest stages of human history and thus with a discussion of "primitive" societies. Primitive societies—hunting and gathering societies such as those of the aboriginal tribes of Australia—have limited structural differentiation. They are almost completely organized around religion and kinship and consequently "the whole society constitutes a single affinal collectivity" that is regulated by prescriptive marriage rules (1966: 36). As these societies become more bounded either in territory or membership—that is to say, when they identify themselves as a "tribe," an ethnic group maintaining jurisdiction over a territorial area—and as their structures of kinship and property become more differentiated, a system of stratification emerges and they become "advanced" primitive societies, of which some of the African kingdoms, such as the Shilluk of the Upper Nile, are prime examples.

Parsons maintains that the crucial "watershed" that allowed for the transition from primitive to intermediate societies was the institutionalization of written language. The intermediate stage requires the differentiation of culture from the specific social systems and personalities with which it is associated. In a society limited to oral tradition, this separation is difficult, but with the appearance of writing cultural values and beliefs become more easily disassociated from their adherents (e.g., priests and political officials), and objectified (written down). What is more, writing allows cultural diffusion to larger groups and greatly aids the inclusion of larger populations with more divergent roles into the same social system.

Parsons divides the intermediate stage into two further substages: the "archaic" and the "advanced intermediate." Archaic societies, such as those of ancient Egypt and Mesopotamia, as well as those in India, China, and Southeast Asia, but also including the New World societies of the Aztecs, Mayans, and Incas, are characterized by the literacy of specialized groups and by cosmological religion. In these societies there emerges a sharper social stratification and a clearer structuring of central political functions into separate governmental institutions. Advanced intermediate societies—examples of which include China and India again, at different periods, the Islamic empires, and Rome—are characterized by, among other things, an "imperial" organization, a fuller elite literacy, and a religion that sharply distinguishes the "supernatural" from the "natural." These advanced intermediate societies contribute to the growth of more universal laws, and in time, to scientific and technological developments as well.

In the West, after the decline of the Roman Empire, modern society developed from medieval Western Christendom when, in the late eleventh century, the Church began to take a strong interest in secular affairs. Then, beginning in the seventeenth century, Europe evolved into a "European system," a truly modern intersocietal system in which lines of structural differentiation followed geographical and regional divisions caused by such splits and conflicts as those between the Eastern and Western Churches, the German north and the Latin south, and so on. Within this European social system the various regions came to be specialized around particular functional processes. Italy, for example, served a primarily pattern-maintenance function in the general European system as it nurtured and transmitted classical culture. Prussia performed a general adaptive function to the European system in becoming the most important stabilizer of Europe's eastern frontier as it pioneered governmental effectiveness. England and France carried out goal-attainment functions given that the most important new institutional developments were emerging there. These nation-states became the "spearhead" of early modernity, and by the late eighteenth and early nineteenth centuries France, with its "democratic revolution," and England, with its "industrial revolution," had become the "lead" societies in the progress toward modernity.

Parsons maintains that the lead in modernity then passed to the United States where a third modern revolution, the "educational revolution," occurred in the twentieth century. The educational revolution successfully synthesized the themes of the industrial and democratic revolutions of England and France—equality of opportunity and equality of citizenship—and fostered the emergence not only of markets and bureaucratic organizations, but also of what Parsons calls "associational organizations." These are voluntary associations, such as political parties, interest groups, business corporations, and professional bodies (e.g., the academic profession), with democratic decision-making apparatuses. The associational organizations play a central role in the overall integration of modern societies. The integrative processes that were pioneered in the associational organizations of the United States, Parsons believed, would eventually spread worldwide.

In *Societies,* and then again in *The System of Modern Societies,* Parsons discusses the sociocultural progression from primitive to intermediate to modern societies with special reference to its implications for the *societal community.* (The societal community as a concept had previously been articulated as "the integrative subsystem of society" by Parsons.) The societal community, Parsons explains, is "constituted both by a normative system of order and by statuses, rights, and obligations pertaining to membership . . . within the community" (1966: 10). Its most general function is to "articulate a system of norms with a collective organization that has unity and cohesion" (1971: 11). In sum, the concept of societal community is similar to Durkheim's notion of social solidarity.

Parsons contends that in the most primitive societies, such as those of aboriginal Australia, the core structure of the societal community was the affinal system. Membership in these societies was based on marital ties. By contrast, the basis of societal community in the intermediate historic empires was their cultural complexes (e.g., religion, polity, economy, law). For example, imperial Rome, with its universalistic legal system, to a limited extent, served to include a whole set of groups associated within it. These complexes were extendable to all who entered the empire's cultural orbit. Finally, societal community in modern multigroup societies, such as the United States, is based on an extended system of common citizenship. The fact that all citizens of a modern, democratic nation-state, irrespective of ethnicity, religion, class origin, or gender, have the same legal rights is what gives them their membership status, as "a company of equals," in an inclusive community. Parsons concludes by stating that "the forces that have transformed the societal community of the United States and promise to continue to transform it are not peculiar to this one society but permeate the whole modern—and 'modernizing'—system" (1971: 121).

As cursory as it may be, this survey of Parsons's life and work should aid in providing an adequate background against which to better understand the ten essays in this collection. Additionally, the essays will no doubt contribute to the conceptual richness and variety of Parsons's theoretical scheme as outlined above.

TEXT AND CONTEXT: THE ESSAYS

Together, the ten chapters that constitute this volume (all, save one, are original to the volume) consider the text and context of Parsons's path-breaking ideas, ideas that continue to have an impact on sociological theory today. As such, the collection analyzes substantive aspects of Parsons's works and discusses certain key concepts explicated in those works. In addition, the collection also examines Parsons's writings in a sociohistorical perspective as it considers the personal, institutional, and social influences on his thinking, from his early ideas in the 1930s to his more mature publications of the 1960s and 1970s. What is more, these chapters, written by some of the leading social theorists in the field, offer a reappraisal—an extension and modification—of Parsons's theoretical scheme. The driving force behind this volume is that in considering Parsons's texts in context we arrive at a fuller understanding and appreciation of his theory and legacy in contemporary sociology.

In the opening chapter Lawrence T. Nichols undertakes a most intriguing contextual analysis of Parsons's first major theoretical text, *The Structure of Social Action*, where he endeavored to lay the foundation for building a systematic sociological paradigm. Drawing upon a wide array of archival materials—especially the personal correspondence of faculty and the official correspondence of administrators at Harvard University—Nichols uses them to shed light on Parsons's orientation toward Harvard's institutional rewards and penalties during the time when he was working on *Structure* and while positioning himself for a permanent academic career at the University. In particular, Nichols identifies those organizational constraints that compelled Parsons to exclude, in *Structure*, a draft chapter on Georg Simmel. He considers how Harvard's culture, but also how two powerful administrators, James B. Conant and Lawrence J. Henderson, exerted certain direct and indirect influences on Parsons to omit references to Simmel, whose sociology was regarded as philosophical and speculative and thus unscientific. By strategically accommodating to these organizational pressures Parsons not only succeeded in securing a permanent faculty position for himself, Nichols maintains, he also made *Structure* more "scientific," at least according to the local understandings of science popular at Harvard during the mid-1930s.

Next, William J. Buxton and David Rehorick examine Parsons's theoretical work immediately following the publication of *The Structure of Social Action* and at a time when Parsons was preoccupied with the work of Max Weber, 1938–1942. During this period Parsons consolidated his previously disparate theoretical and practical work—that is to say, his voluntaristic theory of action and his empirical study of institutions and the professions—into a comparative-institutional analysis of the crises then confronting Western civilization. This synthesis in turn, was grounded in a particular interpretation of Weber's political sociology. In examining the correspondence between Parsons and the political theorist, Eric Voegelin (1901–1985), Buxton and Rehorick identify those domain assumptions that underpinned Parsons's intellectual engagement with Weber and that provided the foundation for his emerging structural functionalism.

In his chapter, "Elias and Parsons: Two Transformations of the Problem-Historical Method," Bruce C. Wearne finds it fruitful to compare Parsons with the German sociologist Norbert Elias (1897–1990) on what they regard to be the historiography of sociology and the proper approach to sociological theorizing. Wearne begins by considering how both Parsons and Elias were influenced by the intellectual debates current in the 1920s, especially in Heidelberg, where they both studied sociology and associated with the Weber circle. Although the two men shared a common historical

background, their epistemology, approaches to theory, and underlying presupposi-
tions stand in stark opposition to each other. Indeed, they represent two wholly different attempts to appropriate the early-twentieth-century intellectual tradition for sociological research. Whereas for Elias the task of sociology is demythologization, for
Parsons the task is to systematically construct a general theory of systems. By comparing Parsons's and Elias's responses to metatheoretical questions Wearne demonstrates
that, from his early work in *The Structure of Social Action* through *The Social System*
and beyond, Parsons's analytical realism—over against Elias's nominalism—relied not
only on theoretical convergence but also on the structural-functional, systemic, and
problem-historical methods.

In the next chapter, Bernard Barber, a student of Parsons at Harvard during the
1930s, relies on voluminous lecture notes that he took in two of Parsons's courses—
one on social institutions, the other on social theory—in detailing chronologically
how Parsons came to develop the notion of "social system." To be sure, by the time
he published *The Social System* in 1951, Parsons had already committed himself to
the social system as his central concept; a concept that, according to Barber, presented at least two limitations to Parsons's later work. Barber concludes that despite
these limitations we nonetheless "need the concept of social system as one of the basic theoretical elements in a scientific sociology."

In the two chapters that follow, Bryan S. Turner and Jonathan H. Turner each focus on certain shortcomings of Parsonian sociology given the many criticisms directed against it—especially in regard to the concepts of social system and the system
requisites. Believing that some of Parsons's ideas need to be reconceptualized, Turner
and Turner, in their respective chapters, attempt, in their own way, to "save" the Parsonian legacy of systems functionalism.

Bryan S. Turner begins his chapter by arguing that Parsons's concept of system is
based on outdated models of science—of space and time—that assume mechanical
and linear notions of causality. Turner states that while Parsonian systems theory was
focused on the processes of modernization (indeed, it is a defense of modernization),
in today's *postmodern* world social systems are more complex, their environments
riskier, and social change more contingent than those of 1950s and 1960s America
that Parsons was studying. Moreover, Parsons's assumption of a set of shared cultural
values in U.S. society today greatly limits his social systems theory because it cannot
account for what Turner sees as the two contradictory processes around which postmodern society is organized: regulation (surveillance and governmentality) and uncertainty (contingency and risk). Thus, in order to better address this postmodern di-
alectic, Turner proposes that Parsonian systems theory, especially its cybernetic
variant, be redeveloped in terms of complexity theory. Only in this way, says Turner,
can the Parsonian legacy survive.

In "Can Functionalism Be Saved?" Jonathan H. Turner addresses those critiques
that have traditionally been leveled at the idea that in order to remain viable, all social systems have to meet certain functional requisites. Three of the most damaging
criticisms are that the system requisites are tautologies, illegitimate teleologies, and
mere taxonomies. Thus, in order to help functional analysis, but in particular Par-

sons's systems functionalism, avoid the pitfalls of tautology, teleology, and taxonomy, Turner proposes a new functionalism. While this new functionalism retains many of the elements of Parsons's functional requisite analysis, it has a more solid foundation in that it rests on four main approaches: (1) it reconnects functionalism to its ecological roots by reintroducing the concept of "selection"; (2) it gives a more dynamic view of subsystems as both a product of selection forces and as a generator of selection pressures on other subsystems; (3) it reconceptualizes systems into the three fundamental levels of social reality—the macro, meso, and micro—where selection forces and pressures operate; and (4) it advances the notion that theoretical explanation revolves not around elaborate taxonomies, but around universal principles such as "force." Turner's attempt to reinvent functionalism in a selectionist mode promises a more fine-grained analysis of system requisites than that previously proffered by Parsons.

In "Networks and Systems," Stephan Fuchs claims that the theory of social systems developed by German sociologist Niklas Luhmann (1927–1998) is the only one to legitimately continue the Parsonian legacy in regard to generality and universality. A one-time student of Parsons at Harvard during the early 1960s, Luhmann, beginning in the mid-1980s, however, began to shift his theoretical orientation away from Parsons's reliance on social action, social order, social integration, and normative consensus. As a consequence of its core concept of "communication," the architecture of Luhmann's social systems theory—especially in its rejection of agency and in its relationalism—more closely resembles network theory than it does Parsons's theory of social systems. A fusion of Luhmann's systems theory with network theory, Fuchs contends, promises to yield a fresh perspective for a general theory of society.

In the next two chapters, Victor Lidz and Uta Gerhardt, respectively, discuss in detail two of Parsons's crucial ideas developed during the 1960s: the generalized symbolic media of interchange and the notion of the societal community. Regrettably, these two conceptions have been largely ignored in the secondary literature. In these essays they are given the serious consideration they deserve as integral components of Parsons's systems-functional sociology.

Lidz examines Parsons's generalized symbolic media of interchange, which are central to his treatment of the processes of social action, and argues that Parsons's conceptual weakness is that he relied on money—with its functions of value and exchange—as the analogue by which an entire family of symbolic media important to total societal functioning (political power, influence, value-commitments, and later, intelligence, affect, collective sentiment, and collective representations) were formulated and compared. Since the mid-1970s Lidz has proposed that it is not money but rather language that is the prototype to be employed in understanding and further developing the media theory of input and output relations. In his chapter, Lidz, borrowing from the work of such diverse scholars as Noam Chomsky, Erving Goffman, and W. I. Thomas, continues to build a language-centered analysis—a "compositional" perspective—that he believes complements well Parsons's focus on the double interchanges between adjacent subsystems of action. The goal, says Lidz, is to integrate his compositional perspective and Parsons's "interchange" perspective in order to develop an orthogonal approach, one that will help us better understand the multidimensional, multistaged processes of social action.

Returning to an explicit consideration of context, Uta Gerhardt painstakingly details the myriad social events and intellectual influences that compelled Parsons, during the 1960s, to reformulate his systems theory to include a major development—his theory of societal community. In what is doubtless the most thorough analysis of Parsons's societal community, Gerhardt carefully delineates his efforts at constructing and reinforcing the theory, which deals principally with social integration, and endeavors to prove its viability by applying it to two issues that currently hold sway not only in academic social science (e.g., in the communitarian literature), but also in the arenas of global politics and international relations. These two issues are the process of globalization and the emergence of civil society. Gerhardt is confident that Parsons's theory of societal community will provide an effective response to the challenges of integration—citizenship—in today's multicultural society and new world order. Gerhardt concludes that "Parsons's theory of societal community is precisely the type of social theory that the sociological community has been looking for since about 1990."

In the final chapter, Mark Gould takes Parsonian sociology from the purely analytic and applies it to legal policy issues. Here, Gould looks at how general, empirical, sociological theory, such as that developed by Parsons, can help resolve important normative questions. By way of example, he argues for the appropriateness of college and university policies regulating consensual sexual relations between employees and students. His systematic argument, which is based on sociological theory in the characteristic manner of Parsons, is able to yield a morally informed, empirical solution to such normative problems. This type of logically coherent, idealist argument considers the moral values, the identity as it were, of the community (e.g., the college) in question. In contrast, Gould shows that the positivist arguments advanced by legal scholar Richard Posner, which are based on neoclassical economic theory (i.e., utilitarianism and rational-choice) can only arrive at an instrumental (i.e., nonmoral) solution to normative problems. Gould's objective is to pave the way for the development of a normative theory of when social relationships should be accepted as legally and morally valid. Accordingly, he relies on Parsons's sociological focus on social values and procedural norms and his contention that all valid social relationships—including, for that matter, consensual sexual relationships—must be justified procedurally and morally legitimated.

Let us now begin the journey through Parsons's rich, if somewhat dense, theoretical landscape. For this we turn to the ten chapters and their consideration of text in context.

REFERENCES

Abbott, A. 1999. *Department and Discipline: Chicago Sociology at One Hundred.* Chicago: University of Chicago Press.

Adriaansens, H. 1980. *Talcott Parsons and the Conceptual Dilemma.* London: Routledge & Kegan Paul.

Alexander, J. C. 1983. *The Modern Reconstruction of Classical Thought: Talcott Parsons. Theoretical Logic in Sociology.* Vol. 4. Berkeley: University of California Press.

———. 1987. *Twenty Lectures: Sociological Theory Since World War II.* New York: Columbia University Press.

———, ed. 1985. *Neofunctionalism.* Beverly Hills, Calif.: Sage.

———. 1988. *Neofunctionalism and After.* London: Blackwell Publishers.

American Sociologist. 1998. (Summer) 29 (2). Edited by L. T. Nichols.

Aronson, R. 1995. *After Marxism.* New York: Guilford Press.

Barber, B., and U. Gerhardt, eds. 1999. *Agenda for Sociology: Classical Sources and Current Uses of Talcott Parsons's Work.* Baden-Baden, Germany: Nomos.

Bierstedt, R. 1981. *American Sociological Theory.* New York: Academic Press.

Bourricaud, F. 1981. *The Sociology of Talcott Parsons.* Chicago: University of Chicago Press.

Bulmer, M. 1984. *The Chicago School of Sociology: Institutionalization, Diversity, and the Rise of Sociological Research.* Chicago: University of Chicago Press.

Buxton, W. 1985. *Talcott Parsons and the Capitalist Nation-State.* Toronto: University of Toronto Press.

Camic, C., ed. 1991. *Talcott Parsons: The Early Essays.* Chicago: University of Chicago Press.

Colomy, P. 1990. *Neofunctionlist Sociology.* Brookfield, Vt.: Elgar Publishing.

Davis, K. 1959. "The Myth of Functional Analysis as a Special Method in Sociology and Anthropology." *American Sociological Review* 24 (6): 757–72.

Faris, R. E. L. 1967. *Chicago Sociology: 1920–1932.* San Francisco: Chandler Publishing.

Fox, R. C. 1997. "Talcott Parsons: My Teacher." *American Scholar* 66 (3): 396–410.

Gerhardt, U., ed. 1993. *Talcott Parsons on National Socialism.* New York: Aldine de Gruyter.

Goudsblom, J. 1987. "The Sociology of Norbert Elias: Its Resonance and Significance." *Theory, Culture & Society* 4 (2–3): 323–38.

Gouldner, A. W. 1970. *The Coming Crisis of Western Sociology.* New York: Basic Books.

Habermas, J. 1981. *Theory of Communicative Action.* Vol. 1. Boston: Beacon Press.

Hamilton, P. 1983. *Talcott Parsons.* London: Tavistock Publications.

Holmwood, J. 1996. *Founding Sociology: Talcott Parsons and the Idea of General Theory.* Essex Eng.: Longman.

Holton, R. J., and B. S. Turner. 1986. *Talcott Parsons on Economy and Society.* London: Routledge.

Kurtz, L. R. 1984. *Evaluating Chicago Sociology.* Chicago: University of Chicago Press.

Lackey, P. N. 1987. *Invitation to Talcott Parsons' Theory.* Houston: Cap and Gown Press.

Levine, D. 1980. *Simmel and Parsons: Two Approaches to the Study of Society.* New York: Arno.

Lidz, V. 1993. "Parsons and Simmel: Convergence, Difference, and Missed Opportunity." *Teoria Sociologica* 1 (1): 130–42.

Luhmann, N. 1995. *Social Systems.* Stanford, Calif.: Stanford University Press.

Luhmann, N., and J. Hebermas. 1971. *Theorie der Gesellschaft oder Sozialtechnologie. Was leistet die Systemforschung.* Frankfurt am Main: Suhrkamp.

Merton, R. K. 1980. "Remembering the Young Talcott Parsons." *American Sociologist* 15: 68–71.

Münch, R. 1982. *Theoriedes Handelns. Zur Rekonstruktion der Beiträge von Talcott Parsons, Emile Durkheim und Max Weber.* Frankfurt am Main: Suhrkamp.

———. 1987. *Theory of Action: Towards a New Synthesis Going Beyond Parsons.* London: Routledge & Kegan Paul.

Parsons, T. 1935. "The Place of Ultimate Values in Sociological Theory." *International Journal of Ethics* 45: 282–316.

———. 1937. *The Structure of Social Action*. New York: McGraw-Hill.

———. 1942. "Propaganda and Social Control." *Psychiatry* 5 (4): 551–72.

———. 1945. "The Present Position and Prospects of Systematic Theory in Sociology. Pp. 42–69 in *Twentieth Century Sociology*, edited by G. Gurvitch and W. E. Moore. New York: Philosophical Library.

———. 1951. *The Social System*. New York: Free Press.

———. 1953. *Working Papers in the Theory of Action*. Glencoe, Ill.: Free Press.

———. 1960. "Pattern Variables Revisited." *American Sociological Review* 25 (4): 467–83.

———. 1963a. "On the Concept of Political Power." *Proceedings of the American Philosophical Society* 107 (3): 232–62.

———. 1963b. "On the Concept of Influence." *Public Opinion Quarterly* 27 (10): 37–62.

———. 1966. *Societies: Evolutionary and Comparative Perspectives*. Englewood Cliffs, N.J.: Prentice-Hall.

———. 1968. "On the Concept of Value Commitments." *Sociological Inquiry* 38 (2): 135–60.

———. 1971. *The System of Modern Societies*. Englewood Cliffs, N.J.: Prentice-Hall.

———. 1977. *Social Systems and the Evolution of Action Theory*. New York: Free Press.

———. 1978. *Action Theory and the Human Condition*. New York: Free Press.

Parsons, T., R. F. Bales, and E. D. Shils. 1953. *Working Papers in the Theory of Action*. New York: Free Press.

Parsons, T., and N. J. Smelser. 1956. *Economy and Society*. New York: Free Press.

Parsons, T., and E. Shils, eds. [1951] 2000. *Toward a General Theory of Action*. With a new introduction by N. J. Smelser. New Brunswick, N.J.: Transaction Publishers.

Parsons, T., E. Shils, K. D. Naegele, and J. R. Pitts, eds. 1961. *Theories of Society*. Vols. I and II. New York: Free Press.

Robertson, R., and B. S. Turner, eds. 1991. *Talcott Parsons: Theorist of Modernity*. London: Sage.

Scott, J. 1995. *Sociological Theory: Contemporary Debates*. Aldershot: Edward Elgar.

Turner, B. S., ed. 1999. *The Talcott Parsons Reader*. Oxford: Blackwell Publishers.

Wearne, B. 1989. *The Theory and Scholarship of Talcott Parsons to 1951: A Critical Commentary*. Cambridge: Cambridge University Press.

1

Parsons and Simmel at Harvard: Scientific Paradigms and Organizational Culture

Lawrence T. Nichols

Most sociologists—certainly including the late Talcott Parsons—would readily acknowledge that social action is always situated or, conversely, that interaction cannot occur without a context.[1] The relationship between context and action, however, is complex and problematic, especially from the distanced perspective of external observers such as historians and sociologists of knowledge and science. Thus, context may be defined in very different ways by both participants and observers, and these competing definitions may all have some validity. There may also be multiple contexts that simultaneously influence the actions of individuals or groups. How, then, to assess the effects of each type vis-à-vis its counterparts? In developing a contextual reading of Parsons's early theoretical work, for example, should one emphasize: (1) Parsons's personal background in Protestant Christianity, biology, and economics (Wearne, 1989); (2) the professional context of a reaction against Chicago-style sociology (Johnston, 1995); (3) the societal setting of a capitalist nation-state (Buxton, 1985); (4) intellectual debates of the era (Camic, 1992); or (5) the overarching context of Western civilization (Sorokin, 1937)? Perhaps some weight should be given to all of these, and to other types of context that have not received systematic analysis.

Contexts can inform, facilitate, or constrain action. They inform actions when they provide reference points in terms of which behavior makes sense. For instance, working to establish a new social science only makes sense with regard to preexisting understandings of science. Contexts facilitate action by providing opportunities and resources (intellectual, material, social). For example, probationary faculty members at research universities are given reduced teaching assignments, as well as equipment, funding, and assistants, in order to enable them to produce original research. Contexts constrain action by imposing structures of rewards and penalties, and by measuring action against preexisting commitments, such as the pursuit of academic preeminence.

Once a contextual method is adopted, moreover, analysts must consider the degree to which action is dependent upon any particular type of context, and the degree to which it may be considered autonomous. There is, regrettably, no established procedure for making such estimates. Karl Marx's writings, for example, make sense only in the context of industrial society, and may therefore be said to depend upon this context. Such dependence, however, does not mean that Marx was compelled to make the theoretical choices for which he is famous.

Contextual analysis can, however, be advanced by analyzing choices in terms of the orientations of participants toward various types of situational factors. In particular, participants are sometimes attuned to contexts in terms of institutionalized rewards and penalties, and they make decisions after assessing likely outcomes. Historical records such as collections of personal and official correspondence may indicate an individual's orientation toward certain types of context (e.g., economic) and a relative indifference to other types (e.g., intellectual). The data presented below will clearly show that Talcott Parsons had a strong orientation toward the reward structure of the organizational context in which he was working, and that he composed and revised his scientific writings with organizational constraints in view.

This chapter will therefore focus on the culture of Harvard University in the mid-1930s, in terms of its significance for understanding the production of Parsons's first major theoretical work, *The Structure of Social Action* (1937a). In particular, the analysis will examine *local understandings of science* and will seek to elucidate their relevance for Parsons's treatise and his academic career. Historical evidence will be presented to show that Parsons was keenly aware of the need to convince two crucial decision makers—one a chemist and the other a physiologist—that *Structure* satisfied their taken-for-granted criteria of scientific work. Failure to do so, it is clear, would have led to a terminating appointment at Harvard.

I shall argue further that dominant local understandings of science worked against inclusion of Parsons's draft chapter on Georg Simmel's sociology, the exclusion of which has become the subject of much discussion in the professional literature. Without denigrating Parsons's creativity and scholarly integrity, and without regarding organizational factors as absolute determinants of his actions (see Alexander and Sciortino, 1996), I shall contend that the Harvard context made it very difficult for Parsons to place Simmel on the same level as the famous quartet of founding figures he celebrated: Max Weber, Émile Durkheim, Vilfredo Pareto, and Alfred Marshall. I will also reconstruct the pressurized situation in which Parsons struggled to bring his ambitious project to completion before his probationary term expired. The emphasis will therefore be upon the risks and contingencies of "scientific work while it is still in the making" (Camic, 1996: 174), as well as on the communication of cues about locally acceptable scientific practice. Drawing upon both archival materials and Parsons's own published reminiscences, finally, I will trace the strategic accommodation that Parsons chose in order to attain scientific stature and academic permanency.[2]

LOCAL CONTEXTS AND SOCIOLOGICAL PARADIGMS

Relationships between local settings and varieties of sociological theory have often been reported in a purely descriptive way. Less frequently, historians have also noted a self-conscious dimension indicative of organizational commitments to paradigms. Thus, in Gary Alan Fine's edited volume on the "second Chicago school," John F. Galliher quotes a colorful recollection by Joseph Gusfield:

> We used to say that a thesis about drinking written by a Harvard student might well be entitled, "Modes of Cultural Release in Western Social Systems"; by a Columbia student it would be entitled, "Latent Functions of Alcohol Use in a National Sample"; and by a Chicago graduate student as, "Social Interaction at Jimmy's: A 55th St. Bar." (Galliher, 1995: 183)

Such relationships, however, have yet to be explored systematically, and thus we know little of the processes that reproduce particular paradigms in specific university settings, especially how faculty are cued or rewarded. A recent adumbration appears in Platt's analysis of research methods in the "second Chicago school."

> What people are likely to mention is . . . a strong emphasis on empirical work with a relative lack of interest in theory. (This tends to be contrasted with what they saw as the contemporary Harvard style.) . . . it is a conception of science which does not seem to have the connotation of following any particular philosophical or methodological prescription so much as staying close to the data. (Platt, 1995: 93)

Abbott and Gaziano (1995) also provide a brief narrative about communicative processes at Chicago that maintained the sense of a distinctive sociological tradition. In 1951, a document entitled "Objectives and Program of the Department of Sociology" emerged from departmental self-examination:

> This was a profoundly conservative document. In its own eyes, at least, the department saw the stratification area as the only seriously new area. . . . Thus, while faculty were willing to think somewhat eclectically in terms of hiring strategy, most still had a pretty clear idea that Chicago stood, and should stand, for a particular approach to social science, enshrined in the justification for objective 1, a sound body of sociological theory interrelated with social life and empirical research. (Abbott and Gaziano, 1995: 230–31)

George Homans has likewise contributed a Harvard anecdote in his autobiography, recalling the efforts of Parsons to create theoretical integration in the Department of Social Relations. Following the 1951 publication of *Toward A General Theory of Action*, edited by Parsons and Edward Shils (and known locally as the "yellow book"), the following interchange occurred:

> Parsons himself laid the "Yellow Book" before a meeting of the whole department, including both tenured and untenured members, urging us all to read it and implying . . . that it ought to be adopted as . . . official doctrine . . . to guide future teaching and research. I was going to have none of that. . . . I spoke up and said in effect: "There must be no implication that this document is to be taken as representing the official doctrine of the department. . . ." A dreadful silence followed . . . But finally Sam Stouffer, a tenured professor and a member of the senior committee . . . declared that the "Yellow Book" ought not be treated as departmental doctrine. There the matter dropped. (Homans, 1984: 303)

More relevant for present purposes are contextual analyses of the production of *The Structure of Social Action* by Buxton (1985, 1996) and Camic (1989, 1992). These observers, however, interpret events in the light of differing definitions of context. For Buxton, the political economy of the capitalist nation-state is the dominant force, while for Camic the keys to *Structure*'s true meaning are the contemporary socio-intellectual milieu and Harvard's local culture.

Thus, Camic argues that every fundamental idea or issue in Parsons's treatise was a defense against assaults on sociology that were widespread in the 1920s and 1930s. *Structure* is seen as a tour de force of rhetorical advocacy, a polemical "charter" disguised as intellectual history. Indeed, Camic concurs with Levine (1989) that *Structure*'s reconstruction of the sociological tradition "must be judged erroneous at every point" (Camic 1989: 56).

Camic also briefly deals with Parsons's deletion of the Simmel chapter, portraying the decision as pragmatic, not theoretical: "Simmel's sociology was not very useful for backing up the historical case his charter was making against economic theory, the ability to do so being the de facto criterion for settling on Marshall, Pareto, Weber and Durkheim" (Camic 1989: 59).

The analysis presented here does not quarrel with Camic's reading of events, but seeks to complement it. In a 1992 publication, Camic presents an argument similar to that developed in this paper. Raising the question of why Parsons, in *Structure*, turned to the Europeans rather than to American economic theorists, he concludes that Parsons could not have built a credible theory by citing Americans whose work had been the object of scorn among Harvard's economists. According to his analysis, Parsons composed *Structure*

> while he was part of a well-signposted intellectual network that warned him of the defectiveness and uselessness of some lines of relevant work while announcing the greatness, brilliance, and fruitfulness of other lines. . . . committed to producing a credible theoretical statement, Parsons heeded the signs, carefully engaging work of the first order that respected local authorities endorsed while slighting what they judged to be inferior pseudoscience. (Camic 1992: 437)

The discussion here, while according with Camic's treatment, focuses on *local understandings of science* rather than on the somewhat narrower issue of "predecessor selection."

Buxton's (1996) analysis of the responses to Parsons and Pitirim A. Sorokin at Harvard in the mid-1930s is also closely related to the present study, because it illumines microprocesses in relation to the validation of theory. Applying a political economy perspective, Buxton concludes that local representatives of national elites rewarded *Structure* (and Parsons's other early works) because these accorded with their own ideological commitments and material interests. In order to appreciate properly the fates of Parsons and Sorokin, Buxton argues,

> we must not only seek to understand the substance of their theoretical systems, but examine what their ideas signified to their contemporaries, and how they were received. . . .

It was because Parsons's vision of professional rationalization was consonant with the views of those who exerted influence that he gained recognition and support. . . . And as persons in influential positions began to actively help Parsons's career, they simultaneously conspired to thwart Sorokin's ambitions and to limit his influence. (1996: 36)

Buxton thus captures the strategic dimension of events that is the particular focus of the present study.[3] The analysis here, however, takes a further step by demonstrating subtle processes affecting not only responses to Parsons's early treatise, but its very composition. This discussion also breaks new ground by examining Parsons's own emergent response to situational pressures, especially what will be called his *strategic accommodation.*

THE "MISSING SIMMEL CHAPTER" CONTROVERSY

In the third edition of his *Structure of Social Action,* Parsons inserted a new, tantalizing footnote:

Along with the American social psychologists, notably Cooley, Mead, and W. I. Thomas, the most important single figure neglected in the Structure of Social Action . . . is probably Simmel. It may be of interest that I actually drafted a chapter on Simmel . . . but partly for reasons of space finally decided not to include it. (1968: xiv)[4]

The draft chapter clearly indicates that Parsons valued Simmel's approach to sociology. Indeed, Parsons raises the issue of whether Simmel's conceptual model surpasses his own "action" framework in terms of its ability to address emergent structures and variation across historical societies:

Thus we may surmise that Simmel's insight was primarily into the importance of what we have called the institutional aspect of social systems. It was clearly thought of as something analytically separable from the immediate "motives" of individuals. . . . It was a "mold" into which the pliable material of action was poured. And this is the emergent quality which arises through the processes of interaction as such. It is this and this only which is the grain of truth in the "organic" theories of society, but as against the "reification" of [such] "mechanistic" schemes as that of economic theory, *it is a profoundly important truth.* Finally, true to the predominant "historicism" of German social thought, it is in this element of "form" that the differentiation of different social structures from each other is to be sought. (Parsons, 1998a: 25, emphasis added)

At another point, Parsons lauds Simmel's approach as an important corrective to the action framework: "On the whole the action schema states social facts in a form which tends to minimize the structural elements. Hence the relationship schema, which throws them directly into the center of attention, is a highly important descriptive corrective" (Parsons, 1998a: 29).[5]

A further indication of Simmel's significance in Parsons's emerging perspective is provided by the Harvard catalogue description of Parsons's course, Sociology 21,

"The Sociological Theories of Hobhouse, Durkheim, Simmel, Tönnies, and Max Weber":

> The course will attempt, in terms of the theories of the above authors and perhaps a less thorough treatment of a few others, to present a comprehensive view of the main tendencies in the development of European sociological thought in the last generation. The main emphasis will be on problems and their interconnections in the work of the various authors rather than on the work of each taken as a separate unit. (Harvard University, 1935: 13)[6]

Thus, Parsons evidently regarded Simmel not only as an important individual thinker, but also as a theorist whose work had "interconnections" with the theories of Durkheim and Weber.[7]

In view of Parsons's engagement with Simmel's thought, his appeal to "reasons of space" as a rationale for excluding the draft chapter may be considered problematic. This assertion may be interpreted in diverse ways: as an adequate explanation by the only person who knows; as a rationalization after the fact, a vocabulary of motive (Mills, 1940) that conceals contemporaneous influences; or as a credible but incomplete account (Scott and Lyman, 1968; Nichols, 1990) that invites further investigation.

Opting for the latter view, Levine (1985) and Jaworski (1997) have published insightful, well-crafted analyses based on careful readings of relevant texts. Both conclude that the deletion resulted from Parsons's judgment that the material in question would have created flaws in his theoretical argument. The analysts, however, differ on the nature of these flaws.

According to Levine, including the Simmel chapter in *Structure* would have undermined the famous "convergence" thesis of the book, which states that positivist and idealist sociologists had increasingly tended toward a new approach that Parsons called the "voluntaristic theory of action." Levine finds support for his interpretation in the timing of Parsons's decision, which occurred not long after the convergence argument took final form. He sees the chapter's removal as a direct consequence of that crystallization, asserting, "There can be no doubt that these two events were connected" (Levine, 1985: 123). His clinching evidence is a letter from Parsons (1979) to Jeffrey Alexander acknowledging that the Simmel chapter did not fit the convergence thesis.

Jaworski (1997) challenges Levine's reading and makes the alternate case that Parsons perceived a clash between Simmel's formalism and his own emphasis on ultimate values. Thus:

> In Parsons's view, moral values, not social forms or structures, provided the source of social cohesion. Simmel's emphasis on forms, therefore, was incompatible with Parsons's solution to the social cohesion problematic. For this reason, it was unlikely that Simmel's sociology would play much of a role in Parsons's general theory. (Jaworski 1997: 51)

By this logic, a full-scale chapter on Simmel was not required, and so Parsons decided to accommodate "Simmel's more positive contribution in a separate section" (Jaworski, 1997: 59).

Interestingly, Jaworski examines selected contextual factors, especially the alleged rivalry between Parsons and Howard P. Becker. In support of this point he cites the 1979 letter to Alexander, which reports Parsons's perception that he and Becker had competed for leadership in introducing German sociology during the 1930s (Jaworski, 1997: 59). In Jaworski's judgment, however, this alleged competition was only a secondary factor in Parsons's decision to remove the Simmel chapter.[8]

Although the fate of a single chapter in an 800-page work may seem rather trivial, it resonates with fundamental issues in the history of sociology, and the sociology of knowledge. This is perhaps most apparent to those who see *Structure* as foundational and agree with Alexander's assertions that the treatise was the "most influential publication of any sociologist since Weber's *Economy and Society*" (1987: 22) and "played a key role, perhaps the key role, in establishing the base line vocabulary for modern sociology" (1988: 97). In the same vein, Levine views Parsons's prepublication decision as relevant to the professional identity of sociology in the United States.

> One notable consequence of the peculiar selectivity of *Structure* has been the exclusion of Simmel from the pantheon of sociological classics, following decades in which Simmel figured as a preeminent original thinker. . . . In other countries, where the Parsonian canon has not been so widely accepted, the last generation has shown a renaissance of interest in Simmel. (Levine, 1989: 114)

LOCAL CULTURE AND CONTINGENCIES AT HARVARD

Before the narrow question of the deletion of the Simmel chapter can be addressed, there must be some understanding of how the larger treatise was produced. The discussion below therefore reviews factors that arguably shaped the situation in which Parsons composed his study, and identifies specific pressures that were inimical to Simmelian sociology. Among the most important elements are the formal governance structure at Harvard; informal networks of political influence; local practices regarding tenure and promotion; local attitudes concerning Harvard's place in academia; the hegemony of natural science over social science; the local hierarchy of social sciences; Harvard's economic losses resulting from the Great Depression; and the attitude of President James B. Conant's administration toward its predecessor, the administration of A. L. Lowell. For present purposes, these situational factors will be combined under two general headings: indirect and direct influences on Parsons.

Indirect Influences

Archival and other sources show clearly that throughout the period in which he composed *Structure,* Parsons had to deal with the demands of Harvard's organizational culture. In Goffman's (1969) terms, he had to make gaming moves. Some situational problems were shared with all faculty, but others were peculiar to his own history. Under conditions of uncertainty and risk, Parsons made commitments to particular projects and sought allies within specific circles. These moves had consequences for *Structure* and its Simmel chapter.

The Vulnerability of Parsons

Assessment of *Structure* requires that analysts bear in mind Parsons's extremely vulnerable position from 1931 through mid-1936. Brought to a successful conclusion, the work had the potential to provide him with employment security during the Great Depression. If, on the other hand, Parsons failed to impress with his treatise he would almost certainly have been forced to leave Harvard and might have been unable to secure another comparable appointment.[9]

Graphic evidence of Parsons's peril appears in a letter from Dean Kenneth B. Murdock to Pitirim A. Sorokin, chair of Sociology, toward the end of Parsons's first semester in the new department:

> I am considerably disturbed by the situation of the two younger instructors in the Department [Parsons and C. S. Joslyn], who . . . *have not proved themselves fit for permanent positions,* and who . . . cannot relieve you as they should from some of the burden of course instruction. Don't you think it would be well to consider, at least, the possibility of *replacing one of them this year* by a new instructor? (Murdock, 1931, emphasis added)[10]

Sorokin (1931a) defended his subordinates, explaining that "the dryness of their lectures is the principal criticism . . . and this is not due to intellectual, but to temperamental factors." A week later, however, in response to another letter from Murdock emphasizing the limits on junior appointments, Sorokin wrote: " I have already warned Dr. Parsons and Dr. Joslyn that they *should not regard their appointments as permanent,* and have advised them not to fail to interest themselves in any considerable offer" (1931b, emphasis added).

Parsons's continuing vulnerability was manifested in an emotional letter to Sorokin, three years later, in which he pleaded his case for promotion to assistant professor:

> In December I shall be 32 years old. I am now in my ninth successive year of full-time college teaching, the eighth at Harvard. . . . four were as non-faculty instructor in Economics . . . and the last four as faculty instructor in Sociology. I fully understand that there were reasons why I was not advanced to a faculty instructorship in economics—I cannot, however, help feeling that Professor Burbank's and Bullock's prejudices against my German training and interests and not merely my lack of ability . . . were in part responsible. (Parsons, 1934)

Thus, Parsons had fallen short of Harvard's standards in economics and was seeking redemption in sociology. His future was in doubt.

Parsons, nevertheless, believed that he was about to demonstrate his true caliber as a theorist, telling Sorokin: " I have not as yet published a major work though I hope to have one ready . . . within a few months. It has taken a long time but . . . I have undertaken a peculiarly difficult job. I could have published a book some time ago—but its quality would have been far inferior to what this will be" (Parsons, 1934). Thus, Parsons himself viewed his book as a strategic gaming move that might transform his status at the University.

Shortly after this letter, Dean Murdock informed Sorokin that he and President James B. Conant were recommending that Parsons be granted sabbatical leave for fall 1935. Murdock (1934) added:

> In view of this absence . . . don't you think it would be interesting to see what some one of the young men of whom we spoke . . . might be able to do here? Do you think that [Howard P.] Becker could be got here for the first half-year . . . or is there some other young man whom you would like to consider? . . . we could try someone who might possibly be *a man we should want to consider for the future at Harvard* (emphasis added).[11]

The dangers to Parsons (already evident under the Lowell administration) had intensified as a result of tough policies that President Conant adopted in 1933. As Conant recalled:

> Dean Kenneth B. Murdock and I had a conference about the general principles which should apply to the reappointment or promotion of junior members of the faculty. In a memorandum summing up our conclusions, I stated that I would be loath to recommend anyone for a fifth year on an annual appointment. I also expressed the view that a second three-year term as faculty instructor should not be offered unless the department felt that within the next year or so it would be ready to make a recommendation for promotion. As to assistant professors, I wrote that after a lapse of six years . . . at this grade, a reappointment would not ordinarily be favored. (1970: 157)

The new approach sent shock waves, as when Conant simultaneously dismissed twelve instructors in English.[12]

The self-righteous zeal of the President's personnel policy can be seen in the following excerpt from his autobiography.

> A university . . . was a collection of eminent scholars. If the permanent professors were the most distinguished in the world, then the university would be the best. . . . I knew how few positions there were . . . where a professor could carry on research. To fill one of these positions with a second-rate person was . . . to be guilty of almost criminal negligence. (Conant, 1970: 83)

Such negligence, from Conant's perspective, would be far worse under conditions of the Great Depression that compelled Harvard to restrict the total number of permanent appointments.

Well aware that he was far beyond the normal probationary term, Parsons sent Conant an anxious letter in the fall of 1935, which Robert K. Merton, Edward P. Hutchinson, and Edward Y. Hartshorne also signed.[13] Rigid application of the new personnel policy, they argued, would be harmful to their young department.

Our one full professor [Sorokin] is slightly under fifty years of age. The two associate professors are respectively about fifty-five [James Ford] and slightly under forty [Carl C. Zimmerman]. According to the usual minimum age of retirement, then, there will be only three vacancies in the permanent staff in somewhat more than ten years, one in about sixteen, and one ten years after that. . . .

This situation is considerably complicated by the presence in the Department of a lecturer [Parsons] whose age is such that he would normally be a member of the permanent staff. (Parsons et al., 1935)

The Vulnerability of Sociology

In the mid-1930s, sociology remained a small field not taught in all American universities. In addition to its general vulnerability, sociology faced serious local obstacles at Harvard, evidenced by the fact that for four decades after the University of Chicago created the first academic department in the field, Harvard refused to take similar action. Only in 1931, two years before the end of President A. Lawrence Lowell's term in office, was a department finally organized (Nichols, 1992). It consisted of three full professors (Sorokin, T. N. Carver, R. Cabot), one associate professor (James Ford), two faculty instructors (Parsons and C. S. Joslyn), one nonfaculty instructor (P. Pigors), several tutors, and numerous "interdepartmental professors."

Having taken office with "a bold reform agenda," however, Conant did not feel bound by the policies of Lowell, who, he believed, "had been leading Harvard downhill" (Hershberg, 1993: 66–67). Prospects for sociology and social science in general were not promising under the new administration.

Conant found it difficult to credit such "unverifiable" disciplines as economics, psychology, government, history, and sociology. At least chemistry and astronomy had shaken off their superstitious shadows, alchemy and astrology. . . . "The real question which I keep turning over and over in my mind," he admitted to a correspondent in early 1936, "*is whether or not the social sciences are the modern equivalents of astrology.*" (Hershberg, 1993: 94, emphasis added)

Organizational Demands for "Empirical Science"

Conant: Naturalistic Social Science

Prior to becoming president of Harvard, James B. Conant had spent a year traveling through Europe, during which he carefully observed the organization of universities (Conant, 1970; Hershberg, 1993). In his judgment, the research university model in Germany was far superior to the British model that had been favored by his predecessor, A. Lawrence Lowell. Indeed, Conant believed there was an urgent need for American science to catch up with its German counterpart, a need which had been demonstrated by the applications of German science during World War I, most dramatically in the form of chemical weapons such as the notorious mustard gas.

Insofar as Conant accepted social science, he desired that it be modeled on the natural sciences. Like physiologist-sociologist Lawrence J. Henderson, he was impressed with history (the only social discipline, Henderson claimed, that had a definite method [Homans, 1984: 123; Whyte, 1994: 22]). Within Harvard, Conant particularly favored the approach of historian Crane Brinton, a protege of Henderson's who lectured in Henderson's case-based course, "Concrete Sociology."[14] A letter to Henderson clearly delineates the type of social science that Conant sought:

> I have just read the first quarter of Brinton's "Anatomy of Revolution." It seems to me a most excellent statement of (1) the fundamental basis of the so-called scientific method and (2) how a social scientist should attack . . . problems. . . . Since I cannot help seeing your influence . . . I am wondering what you would reply to the following question. Granted that Brinton's definition of a social scientist be desirable, would it be sufficient *to include in the University, if possible, only social scientists who had more or less this point of view?*[15]

Conant's letter implies that he would have agreed with Brinton's critique in "What's the Matter with Sociology?"

> All true science is cumulative. Physicists have something they can agree upon. Sociologists can't agree on anything. . . . Natural scientists are certainly not in entire agreement . . . but they dispute about the growing margins, the outside edges, of their discipline, not about its solid and established central core. There just isn't any such central core as yet in sociology. (Brinton, 1939: 14)

Thus, the burden that the organizational context imposed—and the challenge Parsons chose to accept—was to demonstrate the existence of such a core.[16]

Henderson: Behavioristic Functionalism

Nearly two decades before Parsons's 1951 book on the same topic, Henderson was lecturing about social systems in equilibrium. The following passage indicates the analogy that Henderson saw between natural and social science, and also provides insight into the reasons for his eventual support of Parsons's attempt, in *Structure*, to develop a conceptual framework specifying a set of fundamental variables:

> An important characteristic of many of the natural sciences is the concept of a system. . . . In order to fix our ideas we may consider Willard Gibbs's generalized description of a physico-chemical system. . . . It consists of components, which are individual substances, like water or sugar. . . .
> The central feature of Pareto's "General Sociology" . . . is the construction of a similar conceptual scheme; the social system. This system contains individuals; they are analogous to Gibbs's components. . . . As Gibbs considers temperature, pressure, and concentrations, so Pareto considers sentiments, or, strictly speaking, the manifestations of sentiments in words and deeds, verbal elaborations and the economic interests. (Henderson, 1970: 183–84)

Sorokin: Sociology as Generalizing Empirical Science

While Parsons was composing *Structure,* Sorokin was Harvard's best-known sociologist, whose *Contemporary Sociological Theories* (1928) was widely regarded as the
most authoritative survey of the field. The concluding chapter of this work identified
three fundamental divisions of sociology: relationships and correlations between various classes of social phenomena; relationships between social and nonsocial phenomena; and the general characteristics common to all classes of social phenomena.
All were empirical; they would (in Herbert Blumer's phrase) "let the world talk back."

It is also important, in this connection, that *Theories* was presented as an exemplar
of scientific sociology. F. Stuart Chapin, a prominent figure in the profession who was
noted for his hard-headed empiricism, praised the work in a prefatory note:

> Students of sociological theory are prone to fall into two contrasting types of error; either
> they accept speculative explanations of social phenomena with credulity, or they dismiss all
> theorizing as unscientific. . . . Professor Sorokin's book is a sound antidote for both extremes.
>
> By assembling quantitative data on social phenomena from an amazing variety of
> reputable sources, he confronts unfounded speculation with cold facts, and provides the
> student with tangible criteria for evaluating theory. (Chapin, 1928: ix)

Theories sharply criticized efforts to develop conceptual schemes rather than to
conduct empirical research:

> Speculative discussions about what sociology is . . . are examples of "sterile flowers." . . .
> Many sociological works have factually consisted in a mere speculation over these and
> similar problems. . . . Shall we wonder that such "sociologies" have not given us any real
> knowledge of social phenomena, except . . . indefinite words piled upon one another?
> (Sorokin, 1928: 502)

This passage indicates a fundamental difference between the approaches of Sorokin and Parsons. Sorokin believed that sociological theory developed from empiri-
cial studies; whereas Parsons held that fruitful empirical work could not begin until
a conceptual framework had been constructed.

DIRECT INFLUENCES

In order to remain at Harvard, Parsons needed the approval of at least two crucial decision makers. Most important was President Conant, who made all tenure decisions.
Next was Sorokin, Parsons's chairperson and the university's only full professor of
sociology. After encountering resistance from Sorokin, Parsons turned to Henderson,
who would largely displace Sorokin. I shall argue that the situational imperative of
gaining the approval of these persons may have affected the composition of *Structure*
and the specific decision to delete the Simmel chapter. As the following section
demonstrates, moreover, the views of Sorokin and Henderson were pivotal in Parsons's efforts to obtain financial support.

Organizational Funding of *Structure*

In 1929, under a grant from the Laura Spellman Rockefeller Memorial Foundation, Harvard established the Committee on Economic Research. Three years later, following receipt of a second grant, the university replaced it with the Committee on Research in the Social Sciences, whose membership included all full professors in the departments of history, government, economics, and sociology. Most of the committee's work, including the screening of grant proposals, was done by an executive committee of five persons that included a representative from the four participating departments. Since sociology had only one full professor, Sorokin served continuously on the executive committee and participated in all decisions about funding Parsons's research.

Reports of the committee indicate that from 1932 through 1937, Parsons received slightly less than three thousand dollars in support (approximately double the salary of a departmental secretary, and slightly more than the salary of an instructor in the college).[17] Some of this funding went toward his articles on "The Ultimate Place of Values in Sociological Theory" (1935a) and "Education and the Professions" (1937b), but most was directly related to his work on *Structure*. In order to receive this support, Parsons had to convince internal reviewers of the scientific character of his treatise.

Manuscript Reviews

Between 1935 and 1937, the manuscript of *Structure* was revised repeatedly. Some changes resulted from the review process employed by the Committee on Research in the Social Sciences to make funding decisions. Others followed informal readings by friends such as Professor Arthur Darby Nock and Robert K. Merton (Ph.D. 1936).

In the fall of 1935, Parsons also submitted the manuscript to Sorokin, who responded with a lengthy critique, written, he said, in a "friendly spirit." Some of Sorokin's judgments, however, may have intensified Parsons's worries about his future at Harvard:

> I find most essential parts of your work one of the most difficult readings I know of. . . . reading your manuscript proved to be hardly easier, rather more difficult, than my first reading of Kant's *Critique of Pure Reason,* and certainly more difficult than the reading of the "phenomenological" works of Husserl. . . . I feel that your work will be "unreadable" for, say, 90 per cent of sociologists. (Sorokin, 1935a)

Most ominous, in the circumstances, was this summary assessment:

> The reasons are at hand why even for an attentive reader it is exceedingly difficult to follow you. It is not so much in the manner of writing as much as in an unclearness of thought of the author. . . . *the most difficult and the poorest parts of your work appear to me those where you try to give your own constructive scheme.* (Sorokin, 1935a, emphasis added)

Johnston reaches a similar conclusion about the negative implications of Sorokin's assessment: "Judging from this letter, Sorokin may have found Parsons's achievements inadequate for advancement. The difficulties he observed were fundamental and serious" (1995: 99).

Under Harvard's procedures, Sorokin's opposition would ordinarily have been a nearly insurmountable barrier to Parsons's permanency in sociology—in the same way that H. H. Burbank's and C. H. Bullock's negative assessments had blocked his advance in economics. In order to remain at the University, therefore, Parsons needed either to overcome Sorokin's objections or else to locate an alternate means of influencing Conant to grant tenure.[18]

STRATEGIC ACCOMMODATION BY PARSONS

Faced with this urgent problem, Parsons turned to others, especially Lawrence J. Henderson; economic historian and former business school dean, Edwin F. Gay; and professor of religious history, Arthur Darby Nock. Gay had helped Parsons gain his initial appointment in sociology (Nichols, 1992), but he was nearing retirement, and his influence with Conant was not as great as it had been with Lowell. Nock was well respected, but was not a major political broker at Harvard.

Henderson, however, was at the peak of his local influence. A relation of Conant's by marriage, he had continual access to the president, reflected in letters from Conant that begin, "Dear Uncle Lawrence." A member of the faculties of the college (chemistry) and the medical school, Henderson worked mainly at the business school, where his office bordered that of Dean Wallace Donham. He also exercised influence as chairman of Harvard's Society of Fellows, whose members included ex officio both the president of the university and the dean of the faculty of arts and sciences. Conant's confidence in Henderson is evident at many points in their correspondence, which shows that Conant frequently consulted Henderson on a wide range of issues and placed him on important advisory committees.

Most important here is the fact that Conant, members of the Harvard Corporation,[19] and other key administrators and influential members of the faculty *regarded Henderson as Harvard's most authoritative sociologist.* Indeed, Charles P. Curtis, Jr.— while a member of the Corporation—participated in Henderson's seminar on Pareto. William F. Whyte (1994: 56) has likewise recounted how in Harvard's innermost circles, "it was assumed that any social scientist would take Pareto's seminar." George Homans has also recalled how after being invited to enter the Society of Fellows, he sought Henderson's guidance:

> I asked Henderson, in effect, "Master, what shall I do to become a sociologist?" I discovered later that he knew no more about the matter than I did myself, and that he certainly did not propose to consult any of the sociologists, such as Sorokin. . . . Yet his answer was, as always, decided. (1984: 122)

Despite Henderson's limitations (Buxton, 1996; Barber, 1970), he was regarded as Harvard's expert on science whose distinguished research and experience in teaching the history of science for over twenty years qualified him to assess sociology's scientific worth.

Archival documents and Parsons's published reminiscences indicate that Henderson was deeply and continuously involved in the production of *Structure* from 1935 through 1937. Parsons later recalled Henderson's mentoring with unabashed gratitude:

> I had known him . . . before the manuscript of my book was referred to him for critical comment. . . . Instead of the usual limited response, he got in touch with me . . . and started a long series of personal sessions at his house . . . two hours, twice a week for nearly three months. In these sessions he went through the manuscript with me paragraph by paragraph, mainly the sections dealing with Pareto and Durkheim. (Parsons, 1970: 832)

A 1935 letter, however, adds an important correction to Parsons's 1970 statement by showing that *Parsons himself took the initiative and sought Henderson's guidance:*

> I have lately been occupied with the revision, which amounts to an almost complete rewriting, of my study of Pareto. It is to appear as one of the principal parts of a larger book. When it is finished, which should be within a couple of weeks, *I should very much like to submit it to you for your criticism*, if you are willing. The changes will, I think, *bring it considerably more into accord with your own views than was the first version.* . . . Whatever you may think, I shall greatly value your criticisms. (Parsons, 1935b)[20]

Thus, Parsons conceded that his earlier interpretation of Pareto had been inaccurate, and expressed the hope that he was coming to a better understanding as he moved in the direction of Henderson's thinking. Parsons does not say that his approach is identical to Henderson's, but acknowledges a need to modify his own position without suggesting any comparable need on Henderson's part.

Some eighteen months later, Henderson reviewed a subsequent draft of *Structure* and submitted the following recommendation to the Committee on Research in the Social Sciences:

> This seems to me a very important piece of work and I have the impression that Parsons has accomplished his object and proved his case. Moreover, I think that his principal conclusion is likely . . . to be influential. . . . it is a most interesting and weighty contribution to the history . . . of science in the making.
>
> On the other hand, there are in the work a large number of details that I regard as erroneous. . . . Concerning not a few of these *it is my impression that I have convinced Parsons that I am right.* . . .
>
> Because the work seems to me potentially so good I strongly urge that it should be once more revised, but I am of the opinion that the important conclusions are already so firmly established that it justifies an undertaking to spend the necessary funds for its publication. (Henderson, 1937a)[21]

The Parsons-Henderson interaction is consistent with the view that Parsons consciously accommodated himself to Henderson's beliefs as a means of gaining the latter's support for promotion and tenure. Indeed, there does not seem to be another documented instance in which Parsons, who always viewed himself as independent and a "maverick" (Wearne, 1989: 61), submitted to tutelage like Henderson's, which bordered on coauthorship of the Pareto section of *Structure*—if not outright dictation. Given his unique role in Harvard politics (Parascandola, 1992), and especially his influence with Conant, Henderson's backing might have been seen by Parsons as sufficient to offset Sorokin's lack of support.

Parsons's contrasting relationships with his mentor and chairperson are reflected in *Structure*, where Parsons cites Henderson's work seven times and Sorokin's eleven. Interestingly, all of the references to Henderson are favorable, whereas most of the citations of Sorokin are critical. Thus, early in the work Parsons states: "Adapting Professor Henderson's definition, in this study a fact is understood to be an 'empirically verifiable statement about phenomena in terms of a conceptual scheme'" (1937a: 41). Farther on, he likewise observes: "The best general account of Pareto's methodological procedure available is that in L. J. Henderson, *Pareto's General Sociology*" (1937a: 181, n2).

Indeed, Parsons tells readers that Henderson is correct about Pareto, whereas Sorokin's treatment in *Contemporary Sociological Theories* is wrong. Thus, discussing the concepts of "residues" and "derivations," Parsons comments:

> It is very curious that in the great majority of the secondary treatments of Pareto, the residues have been identified with the *A* of the earlier schema, while the derivations have been identified with the *C* of the same schema. This persistent tendency directly in the face of Pareto's perfectly explicit words raises a problem. (1937a: 198–99)

A footnote refers readers to the error on page 50 of *Theories*.

Another footnote, by contrast, comments: "The principal exceptions [i.e., to the mistaken view] are Homans and Curtis, *An Introduction to Pareto* and L. J. Henderson, *Pareto's General Sociology*" (Parsons, 1937a:199, n1). As noted above, however, the views of Homans and Curtis derived from Henderson's seminar (where Pareto's treatise was read in French). As Homans recalled: "Henderson worked slowly through the *Traite*, providing his exegesis of selected passages. After each of these, he would ask for questions. . . . Except from Sorokin, I do not remember that there was much argument" (1984: 105).

Considering that Curtis, as well as Homans's father, were members of the Corporation, it seems fair to conclude that the Henderson circle's view of Pareto—which Parsons embraced in *Structure*—was the official Harvard view of both sociology and science. Farther on, Parsons attacks Sorokin's critiques of both Durkheim and Weber. Regarding the former, he says:

> Professor Sorokin, in quoting Tarde with approval . . . evidently places a quite unduly narrow interpretation on the criterion of constraint, seen in terms of its place in the course of the development of Durkheim's sociological thought. (Parsons, 1937a: 385, n1)

Concerning Weber, he likewise comments:

> it is impossible to agree with Professor Sorokin's contention that Weber failed to establish an adequate distinction between Puritan and Confucian rationalism. . . .

Professor Sorokin also holds . . . the Japanese reception of Western economic organization . . . to be important empirical evidence against Weber's position. . . . Sorokin's point does not seem conclusive. (Parsons, 1937a: 552, n1)

Sorokin, of course, had become aware of such differences during his reading of the earlier draft manuscript, and had told Parsons in his handwritten commentary:

> In your interpretation of the theories analyzed . . . you seem to me twisting the points of the author, if not in their letter then in their meaning. As a case of that, I am ready to take your criticism of my brief characterization of Pareto's "residue": literally you are perfectly right, so far as the text quoted by you is concerned; in the "spirit and meaning" of Pareto, I feel perfectly justified in my characterization. . . . once in a while your analysis becomes so "fine" that in its "fineness" it becomes finicky and misses the elephant in your hunt for the mosquito.
>
> These are the main shortcomings. . . . they do not annul the really fine points of your work. . . . But in your work one finds not only this "gold" but plenty of "pseudo-gold" and something less noble. (Sorokin, 1935a)

Having cast his lot with Henderson, however, Parsons may have felt secure against Sorokin's critical barbs.[22]

Contemporaneous documents indicate that Parsons had by late 1935 convinced Henderson that he possessed the correct "scientific" outlook his mentor demanded. Most informative in this connection are two letters from December 1935. In the first, Henderson supports Parsons's application for a fellowship from the Guggenheim Foundation. The key passage states:

> He is a thoughtful, intellectually enterprising man. While he preserves a little of the metaphysical background of his earlier years—and even a little is too much according to my preference—*he is now thinking in terms of facts and uniformities in facts and the slow building up of sound scientific knowledge.* (Henderson, 1935a)

The second letter, written a day later to Dean George Birkhoff, supports the promotion of Parsons to an assistant professorship. The excerpt below also highlights sociology's tenuous position at Harvard, and shows clearly that the social sciences were to be judged according to the model of natural science:

> I write to say that I have rarely felt more confident about the desirability of promoting a man to an assistant professorship, that this is due to my conviction, based upon first-hand knowledge of a considerable part, say about one-third, of his work of the last few years, that he is fully up to the standard, though not, of course, up to the highest level of assistant professorships in such a subject as mathematics, and that there is probably nobody else in the country . . . who is anywhere near him.
>
> Moreover, since I have known him he seems to me to have been moving steadily away from the habit of thinking in words and vague ideas toward the practice of searching for the facts. And if this tendency continues, there is good prospect that he will become both a distinguished and a trustworthy sociologist, which is a rare combination. . . .

> To sum up, I feel confident that Parsons is up to the standard of assistant professors in the University as a whole, that this is a very exceptional attainment in a sociologist, that *he has been moving in the right direction both in work and in thought and that he is a healthy and level-headed person.* (Henderson, 1935b, emphasis added)

These endorsements were written a few months after the completion of the one-on-one sessions at Henderson's home that had resulted from Parsons's request for Henderson's critical comments.[23]

IMPLICATIONS FOR SIMMEL AS SOCIAL SCIENTIST

The attitudes of key local decision makers about science and its development at Harvard all arguably worked against adoption of a Simmelian approach to sociology. In the case of Sorokin, there is direct evidence on this point, and in the cases of Conant and Henderson, it can be shown indirectly.

Sorokin dealt with Simmel's writings in several of his earlier works, including *Leo Tolstoy as a Philosopher* (1914), *A System of Sociology* (1920), and *Contemporary Sociological Theories* (1928). Although he expressed respect for Simmel as a philosopher, Sorokin's attitude toward Simmel's formalist sociology gradually hardened. This is most evident in *Theories*, which includes a chapter on the formalist approach as a variant of the "sociologistic" school. After reviewing the frameworks of Simmel, Leopold von Wiese, and others, Sorokin concluded:

> What has been said of the fundamental conceptions of Simmelian sociology may be said of its many other propositions. . . . they are stamped by the same vagueness, indefiniteness, changeable meanings. . . . In this respect *they are still in the stage of a purely philosophical or speculative sociology.* (1928: 502, emphasis added)

Sorokin also condemned Simmelian sociology as unscientific on methodological grounds:

> Simmel's method entirely lacks either experimental approach, quantitative investigation, or any systematic factual study. . . . In vain one would look in his work for a systematic method like that of the Le Play school . . . or something like Max Weber's method of the "ideal typology." . . . What there is represents only the speculative generalization of a talented man, backed by the "method of illustration." . . . Without Simmel's talent the same stuff would appear poor. (1928: 502n)

Conant's hard-science orientation has already been noted. The future developer of the atomic bomb was a distinguished experimentalist who had been widely regarded as a potential Nobel Prize winner in chemistry. For him, even more than for Sorokin, Simmel's approach would not have been scientific at all. Thus, had Parsons's *Structure* included Simmel as a foundational thinker, its value would have diminished in the eyes of Harvard's president, the most crucial decision maker regarding Parsons's career.

Henderson's view, grounded in the framework of Pareto, emphasized the concept of equilibrium that Henderson had applied in his famed experiments on acid-base equilibrium in the blood.[24] To become scientific, Henderson believed, sociology would have to work with systems of quantitative variables in relations of mutual dependence—not "forms of sociation" as Simmel advocated.[25]

Other indirect evidence strengthens the inference that Henderson would not have approved of Parsons building a sociological paradigm on Simmelian foundations. These data were produced in connection with two decisions involving prominent sociologists. In 1934, after losing two full professors to retirement (T. N. Carver and R. C. Cabot), the Department of Sociology unanimously recommended that Harvard offer a professorship to Robert M. MacIver of Columbia. Conant solicited Henderson's views, and the latter responded with a fierce debunking of MacIver's works and, more importantly, his approach to science.

Henderson's ten-page document cited objectionable passages from two of MacIver's books, with the following judgments:

I infer from these and many other statements in these two early books that the author:
(1) Habitually mistakes words for things.
(2) Habitually mistakes interactions and mutual dependence for cause and effect.
(3) Habitually interprets in terms of the will and the interests: instinctive action, the results of what is now called conditioning, the passions, emotions, and prejudices of men.
(4) Finally he habitually states as facts his desires. *These are among the chief sources of error in the social sciences in general.* (Henderson, 1934, emphasis added)

Acting partly on this review, Conant rejected the sociology department's strong recommendation and declined to appoint MacIver. There can be little doubt that Henderson would have seen Simmel's writings, even more than MacIver's, as guilty of the above fatal flaws.

The second case, four years later, involved Robert K. Merton, who was then an instructor on a three-year appointment. Conant was considering expanding Harvard's offerings in the history of science, as historian of science George Sarton had been urging the university to do.[26] Several historians and sociologists of science were under discussion as potential Harvard appointees, including Merton, on the strength of his three-hundred-page study, "Science, Technology and Society in Seventeenth Century England" (1938). Asked by Conant to compare Merton with two other candidates, Henderson offered the following observations based on notes he had made while reading Merton's work:

I find . . . that by far the greater part of the criticisms are unimportant except for the purpose that I had in mind, of helping him to consider his procedure, his way of writing, and in particular his use of vague literary and philosophical words in a way that obscured his own thought from himself and from others. All these things I believe to be merely temporary difficulties *that are to be ascribed to his bringing-up in sociology.* [27]

Thus, believing that sociology needed to be liberated from its reliance on "vague literary and philosophical words," Henderson would surely have rejected Simmel's writings as the basis for a scientific sociology.

CONCLUSION

This chapter has called attention to the importance of local contexts and organizational cultures for a complete understanding of sociological work, including theoretical treatises that may appear to be entirely individual efforts. Such contexts do not entirely determine the content of sociological writings, but they do present factors that sociologists must take into consideration, especially prior to receiving academic tenure. It may be that local considerations were more important a century or a half century ago, but they may still exert a significant influence today, for example, in stated or unstated requirements that candidates for tenure receive external funding for their research, which necessitates conformity to the agendas of funding sources, and which may favor quantitative approaches over qualitative work.

A central feature of the analysis has been the question of why Talcott Parsons deleted a chapter on Georg Simmel from his first major work, *The Structure of Social Action* (1937a). Without a "smoking gun" document indicating Parsons's thinking at the time, it is not possible to answer the question definitively. The historical materials cited here have, however, shown clearly that Parsons sought to gain the approval of crucial decision makers, especially Lawrence J. Henderson, who would not have regarded Simmel as a scientist but only as a speculative philosopher. Had Parsons, by contrast, been completing his treatise at the University of Chicago and seeking the final approval of Robert Park, Ernest Burgess, Everett Hughes, or Louis Wirth, he might well have kept the Simmel chapter and modified his discussion of, say, Marshall. Or, had Henderson been as enthusiastic about Simmel as he was about Pareto, the Simmel chapter might have remained in *Structure* and perhaps even been amplified.

Gary Jaworski (1998), writing about academic contexts in the 1950s, has developed a similar argument with regard to Columbia and the New School for Social Research. According to his analysis, Simmel's work was accepted at both institutions, but not in the same way. At Columbia, the overriding emphasis was on extracting Simmel's testable propositions concerning social structure, whereas at the New School Simmel's phenomenological dimension was highly valued. Jaworski attributes these differences to the attitudes of key decision makers at the two universities: Robert Merton and Paul Lazarsfeld and Columbia, and Albert Salomon at the New School. With regard to tangible consequences, Jaworski contends that Lewis Coser's doctoral dissertation and its subsequent publication were altered by the organizational context of Columbia:

> It is well known that *The Functions of Social Conflict* was Coser's doctoral dissertation, written under Merton at Columbia. Less widely known is the fact that the published book is actually only half of his dissertation, and that the other half remains unpublished. The part that has become famous follows Merton's functionalist research program.
>
> The unpublished first part of Coser's dissertation . . . represents a very different research program. . . . In the unpublished material, Coser's basic purpose is to explain the changing status of conflict in American sociological thought from a positive valuation among the founding generation to a negative estimation. (Jaworski 1998: 9)

What is particularly intriguing about the case of Simmel, Parsons, and *The Structure of Social Action* is that key decision makers were outside the Department of Sociology and thus represented a larger, organizational culture dimension. Although space does not permit a detailed treatment here, it is also significant that the natural sciences and their methodology were in the ascendancy at Harvard in the mid-1930s. This was evident not only in the growth of physics and chemistry and their methodologies, but also in some of the social sciences, especially economics, which was rapidly becoming mathematical, and psychology, which was intensifying an emphasis on the biological bases of behavior (see Triplet, 1992). A decade earlier, under the more humanistically oriented administration of A. Lawrence Lowell (who had been a professor of government), the climate would have been more favorable to the inclusion of a figure like Simmel in a work such as *Structure*.

These considerations should be rather obvious, because institutions of learning always have stated or unstated commitments to systems of beliefs and values. Ideology provides perhaps the clearest illustration. Until recently it would have been difficult for an avowed Marxist to gain tenure at a Catholic or fundamentalist Christian university, just as would be the case today in Islamic republics such as Iran. In the former Soviet Union, by contrast, scholars dissenting from the official Marxist-Leninist line were ineligible for academic appointments.

The issue of professional competence is more difficult to analyze. Had Conant and Henderson condemned *The Structure of Social Action,* they would doubtless have articulated their verdict in terms of universal norms of competent science—not ideology. What is especially challenging for sociologists of science and knowledge is the analysis of situations where cues about scientific work are communicated subtly and thus inconspicuously contradict institutional claims about unlimited intellectual freedom. It is difficult even to gauge the extent to which social scientists are aware of organizational cues, and the extent to which they may conform without consciously realizing it. Parsons may have thought he agreed with Henderson and Conant about science, but it is difficult to believe that he actually did so, given the sharp contrasts between his style of work and theirs.

In closing, I would again stress that this analysis is not an attack on the intellectual integrity or the moral courage of Talcott Parsons, both of which have been attested to by colleagues and historians. Thus, in his autobiography, longtime colleague George Homans was emphatic about Parsons's intellectual tenacity: "I came to the conclusion that one could not argue with him, or at least I could not. After I thought I had him convinced, what he wrote down later always turned out to represent his original position" (Homans, 1984: 302). With regard to moral courage, Mike Keen (1999: 137) has uncovered evidence of Parsons's strong stand in support of his colleague Sam Stouffer and other academics during the anti-Communist hysteria of the mid-1950s: "Parsons was unyielding in his support of Stouffer, writing, 'I am in it with you to the death,' and of [Robert] Bellah and [Robert] Oppenheimer as well" (Keen, 1999: 137). Parsons also took a public stand against loyalty oaths for teachers that had been imposed in California in the early 1950s, when such action could—and did—make him a target of FBI surveillance.

Thus, as Alexander and Sciortino have emphasized, the composition of *The Structure of Social Action* was certainly a creative process:

Social scientists and theorists are agents. They possess, protect, and nurture subjectivities that allow them to select, consciously and unconsciously, among the internal and external pressures of their environments, whether these be the reputations of other scientists or the idioms of broad cultural traditions. (1996: 163)

It is, however, equally true, as Camic (1992: 433, 1996: 174) has argued, that the composition of *Structure* did not occur in a social vacuum but rather within an organizational context involving local understandings of science and concomitant reward systems. Further, as Camic has also emphasized, professional scientific activity "involves establishing 'credibility'" in the sense that "natural and social scientists engage . . . in efforts to demonstrate the 'solidity' of their claims so that these will be 'believed in' by fellow specialists or other relevant audiences" (1992: 439). Parsons persuaded Henderson and Conant that in *The Structure of Social Action* he was doing genuine science according to their understanding of scientific practice, and they responded by supporting Parsons for promotion and tenure. In the process, Georg Simmel's sociology may have been an unintended and unnoticed casualty.

NOTES

This analysis has benefited from comments kindly provided by the following colleagues: Bill Buxton, Irving Horowitz, Gary Jaworski, Barry Johnston, Robert K. Merton, Neil Smelser, and Jonathan Turner.

1. In *The Structure of Social Action,* Parsons (1937a: 44) stated that a social act "must be initiated in a 'situation.'"

2. This analysis is based upon research in the extraordinarily rich deposits of the Harvard University Archives (Pusey Library) and the archives of the Harvard Graduate School of Business Administration (Baker Library). The discussion relies upon both official and unofficial sources, including: the correspondence of President James B. Conant, Deans Kenneth B. Murdock, and George Birkhoff, and the Department of Sociology; as well as the faculty papers of Talcott Parsons and Lawrence J. Henderson. The analysis is also informed by other archival sources: the official correspondence of Presidents Charles W. Eliot and A. Lawrence Lowell, the records of the Department of Economics and the Department of Social Ethics, and the faculty papers of James Ford, Richard C. Cabot, Crane Brinton, and Edwin B. Wilson.

All quotations from unpublished sources are printed courtesy of the Harvard University Archives, whose curators and staff have provided invaluable assistance.

3. The network that promoted Parsons's model and opposed Sorokin's theory, according to Buxton, included: Henderson, Conant, Professor of Vital Statistics Edwin B. Wilson, Deans Wallace B. Donham (business school) and David Edsall (medical school), as well as other Harvard figures such as Corporation Secretary Jerome Greene, who had links to the Rockefeller Foundation.

4. Recently, William Buxton (1998) has revealed another dimension to the Parsons-Simmel story, by showing that Parsons wrote a second unpublished paper about Simmel. Interestingly, between the time of the first (1934?) and second papers (1939?), Parsons's thinking had

changed somewhat. Buxton argues that Parsons's engagement with Simmel was more inten-sive and sustained than Parsons's published reminiscences indicated. See Parsons, 1998a and 1998b, and also Buxton, 1998.

5. The original title of *The Structure of Social Action* was *Sociology and the Elements of Hu-man Action,* which Parsons retained as late as his 1936 *curriculum vitae.* The term "elements" indicates his choice of a strategy for theory building that focuses on identifying the simplest components of social life and then developing structures from their combinations. In Sim-mel's writings, by contrast, complex structures such as interpersonal relationships were dis-cussed from the very outset.

6. This course was intended primarily for graduate students, and it was there that some of the best known Ph.D.'s of the 1931–46 Department of Sociology became excited about theory. See Robert K. Merton's memoir (1980).

7. The omission of Pareto from the list of theorists in Sociology 21 is rather striking, not only because of Pareto's importance in *The Structure of Social Action* but also because Parsons had written an article about Pareto's sociology as early as 1932—the year when Sociology 21 was introduced. It may be that Parsons wished to avoid the appearance of competing with Henderson's Pareto seminar.

8. At the time of his possible "rivalry" with Parsons, Becker was a leading exponent of Simmel's sociology, as it had been further developed in Germany by Leopold von Wiese. In 1932, Becker and von Wiese coauthored *Systematic Sociology,* which presented von Wiese's ap-proach. Two years earlier, Parsons had published a translation of Max Weber's influential 1905 study, *The Protestant Ethic and the Spirit of Capitalism.* Both Becker and Parsons were fluent in German, and their efforts to introduce German sociology to English speakers is a good exam-ple of Jaworski's (1997) concept of "translation as social action."

9. The point should not be pushed too far. Although Parsons's situation at Harvard was problematic, other schools were interested in him, including Columbia and the University of Chicago (he had taught summer courses at both), as well as the University of Wisconsin, which offered him a professorship in 1937. Nevertheless, under the conditions of the economic de-pression, finding a job at just the right moment was quite hazardous. Parsons, moreover, had a young family and was reluctant to relocate. Also—and this may be the most crucial consid-eration—he seems to have been determined to prove himself worthy of a permanency at Har-vard. These considerations justify the conclusion that Parsons was risking a great deal on his theory book, and that the assessment of this book would have enormous consequences for his career and professional identity.

10. Sorokin (1963) also claimed that Lowell refused to approve the transfer of Parsons from economics to sociology, and that only Sorokin's intensive lobbying changed the president's mind.

11. Becker's coauthored book on formal sociology was a major reason why he was consid-ered potentially "Harvard caliber." Becker came to Harvard for a semester while Parsons was on sabbatical leave in fall 1935. He taught Sociology 2a, "Conduct and Culture: an Introduc-tion to Psychological Sociology" (enrollment 41), as well as Sociology 14a, "Social Thought be-fore Comte" (enrollment 10), and also participated in the department's proseminar, Sociology 20b, "Sociological Theory" (enrollment 7) along with Sorokin.

12. Conant's policy would generate the famous Walsh-Sweezy controversy of 1937–38, which arose when two popular economics professors with liberal views were informed of terminating appointments. This led to a near mutiny in which over 140 faculty members signed a petition for a formal investigation, and eventuated in two famous reports that be-came the basis for Harvard's "up or out" policy. Indeed, as a result of his personnel policy

and seemingly arbitrary personal style, Conant was nearly forced to resign in 1939 after only six years as president. See Hershberg (1993: 105), and also Harvard University (1939).

13. Hutchinson, Hartshorne, and Merton were then junior faculty in sociology, and the department's main hopes for the future. Hutchinson, a demographer, went on to a career at the University of Maryland. Hartshorne, a social psychologist interested in education, was killed in Germany shortly after the German surrender in 1945. Merton, of course, became the most famous graduate of the 1931–46 Department of Sociology at Harvard.

14. Clarence Crane Brinton (1898–1968) is important for an understanding of the development of sociology at Harvard in the 1930s. An expert on the French Revolution, he was also a member of Harvard's Society of Fellows, which had been largely founded by Henderson. After Henderson's death in 1942, Brinton succeeded him as president of the society. Brinton had also become a member of the exclusive Saturday Club (composed of prominent Bostonians) as a result of Henderson's nomination.

Brinton had other connections with sociology. He mentored the young George Homans during the latter's research as a Junior Fellow on medieval English villages. He lectured in the two-semester course on Social Institutions (Sociology 6) that Parsons coordinated. Brinton also assailed Sorokin's major work, *Social and Cultural Dynamics* (1937), in a review titled "Socio-Astrology" (and received a fierce rejoinder, "Histrionics"). See Brinton (1937) and Sorokin (1938), as well as the Brinton Papers, Harvard University Archives.

15. Conant to Henderson, October 24, 1938, emphasis added. In the Henderson Papers, Baker Library.

16. Parsons sent Brinton an emotionally charged rebuttal, which included the following passage: "you state flat-footedly that 'sociologists can't agree on anything.' This is simply not true. I spent the major effort of an eight hundred page book proving that three sociologists . . . converged on the main outlines of nothing less than a generalized theoretical system, a thing which . . . has appeared in other social sciences only after a relatively mature stage of their developments. . . . "

Although Parsons defended his discipline, he explicitly agreed with Brinton that Sorokin's approach was wrongheaded and therefore could not provide a basis for the development of sociology. Parsons to Brinton, July 11, 1939. In the Parsons Papers, Harvard University Archives.

The timing of the letter is suggestive. Parsons waited until he had been promoted to associate professor with tenure (effective in the fall of 1939) to place in writing this outspoken critique of his senior colleague in history and his department chair.

17. See the annual reports of the committee in the Harvard University Archives, Pusey Library.

18. Despite Sorokin's critical view of Parsons's work, he did support Parsons's promotion to assistant professor (a rank more significant then than it is today). In a December 1935 memorandum to Dean George Birkhoff explaining a series of departmental recommendations, Sorokin wrote: "The main reasons for the recommendation of Dr. Talcott Parsons's promotion are as follows: His second term as instructor on faculty appointment would end next academic year, but as he has been very rapidly growing, has shown considerable efficiency in not only teaching but in rather high grade publications, and as we are informed that other institutions are making definite plans concerning him, and finally as almost all his colleagues of the University who stayed in the Department of Economics are assistant or associate professors, all these reasons motivated the decision of the Department. . . . The Department feels we cannot afford to lose him, and that he deserves unquestionably such a promotion" (Sorokin, 1935b).

19. The Harvard Corporation is an elite group of seven that functions as a self-perpetuating board of directors. Its members include the president and fellows of the university.

20. Parsons to Henderson, May 16, 1935, emphasis added. In the Henderson Papers, Baker Library.

21. Henderson to John D. Black, chair of the Committee on Research in the Social Sciences, January 4, 1937. In the Henderson Papers.

22. Parsons was promoted to assistant professor in 1936, but did not gain permanency until 1939. Thus, while *Structure* was in its final stages, Parsons still had to show deference to Sorokin—though he was less dependent on his chairperson than formerly.

23. Henderson's house, on Willard Street, was only a short walk from Harvard Yard. Interestingly, Parsons developed the practice of holding regular evening discussion groups at his home in Belmont, Massachusetts, which was several miles from the university. Indeed, anyone who wishes to follow the development of Parsons's thought must take account of the numerous discussion groups in which he participated from the mid-1930s through the early 1950s, and in which he was usually the central figure.

One of my former professors at Boston College, John Donovan (who studied under Sorokin and Parsons), used to tell the story of how he was invited to present at one of the Belmont evening groups, because Parsons had liked his paper, "Reflected Status: A Footnote to the Theory of Stratification."

24. Lawrence J. Henderson, *Blood: A Study in General Physiology*. New Haven: Yale University Press, 1928.

25. This is why Henderson advised George Homans to prepare for study in sociology by taking calculus. See Homans (1984).

26. Sarton was a scholar in residence at Harvard, with an office in Widener Library, whose work on the history of science was subsidized by the Carnegie Corporation. He had originally come to the United States from Belgium as a result of World War I. In addition to his own historical survey of the development of science, he created and edited two periodicals, *Isis* and *Osiris*. It was in *Osiris* that Robert K. Merton's study of science in seventeenth-century England appeared in 1938.

27. Henderson to Conant, October 19, 1938, emphasis added. In the Henderson Papers, Baker Library.

REFERENCES

Abbott, A., and E. Gaziano. 1995. "Transition and Tradition: Departmental Faculty in the Era of the Second Chicago School." Pp. 221–72 in *A Second Chicago School?* edited by G. A. Fine. Chicago: University of Chicago Press.

Alexander, J. 1987. *Twenty Lectures: Sociological Theory Since World War II*. New York: Columbia University Press.

———. 1988. "Parsons' *Structure* in American Sociology." *Sociological Theory* 6: 96–102.

Alexander, J., and G. Sciortino. 1996. "On Choosing One's Intellectual Predecessors: The Reductionism of Camic's Treatment of Parsons and the Institutionalists." *Sociological Theory* 14 (2): 154–71.

Barber, B. 1970. *Lawrence J. Henderson on the Social System*, edited by B. Barber. Chicago: University of Chicago Press.

Brinton, C. 1937. "Socio-Astrology." *Southern Review* 3 (autumn): 243–66.

———. 1939. "What's the Matter with Sociology?" *Saturday Review of Literature* (May 6): 3–4, 14.

Buxton, W. 1985. *Talcott Parsons and the Capitalist Nation-State.* Toronto: University of Toronto Press.

———. 1996. "Snakes and Ladders: Parsons and Sorokin at Harvard." Pp. 39–55 in *Sorokin and Civilization: A Centennial Assessment,* edited by J. B. Ford, M. P. Richard, and P. C. Talbutt, Jr. New Brunswick, N.J.: Transaction Publishers.

———. 1998. "From the 'Missing Fragment' to the 'Lost Manuscript': Reflections on Parsons's Engagement with Simmel." *American Sociologist* 29 (2): 57–76.

Camic, C. 1989. "*Structure* after 50 Years: The Anatomy of a Charter." *American Journal of Sociology* 95 (1): 38–107.

———. 1992. "Reputation and Predecessor Selection: Parsons and the Institutionalists." *American Sociological Review* 57: 421–45.

———. 1996. "Alexander's Antisociology." *Sociological Theory* 14 (2): 172–86.

Chapin, F. S. 1928. "Editor's Introduction." Pp. ix–x in *Pitirim A. Sorokin: Contemporary Sociological Theories.* New York: Harper.

Conant, J. B. 1938. Letter to L. J. Henderson, October 24. Henderson Papers, Baker Library.

———. 1970. *My Several Lives.* New York: Harper.

Fine, G. A., ed. 1995. *A Second Chicago School?* Chicago: University of Chicago Press.

Galliher, J. F. 1995. "Chicago's Two Worlds of Deviance Research: Whose Side Are They On?" Pp. 164–87 in *A Second Chicago School?* edited by G. A. Fine. Chicago: University of Chicago Press.

Goffman, E. 1969. *Strategic Interaction.* Philadelphia: University of Pennsylvania Press.

Harvard University. 1935. *Official Register of Harvard University. Division of Sociology.* Cambridge: Harvard University Press.

———. 1939. *Report on Some Problems of Personnel in the Faculty of Arts and Sciences by a Special Committee Appointed by the President of Harvard University.* Cambridge: Harvard University Press.

Henderson, L. J. 1934. "McIver, Robert M." Henderson Papers, Baker Library.

———. 1935a. Letter to the Guggenheim Memorial Foundation, December 10. Henderson Papers, Baker Library.

———. 1935b. Letter to Dean George Birkhoff, December 11. Henderson Papers, Baker Library.

———. 1937a. Letter to John D. Black, January 4. Henderson Papers, Baker Library.

———. 1937b. *Pareto's General Sociology.* Cambridge, Mass.: Harvard University Press.

———. 1938. Letter to James B. Conant, October 19. Henderson Papers, Baker Library.

———. 1970. *Lawrence J. Henderson on the Social System,* edited by B. Barber. Chicago: University of Chicago Press.

Hershberg, J. G. 1993. *James B. Conant: Harvard to Hiroshima and the Making of the Nuclear Age.* New York: Knopf.

Homans, G. C. 1984. *Coming to My Senses: The Autobiography of a Sociologist.* New Brunswick, N.J.: Transaction Publishers.

Jaworski, G. D. 1997. *Georg Simmel and the American Prospect.* Albany: State University of New York Press.

———. 1998. "Contested Canon: Simmel Scholarship at Columbia and the New School." *American Sociologist* 29 (2): 4–18.

Johnston, B. V. 1995. *Pitirim A. Sorokin: An Intellectual Biography.* Lawrence: University of Kansas Press.

Keen, M. F. 1999. *Stalking The Sociological Imagination: J. Edgar Hoover's FBI Surveillance of American Sociology.* Westport, Conn.: Greenwood Press.

Levine, D. N. 1989. "Parsons' *Structure* (and Simmel) Revisited." *Sociological Theory* 7 (1):

110–17.

Merton, R. K. [1938] 1970. "Science, Technology and Society in Seventeenth Century England." Pp. 362–632 in *Osiris*, edited by G. Sarton. Bruges: St. Catherine Press. Second edition, New York: Fertig, 1970. Reprinted 1993.

———. 1980. "Remembering the Young Talcott Parsons." *American Sociologist* 15: 68–71.

Mills, C. W. 1940. "Situated Actions and Vocabularies of Motive." *American Sociological Review* 5: 904–13.

Murdock, K. B. 1931. Letter to Pitirim A. Sorokin, December 16. Papers of the Department of Sociology, Harvard University Archives, Pusey Library.

———. 1934. Letter to Pitirim A. Sorokin, December 31. Papers of the Department of Sociology, Harvard University Archives, Pusey Library.

Nichols, L. T. 1990. "Reconceptualizing Social Accounts: A Framework for Theory Building and Empirical Research." Pp. 113–44 in *Current Perspectives in Social Theory*, edited by J. Wilson, Vol. 10. Stamford, Conn.: JAI Press.

———. 1992. "The Establishment of Sociology at Harvard: A Case of Organizational Ambivalence and Scientific Vulnerability." Pp. 191–222 in *Science at Harvard University: Historical Perspectives*, edited by C. A. Elliott and M. W. Rossiter. Bethlehem, Pa.: Lehigh University Press.

Parascandola, J. 1992. "L. J. Henderson and the Mutual Dependence of Variables: From Physical Chemistry to Pareto." Pp. 167–90 in *Science at Harvard University: Historical Perspectives*, edited by C. A. Elliott and M. W. Rossiter. Bethlehem, Pa.: Lehigh University Press.

Parsons, T. 1930. *Max Weber: The Protestant Ethic and the Spirit of Capitalism*, trans. Talcott Parsons. New York: Scribner's.

———. 1934. Letter to Pitirim A. Sorokin (circa September). Parsons Papers, Pusey Library.

———. 1935a. "The Place of Ultimate Values in Sociological Theory." *Ethics* 45 (April): 282–316.

———. 1935b. Letter to Lawrence J. Henderson, May 16. Henderson Papers, Baker Library.

———. 1937a. *The Structure of Social Action*. New York: McGraw-Hill.

———. 1937b. "Education and the Professions." *International Journal of Ethics* 47: 365–69.

———. 1939. Letter to Crane Brinton, July 11. Henderson Papers, Baker Library.

———. 1951. *The Social System*. New York: Free Press.

———. 1968. *The Structure of Social Action*, 3rd ed. New York: Free Press.

———. 1970. "On Building Social Systems Theory: A Personal History." *Daedalus* 99(4): 826–81.

———. 1979. Letter to Jeffrey Alexander, January 19. Parsons Papers, Harvard University Archives, Pusey Library.

———. [1934?] 1998a. "The 'Fragment' on Simmel [From Draft Chapter XVIII (*Structure of Social Action*): Georg Simmel and Ferdinand Tönnies: Social Relationships and the Elements of Action]." *American Sociologist* 29 (2): 21–30.

———. [1939?] 1998b. "Simmel and the Methodological Problems of Formal Sociology." *American Sociologist* 29 (2): 31–50.

Parsons, T., and E. A. Shils, eds. 1951. *Toward a General Theory of Action*. Cambridge: Harvard University Press.

Parsons, T., R. K. Merton, E. P. Hutchinson, and E. Y. Hartshorne. 1935. Letter to James B. Conant (circa fall). Parsons Papers, Pusey Library.

Platt, J. 1995. "Research Methods and the Second Chicago School." Pp. 82–107 in *A Second Chicago School?* edited by G. A. Fine. Chicago: University of Chicago Press.

Scott, M. B., and S. Lyman. 1968. "Accounts." *American Sociological Review* 33: 46–62.

Sorokin, P. A. [1914] 1998. *Leo Tolstoy as a Philosopher.* Pp. 133–50 in *Pitirim A. Sorokin: On the Practice of Sociology.* edited by Barry V. Johnston, trans. Lawrence T. Nichols. Chicago: University of Chicago Press.

———. 1920. *A System of Sociology.* 2 volumes. Petrograd, Russia.

———. 1928. *Contemporary Sociological Theories.* New York: Harper.

———. 1931a. Letter to Dean Kenneth B. Murdock, December 17. Papers of the Department of Sociology, Pusey Library.

———. 1931b. Letter to Dean Kenneth B. Murdock, December 22. Papers of the Department of Sociology, Pusey Library.

———. 1935a. Letter to Talcott Parsons, November 21. Papers of the Department of Sociology, Pusey Library.

———. 1935b. "Brief Commentaries on Recommendations for 1936–37." Papers of the Department of Sociology, Pusey Library.

———. 1937. *Social and Cultural Dynamics.* 3 Vols. New York: American Book Company.

———. 1938. "Histrionics." *Southern Review* 4 (winter): 555–64.

———. 1963. *A Long Journey.* New Haven, Conn.: College and University Press.

Triplet, R. 1992. "Harvard Psychology, the Psychological Clinic and Henry A. Murray: A Case Study in the Establishment of Disciplinary Boundaries." Pp. 223–50 in *Science at Harvard University: Historical Perspectives,* edited by C. A. Elliot and M. W. Rossiter. Bethlehem, Pa.: Lehigh University Press.

von Wiese, L., and H. P. Becker. 1932. *Systematic Sociology.* New York: Wiley.

Wearne, B. C. 1989. *The Theory and Scholarship of Talcott Parsons to 1951.* New York: Cambridge University Press.

Whyte, W. F. 1994. *Participant Observer: An Autobiography.* Ithaca, N.Y.: ILR Press.

2

The Place of Max Weber in the Post-*Structure* Writings of Talcott Parsons

William J. Buxton and David Rehorick

PARSONS ON WEBER REVISITED

Much has been written about how Talcott Parsons drew on the ideas of classical European social thought in developing his approach to sociological theory. This tendency is quite understandable in that Parsons explicitly grounded his "voluntaristic theory of action"—as developed in *The Structure of Social Action*—in selected traditions from this body of work. Given that the approach developed by Parsons has become so influential, commentators have been obliged to continually reexamine how Parsons situated his own work in relation to the material he chose for consideration (Alexander, 1988; Buxton, 1998; Camic, 1992; Jaworski, 1990; Kivisto and Swatos, 1990; Levine, 1991).

While this strategy has resulted in a more refined assessment of how Parsons's thought, as embodied in *Structure,* was grounded in European thought, it has also led to certain biases in the way that Parsons's early work has been interpreted and periodized. In particular, the foundations of his mature work are generally thought to have been largely determined by his reflections in *Structure* and the cluster of theoretical work (linked to *The Social System*) he produced in the early 1950s (Parsons, 1951, Parsons and Shils, 1951; Parsons, Shils, and Bales, 1953). The work in between has largely been consigned to an amorphous "middle period" during which he supposedly took a leave from his theoretical engagement to undertake practical work and institutional analysis (Gerhardt, 1993). This suggests that Parsons's work vacillated between the "practical/ empirical" and the "theoretical," with these phases quite separate from one another.

We argue in this chapter that this periodization is flawed and has resulted in serious misconceptions about the development of Parsons's ideas. In particular, it largely fails to address how his theoretical work was continually bound up with his ongoing intellectual and practical interests. It is important to recognize that after the completion of *Structure*, Parsons's interests in institutional analysis and the professions did not emerge out of nowhere, as he himself misleadingly suggested (1970). Rather, his study of classical European thought as expressed in *Structure* emerged in tandem with his work on institutional analysis and professional practice, concerns which dated back to at least 1930.[1] Arguably, these two currents of investigation coalesced in the period immediately after *Structure*, during which Parsons developed a framework of the key components of professional practice, the basis for what became the pattern variables. During this period Parsons consolidated his previously disparate theoretical and practical work into a systematic approach to professional practice, which underpinned his emergent structural functionalism. This synthesis, in turn, was grounded in a particular interpretation of Max Weber's thought and influence. What is particularly striking about this brief period is the extent to which Parsons became absorbed with Weber's work.

Parsons's growing engagement with Weber after the publication of *Structure* can be broken down into two interconnected subphases, with somewhat different emphases. The first subphase ran from the beginning of 1938 until the end of 1939. During this time Parsons largely drew on Weber as the basis for developing the foundations of sociological methodology. In effect, he made use of a Weberian framework to construct an authoritative sociological standpoint through which detractors could be silenced and other claimants vying to generate a "systematic sociology" could be effectively challenged. However, with the outbreak of the European War in 1939, Parsons began to use Weberian thought to formulate a comparative-institutional approach to sociological analysis. This took the form of not only affirming what he considered to be the core values and practices of Western civilization, but developing an approach to diagnose departures from this pattern. In this regard, Parsons drew on many of Weber's key concepts in political sociology and transfigured them into his own emergent structural-functional framework. While his concerns during the 1930s were with finding a practical solution to the Hobbesian problem of order, particularly as it pertained to the United States (see Buxton, 1985), his concerns after the publication of *Structure* were more directed toward the role that America could and should play in the emerging world crisis. What this meant in practice was developing a comparative-institutional analysis, capable of diagnosing the extent to which particular nation-states conformed to or deviated from the development of a rational-legal order, which Parsons viewed as the harbinger of modernity. Reflecting this shift, it is instructive that Parsons's interest in Weber gradually moved from his methodological work and toward his comparative political sociology. In effect, Weber was to provide the grounding for a social science capable of contributing to the institutionalization of modernity.

In what follows, we first trace out the major contours of Parsons's work on Weber, giving particular attention to how they formed an interconnected project concentrated into a short time-frame. We then examine in some detail a set of correspondence between Talcott Parsons and Eric Voegelin that took place while this work was under way.[2] We argue that this set of letters makes explicit some of the broader "domain assumptions" that undergirded Parsons's preoccupation with Weber at the onset of World War II. This discussion is embedded also in a wider intellectual exchange, one that encompasses the work and letters of Talcott Parsons, Alfred Schütz, and Eric Voegelin. We have addressed how Voegelin, as a third party, was both witness to and commentator on the exchange between Parsons and Schutz (Rehorick and Buxton, 1988). Our chapter displayed the limitations of viewing the debate between Parsons and Schutz as an isolated dialogue (see Coser, 1979; Embree, 1980; Grathoff, 1978; Natanson, 1978; Rehorick, 1980; Valone, 1979, 1980; Wagner, 1981). However, direct reference to this side of the research literature is beyond the scope of this work.[3]

PARSONS'S ENGAGEMENT WITH WEBER AFTER *STRUCTURE*

Unlike the other thinkers Parsons addressed in his early writings, Max Weber captured his interest by virtue of his spiritual orientation, an outlook that resonated with his own Calvinist background.[4] Parsons always had a special affinity for Weber, as opposed to other thinkers. Initially, it was this spiritual and cultural side of Weber that drew Parsons's attention. This was evident in his Heidelberg dissertation and in his early publications. However, in the process of writing *The Structure of Social Action*, Parsons came to be more attuned to Weber's methodology.[5] Arguably *Structure* represented less a convergence than it did an incorporation of a range of thinkers into a Weberian-inspired framework.

It is noteworthy that among the four major theorists considered by Parsons in *Structure*, Weber was the only one to be given close attention in the period immediately after the publication of his first major work. Weber's frame of reference was very much behind Parsons's critique of Max Lerner's "Materialist Interpretation of History," presented at the 1938 meetings of the Eastern Sociological Society.[6] In contrast with Lerner's one-sided materialist conception of history, Parsons noted that "evidence based primarily on comparative historical material has tended to show that a major differentiating factor in the development of 'material structures' lies in different metaphysical views of the world and man's place in it. In this field the work of Max Weber has been preeminent."[7]

The cornerstone of Parsons's work was his translation of the first four chapters of Weber's *Wirtschaft und Gesellschaft* (1925) accompanied by a lengthy introduction. Parsons had been asked by the British publishing house William Hodge and Company Ltd.[8] to comment on a translation of the first two chapters of the volume that had been made by Arnold Henderson, an economist at the University of Edinburgh, who had completed his work by early 1938.[9] Parsons felt that the translation was "entirely inadequate, and to fall very short of the best that can be done." He strongly advised against its publication, as he did not "think it would be possible for the reader to get anywhere near an adequate understanding of Weber's argument from it as it stands." To be sure, he conceded that "this work, particularly the first chapter, presents one of the very few most difficult problems of translation which I can imagine. . . . It is a highly technical work, and Weber is presenting the barest outline of a conceptual framework without all the detailed explanation and application which would serve to make it much more readily intelligible."[10] Parsons took Henderson to task for having attempted a "direct translation." He felt, rather, "that it is often much better to rephrase the text in such a way as to bring out the author's meaning as accurately as possible than to attempt word-for-word translation." What Parsons recommended was that

> the translation itself be most unusually carefully and skillfully done by someone thoroughly familiar with the subject-matter, but that also it should be very carefully edited, with an extensive introduction which would provide a setting and prepare the reader for the many difficulties of the work, and with quite full explanatory notes wherever misinterpretation seemed at all likely.[11]

He also recommended that chapter 3 of the volume, "Typen der Herrschaft," be included, in order to give "a proper impression of the work" and to convey what Weber had in mind in his discussion of economic organization in Chapter 2."[12] Subsequently, Parsons suggested that "the very brief fourth chapter, Stände und Klassen, which is only four pages," be included as well. In his view:

> This group of chapters was meant by Weber to constitute the outline of the conceptual framework into which the more extended empirical material of the rest of the work was to be fitted. . . . the third chapter contains a vital part of the conceptual scheme without which it is impossible to put the material of the second in its proper perspective.[13]

Parsons had become convinced that the work would constitute "one of the few most important theoretical works in the literature of social sciences to the English reading public." After noting that his "principal motive in undertaking it relates to the scientific importance of the project," he suggested that his total reimbursement for undertaking the translation would be "one hundred pounds total . . . thirty in advance to pay my out of pocket expenses, the balance on submission of the completed manuscript."[14] Hodge agreed to this arrangement, and Parsons received the first of three installments of $117.04 in June of 1939.[15] Parsons was enthusiastic about taking on the project because he believed Weber's volume to be "one of the very few most important general works in the field of social theory" and felt that Hodge was "doing a very great service in making it available to the English-reading public."[16]

Parsons's letters revealed the extent to which he had arrogated himself as the authoritative translator and interpreter of Weber's writings. In arguing against a direct or literal translation of *Wirtschaft und Gesellschaft* in favor of a free or interpretive translation, he wasn't simply stating that the latter was inherently superior. Rather, he wished to claim that an authoritative interpretation of Weber was possible, and, by implication, that he had the requisite knowledge to make it possible. Evidently persuaded by Parsons's forceful assessment of the prospects for translation, Hodge invited him to undertake the translation, largely on the terms that Parsons had suggested.

It is evident that there was much more at issue for Parsons than simply translating some of Weber's work. He believed that this particular material was in some sense foundational, not only for sociology and the social sciences, but as a set of guidelines for making sense of the unfolding of Western civilization.[17] That Parsons viewed sociological theory as having a direct practical bearing on the social order is evident in the assessment of his work offered by Howard Odum, editor of *Social Forces:*

> We like very much your premise expressing the hope that the social sciences will develop an ability to apply generalized theoretical analysis to problems of modern contemporary society. I think you have stated almost the heart of sociological theory when you have said, "The very breadth of the problem of diagnosis of the state of a great civilization creates a strong demand for such a method."[18]

Critical in this respect was Parsons's conviction that these four chapters to be translated contained a distilled version of Weber's approach in the form of a "conceptual scheme." In effect, this was a set of categories that could not only serve as the basis for developing sociology, but could offer a standpoint from which a particular outlook in relation to Western civilization could be cultivated. In this sense, one can understand what was behind the change of title for the volume that Parsons suggested (and was eventually adopted):

> Mr. [A.M.] Henderson gave his draft the title "Economy and Society.". . . I might make the tentative suggestion of "The theory of Social and Economic Organization." The part which we are bringing out is actually the theory as opposed to the concrete application. It is not however either Social theory or Economic theory in the usual sense but is a theory of Organization.[19]

Equally important to Parsons as the translation itself was the lengthy introduction he was to provide. A draft version of the translation was completed by late August, 1939. He enlisted the services of Edwin Gay to go over the translation before he submitted it.[20] In a letter to Gay, Parsons confided that, "Like everybody else [he was] naturally considerably wrought up by the situation in Europe." He also revealed his growing anxiety about the impact of the war on the volume's publication: "Apart from everything else, I cannot help wondering whether war would affect the publication plans for the Weber translation. I should have heard from Mr. Hodge after this crisis is decided one way or the other before the time comes to send the manuscript to you."[21] As these comments indicate, Parsons had originally intended that the work appear when the crisis in Europe was still unfolding.[22]

As it turned out, the war indeed affected the publication date of the volume. Due to various vicissitudes, it did not appear until 1947 (Weber, 1947).[23] Nevertheless, work on the volume proceeded throughout the war, albeit at a snail's pace. Toward the end of 1940, Parsons "entirely completed the text and editorial notes, including practically all of the final checking."[24] By the late summer of 1941, he had also completed the "critical introduction."[25] He finally began to receive page proofs from Hodge toward the end of 1942.[26] It wasn't until the fall of 1944 that Hodge received the corrected galley proofs for the volume.[27] Obviously chafing at the slowness of the process, Parsons repeatedly suggested that an American publisher for the volume be found, and even undertook negotiations with various companies.[28] Such activity appeared to have eventually borne fruit; the volume was ultimately published simultaneously in Britain and in the United States by Collier-Macmillan and The Free Press (a Division of Macmillan Publishing Co. Inc.) respectively.

This translation and introduction was accompanied by a number of other initiatives related to Weber. In the spring of 1939, Parsons's efforts to buttress his approach to sociology with Weber's work were evident in his critique of formal sociology.[29] Here he claimed that Weber's framework was much more promising for sociology than that of Simmel and his proponents.[30] Parsons noted that

> the formal part of Weber's theoretical work is scientifically fruitful precisely because he did not limit himself to Simmel's methodological program, but carried out formal theorizing only in connection with dynamic problems of causation in empirical research, and integrated his formal concepts directly with an analytical system, the concepts of which are essential tools dealing with the same range of empirical problems. What Simmel, failing to live up to his own program, did on a dillentantish, common-sense level, with many brilliant and arresting insights, but no imposing structure of proof of propositions of far-reaching importance, Weber accomplished on a far higher level, meticulously building up a rigorous proof of his theses, in the manner not of a brilliant dilettante, but of a sober professional scientist. Brilliant dilettantes have their place in science, but the progress of science can hardly be left to their efforts alone. (1998b: 48)

Nevertheless, Parsons believed that Weber's approach was not without its limitations:

> In spite of these virtues, there are a number of points at which Weber falls short of the highest level of rigor in his proofs of which his empirical level is capable. Analysis of his work in these respects shows that one main source of his difficulties lies in what, in essence, is the following of a formal procedure in Simmel's sense, where that is not methodologically advisable. This results in a kind of "ideal-type atomism" which unfortunately cannot be dealt with here. (1998b: 48)

These methodological shortcomings notwithstanding, Parsons viewed Weber's approach as the best basis for providing the foundations for sociology. In the summer following the writing of his essay on Simmelian methodology, Parsons had another opportunity to make use of Weber to defend the cause of sociology. He drew on Weber to challenge the dismissal of sociology by his colleague Crane Brinton (1939), provided in his scathing review of Robert Lynd's *Knowledge for What?* (1939). In his copy of Brinton's article, in the section in which Brinton took issue with Lynd's failure to make adequate reference to "W. G. Sumner, Montaigne, Machiavelli, Polybius, . . . Henry Maine . . . North Whitehead, . . . Elton Mayo . . . L. J. Henderson," Parsons added with note (with the names underlined), Pareto, Max Weber—still authentically sociologists (Lynd, 1939).[31] Parsons noted:

> The best work which has been done in the name of Sociology is in my opinion not merely on a level with that in the other social sciences, but fully on a level with that in any scientific field whatever. In particular, Pareto, Max Weber, and Durkheim are with-

out any question minds of the very first caliber, and that in a strictly scientific sense. It is true that Lynd, who as I said has had no real training, is not acquainted with their work; but there is a growing number of sociologists particularly of the younger generation who are well acquainted with it.[32]

Parsons went on to point out to Brinton the preeminence Weber had in the field of economics:

I can claim a certain competence in Economics and I will say flatfootedly that there is no single figure in Economics, at least since [Adam] Smith and [David] Ricardo who is the equal in scientific genius of Max Weber, under which I include analytical acuteness, insight into the significance of problems, and a sheer hardheaded judgment of empirical facts. I deliberately place him head and shoulders above the great [Alfred] Marshall; and since I have studied Marshall's work intensively I feel entitled to have an opinion. In fact I feel there is every reason to believe that Weber is fully equal to the really great figures of natural science. Perhaps it would be sheer sacrilege to mention Newton, but I do not hesitate at all to compare him with Darwin.[33]

These methodological concerns with Weber found expression in a major unpublished theoretical work of Parsons that was completed in the following year (Parsons, 1939).

With the gathering storm in Europe, Parsons began to gradually shift his emphasis away from Weber's methodological contributions and toward his work on institutional analysis and political sociology. This was evident in his discussions with Waldemar Gurian of the University of Notre Dame, editor of *The Review of Politics*, who encouraged Parsons to contribute an article to his journal. In the summer of 1938, Gurian wrote to Parsons asking him to "send us a study on the political ideas of Max Weber."[34] Replying almost immediately to Gurian's request, Parsons agreed to produce something along these lines. Evidently, not having heard back from Parsons for some time thereafter, Gurian again wrote to him in December 1939, reiterating his interest in receiving something from Parsons on Weber's political ideas. He also noted to Parsons that his "work on *The Structure of Social Action* is probably the most important publication written in recent years by an American sociologist." He also was "planning to publish, during the coming year, a special study dealing with your book."[35] This time Parsons was now in a position to respond in a much more definite manner. Likely as a result of having begun the translation of Weber's work (and possibly because of his engagement with the deteriorating situation in Europe), he said he now intended to "write it as soon as I have time . . . while the material was fresh in my mind." He intended to "place the primary emphasis on what may be called his 'political sociology,' especially as developed in the two sections of Typen der Herrschaft in WuG."[36] He felt that he could address Weber's "Politik als Beruf" and his study on parliamentarianism (both requested by Gurian).[37] He now planned to write it in conjunction with his introduction to the translation, and thought it would be ready in the spring of 1940.[38] As it turned out, Parsons was not able to begin his introduction to the translation of *Wirtschaft und Gesellschaft* until the summer of 1940. It was now his intention to write the article after the introduction was completed. He thought that he could send it to Gurian by August so that it could be published in the October 1940 issue.[39] The article finally appeared in a two-part series published in 1942, focusing on the relevance of Weber's political writings to the contemporary political crisis (Parsons, 1942a). Parsons addressed similar aspects of Weber's work in an essay for a volume edited by Harry Elmer Barnes, which was to contain mostly articles by and about European scholars. Again, the publication of the volume was continually pushed back because of wartime circumstances;[40] it did not appear until 1948 (Parsons, 1948).

In another article written around this time, Parsons made use of Weber to address one aspect of the rise of fascism, namely, what it implied for the situation of the Jews in Western Europe.[41] He had evidently been asked by one of the editors of the volume (Isaac Graeber) to contribute to the volume in late 1939. Parsons produced a draft in 1940, which was edited and revised in a manner of which he strongly disapproved (1942b).[42]

Another Weber-related venture that Parsons was involved with was related to Weber's work on law (which Parsons viewed as the foundation of Weber's political sociology). Upon being asked by Dumas Malone, the editor of Harvard University Press, for recommendations about important works to publish, Parsons recommended "the 'Rechtssoziologie' of Max Weber."[43] On a visit to the University of Chicago in January 1939, he had learned about the existence of this volume from Professor Max Rheinstein of the University of Chicago Law School.[44] He indicated to Malone that a translation of the volume had been done under the direction of Frank Knight of the University of Chicago: "It is not in shape for publication but the basic spade work has been done and all that remains is polishing and editorial work." He suggested that Malone contact Knight to find out about the status of the manuscript.[45] In response to Malone's query, Knight noted that he had a rough translation of the work, and would be happy to turn it over to anyone who wished to continue with the project.[46]

The project of translating and editing Weber's *Rechtssoziologie* was taken up by a "group of social scientists and law teachers at the University of Chicago" under the auspices of a "committee of Association of American Law Schools" as part of "the translation and publication of a number of important works on Jurisprudence."[47] Edward Shils agreed to translate the volume, and Jerome Hall of the University of Indiana Law School bore the editorial responsibility. Parsons and Knight were slated to contribute introductory essays to the volume.[48] Responding to Hall's suggestions about what he might write, Parsons suggested that he discuss "the place of Weber's sociology of law in his general sociological system." What he had in mind was "not so much a technical interpretation of Weber's sociology" [but rather a] general appraisal of the kind of thing he was doing and its relation to law." He noted that "it was particularly relevant that Weber started his scholarly career in historical jurisprudence, and that the broad lines of his evolution from that starting point into sociology have a certain interest as positing the problem of the relation between law and the social sciences".[49] Parsons was set to write the introductory essay in August 1941, as he had just completed the introduction to the translated volume, as well as the article on Weber for *The Review of Politics*. He felt that he would "like to clean up this last Weber obligation while [he was] immersed in his work." He volunteered to "look

over the Ms translation critically" and, indeed, preferred to write his essay in connection with the translation.[50] In the meantime, the first draft of the translation was
almost completed, but had been delayed because Shils had been "asked to join the
Neutrality Laws Division of the Department of Justice" in June 1941 and had been
able to make little progress during his summer stint in Washington.[51] Largely because
of wartime restrictions, the volume did not see the light of day until 1954. It finally
appeared as a volume on the sociology of law by Max Weber, translated by Edward
Shils with an introduction by Max Rheinstein (Weber, 1954).

What needs to be stressed is that Parsons viewed his involvement with Weber's
thought as very much part of a collective effort. He kept in close contact with others
who were working on Weber, and shared material willingly with them. Parsons saw his
own work at the center of a movement made up of like-minded interlocutors who were
to take part in developing an authoritative interpretive network and who would help
to shape Weber's canonical work into a foundational work for the Anglo-American
world.[52] At the same time, he discouraged efforts that he thought were potentially at
odds with his own reading of Weber, which he saw as the one faithful to Weber's intent.[53] For instance, in 1942, Parsons received a letter from a graduate student, Ephraim
Fischoff, who "cherished the hope of being able to translate portions of Weber's work
into English, particularly his sociology of religion." Having already translated Alfred
Weber's *Kulturgeschichte als Kultursoziologie*, "undertaken at his behest through the intermediary of Professor Howard Becker," Fischoff sounded out Parsons on the
prospects for his doing a translation of Weber's work.[54] After filling Fischoff in on the
state of the various translation projects under way, Parsons emphatically disagreed with
Fischoff that a condensation of Weber's work was desirable. He also was less than encouraging about Fischoff undertaking a translation of Weber:

> I do not question that you have a very high level of competence in this sort of work but
> it is my experience that it is a particularly difficult kind of undertaking to accomplish
> satisfactorily. . . . in many instances more harm than good has been done by translation
> of great intellectual works, and I have been called upon to give critical opinions of a
> number of translations of different parts of Weber's work, with the result of consider-
> able discouragement.[55]

Among those who figured most prominently in the "interpretive network" of Weberian scholars that Parsons sought to construct was Eric Voegelin. We will now turn
to the correspondence between Parsons and Voegelin, with a view to explicating
some of the "domain assumptions" that undergirded Parsons's intense engagement
with Weber.

We argue that Weber was central to the developing thought of both Parsons and
Voegelin. This centrality, however, was not simply the result of intellectual disposition; it was rooted in the relevance of Weberian thought to the complex of problems
that confronted Western society during the 1940s. By displaying their disagreements
about how Weber could be applied, we will show that it is possible to use Weber as a
key which unlocks the door to the practical intentions in the work of Parsons and
Voegelin.

VOEGELIN AND PARSONS THROUGH WEBER: PREDESTINATION
AND THE INTERPRETATION OF MODERNITY

Between 1940 and 1943, Talcott Parsons and Eric Voegelin shared their intellectual concerns through correspondence.[56] Presumably, they had met during the 1938–39 academic year when Voegelin "held a one year appointment as tutor and instructor at Harvard" (Sandoz, 1981: 71). His appointment had been secured through friends at Harvard (William Y. Elliot, Gottfried von Haberler, and Joseph Schumpeter), all of whom had academic linkages to Parsons.[57]

The correspondence began as an exchange of ideas about Parsons's manuscripts on anti-Semitism (Parsons, 1993; see also Parsons, 1964: 441) along with his "draft of a restatement of the generalized theory of action which [he had] completed in the fall [of 1939].[58] Parsons later sent Voegelin a draft of his translation of four chapters of *Wirtschaft und Gesellschaft* in the summer of 1941.[59] These documents, along with some material that Voegelin sent to Parsons, formed the basis for a wide-ranging discussion of issues related to the origins of fascism, the nature of the Protestant ethic, predestination, and social-scientific methodology. The focal point of their exchange became the issues raised by Max Weber's interpretation of the Protestant ethic, and the status of Weber's overall methodological approach.

While the exchanges were polite and criticisms muted, fundamental disagreements emerged. It is our contention that the basis for disagreement was not simply a matter of intellectual preoccupations. Rather, this incommensurability stemmed from each thinker's theological perspective as to the origins and nature of modernity. Both Voegelin and Parsons were deeply troubled by the concurrent intellectual and political crises of their day. They sought solutions through concerted intellectual engagement. Hence, each viewed the vocation of the intellectual as one of both responsibility and engagement.

As custodians of shared collective values, intellectuals were obliged to actively confront the tendencies that threatened to overwhelm Western civilization. In particular, both thinkers were deeply concerned about the threat posed to Western civilization by the spread and growth of fascism. During the 1930s, Voegelin wrote a number of monographs dealing with totalitarian social movements, including fascism (Voegelin, 1933, 1938). He subsequently contributed a number of articles on fascism to American journals (Voegelin, 1940, 1941, 1944). During the Second World War, Parsons shifted his attention from sociological theory to projects of relevance to the American war effort. Like Voegelin, Parsons was preoccupied with how intellectuals might contribute to strengthening the defense of Western civilization in the face of the fascist onslaught.

This mutual concern with the crisis of Western civilization in the wake of fascism led Voegelin and Parsons to correspond. Moreover, both thinkers used the writings of Max Weber as a point of reference for orienting themselves to the crisis. Nevertheless, they had differing orientations to Weber, reflecting their respective moral-political standpoints, each being informed by their theological assumptions. We turn, now, to an in-depth look at their differing views on predestination.

What gave rise to their differences was Parsons's response to a chapter that Voegelin had written on the Reformation, as part of a longer study on the history of ideas (see Voegelin, 1975). Despite his own uncertainty about the problem, Parsons agreed with Weber "that 'psychologically rather than logically' predestination was a great stimulation to the 'active orientation' of mastery over the world." In this sense, active mastery depends "not on the acceptance of the doctrine but rather upon the attribution of fundamental religious and emotional significance to a certain range of problems revolving about the state of grace."[60]

Parsons stressed that, unlike Catholicism or Lutheranism, the Calvinist "radical doctrine of predestination was one polar solution of the theological problems that revolve about the rationalization of the basic religious attitude." Parsons further contended that "the doctrine ought to be placed in a broader functional context as expressive of the basic attitude I have spoken of."[61]

In his response, Voegelin expressed agreement with both Parsons and Weber that the doctrine of predestination "is a great stimulant to the active orientation of mastery over the world."[62] In response to Parsons's particular comments, Voegelin specified the "broader functional context" by contrasting Lutheranism and Calvinism. Unlike Luther, Calvin had insisted that predestination signifies "'membership in the People of God which collectively acts in history; predestination stresses the soldierly aspect of the person in the collective action against the 'enemy.'"[63] This suggested to Voegelin that "the doctrine of predestination is not introduced by Calvin because the religious experiences connected with the state of grace required it, but because secondary problems, problems of action, recommended it as a creed for the army of the fighting elect." With its emphasis on the chosen people, Calvin's views were "strongly old testament," and in line with his aspirations to organize "a Protestant International in rivalry with the Catholic Church." As Voegelin saw it, the effectiveness of the doctrine in stimulating rational commercial activity was unintended.[64]

Voegelin argued, then, that there was nothing intrinsic about the religious orientation of ascetic Protestantism that induced the attitude of active mastery. Rather, the activism that developed around the time of Calvin could be attributed to his own political designs and his concern to organize people collectively against his religious rivals. Indeed, the active mastery associated with this creed was, in Voegelin's view, purely incidental.[65]

In a later letter, Voegelin clarified that his approach to the problem of predestination was entirely different from that of Max Weber.[66] He noted that Weber, Tawney, and others had focused almost exclusively on "the effects of this doctrine on members of the Calvinist community, and particularly on their ethical, commercial and political attitudes." In contrast, Voegelin was more interested in why the doctrine of predestination, which had been expressed in the letters of St. Paul, became activated only with Calvin. This question, according to Voegelin, was a "terra incognita" in that "nobody seems ever to have been seriously concerned about the causes of this momentous break in Christian history which brought the practical identification between the people as a spiritual community and the people as a political community by means of the collectivist idea of the predestined community of Saints."[67] While Parsons had started with Calvinism as a datum, Voegelin's historical analysis sought to place the Calvinist break with orthodoxy "in the flux of events leading up to it."

If taken at face value, the dispute between Parsons and Voegelin about predestination could be written off as a mere academic quibble. However, this dispute presupposed a much broader disagreement about the emergence of modern rationalized order and the orientation that one should take in relation to it. Their differing interpretations of predestination reflect incompatible theological ideas, which are displayed through their respective views of the nature of modernity.

As Gregor Sebba astutely points out, Voegelin's position could be characterized as one of "Christian philosophy" (though not Christian doctrine):

> Through the Christian "revelation" of grace "as the experienced intrusion of transcendence into human life" philosophy attained the highest level of differentiated knowledge yet. If a philosopher operates on a lower experiential level than this, he disregards a historical fact and its philosophical consequences, which is impermissible. The truth has a history on earth, and no philosopher has the right to disregard it. (Sebba, 1981: 433)

Voegelin adhered to an early Christian ontology, by which one sought transcendental truths through the revelations of God's word in human experience. The possibility of this ultramundane transcendence had become limited by the increasing ascendancy of what he termed "gnostic" movements, which severed the connection between human experience and transcendence (Voegelin, 1952). Gnostics believed that humans could attain salvation through their innerworldly activity within the confines of modern nation-states. It was this gnostic tendency, he argued, that lay at the root of the twentieth-century totalitarian movements of communism and fascism (Voegelin, 1986).

According to Voegelin, the modern age of gnosticism was ushered in by the Puritan revolution of the seventeenth century which had been given "systematic formulation in scriptural terms" by Calvin's *Institutes* (Voegelin, 1952: 138). This work both guided the right reading of Scripture and provided an authentic formulation of truth that would make recourse to earlier literature unnecessary. Voegelin used the Arabic term "Koran" as a technical designation for the newly created study of Gnostic phenomena. Thus, the work of Calvin "may be called the first deliberately created Gnostic Koran." And a man who can break with tradition to write such a text for faith in a new world "must be in a peculiar pneumopathological state" (Voegelin, 1952: 139).

According to Voegelin, "the Gnostic Koran is the codification of truth and as such the spiritual and intellectual nourishment of the faithful." In turn, "the number of faithful may remain small, and expansion and political success will be seriously hampered, if the truth of the Gnostic movement is permanently exposed to effective criticism from various quarters." The Gnostic revolution in the form of Puritanism, then, was characterised by a "taboo on theory in the classic sense." By prohibiting open theoretical debate, Gnostic Puritans exercised control over issues concerning the "truths" of human existence (Voegelin, 1952: 140–43).

Voegelin's views on the intellectual closure of Puritan gnosticism were mirrored in his interpretation of the growth of modern "scientism."

> [The] movement which accompanied the rise of modern mathematics and physics . . . began in a fascination with the new science to the point of underrating and neglecting the concern for experiences of the spirit; they developed into an assumption that the new science could create a world view that would substitute for the religious order of the soul; and they culminated, in the nineteenth century, in the dictatorial prohibition, on the part of the scientistic thinkers, against asking questions of a metaphysical nature. (Voegelin, 1948: 462)

According to Voegelin, scientism, with its roots in gnosticism, implied a serious delimitation of discourse. The modern advance of science is like a cancerous growth, expanding so quickly that the social realization of other values is weakened. The advance of the new sciences will obliterate the possibility of orienting existence toward transcendental reality (Voegelin, 1948: 489).

In contrast, Parsons was much more sanguine about the Puritan revolution and its impact upon modernity. Undoubtedly, this stemmed from his own theological commitments and his Calvinist heritage. Speaking of his troubles with Alfred Schütz, Parsons remarked to Voegelin that:

> I do not want to be a philosopher—I shy away from the philosophical problems underlying my scientific work. By the same token I don't think [Schütz] wants to be a scientist as I understand the term until he has settled all the underlying philosophical difficulties. If the physicists of the 17th century had been Schuetzes there might well have been no Newtonian system.[68]

Further elaborating his position, Parsons contended that

> the whole tenor of Calvinistic religiosity is deeply opposed to philosophical refinement. Faith is the keynote, and he who has faith in that sense does not speculate—to do so would suggest that his faith was not sufficiently strong. Insecurity tends, as you suggest, to be taken out in action, not in speculation. This, it seems to me, has a good deal to do with the basis of the Weber-Merton observation of the relation between Calvinism and science. You may remember Whitehead's remark that, compared with the "rationalism" of the Schoolmen, the early scientists believed in a very simple faith. It was one, in its pattern of the physical world, which fitted the Calvinist theology admirably. But it concealed very difficult and embarrassing philosophical problems. The fact that instead of getting bogged down in these philosophical problems these men proceeded with scientific observation and generalization is at least partly to be attributed to the fact that their faith directly inhibited philosophical refinement.[69]

To some extent, Parsons and Voegelin concurred in their analyses of the impact of seventeenth-century Puritanism on the course of history. Both thinkers perceived how the Calvinist emphasis upon this-worldly activity led to a concern for active mastery of their immediate world, and an eschewal of metaphysical or philosophical concerns. However, while Voegelin believed that this ushered in a period of intense gnosticism culminating in the destructive totalitarian ideologies of the nineteenth century, Parsons celebrated the onset of Calvinist religiosity as the basis for reason and progress. Extending Weber's Protestant Ethic analysis, he noted that:

> The extent to which the Anglo-Saxon peoples seem to have become the overwhelming heirs of the main continuous great tradition of the western world suggests that in the Calvinistic branch of Protestantism there has been a kind of synthesis of the deeper religious orientation with the circumstances of a highly mechanized civilization which the Catholic heritage is notably incapable of achieving, and which also the Germans seem incapable of standing without going off into such a nightmare as Nazism. . . . [W]ith all the modifications and qualifications which the Calvinist attitude must undergo it seems to me to provide a far firmer basis of the orientation to the modern situation than any other of the great movements of our history.[70]

In effect, Parsons believed that the Calvinist legacy of an "activist attitude combined with strong ethical sense and strong sense of community" made for "the relatively greater resistance of the Anglo-Saxon peoples to the encroachments of totalitarianism."[71] In his view, these characteristics could be traced to "the persistent emphasis in the English Puritan literature on the common good, and the idea of the Commonwealth." This meant that there were "basic religious motives for public responsibility." In his letters to Voegelin, Parsons was preoccupied with elaborating ad nauseam how the Calvinist foundations of Anglo-Saxon democracy could be contrasted with the Lutheran and Catholic origins of fascism and authoritarianism respectively.

Given their widely disparate standpoints on the emergence of modernity and the primacy of the secular national-state, it becomes readily apparent why they hold opposing views on the nature and significance of predestination. For Voegelin, Calvin's *Institutes* served to unleash the forces of gnosticism, with its arrogation of the divine to the state and secular society. Hence, his interest in predestination was directed toward understanding why the transcendent features of Christianity, which had been consigned to antiquity, reemerged in the seventeenth century.

In contrast, Parsons viewed the Puritan breakthrough as largely salutary, ushering in an era characterized by ethical responsibility, tolerance, and the growth of reason and science. Parsons was not open to Voegelin's suggestions that Puritanism could be attributed to historical circumstances which predated Calvin. This would be to deny that there was anything inherent in the belief system of Calvinist religiosity that could induce the public virtues of tolerance, responsibility, and active mastery of the world. In effect, Parsons sidestepped the issues raised by Voegelin, choosing to reiterate his own views on how the belief system of Calvinism translated itself into responsible national communities so characteristic of the Anglo-Saxon world.

Parsons saw the link between predestination and active mastery as the basis for understanding how the tolerance, ethical responsibility, and active mastery of the Anglo-Saxon national societies could be consolidated and extended. Specifically, the mantle of the priestly elect of Puritan society had been passed to the professional elite of both the natural and the social sciences. Their efforts would help to build national communities based on the subsumption of individual interests to that of the common good. Hence, Parsons sought to build upon the foundation provided by Weber, with a view toward constituting the Anglo-American national society as a global prototype. That Parsons actively sought to generalize the insights of Weber's *The Protestant Ethic and the Spirit of Capitalism* is evident in his reflections on his early encounter with Weber's work as a student in Germany:

> When I was plunged into the German intellectual world at Heidelberg, I think I can say that I went through a period of considerable intellectual conflict as to where my real interests lay. By contrast with the naive (in the naive sense) empiricism of so much of American and English social science, I was initially attracted by the atmosphere of serious concern with methodological issues. But looking back, I think it is fair to say that I never really became profoundly interested in those things. Undoubtedly the most important single intellectual experience of that period was reading Weber's Protestant Ethic, which from the very first made a tremendous impression upon me; in the first place I suppose the phenomena he was talking about were basic to my own cultural tradition, and at the same time he discussed them in a perspective which was new and fascinating.[72]

Using Weber's proposed link between predestination and active mastery, Parsons sought to develop a systematized basis for social scientific methodology. We turn, now, to an examination of this endeavor, one which was seriously at odds with Voegelin's reflections on how one could go beyond the methodological tenets of Weberian thought.

VOEGELIN AND PARSONS ON METHODOLOGY: DISAGREEMENT OVER WEBER'S CONTRIBUTION

The attraction of Parsons to Weber stemmed from his disillusionment with the formalism and abstraction of "Anglo-American economic thought," which tended to neglect the cultural and temporal differences in patterns of economic activity (Parsons, 1928: 641). In contrast, Weber emphasized not only that capitalism was a historically specific form of economic organization, but that it was rooted in the disinterested, service-oriented value system of ascetic Protestantism (Parsons, 1937: 528).

Parsons was interested particularly in Weber's contention that the rational bureaucratic structure, attendant upon the growth of capitalism, was "in part anchored and in part dependent upon a metaphysical system of ideas" (Parsons, 1937: 510). Drawing this insight from Weber's *Protestant Ethic*, Parsons extended it to include the active mastery of modern science. In the same way that the orientation of "Otherworldliness" of the Calvinist elect would lead to "a kingdom of God on earth," the Weberian-inspired scientist would develop a rational system through which one could objectively affirm the presence or absence of institutions that guided actions of members of society (see Buxton, 1985: ch. 2). In effect, Parsons took the predestination/active mastery linkage as a point of departure for grounding the standpoint of the sociologist in relation to the modern institutional order.

The "sociological calling" was to base itself in a set of "elements of orientation" (asceticism, ethical universalism, functional specificity, and rationality) derived from Weber's sociology of religion.[73] In Parsons's view, this calling could be "acted out in roles such as that of scientist, physician, civil servant, or even Christian minister" (Parsons, 1947: 81). By virtue of acting on the basis of one's calling, and guided by the "elements of orientation" derived from Weber, the social scientist (as a member of the emergent professional stratum) would help constitute "the modern institutional order." Consistent with these designs, Parsons emphasized the institutional side of Weber's work:

> There is a very real sense in which it seems to me that this institutional analysis contains the most important of Weber's scientific contributions, along with the studies in the sociology of religion. If I can help to make the quality of his work in this field better understood I shall be quite satisfied.[74]

Voegelin commended Parsons for having "brought out convincingly the character of Weber's work, as an analysis of the structure of our civilization." He agreed with Parson's view that *The Protestant Ethic* alone does not give a sufficient idea of "Weber's importance as a critic of rational civilization."[75] Nonetheless, Voegelin questioned Parsons's claim that Weber was consistent in his use of the ideal type. In Voegelin's opinion, one could detect two different usages of the ideal type in Weber's work—"historical" and "rational."

Voegelin further claimed that Weber's thoughts on the ideal type evolved from the historical to the rational, and this had "consequences for the interpretation of Weber's work as a whole."[76] Voegelin commended Parsons for showing that Weber's "rational type was deficient" in that it "lacked a good psychology as well as a system of the functional structure of society." All the same, Voegelin was skeptical about the possibility of finding a remedy for such problems. Moreover, Parsons was mistaken in suggesting that he "was on the way to a system of social theory which could be historically understood as a fulfillment of what Weber left unfinished." *Wirtschaft und Gesellschaft* was fragmented, like all of Weber's works. Thus, it is incorrect to depict Weber as a systematic thinker. Moreover, Voegelin was blunt in stating that *The Structure of Social Action* was not a secondary work as Parsons claimed:

> I . . . see your book now as a means for you of arriving in due course of elaboration at your very primary systematic position. Your dynamics of scientific attack are, as far as I can see, entirely different from that of Weber though your problems and topics are related to his.[77]

While Voegelin was willing to commend Parsons for the theoretical position that he was developing, he disagreed that Parsons's approach was an extension and a systematization of Weber's thought. To do so would have been tantamount to approving the gnostic implications of Parsons's project, in which the metaphysical or affective side of Weber's writings was eliminated. Rather than seeking to build on the foundations established by Weber, Voegelin sought to challenge Weber's assumptions, using this critique as a new point of departure.

Voegelin's methodological preferences are revealed clearly in the opening chapter of *The New Science of Politics* (1952), in which he argued for a "retheorization" of political science, in the sense of "a recovery from the destruction of science which characterized the positivistic era in the second half of the nineteenth century" (Voegelin, 1952: 4). In Voegelin's view, it was Max Weber's work that pushed "the 'values' out of science into the position of unquestioned axioms or hypotheses" (Voegelin, 1952: 13).

According to Voegelin, Weber's conception of the "ideal type" embodied the "value-free" precepts of positivism:

> A value-free science meant to Weber the exploration of causes and effects, the construction of ideal types that would permit distinguishing regularities of institutions as well as deviations from them, and especially the construction of typical causal relations. . . . On the one side, there were the "values" of political order beyond critical evaluation; on the other side, there was a science of the structure of social reality that might be used as technical knowledge by the politician. In sharpening the issue of a "value-free" science to this pragmatic point, Weber moved the debate beyond methodological squabbles again to the order of relevance. He wanted science because he wanted clarity about the world in which he passionately participated; he was headed again on the road toward essence. (Voegelin, 1952: 14)

While Weber's solution was theoretically elegant, the fact-value distinction could not be observed in practice.

For Voegelin, Weber's position represented a point of entry through which other values could be invoked as a legitimate part of the scientific endeavor. In the same way that he used Weber's conception of predestination as a starting point for understanding how gnosticism emerged and evolved, Voegelin used Weber's methodological writings as a basis for recovering value-perspectives in the human sciences that had been sacrificed at the altar of positivism.

AGAINST FASCISM: THE PRACTICAL CONCERNS OF PARSONS AND VOEGELIN

In differing ways, both Parsons and Voegelin drew on Weber to formulate positions against emerging fascist views. By systematizing and extending Weber's insights into the linkage between predestination and active mastery, Parsons sought to develop an orientation through which the professional strata (including the social sciences) could help consolidate liberal-democratic orders, thus serving as a bulwark against the growth and development of fascism. In contrast, Voegelin used Weber as a point of departure for retrieving transcendent ideals and wisdom from the past, tendencies that had been lost with the onset of gnosticism, the growth of the nation-state, and the emergence of twentieth-century ideologies such as fascism.

Consistent with their evolving standpoints, it is not surprising that their conceptions of fascism bore little relation to one another. Voegelin viewed fascism as an ideological outburst that could be best described as a "political religion." As he noted, the "severe crisis" and the "process of decay" attendant upon fascism have their "origin in the secularization of the spirit" (Voegelin, 1986: 3). In effect, Voegelin viewed communism as well as fascism as variations on the same theme, namely, the degeneration of secular trends into totalitarian excesses. Such excesses were evident when primacy was given to national political life, and science was harnessed to realize state-defined ends.

What characterized fascism, in particular, was "the race idea" that was used by National Socialism "in order to integrate a community spiritually and politically" (Voegelin, 1940: 283). National Socialism, as characterized by the race idea, became manifest in twentieth-century Germany because its acquisition of political independence was delayed until the twentieth century. Therefore, it lacked "the accumulated weight of centuries of statehood to grant it stability" (311). According to Voegelin, those countries that experienced their revolutions earlier (such as the United States and Great Britain) were resistant to National Socialism because their traditional symbols and values could be more easily retained. However, twentieth-century revolutions, lacking "the authority of established symbol" made unfounded claims that the new symbols that they produced were not based on religion but on science (313).

Although Voegelin's opposition to fascism was unequivocal, he was equally, if not more, concerned about those intellectual trends that fostered the emergence and growth of National Socialism. He maintained that politicizing intellectuals had failed completely as opponents to fascism, and that they were naive in their expectations about the liberating effects of socialism:

> It is always dreadful to hear that National Socialism is a regression to barbarism, to the Dark Ages, to the times before the more recent advances towards humanism, without the speaker's sensing that the secularization of life, which the concept of humanism brought with it, is precisely the soil in which anti-Christian religious movements such as National Socialism could grow. (Voegelin, 1986: 3)

Secular humanism had abetted rather than hindered the growth of National Socialism. In his view, only religious renewal, sparked by great personalities, would allow for the preparation of the "the soil from which the resistance against evil will rise" (Voegelin, 1986: 3).

Consistent with his commitment to the very secular-humanist values that Voegelin condemned, Parsons's views on the relationship between fascism and science differed dramatically. According to Parsons, secular society did not provide the "fertile soil" that nurtured the rise of fascism. Rather, fascism could best be viewed as an irrational response by traditional elements in society to overall trends of rationalization. In this sense, the "National Socialist Movement . . . constitutes a mobilization of the extremely deep-seated romantic tendencies . . . incorporating a fundamentalist revolt against the whole tendency of rationalization in the Western world, and at the same time against its deepest institutionalized foundations" (Parsons, 1964: 123).

Arguably, Parsons's view of fascism as an "irrational response" to rationalization stemmed from his implicit support of Calvinist theological doctrine. In this sense, his explanation could be understood as an instance of the "externalization of evil" that Voegelin had used to describe the onset of Puritan modernity (Voegelin, 1940: 307). Hence, the residual "evil" of fascism, in Parsons's account, could be counterpoised to the inexorable progress of reason in Western capitalist societies.

For Parsons, the secular-humanist state, as the embodiment of reason, served as the standpoint from which externalized evil, in the form of totalitarian tendencies, could be combated. Unlike Voegelin, Parsons discriminated between left and right-wing extremism. While Voegelin viewed them both as similar variants of the race idea taking a national form, Parsons saw them as utilitarian and romantic responses respectively to rationalization (Parsons, 1964: 134). According to Parsons, it was from the emergent standpoint of the secular-rational state that such external sources of evil could be combatted. It is instructive that in his effort to provide the conceptual basis for such an order, he invoked the thought of Max Weber. It was on the basis of Weber's insights into the constitutive features of rational-legal authority that resistance to totalitarian tendencies could be cultivated (Parsons, 1942a).

By contrast, Voegelin viewed Weber as the culmination of positivist thinking, as embodying all the tensions and contradictions of that body of thought. Accordingly, he sought to use Weber's thought as a basis for resurrecting what had been lost with the advent of secularization, modernity, and the formation of nation-states. This involved both an understanding of what historical conditions made for the acceptance of active mastery as a doctrine, and a recoupling of method with transcendent values, a unity that had been violated by contemporary positivist doctrine. It was through the retrieval of earlier conceptions of the social order that Voegelin sought to combat what he considered as "closed societies" dominated by "spiritual eunuchs" (Voegelin, 1948).

AN INEVITABLE PARTING: TERMINATION OF THE PARSONS-VOEGELIN CORRESPONDENCE

Despite the fundamentally different assumptions that informed the standpoints of Voegelin and Parsons, their exchanges were cordial with disagreements muted. In particular, Voegelin never revealed the extent of his dismay with secular modernity, and his abhorrence of the very gnostic trends that Parsons supported. Undoubtedly, as an émigré scholar in a very precarious academic position, he sought to gain support from established scholars such as Parsons, and was therefore not inclined to be overly critical of his work. Indeed, Voegelin asked Parsons to write a recommendation on his behalf for a grant-in-aid from the Social Science Research Council, expressing his gratitude upon learning that Parsons had complied.[78]

Given that their respective views on modernity were both incommensurable and diverging, it is not entirely surprising that their correspondence did not continue beyond the middle of 1944. During the previous year Voegelin's growing discontent with the response of intellectuals to twentieth-century political trends had come to a head. As he described this shift in an autobiographical memoir:

> In 1943 I had arrived at a dead-end in my attempts to find a theory of man, society, and history that would permit an adequate interpretation of the phenomena in my chosen field of studies. The analysis of the movements of Communism, Fascism, National Socialism, and racism . . . had made it clear beyond a doubt that the center of a philosophy

of politics had to be a theory of consciousness: but the academic institutions of the Western world, the various schools of philosophy, the rich manifold of methodologies, did not offer the intellectual instruments that would make the political events and movements intelligible. (Voegelin, 1978: 3)

Among the school philosophies that did not "provide an answer" to the concerns troubling Voegelin was "the value-free science of Max Weber."

Voegelin's rejection of these "school-philosophies" had profound implications for his own intellectual orientation. Specifically, he embarked on an effort to expand his own "horizon of consciousness" through a "ceaseless action of expanding, ordering, articulating, and correcting itself" (Voegelin, 1978: 4).[79] This meant avoiding the self-destructive fantasy of believing the reality of which it is a part to be an object external to itself that can be mastered by bringing it into the form of a system. At the moment that Voegelin was in the process of rejecting the mastery of the world as a mode of being, Parsons's commitments to activity in the secular world were increasing. In support of the American war effort, he suspended his research on theoretical sociology, preferring to work in a much more applied vein. In addition to educating military administrative personnel, he arranged to be hired as a consultant for the Foreign Enemy Branch, whose mandate was to design policy for the anticipated occupation of Germany and Japan (Parsons, 1945). In view of their rapidly diverging perspectives on the vocation of the intellectual, there was little basis for any further exchange between Parsons and Voegelin.

For all its intellectual intensity, the correspondence between Parsons and Voegelin generated little light and even less heat. Both individuals put great effort into explicating their positions for one another, yet neither was willing to question assumptions and drive home disagreements. Given the lack of real communication about fundamental issues, it is doubtful whether either of them changed his views significantly as a result of the correspondence.

Its communicative shortcomings aside, the exchange of letters between Parsons and Voegelin is revealing in ways fully unintended by the correspondents. In responding to each other's queries and puzzlement, they inadvertently threw their most deeply held assumptions on the intellectual vocation into bold relief. And in doing so, they have afforded us some rare glimpses into their respective testaments to the ghost of Max Weber.

CONCLUSION

That Parsons continued to view Weber in this fashion long after his correspondence with Voegelin is evident in the address he gave at the Weber Centenary Conference, held in Heidelberg in 1964. His analysis of Weber in relation to the crisis of his time sheds light on his invocation of Weber during the emergent crisis of World War II, a quarter century earlier. Parsons noted that "Weber's peak of intellectual maturity coincided remarkably with the outbreak of the great crisis of the century in the social and political order of the Western world, both internally and in its relation to the rest of the world." He saw Weber as a member of "the generation spanning the turn to the twentieth century [which] saw the decisive initial steps taken in a profound intellectual and cultural transformation, the full consequences of which are even now only beginning to emerge" (Parsons 1967: 81). He was particularly interested in the approach for the social scientist which Weber advocated: "It is not an advocacy that the social scientist abstain from all value commitments. . . . The point is rather that *in his role* as scientist a particular subvalue system must be paramount for the investigator" (86). But these values underpinning science were not autonomous. "Science," in his view, "must in the nature of the case be socially organized." Moreover, "it is essential that it should be integrated to a degree in the value consensus of the community in which it takes place, not totally absorbed, but accorded the kind of place that it is essential to its support in a broadly political sense" (87).

What Parsons wished to emphasize was that "Weber stood at a very crucial juncture in the whole development of Western civilization. He understood, as hardly any of his contemporaries did, the fact and nature of the breakup of the older system, and he contributed more than any single figure to the outline of a new intellectual orientation which promises to be of constitutive importance in defining the situation of the emerging social world." In his view, Weber's conception of sociology had great significance for the fate of western civilization:

> The emergence of the science of sociology, of which I regard Max Weber as one of the very few true founders, is a harbinger of these great changes; and that our science may well be destined to play a major role, not only its primary task of understanding the social and cultural world we live in as an object of its investigation, but, in ways, which cannot now be foreseen, in actually shaping that world. In this sense it may possibly turn out to be the most important heir of the great ideologies of the turn of the last century. The possibility is perhaps the truest measure of the greatness of Max Weber. (Parsons, 1967: 101)

These statements reveal an enduring feature of Parsons's engagement with Weber, namely an effort to draw upon Weberian thought to generate practical guidelines for the social sciences. Yet most interpretations of how Parsons made use of Weber and other classical thinkers have largely confined themselves to analytical aspects of writings, largely as they pertain to his general theory. This has meant that commentary has tended to focus on Parsons's discussion of Weber in *The Structure of Social Action*, which has commonly been viewed as the foundation of his scholarly activity. However, if one places shifting patterns of Parsons's intellectual engagement at the center of the discussion, a different picture emerges. In this respect, *Structure* is examined not as an autonomous body of sociological theory, but as a form of intellectual activity bound up with Parsons's broader reflections on how the institutionalization of professional practice would provide a solution to the "Hobbesian problem of order" (see Buxton, 1985). In the aftermath of *Structure*, one can observe a convergence between the two streams of Parsons's thought, namely, his efforts to ground a theoretical standpoint for sociology (the voluntaristic theory of action) and his project of laying out the contours of social organization, as rooted in the practice of professionals. In doing so, he relied heavily on the writings of Max Weber. Initially, this involved deploying Weber to shore up the methodological foundations of sociology. But as the war in Europe became a reality, Parsons began to rely on Weber as the basis for developing a comparative-institutional analysis. This involved an effort to bring together a community of like-minded interlocutors, who, in subscribing to the views on society and politics that informed Parsons's depiction of Weber's central conceptual scheme, were to provide the bearings for the course of Western civilization.

This means that in order to understand how Weber fit into Parsons's emergent theory one can't simply focus on *Structure* complemented by a few other selected writings from Parsons's oeuvres. Rather, it is necessary to examine in detail what lay behind that relatively brief time period when, echoing his earlier fascination with *The Protestant Ethic and the Spirit of Capitalism,* Weber's writings gripped his "intense interest" and had a "powerful impact" upon his thinking (Parsons, 1980: 39).

NOTES

This is a revised version of a paper that was originally presented at the annual meetings of the Canadian Sociology and Anthropology Association, held at McMaster University in Hamilton, Ontario, June 1987 and at the meetings of History of Sociology section of the International Sociological Association held at Madrid in 1988. We wish to thank Larry Nichols and John Drysdale for their helpful comments on an earlier draft of this chapter. Material from the Parsons Papers and the letters from Eric Voegelin have been published by permission of the Harvard University Archives and the estate of Eric Voegelin, respectively.

1. Parsons's approach to institutional analysis developed through his role as the coordinator of Sociology 6, "Social Institutions," a course he both designed and continually revised. His involvement with the professions appears to have had its origin in his response to the debates about national health insurance during the early New Deal.

2. Eric Voegelin (1901–1985) was a creative and prolific thinker who is particularly well known for his highly original work in political theory. He was born in Cologne but was raised in Vienna, where his family had relocated in 1910. He completed his doctorate at the University of Vienna in 1922, and then served as an assistant in the Law Faculty to Hans Kelsen, whose neo-Kantian views were to influence Voegelin's early work. From 1924 to 1927 he spent time in the United States, France, and England, supported by a Laura Spelman Rockefeller Fellowship. After returning to Austria, Voegelin became an associate professor of law at Vienna. Upon the Nazi annexation of Austria in 1938, Voegelin was forced to resign his position, escaping to Switzerland. He then immigrated to the United States and taught briefly at Harvard University, Bennington College, Northwestern University, and the University of Alabama. In 1943, he was invited to Louisiana State University, where he taught government for many years. In 1958 he accepted a prestigious professorship (along with the directorship of the Institute for Political Science) at the University of Münich. Upon his retirement from this position in 1969, Voegelin returned to the United States (where he had become a naturalized citizen), serving as a senior research fellow at the Hoover Institution. He lived in Stanford, California, until his death there in 1985.

While interest in Voegelin's work has been steadily increasing in recent years (Cooper, 1986, 1999; Germino, 1979, 1982; Hallowell, 1975; Kirby and Thompson, 1983; McKnight, 1978; Morrisey, 1994; Sebba and Opitz, 1981; Sandoz, 1981; Webb, 1981), his vision and life's work has largely been misplaced and misunderstood within his disciplinary locus, political science.

In published books, articles, and essays spanning more than half a century, Voegelin sought to address the "whole history and hierarchy of human existence with special emphasis upon the modes of man's [people's] participation in the divine as reflected in documented experience" (Sandoz, 1981: 15). He was not a system builder, but someone who sought to uncover truths at the level of experience and to show that the meaning of history is a refection of the modes of consciousness of the individual and the times. Sandoz (253–60) provides an excellent intellectual biography of Voegelin along with a comprehensive bibliography of his writings.

3. Continuing discussion of the Parsons-Schütz exchange is expressed by Kassab (1991) and Buxton (1994).

4. As Parsons noted in a letter to Herbert Heaton with reference to Edwin Gay (one of his mentors) upon the latter's death: "Gay was a strong admirer of Max Weber. I discussed this with him on a number of occasions. He felt, also, that many of the economic historians, who were strongly hostile to Weber, were badly off base and did not really know what they were talking about. . . . One point he made was that these people were Anglicans, who didn't know what a real Calvinist was like, whereas he said he and I, both being brought up Puritan backgrounds, had it in our bones." Talcott Parsons to Herbert Heaton, March 23, 1949. Harvard University Archives (hereafter HUA). Parsons Papers (hereafter PP). HUG(FP) 42.8.4, Correspondence and Other Papers, 1935–55. Box 11. File: "H," 1947–49.

5. Undoubtedly, this was fueled by his critique of H. M. Robertson's (1933) treatise on Weber (Parsons, 1935) and his reading of Alexander von Schelting's analysis of Weber's methodology (1934), which seemed to have exerted a powerful influence upon him (see Parsons, 1936).

6. Max Lerner, "The Materialist Interpretation of History." HUA. PP. HUG(FP) 15.75. Box 3.

7. Talcott Parsons, "vs. Max Lerner." HUA. PP. HUG(FP) 15.75. Box 3.

8. Parsons's name had been given to Hodge by Professor Friedrich von Hayek of the London School of Economics. Professor Fritz Machlup of Princeton University served as an intermediary.

9. Fritz Machlup to Talcott Parsons, February 16, 1938. HUA. PP. HUG(FP) 42.8.2. Correspondence and Related Papers (hereafter CRP), 1923–40. Box 3. File: Correspondence re: publications, reviews etc. 1937–40.

10. Talcott Parsons to James Hodge, January 26, 1939. HUA. PP. HUG(FP) 1930–59, CRP 1923–40. Box 13. File: Hodge, 1938–44.

11. Talcott Parsons to James Hodge, January 26, 1939. HUA. PP. HUG(FP) 15.2, CRP 1930–59. Box 13. File: Hodge, 1938–44.

12. Talcott Parsons to James Hodge, January 26, 1939. HUA. PP. HUG(FP) 15.2, CRP 1930–59. Box 13. File: Hodge, 1938–44.

13. Talcott Parsons to James Hodge, April 13, 1939. HUA. PP. HUG(FP) 15.2, CRP 1930–59. Box 13. File: Hodge, 1938–44.

14. Talcott Parsons to James Hodge, April 13, 1939. HUA. PP. HUG(FP) 15.2, CRP 1930–59. Box 13. File: Hodge, 1938–44.

15. Eventually, however, Parsons quite generously declined to accept further payments for his work. As the war in Europe deepened, he felt that "in view of the difficulties of the British position the other payments be omitted. Of the remainder perhaps half could be retained by the firm in . . . partial recognition of their courageous devotion to international scholarship in bringing out such a volume at such a time, and the other half given on my behalf to the fund which takes care of families rendered homeless by bombing." Talcott Parsons to James Hodge, August 12, 1941. HUA. PP. HUG(FP) 15.2, CRP 1930–59. Box 13. File: Hodge, 1938–44.

16. Talcott Parsons to James Hodge, May 17, 1939. HUA. PP. HUG(FP) 42.8.2, CRP 1923–40. Box 3. File: Publications etc. 1937–40.

17. In this respect, there are some similarities between Parsons's analysis of civilization and those of Sorokin, Mannheim, Spengler, and Toynbee. It is rather ironic that around the time that Parsons was engaged in this sort of work, he was suggesting that Pitirim Sorokin, the chair of the Sociology Department at Harvard, should be appointed as a philosopher of history instead. I am indebted to Larry Nichols for these insights.

18. Howard A. Odum to Talcott Parsons, September 23, 1942. HUA. PP. HUG(FP) 15.2, CRP 1930–59. Box 19. File: Publications, 1939–43.

19. Talcott Parsons to James Hodge, June 28, 1939. HUA. PP. HUG(FP) 15.2, CRP 1930–59. Box 13, File: Hodge, 1938–44.

20. Talcott Parsons to Edwin Gay, August 28, 1939. HUA. PP. HUG(FP) 42.8.2, CRP 1923–40. Box 3. File: Publications etc. 1937–40.

21. Talcott Parsons to Edwin Gay, August 28, 1939. HUA. PP. HUG(FP) 42.8.2, CRP 1923–59. Box 3. File: Publications etc. 1937–40.

22. As he noted in a letter to Frank Knight in the spring of 1939, "My plan is to try to get the work done this summer, so there is a chance of its being published some time next year. So at last it looks as if things were moving in this field." Talcott Parsons to Frank Knight, May 17, 1939. HUA. PP. HUG(FP) 42.8.2, CRP 1923–40. Box 3. File: Publications etc. 1937–40.

23. At one point, some material that Parsons sent was "lost in the sinking of a steamer due to war causes." Post Office Department, Bureau in Charge of the Chief Inspector, Inspector in charge of Boston Division to Talcott Parsons, October 15, 1943. HUA. PP. HUG(FP) 15.2, CRP 1930–59. Box 13. File: Hodge, W. H. and Company, 1938–44. The production of the book was also slowed by the fact that both Hodge and Henderson went into the war service. After an exchange of letters in early 1939, Parsons never heard from Henderson again.

24. Talcott Parsons to James Hodge, November 14, 1940. HUA. PP. HUG(FP) 15.2, CRP 1923–40. Box 13. File: Hodge, 1938–44.

25. Talcott Parsons to James Hodge, August 12, 1941. HUA. PP. HUG(FP) 15.2, CRP 1930–59. Box 13. File: Hodge, 1938–44.

26. Talcott Parsons to Hans Gerth, December 9, 1942. HUA. PP. HUG(FP) 15.2, CRP 1930–59. Box 19. File: Professional Colleagues, corr. with, 1942–43.

27. Talcott Parsons to William Hodge and Co. Ltd., September 29, 1944. HUA. PP. HUG(FP) 15.2, CRP 1930–59. Box 13. File: Hodge, W. H. and Company, 1938–44.

28. He noted at one point that "it would pay to make an arrangement with an American publisher to take a substantial number of sheets . . . one of my colleagues has discussed the question of the translation of Weber's works with McMillan and thinks they would be interested." Talcott Parsons to James Hodge, June 28, 1939. HUA. PP. HUG(FP) 15.2, CRP 1930–59. Box 13. File: Hodge, 1938–44. He later revealed that he had been "approached on behalf of two publishers with the possible view to publication here in case you wished to be relieved of the responsibility. These are the MacMillan Company, through Professor Louis Wirth of the University of Chicago, and D. C. Heath Company, through Professor Howard Becker of the University of Wisconsin." Talcott Parsons to Niold Manhaad, February 10, 1941. HUA. PP. HUG(FP) 15.2, CRP 1930–59. Box 13. File: Hodge, 1938–44.

29. This manuscript was entitled "Simmel and the Methodological Problems of Formal Sociology." It has recently been published (Parsons, 1998b) along with Edward Shils's comments on the document (1998), Parsons's "fragment" on Simmel from the draft chapter XIII from *The Structure of Social Action* (Parsons, 1998a), and a commentary by William J. Buxton (1998).

30. He gave particular attention to work in the area of "formal sociology," as developed by Leopold von Wiese and Howard Becker (1932).

31. This copy can be found in the Parsons Papers. HUA. PP. HUG(FP) 15.75. Box 3.

32. Talcott Parsons to Crane Brinton, July 11, 1939. HUA. PP. HUG(FP) 42.8.2, CRP 1923–40.

33. Talcott Parsons to Crane Brinton, July 11, 1939. HUA. PP. HUG(FP) 42.8.2, CRP 1923–40.

34. Waldemar Gurian to Talcott Parsons, August 12, 1938. HUA. PP. HUG(FP) 42.8.2, CRP 1923–40. Box 3. File: Publications etc. 1937–40.

35. Waldemar Gurian to Talcott Parsons, December 11, 1939. HUA. PP. HUG(FP) 15.2, CRP 1930–59. Box 19. File: Publications 1939–43.

36. Talcott Parsons to Waldemar Gurian, December 21, 1939. HUA. PP. HUG(FP) 15.2, CRP 1930–59. Box 13. File: Publications, 1939–43.

37. Waldemar Gurian to Talcott Parsons, January 3, 1940. HUA. PP. HUG(FP) 15.2, CRP 1930–59. Box 17. File: Publications, 1939–43.

38. Talcott Parsons to Waldemar Gurian, January 10, 1940. HUA. PP. HUG(FP) 15.2, CRP 1930–59. Box 19. File: Publications, 1939–43.

39. Talcott Parsons to Waldemar Gurian, July 6, 1940. HUA. PP. HUG(FP) 42.8.2, CRP 1923–40. Box 3. File: Correspondence re: publications, reviews etc. 1937–40.

40. Savoie Bottinville to Talcott Parsons, April 5, 1943. HUA. PP. HUG(FP) 15.2, CRP 1930–59. Box 19. File: Publications, 1939–43.

41. Parsons sent a draft of the article to Eric Voegelin. In responding to Voegelin's comments, he noted the influence of Weber upon his thinking:

I am delighted that you liked the article on Anti-Semitism. There is very little that is original in it. . . . the analysis of the historical elements of the Jewish tradition is overwhelmingly indebted to Max Weber. I have read his *Antike Judentum* three or four times and, I think, am more impressed with it each time. . . . it seems to me certain of these things stand out with beautiful clarity and throw a remarkable light on certain of the features even of the modern Jewish problem. My impressions from Weber have, however, been very strongly confirmed from other sources.

Talcott Parsons to Eric Voegelin, September 27, 1940. HUA. PP. HUG(FP) 42.8.2, CRP 1923–40. Box 3. File: Correspondence, 1940.

42. Gerhardt (1993: 20–22). The original draft has been reconstructed and republished in this volume. See Parsons (1993).

43. Talcott Parsons to Dumas Malone, February 25, 1939. HUA. PP. HUG(FP) 42.8.2, CRP 1923–40. Box 3. File: Publications etc. 1937–40.

44. Talcott Parsons to Frank Knight, May 17, 1939. HUA. PP. HUG(FP) 42.8.2, CRP 1923–40. Box 3. File: Publications etc. 1937–40.

45. Talcott Parsons to Dumas Malone, February 25, 1939. HUA. PP. HUG(FP) 42.8.2, CRP 1923–40. Box 3. File: Publications etc. 1937–40.

46. Frank Knight to Dumas Malone, May 20, 1939. HUA. PP. HUG(FP) 42.8.2, CRP 1923–40. Box 3. File: Publications etc. 1937–40.

47. Jerome Hall to Talcott Parsons, May 29, 1940. HUA. PP. HUG(FP) 15.2, CRP 1930–59. Box 19. File: publications, 1939–43.

48. Jerome Hall to Talcott Parsons, April 8, 1941. HUA. PP. HUG(FP) 15.2, CRP 1930–59. Box 27. File: Weber Translation corr., 1940–42. Knight eventually decided not to contribute to the volume because of poor health and an excess of work.

49. Talcott Parsons to Jerome Hall, March 14, 1941. HUA. PP. HUG(FP) 15.2. CRP 1930–59. Box 27. File: Weber translation corr., 1940–42.

50. Talcott Parsons to Jerome Hall, August 18, 1941. HUA. PP. HUG(FP) 15.2, CRP 1930–59. Box 27. File: Weber translation corr., 1940–42.

54 Buxton and Rehorick

51. Talcott Parsons to Edward Shils, September 7, 1941. HUA. PP. HUG(FP) 15.2, CRP 1930–59. Box 27. File: Weber translation corr., 1940–42.

52. This sense of building an interpretive network appears to have been given impetus by Parsons's visit to Chicago in January 1939. He evidently discussed the prospects for translations of Weber's work with a number of faculty at the University of Chicago including Frank Knight, Edward Shils, Louis Wirth, and Max Rheinstein. He suggested that he make use of a translation by Shils and Alexander von Schelting rather than by Henderson. Other persons whom Parsons wished to bring into this network included Howard Becker and Albert Salomon.

53. These included Henderson's original translation, along with another project contemplated by the publishing firm of Kurt Wolff. Parsons also sought to cultivate an interpretation of Weber that was at odds with that developed by both Karl Mannheim and Alfred Schütz. While his relations with Hans Gerth were cordial, there is some evidence that he felt that his Weber translation project was in competition with that of Gerth and Mills.

54. Ephraim Fischoff to Talcott Parsons, April 6, 1942. HUA. PP. HUG(FP) 15.2, CRP 1930–59. Box 27. File: Weber translation corr., 1940–42.

55. Talcott Parsons to Ephraim Fischoff, April 21, 1942. HUA. PP. HUG(FP) 15.2, CRP 1930–59. Box 27. File: Weber translation corr., 1940–42. It is somewhat ironic that it was Fischoff who eventually translated Weber's *Sociology of Religion* for which Parsons provided the introduction (Weber, 1963).

56. A total of sixteen letters (ten from Voegelin and six from Parsons) can be found in the Parsons Papers at the Harvard University Archives. An additional letter (Parsons to Voegelin, January 8, 1943) is missing from the collection. Evidently, other correspondence between Parsons and Voegelin can be found in the Voegelin Papers, which are held at the Hoover Institution Archives in Stanford, California (Cooper, 1999). Increasing interest in the Parsons-Voegelin exchange is reflected in the recent translation of the letters into Italian. See Bortolini (2000).

57. Details about the circumstances leading up to Voegelin's appointment at Harvard can be found in Cooper (1999: 15–21).

58. Talcott Parsons to Eric Voegelin, February 8, 1940. HUA. PP. HUG(FP) 42.8.2, CRP 1923–40. Box 3. File: Correspondence, 1940. He was likely referring to his 1939 manuscript (Parsons, 1939).

59. Voegelin was unequivocal in his praise of the manuscript:

> I was at first quite surprised at the bulk because somehow I had misunderstood you and believed it would be a translation only of the First *Chapter*. Now I am rather overwhelmed; this is a tremendous piece of work. . . . It would be desirable to have it published as soon as possible.

Eric Voegelin to Talcott Parsons. HUA. PP. HUG(FP) 15.2, CRP 1930–59. Box 27. File: Voegelin, Eric.

60. Talcott Parsons to Eric Voegelin, August 1, 1941. HUA. PP. HUG(FP) 15.2, CRP 1930–59. Box 24. File: Voegelin, Eric.

61. Talcott Parsons to Eric Voegelin, August 1, 1941. HUA. PP. HUG(FP) 15.2, CRP 1930–59. Box 24. File: Voegelin, Eric.

62. Eric Voegelin to Talcott Parsons, August 4, 1941. HUA. PP. HUG(FP) 15.2, CRP 1930–59. Box 24. File: Voegelin, Eric.

63. Eric Voegelin to Talcott Parsons, August 4, 1941. HUA. PP. HUG(FP) 15.2, CRP 1930–59. Box 24. File: Voegelin, Eric.

64. Eric Voegelin to Talcott Parsons, August 4, 1941. HUA. PP. HUG(FP) 15.2, CRP 1930–59. Box 24. File: Voegelin, Eric.

65. Eric Voegelin to Talcott Parsons, August 4, 1941. HUA. PP. HUG(FP) 15.2, CRP 1930–59. Box 24. File: Voegelin, Eric.

66. Eric Voegelin to Talcott Parsons, October 19, 1941. HUA. PP. HUG(FP) 15.2, CRP 1930–59. Box 24. File: Voegelin, Eric.

67. Eric Voegelin to Talcott Parsons, October 19, 1941. HUA. PP. HUG(FP) 15.2, CRP 1930–59. Box 24. File: Voegelin, Eric.

68. Talcott Parsons to Eric Voegelin, October 19, 1941. HUA. PP. HUG(FP) 15.2, CRP 1930–59. Box 24. File: Voegelin, Eric.

69. Talcott Parsons to Eric Voegelin, August 18, 1941. HUA. PP. HUG(FP) 15.2, CRP 1930–59. Box 24. File: Voegelin, Eric.

70. Talcott Parsons to Eric Voegelin, May 13, 1941. HUA. PP. HUG(FP) 15.2, CRP 1930–59. Box 24. File: Voegelin, Eric.

71. Talcott Parsons to Eric Voegelin, May 13, 1941. HUA. PP. HUG(FP) 15.2, CRP 1930–59. Box 24. File: Voegelin, Eric.

72. Talcott Parsons to Eric Voegelin, October 2, 1941. HUA. PP. HUG(FP) 15.2, CRP 1930–59. Box 24. File: Voegelin, Eric.

73. These elements of orientation were in fact a restatement of the "modern" half of the pattern variables, which Parsons had previously used to describe the patterned action of the professional stratum. He previously claimed that he had derived them from a field study of medical practitioners. However, given that they were virtually interchangeable with elements of orientation derived from Weber's writings on ascetic Protestantism, it is arguable that he projected his own theological commitments upon medicine, rather then deriving them from actual study and observation (see Buxton, 1985: ch. 5).

74. Talcott Parsons to Eric Voegelin, October 2, 1941. HUA. PP. HUG(FP) 15.2, CRP 1930–59. Box 24. File: Voegelin, Eric.

75. Eric Voegelin to Talcott Parsons, September 24, 1941. HUA. PP. HUG(FP) 15.2, CRP 1930–59. Box 24. File: Voegelin, Eric.

76. Eric Voegelin to Talcott Parsons, September 24, 1941. HUA. PP. HUG(FP) 15.2, CRP 1930–59. Box 24. File: Voegelin, Eric.

77. Eric Voegelin to Talcott Parsons, September 24, 1941. HUA. PP. HUG(FP) 15.2, CRP 1930–59. Box 24. File: Voegelin, Eric.

78. Eric Voegelin to Talcott Parsons, January 16, 1943. HUA. PP. HUG(FP) 15.2, CRP 1930–59. Box 24. File: Voegelin, Eric.

79. As Dante Germino (1979: 787–88) describes Voegelin's new departure, "In 1943 he abandoned a lengthy 'History of Political Ideas' that followed conventional chronological organization to work out an important new theory of experience and its symbolization. This theory became the basis for *Order and History.*" (Voegelin, 1956–87).

REFERENCES

Alexander, J. 1988. "Parsons's Structure in American Sociology." *Sociological Theory* 6: 96–102.

Bortolini, M., ed. 2000. "Il carteggio Tra Eric Voegelin." Pp. 129–33 in *La Societa Accaduti: Tracce di una "nuova" scienza sociale in Eric Voegelin*, edited by E. Morandi. Milano: Angeli.

Brinton, C. 1939. "What's the Matter With Sociology?" *Saturday Review of Literature* 6 (May): 4–5, 14.

Buxton, W. J. 1985. *Talcott Parsons and the Capitalist-Nation State: Political Sociology as a Strategic Vocation.* Toronto: University of Toronto Press.

———. 1994. "Academic Dispute or Clash of Commitments: The Schutz-Parsons Exchange Reconsidered." *Human Studies* 17 (2): 267–75.

———. 1998. "From the 'Missing Fragment' to the 'Lost Manuscript': Reflections on the Place of Georg Simmel in the Thought of Talcott Parsons." *American Sociologist* 29 (2): 75–93.

Camic, C. 1992. "Reputation and Predecessor Selection: Parsons and the Institutionalists." *American Sociological Review* 57: 421–45.

Cooper, B. 1986. *The Political Theory of Eric Voegelin.* Toronto: Mellen.

———. 1999. *Eric Voegelin and the Foundations of Modern Political Science.* Columbia: University of Missouri Press.

Coser, L. A. 1979. "A Dialogue of the Deaf." *Contemporary Sociology* 8: 680–82.

Embree, L. 1980. "Methodology Is Where Human Scientists and Philosophers Can Meet: Reflections on the Schutz-Parsons Exchange." *Human Studies* 3 (4): 367–73.

Gerhardt, U., ed. 1993. *Talcott Parsons on National Socialism.* New York: Aldine de Gruyter.

Germino, D. 1979. "Voegelin, Eric." Pp. 787–90 in *International Encyclopedia of the Social Sciences,* Vol. 18, edited by David Sills. New York: Free Press.

———. 1982. *Political Philosophy and the Open Society.* Baton Rouge: Louisiana State University Press.

Grathoff, R., ed. 1978. *The Theory of Social Action: The Correspondence of Alfred Schutz and Talcott Parsons.* Bloomington: Indiana University Press.

Hallowell, J. H., ed. 1975. *Eric Voegelin: From Enlightenment to Revolution.* Durham, N.C.: Duke University Press.

Jaworski, G. D. 1990. "Simmel's Contribution to Parsons' Action Theory and its Fate." Pp. 109–30 in *Georg Simmel and Contemporary Sociology,* edited by M. Kaern, B. S. Phillips, and R. S. Cohen. Dordrecht: Kluwer.

Kassab, E. 1991. *The Theory of Social Action in the Schutz-Parsons Debate.* Freiburg: Éditions Universitaires Freiburg Suisse.

Kirby, J., and W. M. Thompson, eds. 1983. *Voegelin and the Theologians: Ten Studies in Interpretation.* Toronto: Mellen.

Kivisto, P., and W. H. Swatos, Jr. 1990. "Weber and Interpretive Sociology in America." *Sociological Quarterly* 31 (1): 149–63.

Levine, D. 1991. "Simmel and Parsons Reconsidered." *American Journal of Sociology* 96 (5): 1097–116.

Lynd, R. S. 1939. *Knowledge for What?: The Place of the Social Sciences in American Culture.* Princeton: Princeton University Press.

McKnight, S. A. 1978. *Eric Voegelin's Search for Order in History.* Baton Rouge and London: Louisiana State University Press.

Morrisey, M. P. 1994. *Consciousness and Transcendence: The Theology of Eric Voegelin.* Notre Dame, Ind.: Notre Dame University Press.

Natanson, Maurice. 1978. "Foreword." Pp. ix–xvi in *The Theory of Social Action: The Correspondence of Alfred Schutz and Talcott Parsons,* edited by R. Grathoff. Bloomington: Indiana University Press.

Parsons, T. 1928. "'Capitalism' in Recent German Literature: Sombart and Weber I." *Journal of Political Economy* 36: 641–61.

———. 1935. "H. M. Robertson on Max Weber and His School." *Quarterly Journal of Economics* 43: 688–96.

————. 1936. Review of *Max Weber's Wissenschaftslehre* by Alexander von Schelting. *American Sociological Review* 1: 675–81.

————. 1937. *The Structure of Social Action.* New York: McGraw-Hill.

————. 1939. "Action, Theory, and Normative Pattern (date approximate, 175 typed pages). HUA. PP. HUG(FP) 42.45. Box 1. File: Manuscripts of articles and essays, 1937–c.1970. (German translation by Harold Wenzel, published by Suhrkamp Verlag, 1986).

————. 1942a. "Max Weber and the Contemporary Political Crisis." *Review of Politics* 4: 155–72.

————. 1942b. "The Sociology of Modern Anti-Semitism." Pp. 101–22 in *Jews in a Gentile World*, edited by I. Graeber and S. H. Britt. New York: Macmillan.

————. 1945. "The Social and Psychological Aspects of the F.E.A. Disarmament Program." Parsons Papers, Harvard University Archives.

————. 1947. "Introduction to *The Theory of Social and Economic Organization* by Max Weber." Trans. A. M. Henderson and T. Parsons. Edited by T. Parsons. New York: Free Press.

————. 1948. Max Weber's Sociological Analysis of Capitalism and Modern Institutions. Pp. 287–308 in *An Introduction to the History of Sociology*, edited by H. E. Barnes. Chicago: University of Chicago Press.

————. 1951. *The Social System.* New York: Free Press.

————. 1963. Introduction to Max Weber's *The Sociology of Religion*, translated by E. Fischoff. Boston: Beacon Press.

————. 1964. *Essays in Sociological Theory.* New York: Free Press.

————. 1967. "Evaluation and Objectivity in Social Science: An Interpretation of Max Weber's Contributions." Pp. 79–101 in *Sociological Theory and Modern Society.* New York: Free Press. (Originally delivered at the Weber Centennial, April 1964, Heidelberg.)

————. 1970. "On Building Social System Theory: A Personal History." *Daedalus* 99 (Part 2): 826–81.

————. 1974. "A 1974 Retrospective Perspective." Pp. 115–30 in *The Theory of Social Action: The Correspondence of Alfred Schutz and Talcott Parsons*, edited by R. Grathoff. Bloomington: Indiana University Press.

————. 1980. "The Circumstances of my Encounter with Max Weber." Pp. 37–43 in *Sociological Traditions from Generation to Generation: Glimpses of the American Experience*, edited by R. K. Merton and M. W. Riley. Norwood, N.J.: Ablex.

————. 1993. "The Sociology of Modern Anti-Semitism." Pp. 131–53 in *Talcott Parsons on National Socialism*, edited by U. Gerhardt. New York: Aldine de Gruyter.

————. 1998a. "The 'Fragment' on Simmel. From Draft Chapter XVIII [Structure of Social Action]: Georg Simmel and Ferdinand Tönnies: Social Relationships and the Elements of Action." *American Sociologist* 29 (2): 39–48.

————. 1998b. "Simmel and the Methodological Problems of Formal Sociology." *American Sociologist* 29 (2): 49–68.

Parsons, T., and E. Shils. 1951. *Towards a General Theory of Action.* Cambridge: Harvard University Press.

Parsons, T., E. Shils, and R. F. Bales. 1953. *Working Papers in the Theory of Action.* New York: Free Press.

Rehorick, D. A. 1980. "Schutz and Parsons: Debate or Dialogue?" *Human Studies* 3(4): 347–55.

Rehorick, D. A., and W. J. Buxton. 1988. "Recasting the Parsons-Schutz Dialogue: The Hidden Participation of Eric Voegelin." Pp. 151–69 in *Worldly Phenomenology: The Continuing Influence of Alfred Schutz on North American Human Science*, edited by L. Embree. Washington, D.C.: Center for Advanced Research in Phenomenology and University Press of America.

Robertson, H. M. 1933. *Aspects of the Rise of Economic Individualism—A Critique of Max Weber and His School.* Cambridge: Cambridge University Press.

Sandoz, E. 1981. *The Voegelinian Revolution: A Biographical Introduction.* Baton Rouge: Louisiana State University Press.

Schelting, A. von. 1934. *Max Weber's Wissenschaftslehre.* Tübingen: J.C.B. Mohr.

Sebba, G. 1981. "Documentary Appendix (Schutz-Voegelin Correspondence)." Pp. 431–65 in *The Philosophy of Order: Essays on History, Consciousness and Politics,* edited by G. Sebba and P. J. Opitz. Stuttgart: Klett-Cotta.

Sebba, G., and P. J. Opitz, eds. 1981. *The Philosophy of Order: Essays on History, Consciousness and Politics.* Stuttgart: Klett-Cotta.

Shils, E. 1998. "Comments on Parsons's 'Simmel and the Methodological Problems of Formal Sociology.'" *American Sociologist* 29 (2): 69–74.

Valone, J. J. 1979. "Two Social Theorists and a Second Look." *Phenomenology and Social Science Newsletter* 7 (2–3): 2–7, 4–6.

———. 1980. "Parsons' Contributions to Sociological Theory: Reflections on the Schutz-Parsons Correspondence." *Human Studies* 3 (4): 375–86.

Voegelin, E. 1933. *Rasse und Staat.* Tübingen: J.C.B. Mohr.

———. 1938. *Die Politischen Religionen.* Vienna: Bermann-Fischer.

———. 1940. "The Growth of the Race Idea." *Review of Politics* 2: 283–317.

———. 1941. "Some Problems of German Hegemony." *Journal of Politics* 3: 154–68.

———. 1944. "Nietzsche, the Crisis and the War." *Journal of Politics* 6: 177–212.

———. 1948. "The Origins of Scientism." *Social Research* 15 (1): 462–94.

———. 1952. *The New Science of Politics: An Introduction.* Chicago: University of Chicago Press.

———. 1975. *From Enlightenment to Revolution.* Durham, N.C.: Duke University Press.

———. 1978. *Anamnesis.* Notre Dame, Ind.: University of Notre Dame Press.

———. 1986. *Political Religions.* Trans. T. J. DiNapoli and E. S. Easterly III. Lewiston: Edwin Mellen Press.

———. 1956–87. *Order and History.* 5 vols. Baton Rouge: Louisiana State University Press. Volume 1: *Israel and Revelation,* 1956. Volume 2: *The World of the Polis,* 1957. Volume 3: *Plato and Aristotle,* 1957. Volume 4: *The Ecumenic Age,* 1974. Volume 5: *In Search of Order,* 1987.

Wagner, H. R. 1979. "Theory of Action and Sociology of the Lifeworld." *Contemporary Sociology* 8: 685–87.

———. 1980. "Reflections on Parsons' '1974 Retrospective Perspective' on Alfred Schutz." *Human Studies* 3 (4): 387–402.

———. 1981. "Agreement in Discord: Alfred Schutz and Eric Voegelin." Pp. 74–90 in *The Philosophy of Order,* edited by G. Sebba and P. J. Opitz. Stuttgart: Klett-Cotta.

Webb, E. 1981. *Eric Voegelin: Philosopher of History.* Seattle: University of Washington Press.

Weber, M. 1925. *Grundriss der Sozialoekonimuk. III. Abteilung: Wirtschaft und Gesellschaft,* 2 vols. Tübingen: J.C.B. Mohr.

———. 1947. *The Theory of Social and Economic Organization.* Trans. A. M. Henderson and T. Parsons. Edited with an Introduction by T. Parsons. New York: Free Press.

———. 1954. *Max Weber on Law in Economy and Society,* edited by E. Shils with an Introduction by M. Rheinstein. Cambridge: Harvard University Press.

———. 1963. *The Sociology of Religion.* Trans. by E. Fischoff with an Introduction by T. Parsons. Boston: Beacon Press.

Wiese, L. von, and H. Becker. 1932. *Systematic Sociology on the Basis of the "Beziehungslehre" and "Gebildlehre."* New York: Wiley.

Parsons-Voegelin Correspondence, Harvard University Archives, Parsons Papers

Talcott Parsons to Eric Voegelin, September 27, 1940
Talcott Parsons to Eric Voegelin, May 13, 1941
Talcott Parsons to Eric Voegelin, August 1, 1941
Talcott Parsons to Eric Voegelin, August 18, 1941
Talcott Parsons to Eric Voegelin, October 2, 1941
Talcott Parsons to Eric Voegelin, December 17, 1943
Eric Voegelin to Talcott Parsons, September 11, 1940
Eric Voegelin to Talcott Parsons, May 9, 1941
Eric Voegelin to Talcott Parsons, May 28, 1941
Eric Voegelin to Talcott Parsons, June 17, 1941
Eric Voegelin to Talcott Parsons, August 4, 1941
Eric Voegelin to Talcott Parsons, September 3, 1941
Eric Voegelin to Talcott Parsons, September 24, 1941
Eric Voegelin to Talcott Parsons, October 19, 1941
Eric Voegelin to Talcott Parsons, January 16, 1943
Eric Voegelin to Talcott Parsons, June 9, 1944

3

Elias and Parsons: Two Transformations of the Problem-Historical Method

Bruce C. Wearne

In this chapter I examine the relation between sociology and history as academic disciplines in the context of a comparison between the approaches of Norbert Elias and Talcott Parsons. Elias's *figurational sociology* is contrasted with Parsons's *structural functional* concern for the analysis of social systems. Both Elias and Parsons developed their contributions to sociology in response to philosophical questions dominant in the early decades of the twentieth century. To adequately describe the point at which their post–neo-Kantianism diverges, I also consider their differing approaches to the historiography of sociological theory.

Parsons's theoretical *convergence* presupposes the *Problemgeschichte Methode;* structural functionalism also requires a specific approach to the historiography of sociological theory. Moreover, structural functionalism is a form of sociological theory that reapplies the basic ideas of the problem-historical method to the historiography of theoretical reflection about the structure and function of modern society.

Elias rejected *Problemgeschichte* and turned away from any similar tendency in social thought and avoided any alignment of his own thinking with "grand historical systems." He believed that grand historical systems would narrow the historical focus upon the past to what is asserted to be relevant for the discipline by its present-day practitioners. Such a method must be opposed to genuine historical and sociological knowledge. The history of sociological theory is no definitive discipline but should be viewed as one side of the social historical analysis of time and context. For Elias, the sociologist of the long-term social processes which lead to the configurations of civilization, is as much involved as a social historian and as an historian of sociological ideas.

When Parsons and Elias are discussed together they can highlight aspects of early twentieth-century intellectual tradition. Their embeddedness within varying streams of the same western community of thought makes comparison a fruitful exercise.

THE COMMON HISTORICAL CONTEXT

During his Heidelberg days (1925–1927) Parsons made the acquaintance of Mari-
anne Weber and the Weber circle. Alfred Weber, Emil Lederer, and Karl Jaspers were
his examiners. Edgar Salin was his supervisor. Arnold Bergstraesser, a research assistant, was an associate to whom Parsons reputedly gave the famous "lost chapter on
Marx." The material in the German version of Parsons's doctoral dissertation, *Kapitalismus bei Sombart und Max Weber,* really doesn't discuss Marx much at all; rather
it begins with a discussion of Richard Passows's definition of the term *capitalism.*[1]
The opening introduction is, in its own way, reminiscent of Weber's discussion of
Beruf. The historical discussion of terms serves as prolegomenon to an analytical
project of wider sociocultural significance. By addressing the lingual use of words
Parsons identifies where we are historically. Then he moves on to a discussion of
Werner Sombart, whose wide-ranging and detailed historiography is, in some re-
spects, reminiscent of Elias. And then, of course, he considered Max Weber.

If one thing characterizes the work of Heidelberg neo-Kantianism in the social sciences, which Parsons also imbibed, it was the search for a disciplined and systematic
approach. It may not have been scientific in a *naturalistic* (positivist) sense, but the
neo-Kantian program in sociology could not avoid a concerted systematic attempt to
redefine science.

Elias's involvement in Heidelberg, on the other hand, is somewhat harder to define. He is not mentioned in the parts pertaining to Heidelberg in the 1920s in Fritz
K. Ringer's magisterial study *The Decline of the German Mandarins* (1965)—but then
neither is Parsons. Parsons's teachers, however, do figure prominently; and Richard
Hönigswald, Elias's mentor, with whom he later came to express profound disagreement, is also referred to. Can any significance be made of this? Ringer makes a point
in a footnote that alerts us to Hönigswald's intellectual orientation, and by implication we might begin to see how Elias was postured over against other neo-Kantians
and the intellectual stream. Ringer writes:

> When describing the revival in German philosophy during the later nineteenth century,
> the mandarins of the 1920's generally gave qualified praise to the neo-Kantian tradition.
> More specifically, they distinguished between two major strands within that movement:
> a primarily critical wing and a more constructively Idealistic tendency. (1965: 305)

At this point Ringer interrupts his narrative with a footnote: "The two fairly prominent neo-Kantians, Alois Riehl (1844–1924) and Richard Hönigswald (1875–1947),
are hard to assign to either of the major wings" (1965: 305).

So, historically, we can suggest that Elias's predisposition to marginality within the
discipline of sociology may not have been totally absent from the outset. By marginality we cannot only mean that his career was severely disrupted and that his writings
took on published form at a time in life when most other scholars would have retired.
It also has to do with the very singular nature of Elias's view of his own engagement
in the discipline. It was back in the 1920s that the foundations of Elias's approach
were poured, or prefigured, and by the time he came to formulate his mature

thought, debate about *Problemgeschichte* with its inner contradictions was no longer in vogue. This might also help explain why we do not get a very systematic theoretical statement of Elias's dissent from Heidelberg neo-Kantianism.

THE PROBLEM-HISTORICAL METHOD AS A POINT FOR COMPARISON

Parsons and Elias should be discussed together because they represent two early twentieth-century attempts to appropriate the insights of the intellectual tradition for sociological research. Their embeddedness within varying streams of the same western "community of argument" makes comparison a fruitful exercise.

What is the relation between theory-building on the one hand and the historiography of theoretical reflection on the other? Or, to put it another way, what place does the historiography of social theory have within the task of social theory? Or, conversely, within what frame of reference is the story of social theory to be plotted?

Parsons and Elias enjoy quite distinct reputations. Yet they both developed approaches to sociological theory and research that are implicit criticisms of the "*two major wings*" of neo-Kantianism as well as the middling attempt to construct that *via media* between rationalistic positivism and relativistic historicism that has become associated with Karl Mannheim.[2] Any attempt to read Parsons and Elias as "converging" should keep in mind that they took *alternative* pathways *away* from the neo-Kantian paradigm. The neo-Kantian tradition has its fair share of independent spirits and deviant theorists—for example, Karl Jaspers and Karl Mannheim[3]—but we should not too quickly overlook their dissent from the prevailing tradition. To contrast Elias's critical divergence from Hönigswald[4] with Parsons's attempt to launch a new post–neo-Kantian form of the historiography of the theory of social action is to identify their important contributions to the shape of twentieth-century historiography of sociology, even if from radically opposed standpoints.[5]

The so-called problem-historical method (*Problemgeschichte Methode*) may have an exalted name for us in English-speaking countries, but its basic ideas are quite simple. *Problemgeschichte* is a method in which the history of ideas is read in terms of the abiding questions that theorists in times past put to themselves *in* their theorizing.[6]

It now becomes clear why a comparison of Parsons with Elias has analytic and historical potential. It reminds us that sociology has also been formed in the midst of attempts to resolve the problems that arise from a recognition of the historicity of human life, thought, and experience. Such problems are not just sociology-specific but relate to the structure of the scientific encyclopaedia in its entirety. Parsons and Elias, each in his own way, highlighted the fact that sociological theory pushes beyond the traditional boundaries of a narrowly conceived specialist discipline. Sociology becomes enmeshed in a widespread conceptual attempt to solve the theoretical problems that arise when science is viewed in terms of its own evolving historicity.

Put simply, Parsons's modified use of the a priori for sociological theory is an historical derivative of *Problemgeschichte* in the following sense. The questions are "immanent methodological a prioris";[7] and when they take the form of the pattern variables, these are the abiding questions any society has to "answer" if it is to be, and remain, a "going concern." Later on as Parsons refined (rather than re-defined) his definitive exposition of his theory, the AGIL scheme also emerged as the analytical framework within which the theorist theorizes, and the empirical sociological researcher collects and arranges data for systematic empirical and theoretical articulation. AGIL is, of course, *Problemgeschichtlich,* setting the framework in which relevant socio*logical* questions will be framed for the cross-examination of the data. Parsons referred to the similarities between such general theory and the work of the competent common-law appellate judge.[8]

In Elias, the approach to sociological theory is much different. What is more, the philosophical problems we might encounter in cross-examining Elias are also quite different. It would seem that Elias, the teacher, preferred to have worked with questions which he viewed to be on the periphery of sociological reflection, philosophical questions about meaning, the meaning of theorizing, the nature of mythology, and so on.

Elias: Sociologist as Destroyer of Myth

Elias is not only "hard to pin down"; he is occasionally revealed as a scholar who doesn't suffer philosophical questions lightly. For him the task of sociology is indeed *demythologization*; the sociologist is nothing other that the destroyer of myths. He elaborates upon this in the interviews now recorded in the late-in-life autobiographical *Reflections on a Life* (1994). Having just touched upon the evil of nationalism as myth, which needs ongoing unmasking, the interviewer moves on to a logical implication that has a bearing upon Elias's meaning and his worldview.

Is every ideology a mythology?
Yes. In my book *What is Sociology?* there is a chapter: *The sociologist as the destroyer of myths.* That puts it in a nutshell.

Have you never thought that people need myths?
Yes, but then they ought to write poetry, as I have done. I needed myths, too—and paintings.

But many people need myths in daily life: myths about their party, their country, their football club. . . .
People do need myths, but not in order to arrange their social life. It is my conviction that people would live together better without myths. I think myths come back on one with a vengeance.

So you do not agree with the idea that myths are indispensable in social life?
Why should they be? Certainly, reality has some extremely unpleasant aspects—for instance, the fact that life is completely meaningless. But one has to face up to that because it is the condition of one's effort to give it a meaning. Only people can do that for each other. Seen in this way, the illusion of a given meaning is harmful.

You do not like illusions.
What do you mean: You do not like illusions? I *know* that they are harmful. Why do you immediately translate that into likes and dislikes? What kind of language is that? I am speaking of knowledge. If you said one cannot live without fantasies—that's something different.

Is there such a sharp difference between myth and fantasy?
The difference is whether you know that they are fantasies, or whether you regard them as a reality. In the latter case you cheat yourself, and that, of course, one should not do. One should not cheat oneself, and one should not cheat others with one's own myths. I very sincerely think that we live in a forest of mythologies and that at the moment one of the main tasks is to clear it away. A great spring cleaning—that is really what has to be done. (Elias, 1994: 39–40)

Parsons: Facts and Myth

But this was not the approach taken by Parsons. In his early career he moved decisively away from any "fiction view" of social theory and empirical research, as represented in Hans Vaihinger's *Philosophy of As If*.[9] But as the articulation of his theoretical scheme progressed, and he found himself required to give an account of the relation of ideas to that mode of action called theorizing, Parsons did indeed articulate his modified a priorism, with an outlook which was more or less philosophical. It was steeped in the neo-Kantian evaluation of "theory," namely, that in the history of thought theory is itself a dependent and independent variable. Or in other words, the social system is an articulated set of interdependent independent variables. I have pointed out elsewhere (Wearne, 1989) that Parsons's theoretical development needs to be assessed in terms of the various phases through which his pretheoretical commitment to the dogma of the autonomy of theoretical thought has passed.

When it comes to a discussion of "mythology" the opposition between Parsons's theoretical trajectory and that taken by Elias's could not be sharper. Parsons adopted a modified a priori approach and embraced the neo-Kantian *Problemstellung*. Any appropriation of insight from the positivist heritage was undertaken from this angle. Parsons did not see his adoption of philosophical or quasi-philosophical modes of analytic discourse as in any way contrary to his scientific intention in theory-building. He did not view the adoption of a philosophical mode of discourse as contradictory to his scientific aspiration.

In contrast with Elias, for whom the sociologist is the quintessential destroyer of myths, including philosophical ones, Parsons had imbibed Pareto's emphasis upon the nonlogical residues of logical action. This may be indicative of a built-in *arrière pensée* in his theoretical development, but Parsons had trained himself to see the philosophical interdependence implied in and by his independent theoretical constructions. With time and ongoing "re-visits" to such thinkers as Claude Bernard and Alfred North Whitehead,[10] Parsons continued to seek philosophical insight into that concept that was fundamental to his entire project: *system*. Maybe this was not possible without further philosophical reflection, but in the process it seems that a shift occurs, a shift of some significance for our systematic assessment of his theoretical work.

PARSONS'S KANT AND THE NEW ENGLAND WEBER

Parsons's first reading of Kant occurred when his studies, with his plans to study more sociology, Amherst-style,[11] were disrupted at Amherst during the 1922–23 academic year by the sacking of Alexander Meiklejohn and the departure of Clarence Ayres. Otto Manthey-Zorn was his teacher. Manthey-Zorn, a philosophical commentator in his own right,[12] encouraged Parsons in his intellectual odyssey in these terms:

> It is a great delight to me to see that your interests are turning more and more to the philosophical aspects of things. I suppose it is the philosophy of history that is really demanding your attention, and good old father history is certainly more in need of such understanding than any of his lesser children.[13]

The famous statement in *The Structure of Social Action* is indicative of Parsons's philosophical predilection to attempt to place things in a larger frame of reference. It indicates Parsons ongoing epistemological search for *analytic* and *conceptual* order in which the flux of social structure could be grasped and analytical progress made:

> The god of science is, indeed, Evolution. But for those who pay their obeisance in a true scientific spirit, the fact that science evolves beyond the points they have themselves attained is not to be interpreted as a betrayal of them. It is the fulfillment of their own highest hopes. (Parsons, 1937b: 41)

The "nonrigid" boundedness of philosophy's relationship to scientific social theory meant that *The Social System* assumed a philosophical assumption about philosophy: in the philosophical sphere where theory can be considered "pure," theoretical thought is, and ought to be, autonomous and self-defining. In social theoretical thought, on the other hand, there need be no *rigid* adherence to this dogma. After all what is being put forward about the "ultimate reality" of social structure is merely a *conceptual* frame of reference, a theoretical construct. When it came to a sociological analysis of social structure the social theorist confronts change; what is the response of social theory to be? According to Parsons, "[t]he specificities of significant change could not even be identified if there were no *relative* background of non-change to relate them to" (1961: 220).

For Parsons this 1961 statement is quite consistent with the view he had articulated when his academic orientation was being decisively formed back in the 1920s and 1930s. Yet as his career progressed and as his writings covered the entire field of sociology, Parsons's philosophical reflections would frequently conflict, or appear to conflict, with his more strictly theoretical formulations. His late-in-life reflections also give an impression of humankind being totally enclosed within "cultural systems" as the ultimate reality. On other occasions he seems to have implied that "cultural systems" provide some kind of transcendental "exit" from the systems of natural laws and rational action.

A 1973 comment made by Parsons in concluding the Colver Lectures at Brown University entitled *Religion and Science in the Modern World* is a case in point. Clearly building upon the thesis Whitehead had developed in *Science and the Modern World*, Parsons concluded his diagnosis of our times in these terms:

I think that I had better conclude with simply a mention of the very *deep dilemma* that is presented by the religio-ethical permeation of the contemporary world: of pre-occupation with this kind of problem, and with the fact that we have pretty well *deprived ourselves of a recourse to a transcendental solution.* In other words we can no longer say life in this world, temporal life, is corrupt but then there will be salvation in heaven after death. I think *we're stuck* with the attempt to make life in this world religiously tolerable. (1973: 12)

This statement is poignant for its "almost existentialist" style and its persistent echo of Parsons's New England Protestantism and his reconstruction of it with the help of his hero, Max Weber. It is clear that in some very important respects Parsons saw himself as a modern man immersed, if not "stuck," in the historical consequences of the demise of the Calvinistic *Weltanschauung* in the western world.

Almost seventy years earlier, his father, Edward Smith Parsons, immersed in the challenges that were presenting themselves to Christianity in education and science, had struck a chord, a piety that still clung to its hope in God:

Rather, welcome scientific investigation, higher criticism, rationalism, philosophical speculation—welcome every storm which beats upon the rock of faith. If it is rock it will stand; if it does not stand, our hearts tell us that God will provide for our feet some surer, safer resting place. (E. S. Parsons, 1904: 95)

In a post-Christian sense, the younger Parsons had used the sociological frame of reference to rework his openly spiritual view of humankind in the cosmos. He concluded, like Weber had done, that the Protestant *innerweltliche askese* was still powerfully alive at some subliminal level, even if its relevance was now only applicable to our being fated to be "stuck" in this world for a time. The Christian civic virtue of tolerance is carried to a higher plane; making this life tolerable becomes a personal ethic. Here Parsons's post-Calvinism indeed sounds like Elias's nihilistic profession: "Certainly, reality has some extremely unpleasant aspects—for instance, the fact that life is completely meaningless" (Elias, 1994: 39–40). But what are we to make of Parsons's and Ackerman's comments of 1966? "The 'facts' of science are myths . . . analytical thought itself is mythologization" (Parsons and Ackerman, 1966: 25, 27).

PROBLEM-HISTORICAL AND/OR OPERATIONALIST METHOD?

To answer this and to better appreciate why the sociological theories of Parsons and Elias are so deeply at cross-purposes we need to look again at Parsons's method and his acceptance of Lawrence J. Henderson's definition of fact. According to Henderson, a fact is the statement about the phenomena, not the phenomena itself. This idea is important to keep in mind; it works its way into everything Parsons wrote (Barber, 1986: 123–30), and shows Parsons responding in a systematic way to the challenge originally thrown down, not by Kant or neo-Kantianism, but by Whitehead in *Science in the Modern World*:

The progress of science has now reached a turning point. . . . . The old foundations of scientific thought are becoming unintelligible. Time, space, matter, material, ether,

electricity, mechanism, organism, configuration, structure, pattern, function, all require re-interpretation. What is the sense of talking about a mechanical explanation
when you do not know what you mean by mechanics? (Whitehead, 1925: 21)

The problem-historical method is a method of doing history (or doing science or
doing social theory) that indicates a turn to the scientific *subject*, focusing upon the
theorist rather than upon the theorized. It highlights the *questions* which the historians
(or scientists or social theorists) typically ask in the exercise of their scientific vocation.
It is an approach taken to the history of science similar to the one enunciated by Whitehead, Percy W. Bridgman, Suzanne K. Langer, and L. J. Henderson. Bridgman writes:

> In his [the scientist's] attack on his specific problem he suffers no inhibitions of prece-
> dent or authority but is completely free to adopt any course that his ingenuity is capable
> of suggesting to him. No one standing on the outside can predict what the individual sci-
> entist will do or what method he will follow. In short science is what scientists do and
> there are as many scientific methods as there are individual scientists. (1955: 83)

Bridgman is *problem-historical* in the sense that the story of science becomes the
story of the scientist's attempts to transform experimental problems into theoretical
questions. The story develops through the examination of the ways in which the
community of scientists, from generation to generation, creatively developed these
questions.

Langer in her defense of *Philosophy in a New Key* says that a philosophical movement is known by the questions it asks:

> Its answers establish an edifice of facts; but its questions make the frame in which the
> picture of facts is plotted. They make more than the frame; they give the angle of per-
> spective, the palette, the style in which the picture is drawn—everything except the sub-
> ject. In our questions lie our principles of analysis and our answers may express what-
> ever those principles are able to yield. (1951: 16)

The history of philosophy is therefore very much concerned with how one question
(or set of questions) gives way to a new approach of the issues. But again the question
arises: What kind of data need to be examined to establish the nature of this transition? Is it a matter of the breakdown in the accepted logic of philosophical argument
or is it a matter of studying the context in which the questions are formulated?

Henderson was an important adviser in the development of sociological thought
at Harvard in the 1930s. It was his definition of *fact*[14] that underlay Parsons's method
in *The Structure of Social Action,* and it was Henderson's mediation of the concept of
social system that Parsons acknowledged to be central to his 1951 magnum opus, *The
Social System.* Henderson also adopted this Paretian approach when he applied
Pareto's elite concept to the history of sociological thought, while warning Parsons of
the dangers he faced:

> In the first place, I shall define sociology as what sociologists do and say and think, and
> sociologists are, for my purposes, the people called sociologists and predecessors whom

they so classify. Let me remind you of what Pareto says of the use of the words "real" and "true" in making derivations. . . . the sociologists of the present time, are in general and on balance, doing what I regard as harm rather than good. . . . they are misleading their pupils and, so far as they have influence, the public, and they are not giving their publics that kind of discipline that seems to me, as an induction from experience, to be a part of effective scientific training.[15]

HISTORIOGRAPHY AND SOCIAL THEORY

Having reviewed the intellectual orientation of *Problemgeschichtlichkeit* it is not difficult to see why the historiography of sociological theory is so controversial in the sociohistorical disciplines. It is a question of how the philosophical genealogy of sociology (from Kant and Comte) is integrated with theorizing in the discipline. We can anticipate two possible ways in which the historiography will be related to the systematic theoretical task. On the one hand these two academic pursuits could be seen as *different areas* of academic engagement with some overlap. On the other hand, they could be viewed as the *same general area* of theoretical concern with some differing methodological emphases. In this discussion both Parsons and Elias are viewed as sociologists who developed their respective theoretical approaches by responding to, modifying, and correcting this particular conundrum.

Parsons construed the historiography of sociology in ways similar to the manner he approached the task of a general theory within sociology; not exactly the same as, but not separate from, the task of sociologically studying society. The historiography of sociological theory is a matter of the internal differentiation within the discipline itself. It emerges as an independent and dependent aspect within the system of sociological theory, always keeping in mind that Parsons saw that at *this stage in its development* what was in view was the general theory of systems, not a system of theory. This returns us to his view that theory is a dependent and independent variable in the historical disclosure of knowledge. What kind of theoretical statement is this? A limit in our critical confrontation with Parsons's theoretical/philosophical orientation is reached. It is simply taken for granted that within the sphere of philosophical reflection the dependent and independent activity of theory is autonomous and self-defining.

In our examination of the sociology of Elias we arrive at a similar philosophical dogma, but we do so via an altogether dissimilar route. We would have to admit that it is tempting to say that it is exactly the same starting point *except* for the fact that everything that follows is in such radical opposition. Parsons's "modified a priorism" does not have an exclusive corner on dogmatism. Elias's historicism nestles the dogma of the autonomy of theoretical thought in its own way.

Elias also views the development of the historiography of sociology in ways similar to the manner he construes the task of theorizing. Sociological theorizing, for Elias, is that mode of theorizing which brings theorizing to its culmination; he is *positivist*, but not in terms of any *static* construal of any classic Comteian distinction between social dynamics and social statics, which he says is characteristic of the ground-problem of

Durkheimian positivism.[16] Elias embraces historicity, and his sociology is thus a wholehearted historicism. If Parsons takes up Whitehead's cosmology and declares that "he has not gone far enough," Elias appropriates Mannheim and radicalizes his sociology of knowledge. He radicalizes the Mannheimian aphorism to the heart of his social dynamics: "The world of external objects and of psychic experiences," Mannheim wrote, "appears to be in a continuous flux. Verbs are more adequate symbols for this situation than nouns" (1936: 20). Knowledge about the historical character of scientific concepts is central to getting the sociological frame of reference right in Elias's view. Any logical juxtapositions within the theoretical frame of reference need to be made with an understanding that the theoretical frame of reference is itself a matter of an evolving historical understanding that is passed from one generation to the next. History is integral to, and not to be understood as artificially (and statically) standing over against, the theorist as a social actor. *Gegenstandlichkeit* is always to be understood as a process of actively standing over against whatever is in view. It is not eternally passive—and should not be thought of as such even in some fictitious sense—but part of an active historical engagement.

To put it in other words: Elias's theory is based on the conviction that the possibility of taking a detached scientific view presupposes an ongoing historical process in which incremental changes have been added over the long term, thus making scientific detachment possible. The possibility of taking a scientific view of human society is itself conditioned by social processes that the science of society must consider in painstaking, detailed, and deliberate fashion; otherwise it cannot be science in its own right.

The historiography of sociological theory is no independent and dependent variable within sociological theory, construed as a system, but simply disciplined sociological insight, one possible theme of the all-encompassing scientific outlook, which sociology represents. When we then seek to clarify the character of this approach we reach the realistic limit of Elias's nominalism, the taken-for-granted assumption in his non-apriori, the deductive application of his inductivism and his idealistic version of a positivism retreating into his own present. The Comtean "law of the three stages" is not only a guide for viewing the social-historical process but it is also an indicator for how one's own thinking has become more and more immersed in that overriding reality which Elias's theory represents:

> Sociological theories of knowledge have to break with the firmly entrenched tradition according to which every person in terms of his or her own knowledge is a beginning. No person ever is. Every person from the word go, enters a pre-existing knowledge stream. He or she may later improve or augment it. But it is always an already existing social fund of knowledge which is advanced in this manner, or perhaps made to decline. (Elias, 1987: xviii)

Elias's nominalism stands over against Parsons's analytical realism. Elias's anti–a prioristic positivism stands over against Parsons's analytical concern for "theoretical convergence" of the analytical schemes of the previous generation of social theorists. This is not a minor point where abstract detail meets abstract detail. This is where Parsons's theory conflicts with Elias at a deep, if not *the* deepest, level; and Elias's answer to the question "What is sociology?" contradicts Parsons's way of asking that question. Looked at historically Elias and Parsons may represent different though related ways of mixing and matching the idealist and positivist traditions. But Elias's attempt is to radically diverge from that mode of intellectual engagement by which Parsons accommodated *Problemgeschichte*.

HOW IS SOCIOLOGY POSSIBLE? ELIAS'S COMTE

Elias's rebellion against Kantianism, neo-Kantianism, and all things a priori leaves us breathless. His dogmatism is confirmed in his claim to leave all dogmatism behind. He saw himself "getting on with the job," standing actively in the historical midstream, viewing society in the long-term, amidst all the results of science, scholarship, and whatever contributes to sociological scholarship broadly conceived. The critical question is whether those who have "learned their sociology," or taken their historical/historicist cue from Elias, will sooner or later come under Elias's judgment of being "newcomers [who] follow the authoritative . . . imperatives" (1987: xix) not of Descartes, Husserl, and Sartre, but of Elias himself.

On the other hand, Elias's historicism has led him to ask some extremely pertinent questions, whether or not we would want to address those questions in the way that he intended them to be addressed. For instance, in *What is Sociology?* he claims to ask a fundamental question for the first time. This question, as Elias intended it, may even be anti-Kantian, and immanentistically anti–a priori, but it cannot now be considered and answered without some reflection on its historical relation to Kant's transcendental philosophy.

Kant had been preoccupied with the question How is philosophy possible? Elias constructed his approach presupposing a priori the necessary consideration of this question: "how and under what conditions [is] non-ideological, scientific knowledge of natural and social relationships . . . possible" (1978: 54).

Later Elias elaborates further and implies that it is only as people address this question that they will rid themselves of all the myths that scientists, and in particular social scientists, have constructed out of their fantasy. Only then can social science come into its own as a distinct and autonomous scientific activity, with a distinct and autonomous scientific focus. Sociologists, Elias maintains, need to clarify how their theories differ from social ideologies:

> The prevailing sociology of knowledge, like the philosophical theory of knowledge, neglects the question of what conditions allow prescientific myths and ideologies to develop into scientific theories, either about nature or about society.
> The sociological theory of science, which first began to emerge in the work of Comte and is now at last becoming more intelligible, puts these very problems in a position of central importance. It poses a key question. Under what social conditions did people

succeed in expanding their knowledge of human societies and in continually reconciling their knowledge with observed facts? It cannot yet be said with certainty that overall social development will necessarily lead to the progressive emancipation of the social sciences as it did for the natural sciences. It is too early to tell; we are still caught up in the process of emancipation. (Elias, 1978: 54)

For Elias, a sense of complete uncertainty is avoided if we allow the sociological study of science to give us a better scientific understanding of the social development of science. Mythology, also within the realm of science, has to be overcome. Any theory of science must first assimilate data from a scientific study of the sciences.

In sociology the development of an autonomous disciplinary understanding is marked by the move from studies which concentrate upon *action* to those which concentrate upon *function*. Theories can then be constructed about observed relationships as well as tested systematically. But as this scientific mode of thinking about society develops Elias perceives a tendency in scientists to cognitively resist the "purposeless, meaningless functional interconnections" which scientific analysis brings to light. Scientific enlightenment has often brought in its trains a sense of blind, purposeless meaninglessness.

> Many people find the idea repugnant. It is frightening to realize that people form functional interconnections within which much of what they do is blind, purposeless and involuntary. It is much more reassuring to believe that history—which is of course always the history of particular human societies—has a meaning, a destination, perhaps even a purpose. And indeed there is always a supply of people willing to tell us what that meaning is. (Elias, 1978: 58)

At this point Elias's *practical* scientific attitude may indicate an appropriation of positivism in a nihilistic direction. But it is as if he turns to his scientific work with the view that nihilism cannot be anything other than meaningless. The Elias sociological project still intends taking up the role, if not getting "stuck" in it, of the destroyer of myths. The critical point comes when, at the limit of Elias's historicism, he acknowledges that

> the origins of sociology cannot be understood apart from this radical transformation of society. Society oligarchically ruled by the hereditarily privileged were transformed into societies ruled by the recallable representatives of mass political parties. The shift in the internal balance of power is symptomatic of the overall transformation of society. The social sciences, especially sociology, can be said to have the same social parentage as the belief-systems of the great mass parties, the major social ideologies of our age. However disparate social science and social ideology may be, both are manifestations of the same transformations in the structure of society. (Elias, 1978: 65)

Several critical questions emerge: What is the status of this statement? Is it a statement that is edifying and reassuring in nature? Is not Elias trying to help those who follow his path into developmental sociology to get some sense of their historical bearings? Is this statement not a *relatively* constant background within which sociologists can assess the (changing) meaning of their own work?

Could it not also be a hypothesis, a theory of science, which has to be tested through what can actually be observed in the scientific study of sociological research? In which case, it is a deceptive statement, which indicates Elias's idea of what sociology should be, but it is put forward under a pretext of it being an empirical conclusion about how sociology has evolved. Is not this the beginning of Elias's own positivist myth, despite his protestation that "the work of Comte is now at last becoming more intelligible"? The elision here is the double-meaning—it seems that Elias is claiming that he has come to a better understanding of Comte, at *precisely the time* he divines a general improvement in the understanding of what Comte's positivism stood for. The mythic phase of Comte-reception has come to a close; the time for the truly scientific reception of Comte has now arrived. Moreover, the subjection of the history of Comte-reception to analysis in terms of the "law of the three stages" implies a priori acceptance of the positivist law to begin with.

HOW IS SOCIOLOGY POSSIBLE? PARSONS'S FACT OF CONVERGENCE

Parsons's solution of the problem of the relationship between the historiography implicit in "convergence" and the theory identified through his secondary study of a group of recent European writers is to state that *The Structure of Social Action* "is a study in social *theory,* not *theories*" (1937b: v). Twelve years later, in the preface to the second edition, Parsons stated that that book "was intended to be primarily a contribution to systematic social science and not to history, that is the history of social thought" (1937b: A-B). This does not address the question of how "convergence" as a secondary study can also function as a form of analytic historiography. Instead the resolution is the implication that *within* sociological theory historical consciousness has a function in assisting the sociologist to identify analytically the emergent structure of that frame of reference to which past and present societies can be subjected to structural-functional sociological analysis. And so sociology is accepted a priori as not historical analysis per se, even if Parsons's constructed convergence as "a relative background of non-change"[17] to ensure that logical and analytical order is maintained *within* the theoretical frame of reference. But convergence is constructed on the basis of a distinction between the historical sciences, oriented to the concrete and the analytic sciences, whose major focus is "systems of general theory verifiable in terms of and applicable to a wide range of concrete phenomena" (Parsons, 1937b: 598). But without historical convergences an anarchy of facts—an orderless diffusion—will prevail without any theoretical ordering principle for the analytic social sciences:

> For the historical sciences theoretical concepts are means to understanding the concrete historical individual. For the analytical sciences, on the other hand, the reverse is true; concrete historical individuals are means, "cases" in terms of which the validity of the theoretical system may be tested by "verification." (Parsons, 1937b: 598, n. 2)[18]

74   *Wearne*

But Parsons avoids addressing the question of the *principles* for the historiography of sociological theory as such. It is as if he were too busy applying the results of his study of theory's *historical individuals* (i.e., the ideal types of Weber, Durkheim, and others) to his analytical system, and then too busy seeing how this analytical system could be applied to the historical study of concrete historical phenomena. History in the sense of the recent history of sociological thought is conscripted (unintentionally?) into the parameters of social theory. Parsons's *intention* to contribute to systematic social science, and not to the history of social thought, cannot substitute for a principled statement of how to write the historiography of sociological theory.

The continuity between *The Structure of Social Action* (1937) and *The Social System* (1951) is confirmed not only by an argument that shows that the latter elaborated theory is implicit in the earlier (historical and analytic) statement of convergence. It also has to be noted that the convergence of Alfred Marshall, Weber, Durkheim, and Pareto (and later, Freud) is itself a theoretical view that is structural-functional in character. As such it distinguishes Parsons's contribution to sociology from all those who would follow in his lead analytically, but leave out the "convergence" focus. A more exact approach suggests that "'convergence' is the structural-functional approach to the historiography of sociology" (Wearne, 1989: 76–88).

It is easy to see why Elias has affinity with Parsons. Both deal with the big picture but both diverge from Sombart, Spengler, Sorokin, and Toynbee.[19] Parsons theorized in terms of the options raised by the *Problemgeschichte Methode*, namely searching for the *one* set of questions to which all social theory will have to provide answers. He later claimed to find these questions in the pattern variables. These four (or five or six) questions—those which any society must answer if its social structure is to be maintained—are also the basic questions the historian of sociological theory will have to ask in the analysis of theory's pilgrimage toward convergence! Convergence and the pattern variables in Parsons are evidence of the residual problem-historical methodology which Elias (and Rorty) fulminated against. For Parsons they indicate how the *study* of the history of theory converges with the *task* of system-building itself. The historiography of sociology is nothing other than a structural-functional methodology. Structural functionalism is the *Problemgeschichte* approach to sociology. For Parsons, *The Structure of Social Action* and *The Social System* clarify the same theoretical scheme. The results amount to essentially the same "thing."

CONCLUSION: PARSONS'S NEO-KANTIAN MYTH AND ELIAS'S POSITIVIST A PRIORI

If Parsons's neo-Kantianism merges with the logical positivist concern for defining *fact* and *structure*, Elias is positivist in terms of a return to a view of history and historiography that admits its indebtedness to Comte. Parsons's convergence sees idealism and positivism coming together in a new constellation (Parsons, 1937b: 774). In that sense the ongoing contribution of the theories of Parsons and Elias is to be found in the renewal of academic interest in a group of analytic *and* historical questions that lie close to the surface of the twentieth-century sociological tradition. A theorizing led by a pragmatic pedagogy might wish to announce the convergence of Parsons and Elias, but continued reflection comparing their divergent contributions is called for. The singular virtue of Elias for students of sociology derives from his emphasis upon the historicity of the central concepts of the scientific outlook. Not only do *reflexivity* and other metatheoretical (or methodological) concepts have a history of their own, but so do the everyday concepts that inevitably have a part to play in sociological reflection. Elias therefore opens the possibility for an analysis of social reality via the historical investigation of word usage and meaning. This is in stark contrast to Parsons, who, following Weber in *Die Protestantische Ethik*, began philologically (as in his doctoral dissertation examination of *Kapitalismus*) but then turned away seemingly never to return. Elias, at the end of the day, leaves us with a massive task begun with a carefully articulated sense of the linguistic framework from out of which our historicity is nourished.

The approaches of both Elias and Parsons stand starkly opposed to each other. They share a common historical background with roots in Heidelberg and the early years of the sociology of knowledge. They both give evidence of understanding the theoretical problems that have become associated with *Methodenstreit* and Max Weber. They both are greatly concerned about the status of sociology as a science, and the way to understand sociology's own historicity. Both accept that the idea of function is a central concept for the ongoing development of sociological theorizing in the social sciences. Both allow for compromise, accommodating theoretically insights gleaned from the polar opposite standpoint. Parsons's realism was (occasionally) modified by his acquiescence in a nominalistic view of facts, as a peculiar form of mythology; Elias's nominalism reaches its limit with a realistic positivist rendering of the stages through which Comte's philosophy had to pass until it could be finally understood (in a scientific way). Both theorists demand a peculiar personal loyalty by their readers to their stated intentions. Elias and Parsons are almost as far apart as any two twentieth-century sociologists could be.

NOTES

1. In the typescript of the dissertation the reference is simply to Richard Passow's "Kapitalismus" (und). The full title of the typescript is "Der Kapitalismus bei Sombart under Max Weber"—Inaugural Dissertation zur Erlangung der Doktorwuerd. It was presented to the Philosophical Faculty of Ruperto-Carola University of Heidelberg. There are six chapters and it is 141 pages in length. But the doctoral degree (D.Phil.) was granted on the basis of the revised English version subsequently published in two parts as "Capitalism in Recent German Literature: Sombart and Weber" in the *Journal of Political Economy*, which differs significantly in content and style (Parsons, 1927: 1928; 1929). It is still a puzzle that the German-language form of the dissertation should have remained unpublished and untranslated after all these years.

2. See Parsons's 1936 essay, "Review of *Max Weber's Wissenschaftslehre* by Alexander von Schelting" in Camic (1991: 123–31, particularly at p. 130). See also Parsons (1937a: 279–83 particularly at p. 280).

3. See Wilterdink (1977).

4. See Wolandt (1977).

5. In this paper I dissent mildly from the position presented by Mennell (1989). In my view Mennell mutes the radical difference between the two theorists.

6. It is also the view to which Rorty takes such exception in his attempt to undermine the mythologies of foundationalism. Rorty (1980) develops a systematic approach self-consciously opposing the problem-historical method. Reading Rorty one could conclude that the approach to Hönigswald and Hartmann is an ideal-type of the entire philosophical tradition from which Rorty launches his antifoundational dissent. Rorty theorizes against "the assumption that human beings have a natural center that philosophical inquiry can locate and illuminate." He emphasizes "the view that human beings are centerless networks of beliefs and desires and that their vocabularies and opinions are determined by historical circumstance." He would allow for the "possibility that there may not be enough overlap between two such networks to make possible agreement about political topics or even profitable discussion of such topics" (Rorty, 1991: 191). Perhaps a careful comparison between Rorty and Elias is called for, and may help us not only to better grasp the sociology and philosophy of each, but to elucidate how Elias anticipated anti-foundationalist philosophy.

7. See Brecht (1970: 508).

8. See Parsons (1977b: 68).

9. See his reference to this in Parsons (1977b: 27).

10. Whitehead, Parsons tells us, did not "go far enough." See Parsons (1977c: 122–34).

11. Parsons ([1923] 1996: 24–37).

12. Otto Manthey-Zorn wrote the "Introduction" to the 1938 Appleton Century-Crofts edition of Kant's *The Fundamental Principles of the Metaphysics of Morals*. He also wrote *Dionysus: The Tragedy of Nietzsche* (Amherst College Press, 1956; reprinted by Greenwood Press, 1975). As further work is done on Parsons's involvement in the culture of institutionalism, and institutionalism's involvement in early waves of German neo-Kantianism and *Methodenstreit* in the United States, attention should be given to the Kantianism represented not only by Manthey-Zorn but also by Meiklejohn. Meiklejohn wrote a doctoral dissertation, *Kant's Theory of Substance*, at Cornell in 1897.

13. Manthey-Zorn letter to Parsons dated January 27, 1925.

14. See here Parsons (1937b: 28; 41–42). The reference is to Henderson's "An Approximate Definition of Fact," which has been reprinted in Barber (1970).

15. Letter to Talcott Parsons dated July 17, 1939.

16. Elias (1978: 117–18).

17. The way he expresses this is as follows: "The specifics of significant change could not be identified if there were no relative background of nonchange to relate them to" (Parsons, 1961: 220).

18. Parsons goes on in this footnote to identify the "two different possible meanings of the term 'theory' which are often confused." But it is not only "theory" which is confused or confused in Parsons's convergence thesis. Later on, in "Tentative Methodological Implications" concerning the place of sociology, he notes: "History may be regarded primarily as the general historical science concerned with human action" (1937b: 771). Again, in a footnote he states: "As distinguished from what, reviving an old term, may be called natural history, on the one hand, history of ideas and other cultural systems, on the other" (Parsons, 1937b: 771, n. 2).

19. In this context a quotation from Toynbee might be appropriate: "the concept of continuity is only significant as a symbolic mental background on which we can plot out perceptions of discontinuity in all their actual variety and complexity" (1935: 43). See also Sorokin

(1940; 1950; 1962); Sorokin and Merton (1937); Merton (1936; 1967); and Geyl et. al (1949). This issue upon which so much depends in the history and historiography of twentieth-century American sociology has of late emerged again in the debate in the leading American journals. It centers upon the right interpretation of Parsons's theoretical development (Camic, 1992; 1996 and Alexander and Siortino, 1996).

REFERENCES

Alexander, J. C., and G. Sciortino. 1996. "On Choosing One's Intellectual Predecessors: The Reductionism of Camic's Treatment of Parsons and the Institutionalists." *Sociological Theory* 14 (2): 154–71.

Barber, B. 1986. "Theory and Fact in the Work of Talcott Parsons." Pp. 123–30 in *The Nationalization of the Social Sciences*, edited by S. Z. Klausner and V. M. Lidz. Philadelphia: University of Pennsylvania Press.

———, ed. 1970. *L. J. Henderson on the Social System*. Chicago: Chicago University Press.

Brecht, A. 1970. *Political Theory: The Foundations of Twentieth-Century Political Thought*. Princeton, N.J.: Princeton University Press.

Bridgman, P. W. 1955. *Reflections of a Physicist*. New York: Macmillan.

Camic, C. 1992. "Reputation and Predecessor Selection: Parsons and the Institutionalists." *American Sociological Review* 57: 421–45.

———. 1996. "Alexander's Anti-Sociology." *Sociological Theory* 14 (2): 172–86.

———, ed. 1991. *Talcott Parsons: The Early Essays*. Chicago: University of Chicago Press.

Elias, N. 1978. *What Is Sociology?* London: Hutchinson.

———. 1987. *Involvement and Detachment*. Oxford, England: Basil Blackwell.

———. 1994. *Reflections on a Life*. Cambridge, Eng.: Polity Press.

Geyl, P., A. J. Toynbee, and P. A. Sorokin 1949. *The Pattern of the Past: Can We Determine It?* Boston: Beacon Press.

Gleichmann, R., ed. 1977. *Human Figurations: Essays for Norbert Elias*. Amsterdam: Amsterdams Sociologische Tijdschrift.

Henderson, L. J. 1939. Letter to Talcott Parsons dated July 17, 1939 in "Correspondence 1939." Miscellaneous correspondence and papers in the Harvard University Archives Collection of the Parsons Papers.

Langer, S. K. 1951. *Philosophy in a New Key*. 2nd ed. New York: Mentor.

Mannheim, K. 1936. *Ideology and Utopia*. London: Routledge and Kegan Paul.

Manthey-Zorn, O. 1956. *Dionysus: the Tragedy of Nietzsche*. Amherst: Amherst College Press.

Mennell, S. 1989. "Parsons et Elias." *Sociologie et societe* 21 (1): 69–86.

Merton, R. K. 1936. "Civilization and Culture." *Sociology and Social Research* 21 (2): 103–13.

———. 1967. "On the History and Systematics of Sociological Theory. Pp.1–37 in *On Theoretical Sociology: Five Essays Old and New*. New York: Free Press.

Parsons, E. S. 1904. *The Church and Education*. Colorado College Series, Colorado Springs.

Parsons, T. [1923] 1996. "A Behavioristic Conception of the Nature of Morals." *American Sociologist* 27 (4): 24–37.

———. 1927. "Der Kapitalismus bei Sombart under Max Weber"—Inaugural-Dissertation zur Erlangung der Doktorwuerd. Presented to the Philosophical Faculty of Ruperto-Carola University of Heidelberg. Located in the Parsons Papers, Harvard University Archives.

———. 1928. "'Capitalism' in Recent German Literature: Sombart and Weber, I." *Journal of Political Economy* 36: 641–44.

78   *Wearne*

——. 1929. " 'Capitalism' in Recent German Literature: Sombart and Weber, II." *Journal of Political Economy* 37: 31–51.

——. 1936. "Review of *Max Weber's Wissenschaftslehre* by Alexander von Schelting." Pp. 123–31 in *Talcott Parsons: The Early Essays*, edited by C. Camic. Chicago: University of Chicago Press.

——. 1937a. "Review of *Economics and Sociology* by Adolph Lowe." Pp. 279–83 in *Talcott Parsons: the Early Essays*, edited by C. Camic. Chicago: University of Chicago Press.

——. 1937b. *The Structure of Social Action.* New York: Free Press.

——. 1951. *The Social System.* New York: Free Press.

——. 1961. "Some Considerations on the Theory of Social Change." *Rural Sociology* 26 (3): 219–39.

——. 1973. *Religion and Science in the Modern World.* Lecture 3. Colver Lectures, Brown University. Harvard University Archives. Parsons Papers.

——. 1977a. *Social Systems and the Evolution of Action Theory.* New York: Free Press.

——. 1977b. "On Building Social Systems Theory: A Personal History." Pp. 22–76 in *Social Systems and the Evolution of Action Theory*, edited by T. Parsons. New York: Free Press.

——. 1977c. "Review of Harold J. Bershady *Ideology and Social Knowledge*." Pp. 122–34 in *Social Systems and the Evolution of Action Theory*, edited by T. Parsons. New York: Free Press.

Parsons, T., and C. Ackerman. 1966. "The Concept of 'Social System' as a Theoretical Device." Pp. 24–40 in *Concepts, Theory and Explanation in the Behavioral Sciences*, edited by G. J. DiRenzo. New York: Random House.

Ringer, F. K. 1965. *The Decline of the Mandarins.* Cambridge, Mass.: Harvard University Press.

Rorty, R. 1980. *Philosophy and the Mirror of Nature.* Oxford: Basil Blackwell.

——. 1991. *Objectivity, Relativism and Truth: Philosophical Papers*, Vol. 1. Cambridge: Cambridge University Press.

Sorokin, P. A. 1940. "Toynbee's Philosophy of History." Pp. 95–126 in *The Pattern of the Past: Can We Determine It?*, edited by P. Geyl, et al. Boston: Beacon Press.

——. 1950. "Notes on the Interdependence of Philosophy and Sociology." *Revue Internationale de Philosophie* (July): 268–77.

——. 1962. "Theses on the Role of Historical Method in the Social Sciences." Pp. 235–54 in *Transactions of the Fifth World Congress of Sociology.* Washington, D.C.

Sorokin, P. A., and R. K. Merton. 1937. "Social Time: A Methodological and Functional Analysis." *American Journal of Sociology* 42 (5): 615–29.

Toynbee, A. J. 1935. *A Study of History*, Vol 1. London: Oxford University.

Wearne, B. C. 1989. *The Theory and Scholarship of Talcott Parsons to 1951: A Critical Commentary.* Cambridge: Cambridge University Press.

Whitehead, A. N. 1925. *Science and the Modern World.* New York: Macmillan.

Wilterdink, N. 1977. "Norbert Elias's Sociology of Knowledge and Its Significance for the Study of the Sciences." Pp. 127–35 in *Human Figurations: Essays for Norbert Elias*, edited by R. Gleichmann. Amsterdam: Amsterdams Sociologische Tijdschrift.

Wolandt, G. 1977. "Norbert Elias und Richard Hönigswald." Pp. 127–32 in *Human Figurations: Essays for Norbert Elias*, edited by R. Gleichmann. Amsterdam: Amsterdams Sociologische Tijdschrift.

4

Parsons's Second Project: The Social System— Sources, Development, and Limitations

Bernard Barber

The purpose of this chapter is to stir up interest, to "clarify and elaborate" (to use terms that Parsons himself employed in discussing his own work toward the end of his life) what I am calling "Parsons's Second Project," that is, his work on the concept and substance of the social system. It was a project that preoccupied him for a good part of his life after the publication of his early masterwork, *The Structure of Social Action* (1937).[1]

In this chapter I write about three matters: the sources, the development, and the limitations of Parsons's work on his Second Project. Elsewhere, as my citations in note 2 indicate, I have dealt with these matters at greater length, and I hope I can enlarge my treatment in the future. Like the writings of two of our other great modern sociologists, Weber and Durkheim, Parsons's massive *oeuvre* has a protean quality, with many obscurities, ambiguities, inconsistencies, and side-trails, along with its clear main themes, its central messages. The inevitable result has been frequent differences of interpretation of his work and also different scholarly decisions about what to emphasize and what to follow up, not only by those who came to his work after his death but by those who knew him and studied with him during his lifetime. I fall into the latter category; I have studied with Parsons, beginning in the 1930s, first as an undergraduate and later as a graduate student, and then closely followed his writing until his death.

Despite this long experience, I wish to enter a qualification: I make no claim in this article to any final accuracy of my account. Also, I hasten to say that at a certain later point, as I will tell soon, I diverged from Parsons's own later primary emphasis and attempted to elaborate his work on the basis of my interpretation of his earlier work. My conception of the social system became quite different from Parsons's own in his later work.

SOME SOURCES OF PARSONS'S SECOND PROJECT

In 1969, when Parsons was asked by the American Academy of Arts and Sciences to describe his intellectual career for an issue of its journal, *Daedalus,* he titled his essay "On Building Social Systems Theory: A Personal History." In this essay, especially, but also elsewhere and frequently, Parsons emphasized the importance of the concepts of system and social system. Parsons tells us a good deal about those who made him appreciate the importance of the *general* concept of system, but nowhere does he tell us explicitly how he came to the *more specific* idea of the social system.

He learned about the importance of the general concept of system, he tells us, from biologists like Walter B. Cannon and Lawrence J. Henderson, from philosopher Alfred North Whitehead, from economists like Vilfredo Pareto and Joseph Schumpeter, but not from any sociologist. That is not surprising, since no sociologists of the time, either American or European, thought explicitly in terms of social systems. From his European sources, Weber and Durkheim, he learned instead about the voluntaristic theory of action. It is Talcott Parsons who brought the concept of social system directly into sociology.

I shall come in a moment to his first and very important statement about this concept in his book *The Social System* (1951), but first I want to examine some unpublished earlier materials where he might well have used the term but did not. These materials help us understand the beginnings of the development of Parsons's commitment to the concept of social system.

The first set of materials is the voluminous amount of notes I took on the lectures in Parsons's two-semester undergraduate/graduate, Sociology 6, "Comparative Social Institutions," in the academic year 1937–38. Parsons, naturally, was the organizer and theorist in this course, but he was assisted by a set of specialist Harvard colleagues whom he invited to lecture on various major social institutions in such very different societies around the world as China, India, the *ancien régime* in France, Navaho Indians in the United States, Antonine Rome, the Ottoman Empire, Victorian England, ancient Greece, and mediaeval Europe. Parsons's purpose in inviting these lectures was to provide expert demonstrations of both the constants and the great historical and societal variability in such social institutions as kinship, stratification, religion, law, education, and politics. For it was "social institutions," he said explicitly in his opening theoretical statement, that were the central concept necessary for the analysis of societal structure and variation. Sociology, he said, had to be theoretical, had to have a way of selecting the constants and variants in social behavior, and social institutions was what he had chosen. Thus, in 1937–39, there was no mention, as there might well have been, of the social system; instead, social institutions was what he called the "central concept." To anticipate what will be said further on, it was this course that set me on the path I eventually took to the goal of constructing an empirically based, comparative, relatively complete theoretical model of the social system. For me at least, the concept of social system was implicit already.

We might pause here to ask why the concept of "social institutions" rather than "social system" was of premier importance for Parsons. After all, he not only knew about the importance attached to the concept of system by Pareto and Henderson, but he counted himself a follower of both of them. Nevertheless, he preferred "institutions" to "system."

We must remember that Parsons's great purpose at this time in *The Structure of Social Action* (1937) was to create a new theory of action, one in which the element of *normativity* was of central importance. This was counter to the predominant utilitarian social theory of the time, which had no place for normativity. For Parsons, institutions were not normally neutral social and cultural structures; rather, they were *normative* structures. They were moral reference points for the actors in a society, often binding reference points.

The second set of materials I possess in this mini-archive consists of the notes I took the following year, in the spring 1939 term, in Parsons's course in social theory. This course was given after the publication of *Structure*, in which, we should definitely note, there is no mention of the concept of social system. After the publication of *Structure*, Parsons realized that its theoretical basis, the "unit act" with its normative component, had limited usefulness in analyzing actual concrete social reality. In the 1939 theory course, he offered for this analytic purpose the new theoretical pair, "Actor-Situation," as emergent from action theory and more convenient for analyzing the reality of concrete social phenomena. This, however, was still an approach from the point of view of the individual, and there was still no direct or intensive discussion of the concept of social system.

As he proceeded in his lectures to discuss various aspects of the individual actor's orientation to his/her situation, he mentioned, *but only in passing,* that part of the actor's situation is the existence of other actors. For example, there are at least four cases where he said the social situation is essential: (1) the problem of order; (2) the practice of mutual evaluations resulting in systems of stratification; (3) the problem of power and social control; and (4) the problem of social change. Surely, it would be only another easy theoretical step to conceptualize the social system explicitly as an essential context for the actor. That step would integrate the concepts of the individual and the system.

DEVELOPMENT OF THE SECOND PROJECT

Given his strong conviction regarding the theoretical importance of the system concept, his turn in the 1939 theory course from the unit-act concept to the actor-situation concept and, finally, his realization, if only in passing, that the actor's situation involved a social system, it is not surprising that Parsons eventually developed the social system approach fully and made it central to his work for the rest of his life. Indeed, in his *Daedalus* memoir, he spoke, incorrectly, as if the concept of social system had antedated *Structure*.

Because of his devoted commitment during the period from 1940–45 to teaching about, and various advisory activities connected with, World War II (so well reported recently from her archival research by Professor Gerhardt) and because of his duties and activities as the central founder and first chair of the new multi-disciplinary Social Relations Department at Harvard beginning in 1946, Parsons delayed taking up intensive work on the concept of the social system until toward the end of the 1940s. He had not, of course, lost interest in the social system; indeed, in 1947 he held a seminar on "The Theory of Social Systems." Finally, in 1951, he presented his first set of mature ideas on the subject in the book *The Social System*.

Parsons states his goal for the book in the very first sentence of the preface: "The present volume is an attempt to bring together, in systematic and generalized form, the main outlines of a conceptual scheme for the analysis of the structure and processes of social systems." *The Social System* (hereinafter *S.S.*) is a wonderful book, still immensely illuminating but, as Parsons himself also says in the preface, somewhat "inconsistent" because it was worked upon simultaneously with his further work on action theory in close collaboration with Professor Edward Shils of the University of Chicago. Shils came on leave to Cambridge to work intensively with Parsons on the volume *Toward a General Theory of Action*. *The Social System* is rich but confusing, as there is no orderly presentation of a comprehensive, empirically grounded model for the social system. Instead, there are analyses of some functionally essential social, structural, and cultural elements of a generalized model of society as a social system, such as kinship, stratification, power, and socialization (education) mixed with cultural elements such as religion, science, ideology, and values. Interspersed among these analyses are discussions of deviancy and social control in social systems and also various processes of change in social systems. There is even a section on "Modern Medical Practice" as a "case" to illustrate "social structure and dynamic processes." It is a book still well worth studying for its theoretical and empirical substance.

After *S.S.*, Parsons's writings on the social system develop in quite a new way. Indeed, in the preface to *S.S.*, Parsons speaks of the rapid theoretical development that had been occurring during the very writing of that book as a result of his work with Shils on the monograph *Toward a General Theory of Action*. In his *Daedalus* memoir Parsons also notes the rapidity with which his ideas changed at the time, and mentions the fact that he experienced what he liked to call a theoretical "breakthrough." He says: "In my book, *The Social System* (1951), I made an attempt of that sort [i.e., to write a comprehensive statement on the social system] only to find that my own thinking . . . had evolved beyond the stage reached in that book, almost before it was published" (p. ix). This was probably a part of the breakthrough to his four-function, AGIL theory for the analysis of social systems and social exchange processes, the theory he elaborated for the rest of his life.

Indeed, in *S.S.*, there are already manifestations of his later style and substance. For the first time there appear frequent abstract lists, diagrams, and sets of theoretical boxes of the kind that became so prominent in much of his later work. These are the kinds of abstract formulations that led to the charge by such critics as C. Wright Mills (1959) that Parsons's work consisted of "Grand Theory," the mere "associating and dissociating of concepts."

LIMITATIONS OF PARSONS'S LATER WORK ON THE SECOND PROJECT

There are at least two limitations in Parsons's later work on the social system. The first is his confusing use of the term "social system." Perhaps first in *S.S.* and then thereafter, Parsons uses the concept of social system in different and therefore confusing ways. Sometimes he used it to refer to a total social system, a society, called in the later phase of his work a "societal community." More often, he used it to refer to one of the three subsystems of any society or total social system, that is, social systems as against culture and personality. This usage became more common as his theoretical interests shifted somewhat away from the study of social structure to the study of the two other subsystems, culture and personality. His emphasis also shifted to what he called "the general system of action."

We can clarify this confusion of conceptual terms in the following way. *General system of action* should be used to refer to the special basic stuff, human action, distinguishing it from those other two basic stuffs, life and matter, each of which is the focus of a general system of theory. *Social system* or *society* should be used to refer to total social systems, or societies, composed of three basic analytic subsystems: social structure, culture, and personality, each of which in turn has its own subsystems.[2] This terminology eliminates confusion and makes explicit the importance in sociology of social structure. Parsons himself, of course, had made notable contributions to the analysis of social structure in his various essays on kinship, social stratification, occupations, organization, the polity, and education. By failing to emphasize the term, social structure, Parsons may have confirmed the mistaken idea of many of his colleagues that his theory of the social systems was basically "cultural." The extreme version of this mistake was the allegation that Parsons was a value-absolutist.

The second limitation of Parsons's later work on the social system is his move to the *AGIL* scheme. I have long felt that his four-function paradigm, his AGIL scheme, for the analysis of concrete social systems was too abstract for many purposes of empirical work. Parsons's own use of this conceptual scheme was not particularly helpful for empirical analysis; I frequently lost the sense that I always had in his earlier courses and essays that Parsons had new insights into basic problems of social reality. And few of his students, or their students, have found this schema productive in empirical work. Even Neil Smelser and Jeffrey Alexander, two of his most productive students, have not used this scheme in their empirical work, although they are otherwise much indebted to Parsons.

This is not the place to present more than a mention of a different path that Parsons took to the elaboration of the social system concept. As I mentioned earlier, inspired by the "Comparative Institutions" course, I have formulated a model of society as a social system, keeping the idea of the three basic subsystems and working out a comprehensive set of subsystems for social structural and cultural systems. I have used it in my work in the sociology of science, stratification, the professions, trust, and elsewhere. It is intended as generalized, comprehensive, empirically useful, endlessly provisional, and improvable. This model, its rationale, and substance are spelled out in my recent book, *Constructing the Social System* (1993), with illustrations of its empirical usefulness in some twenty-five of my articles written over the last fifty years. It takes social system analysis in a direction that I think Parsons would have approved, though less so than his favored AGIL model. We need the concept of social system as one of the basic theoretical elements in a scientific sociology.

NOTES

An earlier version of this chapter was presented at an international conference at Heidelberg University, Germany, June 26–27, 1997. The theme of the conference, organized by myself and Professor Uta Gerhardt of Heidelberg University, was "A Legacy of '*Verantwortungsetbik*': Talcott Parsons's *The Strucutre of Social Action* after Sixty Years." For help in the revision of this chapter, I thank Larry Nichols, editor of this journal [*The American Sociologist*—ed.], for useful comments and questions.

1. My concern for the clarification and use of Parsons's theory has been longstanding and continuous. In addition to the present chapter, see my other writings on this topic: "Biographical Sketch," in Talcott Parsons *Essays in Sociological Theory: Pure and Applied* (Glencoe, Ill.: Free Press, 1949); "Beyond Parsons' Theory of the Professions," in *Neofunctionalism*, edited by Jeffrey Alexander (Beverly Hills, Calif.: Sage, 1985); "Fact and Theory in the Work of Talcott Parsons," in *The Nationalization of the Social Sciences*, edited by Samuel Z. Klausner and Victor M. Lidz (Philadelphia: University of Pennsylvania Press, 1986); "Talcott Parsons and the Sociology of Science: An Essay in Appreciation and Remembrance," *Theory, Culture and Society* 6 (1989): 623–35; "Talcott Parsons on the Social System: An Essay in Clarification and Elaboration," *Sociological Theory* 12 (1994): 101–5.

2. For a more complete clarification, see my *Constructing the Social System* (New Brunswick, N.J.: Transaction Books, 1993).

REFERENCES

Mills, C. W. 1959. *The Sociological Imagination.* New York: Oxford University Press.
Parsons, T. 1937. *The Structure of Social Action.* New York: McGraw-Hill.
———. 1951. *The Social System.* New York: Free Press.

5

Social Systems and Complexity Theory

Bryan S. Turner

SOCIAL SYSTEMS AND SOCIAL SCIENCES

The history of efforts to develop a theory of social systems is both closely connected with the processes by which the social sciences have borrowed from the natural sciences and with attempts to control and regulate society. Early social systems theory was connected with the growth of social Darwinism and with the notion that the law-like progress of societies could be mapped out by notions of evolutionary growth through differentiation and specialization. Herbert Spencer's conceptualization of the mechanisms of social change in *Principles of Sociology* (1876) now look decidedly dated, mainly because we know that the biology on which his ideas were based has been superseded. Perhaps the most important developments in systems theory in the twentieth century have been sparked off by theories of information and communication. Norbert Wiener's *Cybernetics, or Control and Communication in the Animal and the Machine* (1948) clearly grasped the connection between regulating and communicating, a connection that persists in contemporary sociologies of communication.

The argument of this chapter is that Parsons's concept of "system" and contemporary sociology generally are operating, at least implicitly, with outdated models of science, and therefore with concepts of space and time that are in some respects Newtonian. In a similar fashion, I have argued elsewhere (Turner, 1996) that sociology has been working on implicit models of human embodiment that are Cartesian, but that problem need not disturb us in this discussion of systems. The sociology of space has obviously grasped the importance, via the new social geography, of reconceptualizing our understanding, but these notions have yet to reorganize social theory as a whole (Urry, 1996). It has been argued (Soja, 1989) that the technological changes that transformed the spatial foundations of society—the telegraph, telephone, X-ray, and radio—in the first half of the twentieth century had little impact on social theory. My argument here is that whereas in the natural sciences the notion of system has been transformed, much of sociology still operates with relatively mechanical and linear

notions of causality. Complexity theory promises to provide a framework for rethinking social systems, but I conclude this paper by suggesting that complexity theory retains a strong notion of order, control, and "systemicity." In a postmodern environment, there is a new level of complexity, fussiness, and overload that is not as yet
adequately understood in terms of complexity theory.

In this paper I make two claims. The first is that complexity theory offers some
promising *theoretical* developments and refinements of Parsons's systems theory. The
second is that *empirically* societies have become more complex, the environment
more risky, and social change more contingent. Complexity theory in many ways fits
this empirical complexity and attempts to explain it. In an ironic fashion, some arguments about social and cultural complexity fit quite well with arguments from postmodernism. We need to change many of the assumptions about the media of exchange to take into account the complexity, fragmentation, and simulation of cultural
messages, the ambiguities and uncertainties of identity and commitment, and the
growing self-reflexivity of system relationships. In this respect my argument follows
the criticisms of systems theory in Danilo Zolo's (1992: 5) *Democracy and Complexity* in which he argues that, in post-industrial societies, "social complexity manifests
itself as the variety and semantic discontinuity of the languages, understandings,
techniques and values which are practiced within each subsystem." As the risks of the
internal and external social environment increase, social systems respond with new
forms of regulation and surveillance, because the cultural underpinnings of social
systems have eroded. There are major crises facing, in Parsonian terms, the integration and latency subsystems, but these cannot be resolved by system rigidity. Complexity requires new strategies of flexibility, reflexivity, and experimentation.

We should probably distinguish two forms of complexity theory. Firstly, there is a
position in complexity theory that accepts a realist epistemology and regards structures as products of causal chains. The principal components of realist complexity
theory can be briefly stated (Byrne, 1998; Eve, Horsfall, and Lee, 1997). Complexity
theory can be defined as a type of systems theory that provides explanations in a language of cause and effect, but at the same time seeks to avoid any mechanistic and
deterministic view of causality. It sees the interaction between system and environment in terms of a series of feedbacks. Social phenomena have to be conceived in
terms of nonlinear sequences. Although complexity theory offers explanations in
terms of complex chains of cause and effect, it assumes that the states of systems are
not ultimately predictable.

Secondly, the development of theories of complex communication systems have
not characteristically followed this realist language of causality. The sociology of
Niklas Luhmann is probably one of the best examples of the use of notions about
contingency, communication, and reflexivity to develop Parsons's structural-
functionalist approach to social systems. Luhmann has clearly followed Parsons's systems theory, but he has also made major changes to it (Luhmann, 1976). One important difference is that for Luhmann system and environment are used to define
action, and therefore systems theory is more fundamental than action theory. System
exists for Luhmann because any communication between social actors produces a

certain amount of redundancy, that is it defines a set of possiblilities, most of which are not relevant to the actual communication. A system reduces the amount of complexity and uncertainty in the environment of social actors (Luhmann, 1995). In this sense, systems are recursive properties of reflexive actions where the next "event" is unstable and uncertain. Systems emerge out of the very indeterminateness of social life as partial solutions to complexity. System is a by-product of the *Unverstandlichkeit* of the properties of relations. Luhmann's study of love as passion (1986) attempts to show how love, which is ineffable, is communicated through a semantics of love, namely through a codification of intimacy. Codes of love make the ineffable in human relationships speakable.

THE SOCIAL SYSTEM AND PARSONS'S AMERICA

Talcott Parsons developed social systems theory for a great variety of different reasons. Firstly, it seems likely that it was a product of the influence of Paretian economic theory, the work of the biochemist Lawrence J. Henderson, and Parsons's own interests in biological theories. Secondly, in his early career at Harvard, it provided him with a method of thinking more clearly about the problems of interdisciplinarity (between sociology, politics, economics, and psychology) in the context of the Harvard Department of Social Relations, where Parsons was chairman until 1956. Thirdly, it provided an analytically neat way of bringing together his interests in the work of Clyde Kluckhohn and Émile Durkheim on religion in relation to questions of social solidarity, and the work of Alfred Marshall and Max Weber on questions of scarcity. These two themes—scarcity with respect to the external environment and solidarity with respect to the internal problems of motivation and value commitments—shaped the development of the AGIL system around the two functions of allocation and integration. Finally, system theory reflected Parsons's postwar confidence in the capacity of American society in particular and western industrial society in general to evolve as progressive and democratic societies, namely to achieve the evolutionary upgrading of capitalism along the lines suggested by T. H. Marshall's theory of the development of citizenship. Systems theory was combined with Parsons's growing commitment to the theme of modernization to provide an optimistic view of adaptive capacity of American society.

One aspect of this commentary of Parsonian structural-functionalism is to suggest that systems theory as a whole is expressive of postwar modernization theory; it expressed a liberal hope in favor of evolutionary patterns of adaptation and system upgrading as a model of social change. I have argued elsewhere that:

> Much of the opposition to Parsons appears to be based on the fact that Parsons, almost alone among modern sociologists, was essentially optimistic about the long-term future of American society. . . . Parsons saw modern societies (at least modern, industrial, western societies) as embodiments of Christian culture, especially individualism, the separation of religion and politics, and tolerance for intellectual values. . . . In this respect, we

might usefully conceive Parsons' analysis of modern societies as an extension and application of Marshall's analysis of citizenship. (Holton and Turner, 1986: 21–22)

Parsons's positive view of American society's capacity to resolve, for example, the racial conflicts between black and white communities (Parsons and Clark, 1966) and its capacity to survive McCarthyism (Parsons, 1955) was part of a broader range of comparisons that he drew with authoritarian regimes in Nazi Germany (Parsons, 1942) and the Soviet Union (Parsons, 1964). We can see the work of the mature Parsons pointing towards a large scale but incomplete study of American society (with Winston White) in which Parsons wanted to show through a Weberian analysis of "the relevance of values" to social science that (1) America was becoming a more complex society but there were underlying structures and values of continuity and consistency that were robust and resilient, and (2) given the complexity of modern society no single elite or class could ever be dominant (Lidz, 1991). These essays, which were intended to be a critique of the sociology of American society represented, for example, by the work of C. Wright Mills, were never completed, although "A Tentative Outline of American Values" (Parsons, 1991) gives some flavor of the project.

Part of my argument is that (Parsonian) social systems theory represents a theoretical response to modernization processes and to an optimistic stage in postwar American politics, where American society in a cold-war environment was seen to be the cutting edge of these modernization processes. The rise of complexity theory, chaos theory, and postmodern theories of organization represents both a greater sense of anxiety about the complexities of modern society and an attempt to refashion systems theory through cybernetic models to make more sense of these new levels of cultural and social complexity. The popularity and influence of a book like Ulrich Beck's *Risk Society* (1992) reflects public concern about the political consequences of contingency and complexity in modern society. However, the increasing levels of complexity and deregulation result in new levels of regulation and surveillance. As a result, modern societies appear to be organized around two apparently contradictory processes—flexibility, contingency, and risk, on the one hand, and regulation, surveillance and governmentality on the other. I argue that the task facing modern systems theory would be to conceptualize these different and apparently contradictory aspects of social relations.

PARSONIAN SYSTEMS THEORY AND ITS CRITICS

During the development of Parsons's social systems theory, a variety of models of system influenced his thought. We can detect three basic versions of systems theory in Parsonian sociology: biological, structural-functional, and cybernetic. These three models often overlap in his work, but it is useful to isolate them in order to understand the complexity and promise of his systems theory. The first approach is no longer persuasive since the biological perspective rests on a weak organic analogy that offers low analytical rewards for sociology. The structural-functionalist version rests on analogies taken from mathematics and mechanics, and has to postulate system needs, the satisfaction of which produces circular sociological explanations. The idea of dysfunction is largely inexplicable in these terms. The final cybernetic model offers a more robust analytical tradition by an examination of media of exchange, communication, and hierarchies of control. Parsons's notion of symbolic media of exchange (money, power, authority, and value commitments) has been neglected and, although some expositions have recognized the innovative qualities of Parsons's theory of money, the relevance of this approach to system complexity needs further exploration.

The argument of this chapter is that cybernetic models can be (re)developed in terms of complexity theory to produce interesting responses to theories of risk society and postmodernization. Luhmann's version of complexity as differentiation has however been an unpromising response to questions of complexity and contingency because it tends to assume an evolutionary unfolding of structural differentiation and that in empirical terms, modern social systems are subject to two apparently contradictory cybernetic processes, namely increasing deregulation (uncertainty, contingency, and risk) and increasing regulation (McDonaldization, surveillance, and control). We can think of the systemic features of this contrast between risk and regulation in terms of a system loop. The greater the degree of risk encountered by a social system, the greater the need for regulation and surveillance. However, the pattern of regulation required by social systems in a deregulated context will have to be flexible and responsive. This discussion of risk and regulation leads through a critique of risk-society theory to an exploration of how complexity theory might assist rethinking systems theory. Complexity theory offers some promise of explaining and resolving these contradictory pressures in social systems; and if the Parsonian legacy is to survive, it will need to address these sociological issues in a theoretical strategy which goes well beyond the organic and mechanistic metaphors of early systems theory. The key to rethinking Parsonian systems theory in this context can be found in the notion of the media of exchange.

Parsons's approach to systems theory represented a modernist understanding of social systems that reflected the processes of modernization that were characteristic of the first half of the twentieth century. The impact of postmodern theory has been to question notions of hierarchy, linear notions of time, and unidimensional views of structure. If social systems theory is to survive, it has to come to terms with new theories of time and space, especially theories that have embraced the notion of complexity.

Biological and medical models were influential in Parsons's early encounter with social theory through the influence of Pareto and L. J. Henderson. In this early work, there was the notion that human society has an organic character and that the organic analogy is theoretically useful for sociological analysis. Parsons's thinking about systems was shaped by his reading of W. B. Cannon's *The Wisdom of the Body* (1932). At this stage, he conceived of social systems as having three fundamental categories—action, situation, and normative pattern—as outlined in the manuscript of 1939 (Parsons, 1986).

During the 1940s Parsons came to see sociology as a science of institutions, and his main scholarly objective was to create a theory of social systems from the foundation of the unit act. Criticism that Parsons's sociology represents an unresolved tension between system and action fail to understand Parsons's sophisticated notions of the systemic properties of action-systems. His theory had relatively little significant connection with organic analogies, and Parsons began to adopt the language of structural-functionalism, which in some respects was derived from mathematics and mechanics. Parsons's view of systems analysis was shaped by the interdisciplinary agenda of the Department of Social Relations at Harvard from 1946 and by the impact of his interest in Freudian psychoanalysis and the cultural anthropology of Clyde Kluckhohn. These influences led him to think about system in terms of personality, society, and culture. In 1951 *The Social System* began to treat the orientation of the actor in terms of a set of pattern variables, and provided a general theory of social action within which different disciplines (especially economics, politics, sociology, and social psychology) could find a place. *Toward a General Theory of Action* (1951) attempts to develop a systems approach to action that integrates sociology and psychology. In the 1950s, Parsons also developed the famous AGIL system around the two axes of allocative problems of scarcity (involving economics and politics) and the integrative problems of solidarity and commitment (the domain of sociology and psychology). Social systems survive insofar as they can resolve the complex balance between "external" problems of resources in relationship to their environment and "internal" problems of motivation and commitment (through processes of socialization and internalization).

There is a third model of the social system in which Parsons imported ideas from cybernetics and came to see the social system more in terms of communication and hierarchies of control and regulation. The social system was now a complex set of exchanges between these subsystems in terms of the media of exchange. These models of exchange and their relevant media were developed by Parsons in the 1960s in his essays on power and influence. These notions were given a more formal statement in, for example, the article on "Some Problems of General Theory in Sociology" (1970). Although in these articles Parsons attempted to preserve some continuity with both biological and structural-functional approaches, his conception of media of exchange (in terms of money, power, influence, and value commitments) represents an innovative advance. Social systems involve patterns of exchange of symbolic media that provide information and regulation.

It is well known that Parsons's structural functionalism came under extensive and penetrating criticism in the 1960s and 1970s. There is no need to explore these criticisms at this stage, because they are too well known to require further elaboration (see Alexander, 1985). The essence of these criticisms was that functionalism could not explain change and conflict. Parsons use of the AGIL system became too formalistic and indeed ritualistic. It became a conceptual grid through which any phenomenon could be routinely processed. The social system concept was developed at a level of high abstraction that precluded its successful application in empirical research and as a result had little impact on mainstream sociological research. Finally, the analogy with biological organisms produced an evolutionary functionalism that in, for example, the concept of structural differentiation, produced unhelpful and untestable assumptions about social complexity. Various attempts have been made to correct and cope with these critical objections (Alexander, 1998). The point of my argument in this chapter is to suggest that these criticisms could be summarized by saying that Parsons's social system was too systemic.

RISK, REGULATION, AND COMPLEXITY

The contradictory nature of contemporary societies can be neatly illustrated by the popularity of Ulrich Beck's *Risk Society* (1992) and George Ritzer's study of McDonaldization (1993). According to Ritzer, contemporary societies are influenced by a process of general rationalization that we can call by the generic title "McDonaldization," that is, by the regulation of actions by methods that depend significantly on the principles of Taylorism and Fordism; but they also appear to be influenced by the breakdown of stability and predictability, that is, by a growth in the risky nature of society. What is the relationship between the theory of risk society and the McDonaldization of society? On the surface, these two processes of increasing risk and uncertainty on the one hand and increasing rationalization and McDonaldization on the other appear to be entirely contradictory. They appear to indicate entirely different processes in contemporary society, pointing toward radically alternative futures. In response to the thesis of McDonaldization, one could argue that McDonaldization represents an early stage of modernization prior to the development of risk society with its ethic of self-reflexivity. Specifically, McDonaldization corresponds to Fordism and Taylorism in the period of industrial society, but it does not correspond to reflexive modernization, which attempts to cope with increasing cultural diversity, social differentiation, political fragmentation, and a more unpredictable economic environment. The process of individualization would require a more flexible and pluralistic food industry to correspond with a stage of capitalism involving reflexive modernization. If this were the case, one would expect that McDonaldization as a set organizational principles would decline as more reflexive and flexible patterns associated with risk society began to dominate.

An alternative scenario would be that the principles of risk society and McDonaldization would exist simultaneously, not as a premodern stage of rationalization, but at different levels. One might argue that deregulation and uncertainty have been more prevalent at the global and macrolevel, whereas at the local and microlevel processes of discipline, administration, and bureaucratization (that is, McDonaldization) have been more common. Risk society in this case is primarily an account of deregulation of the macroeconomy (type one risks) and its negative cultural consequences (type two risks). The best illustration of these processes has been in finance markets resulting in spectacular economic uncertainty and unpredictability. Macroderegulation has resulted in global uncertainty about economic futures, in which governments are unable either to predict or to control the external environment of the national economy. By contrast McDonaldization would refer to microrationalization of social or economically productive units. For example, while banking units operate in a highly uncertain financial environment, individual banks are highly rational, highly organized, and very predictable. In fact one could imagine the McDonaldization of banking occurring in a context of macrorisk and uncertainty. With external tellers, banks already have some elements of McDonaldization involving the concept of the drive-in bank providing a minimal set of functions to a mass audience where services are relatively undifferentiated. In this case risk and McDonaldization would be simultaneous social processes where one would expect uncertainty at the macrolevel. Ritzer's *Expressing America* (1995) can be read as an account of this standardization of banking services (to provide cheap, efficient, and reliable services to customers) in a context of global economic risk. Globalized uncertainties require, at a different level, increasing patterns and mechanisms of control, regulation, and surveillance (Turner, 1997: xviii).

Of course one objection to this argument would be that McDonaldization creates an impression of certainty and safety that in reality are not present. McDonald's eating outlets are safe in the limited sense that one is unlikely to get serious food poisoning as a client of McDonald's, but a McDonald's diet, as a lifestyle, would expose one to the possible risks, in the long term, of stomach cancer, type-two diabetes, and obesity. A diet based almost exclusively on McDonald's products would expose one to the risk of a low fiber diet with high cholesterol intake, which from a nutritional point of view is not a form of safe eating. These would be significant type-one risks, with the added possibility of type-two risks (of cultural pollution). Here again risk and rationalization would be closely interconnected, occurring simultaneously and representing two facets of modern society.

One might say in defense of Beck's attempt to differentiate between traditional and modern risk, that in traditional societies risks were somewhat random rather than systematic. Risk, for Beck, is a *systemic* feature of modernization, not an unanticipated and random outcome of social change. Nevertheless, these historical doubts about Beck's account lead me to suggest that we need to distinguish between two types of risk and that Beck's failure to provide a definition lies at the root of his somewhat undifferentiated approach to the nature of risks. I shall call technoenvironmental risks "type-one risks." In fact most of Beck's illustrations have to do with ecological politics. They involve industrial pollution of the environment, industrial hazards, and technological disasters. Beck feels that sociology has a special duty to address green issues because in Germany these issues are seen by the general population to be fundamental to modern politics. His recent work (Beck, 1995) is indeed primarily about the relationship between ecological crisis, political debate, and the role of sociology as a critical discipline.

We need to distinguish these type-one risks, which are basically about hazard, from type-two risks, which we can describe as "socio-cultural risks." Of course, Beck wants to extend the idea of hazard more broadly to the analysis of social-cultural economic risks. However, he attempts to analyze political risk and cultural risk within the same paradigm or framework as type-one (environmental) risks. Now the concept of social risk (such as uncertainty) has been fundamental to economic theory since the foundations of capitalism with the development of international trade risks and investment risks. The notion of risk, uncertainty, and danger have also been extensively explored by anthropologists in their work on taboo, pollution, and magic (Douglas, 1966). The anthropological study of magic suggests that magical practices and beliefs are present in social circumstances where risk and uncertainty are maximized and the outcomes of social action are not clearly understood by social actors. Magical practices in response to risk decline as social circumstances become more predictable and understandable. One minor criticism of Beck is that his theory has neglected, for example, the work of Mary Douglas and the history of economic theory in relation to risk and uncertainty.

Beck, in fact, covers the idea of social risk (type-two risks) in his work on so-called individualization theory (Beck, 1994). Individualization theory was concerned to defend six basic ideas or theses about the nature of reflexive modernization, risk society, and detraditionalization. First, the argument was that class, culture, and consciousness in capitalist society had been both detraditionalized and individualized, producing a society that is described as capitalism without classes, but with a continuity of individualized forms of social inequality and their related problems. Thus inequality has become individualized and is no longer collective. A second and related argument was that the labor market had become flexible, fragmented, and uncertain. Notions of class community and political struggle could no longer adequately address a society in which large sections of the youth population might never experience work. Thus individualization theory is part of a broader argument that suggests that class analysis in its strong form is obsolete and redundant (Lee and Turner, 1996). His third thesis was that there has been a significant decline in status and class characteristics, which again have become increasingly individualized, and that new forms of poverty through the feminization of poverty have significantly changed the traditional nature of status and class positions. Fourth, with the decline of these traditional structures the individual becomes the basic unit of the social in the life world (Beck, 1994). In short, in reflexive modernity, the self becomes a project. His fifth thesis is that individualization and standardization are ironically and paradoxically merely two sides of the same coin. There has been a profound detraditionalization of individuals who become dependent, as a result, on social arrangements that provide regulation and control of the life world. The result is that there is the emergence of new and special forms of social control that address the individualization of social issues and social problems. Finally we should understand individualization as a contradictory process of "societalization."

We have already seen that Beck derives social and cultural risk (type-two risks) from changes in the economy, particularly changes in the labor force and labor market. Casualization and flexibility in employment practices are part of the economic scenario of late modernity, because they offer the employer a more sensitive strategy for coping with rapid changes in the nature of demand for commodities. Employers do not want to be committed in the long term to an inflexible labor force, and casualization offers them opportunities for responding rapidly to changing political and economic circumstances. However, the consequences of casualization, particularly for young people, are negative, because they do not provide for a stable employment career path and they imply instability in lifestyles and life courses. One can argue that extensive McDonaldization also implies a process of deskilling. In fact, the debate over the nature of employment in late capitalism is yet another illustration of the contrasting paradigms of individualization in Beck's sociology and McDonaldization in Ritzer's version of Weber's theory of bureaucratization. Whereas the deskilling thesis (Braverman, 1974) was associated with fordism, the theory of flexible specialization (Piorie and Sabel, 1984) is associated with post-Fordist labor processes. A fordist labor market corresponds to a mass production system, whereas flexible specialization is focused on niche markets where production processes are highly differentiated and specialized. Labor flexibility is required by a post-Fordist economy in order to allow employers to respond to the systemic uncertainty of an advanced industrial system. The implications of a risk society environment for youth unemployment is therefore pessimistic in the sense that there will be an extensive casualization of blue-collar manual and white-collar employment. The growth of flexible specialization would suggest that Beck's account of the labor market is a more valid analysis and description of current labor market developments, but one can also expect a fairly extensive McDonaldization of the service sector involving a process of deskilling.

THE POSTMODERNIZATION OF SOCIAL SYSTEMS

The contradictions and tensions behind these two empirical processes (regulation and uncertainty) in contemporary societies accurately describe or indicate the limitations of traditional social systems theory. We need an understanding of system that expresses this dialectical and reflexive process between an increasing pattern of regulation in social life and increasing uncertainty and contingency. One can imagine a complex interaction between these patterns of regulation and deregulation. Luhmann's approach to the problem of complexity and contingency is promising in that he recognized that in general a system represents an attempt to reduce complexity by institutionalization—by creating systems.

In this chapter, I am also trying to express the notion that modern systems theory cannot assume (in Parsonian terms) a system of shared values and that in everyday life there has been a deinstitutionalization of meanings and practices. If a social system is a complex of institutions for reducing the complexities of social life, then Beck's notion of detraditionalization suggests a desystematization of social phenomena. The notion that society is more fragmented, uncertain, and more complex is often described as "the postmodernization of society." We could argue that postmodern societies are societies in which Beck type-two risks are maximized. They are societies characterized by confusing and complex communications, by an overload of communication, by irony and simulation, and by the dominance of the commodification of information.

These perspectives on social change have intellectually a close relationship with earlier notions of social order and disorder, for example in the sociology of knowledge of Peter L. Berger and Thomas Luckmann (1966), who in turn derived their understanding of meaningful everyday knowledge from the German philosophical anthropologist Arnold Gehlen (1980). The core of Gehlen's work is a theory of institutions. Human beings are characterized by their "instinctual deprivation" and therefore humans do not have a stable structure within which to operate. Humans are defined by their "world openness" because they are not equipped instinctively for a specific environment, and as a result they have to build or construct their own environment, a construction that requires the building of institutions. Social institutions are the bridges between humans and their physical environment; and it is through these institutions that human life becomes coherent, meaningful, and continuous. In filling the gap created by instinctual deprivation, institutions provide humans with relief from the tensions generated by undirected instinctual drives. Over time, these institutions are taken for granted and become part of the background of social action. The foreground is occupied by reflexive, practical, and conscious activities. With modernization, there is a process of deinstitutionalization with the result that the background becomes less reliable, more open to negotiation, culturally thinner, and increasingly an object of reflection. Accordingly the foreground expands, and life is seen to be risky and reflexive. The objective and sacred institutions of the past recede, and modern life becomes subjective, contingent, and uncertain. In fact, we live in a world of secondary or quasi-institutions. There are profound psychological consequences associated with these changes. Archaic human beings had character, that is, a firm and definite psychological structure that corresponded with the reliable background institutions. In modern societies, people have personalities that are fluid and flexible, like the institutions in which they live. The existential pressures on human beings are very profound and to some extent contemporary people are confronted with the uncertainties of a "homeless mind" (Berger, Berger, and Kellner, 1973).

CONCLUSION

One could argue that society is imploding on itself and that the regulatory framework of industrial society does not provide an effective or adequate system of control. The growth in the scale and complexity of communication has dangerous and negative political consequences. For example, there is an increasing gap between the complexity of information and the competence of individuals to evaluate information. Social systems operate therefore by depending more and more on expert opinion, where expert systems filter information to lay persons and reinforce citizenship passivity. These developments are incompatible with the democratic ideals of "education for citizenship" (Bobbio, 1987). Parsons's confidence in the capacity of citizenship institutions to resolve the internal tensions and contradictions of modern society now appears problematic. The inherent tensions in American "civic ideals" (Smith, 1997) between state and local authority, between republican universalism and ethnic differences, between equality and individualism, illustrate the problems of securing minimal agreements to make social policies effective.

Bruce Wearne (1989: 183) has perceptively observed that *The Social System* was Parsons's attempt to provide a theory of capitalism via an ideal type formulation of human society in its entirety, "constructing the general theory which he could not find in Weber's work." My argument is that capitalism has changed, becoming a more complex and dynamic system. In Parsons's theory, it was possible to make assumptions about the existence of a common set of values, underpinning American capitalism. He also assumed that a Marshallian version of citizenship would provide a common institutional framework within which migrant and minority groups could be incorporated. If postmodernization is a valid account of the fragmentation of authority in contemporary society, then the systemic assumptions of Parsons's treatment of the personality-culture-society complex or the pattern variables no longer hold. Recent theories of postmodernism, risk society, and contingency theory reflect the growing empirical complexity of contemporary industrial society. But if Parsons's systems theory was both a theory of American society and a product of its postwar optimism, complexity theory is a product of the "cultural curcuit of global capitalism" (Thrift, 1999), where theories of complex management systems have replaced the traditional models. Nigel Thrift (1999: 47) produces a useful comparison of the two models:

Old Paradigm	*New Paradigm*
reductive	emergent
isolated and controlled	contextual and self-organizing
parts completely define the whole	whole is greater than parts
top-down management	bottom-up leadership
reactive	imaginative and experimental

The new paradigm, as Thrift calls it, may hold an interesting relationship to what Michel Foucault called "governmentality" (Foucault, 1991). The idea of governmentality attempts to express the idea that power has become less a top-down constraint on the economy and more a bottom-up productive regulation. A variety of social scientists have recognized the importance of Foucault's concept of "governmentality" as a paradigm for understanding the microprocesses of administration and control within which self-regulation and social regulation are united. The concept of "governmentality," which appears late in Foucault's writing, provides an integrating theme that was concerned with the sociopolitical practices or technologies by which the self is constructed. "Governance" or "governmentality" refers to the administrative structures of the state, the patterns of self-government of individuals, and the regulatory principles of modern society. Foucault argued that governmentality has become the common foundation of all forms of modern political rationality; that is, the administrative systems of the state have been extended in order to maximize state control over the processes of the population. This extension of administrative rationality was first concerned with demographic processes of birth, morbidity, and death, and later with the psychological health of the population.

Foucault's research gave rise to a distinctive notion of power in which he empha-sized the importance of its local or micromanifestations, the role of professional knowledge in the legitimation of such power relationships, and the productive rather than negative characteristics of the effects of power. His approach can be contrasted usefully with the concept of power in Marxist sociology, where power is visible in terms of the police and army, concentrated in the state and ultimately explained by the ownership of the economic means of production. Foucault's view of power is more subtle with an emphasis on the importance of knowledge and information in modern means of surveillance.

Governmentality is the generic term for these power relations. It was defined as "the ensemble formed by the institutions, procedures, analyses and reflections, the calculations and tactics, that allow the exercise of this very specific albeit complex form of power, which has as its target populations" (Foucault, 1991: 102). The im-portance of this definition is that historically the power of the state is less con-cerned with sovereignty over things (land and wealth) and more concerned with maximizing the productive power of administration over population and repro-duction. Furthermore, Foucault interpreted the exercise of administrative power in productive terms, that is, enhancing population potential through, for example, state support for the family. In our view, the state's involvement in and regulation of reproductive technology is an important example of governmentality in which the desire of couples to reproduce is enhanced through the state's support of new technologies.

In an age of complexity, social systems have to work overtime because the back-ground assumptions of more traditional societies are routinely and regularly ques-tioned as a consequence of the erosion of the authority of more general value sys-tems, and in response to what we might call the "foregrounding" of social relations, there has to be higher and more subtle levels of governmentality and surveillance. It is this combination that explains the existential paradox of modern societies—more personal negative freedoms and greater but less obvious social surveillance. This no-tion that modern societies produce both a wider sphere of liberal individualism and more subtle, systematic, and successful patterns of surveillance is related to an in-quiry in *Sovereign Individuals of Capitalism* (Abercrombie, Hill, and Turner, 1986: 180) that we called "the Foucault Paradox." The notion of a Foucauldian paradox is simply that individualism and governmentality are not mutually exclusive. Mc-Donaldization and individualization may be interrelated and interdependent processes within the same social system of institutions. One can argue that modern citizenship is indeed the regulatory framework within which the sovereign individu-alism of capitalism and welfare governmentality are conjoined, and that it is social citizenship that provides some of the social glue that Parsons argued was a necessary underpinning of a social system. The conclusion of this chapter is that citizenship is likely to be a fragile and uncertain framework for a regulatory regime, because the notions of a common culture or civic virtue that underpinned the Marshallian-Parsonian model are constantly questioned and challenged. The modern social sys-tem is a precarious balance of processes of risk and regulation.

REFERENCES

Abercrombie, N., S. Hill, and B. S. Turner. 1986. *Sovereign Individuals of Capitalism*. London: Allen & Unwin.

Alexander, J. C., ed. 1985. *Neofunctionalism*. Beverly Hills, Calif.: Sage.

———, ed. 1998. *Neofunctionalism and After*. Oxford: Blackwell.

Beck, U. 1992. *Risk Society: Towards a New Modernity*. London: Sage.

———. 1994. "The Reinvention of Politics: Towards a Theory of Reflexive Modernization." Pp. 1–55 in *Reflexive Modernization: Politics, Tradition, and Aesthetics in the Modern Social Order*, edited by U. Beck, A. Giddens, and S. Lash. Cambridge, Eng.: Polity Press.

———. 1995. *Ecological Politics in an Age of Risk*. Cambridge, Eng.: Polity Press.

Berger, P. L., and T. Luckmann. 1966. *The Social Construction of Reality*. Garden City, N.Y.: Doubleday.

Berger, P. L., B. Berger, and H. Kellner. 1973. *The Homeless Mind*. New York: Random House.

Bobbio, N. 1987. *The Future of Democracy*. Cambridge, Eng.: Polity Press.

Braverman, H. 1974. *Labor and Monopoly Capitalism: The Degradation of Work in the Twentieth Century*. New York: Monthly Review Press.

Byrne, D. 1998. *Complexity Theory and the Social Sciences*. London: Routledge.

Cannon, W. B. 1932. *The Wisdom of the Body*. New York: Norton.

Douglas, M. 1966. *Purity and Danger: An Analysis of the Concepts of Pollution and Taboo*. London: Routledge & Kegan Paul.

Eve, R. A., S. Horsfall, and M. E. Lee. 1997. *Chaos, Complexity and Sociology*. London: Sage.

Foucault, M. 1991. "Governmentality." Pp. 87–104 in *The Foucault Effect: Studies in Governmentality*, edited by G. Burchell, C. Gordon, and P. Miller. Oxford: Blackwell.

Gehlen, A. 1980. *Man in the Age of Technology*. New York: University of Columbia Press.

Holton, J., and B. S. Turner. 1986. *Talcott Parsons on Economy and Society*. London: Routledge.

Lee, D., and B. S. Turner, eds. 1996. *Conflicts about Class: Debating Inequality in Late Industrialism*. London: Longman.

Lidz, V. 1991. "The American Value System: A Commentary on Talcott Parsons's Perspective and Understanding." Pp. 22–36 in *Talcott Parsons: Theorist of Modernity*, edited by R. Robertson and B. S. Turner. London: Sage.

Luhmann, N. 1976. "Generalized Media and the Problem of Contingency." Pp. 507–32 in *Explorations in General Theory in Social Science: Essays in Honor of Talcott Parsons*, vol. 2, edited by J. J. Loubser, R. C. Baum, A. Effrat, and V. M. Lidz. New York: Free Press.

———. 1986. *Love as Passion*. Cambridge, Eng.: Polity Press.

———. 1995. *Social Systems*. Stanford, Calif.: Stanford University Press.

Parsons, T. 1942. "Democracy and the Social Structure in Pre-Nazi Germany." *Journal of Legal and Political Sociology* 1: 96–114.

———. 1951. *The Social System*. London: Routledge & Kegan Paul.

———. 1955. "'McCarthyism' and American Social Tensions: A Sociologist's View." *Yale Review* 44: 226–45.

———. 1964. "Communism and the West: The Sociology of the Conflict." Pp. 390–9 in *Social Change, Sources, Patterns and Consequences*, edited by A. Etzioni and E. Etzioni. New York: Basic Books.

———. 1970. "Some Problems of General Theory in Sociology." Pp 26–68 in *Theoretical Sociology: Perspectives and Developments*, edited by J. C. McKinney and E. A. Tiryakian. New York: Appleton-Century-Crofts.

———. 1986. *Aktor, Situation und normative Muster. Ein Essay zur Theorie sozialen Handelns.* Frankfurt: Suhrkamp.

———. 1991. "A Tentative Outline of American Values." Pp. 37–65 in *Talcott Parsons: Theorist of Modernity,* edited by R. Roberston and B. S. Turner. London: Sage.

Parsons, T., and E. A. Shils, eds. 1951. *Toward a General Theory of Action.* Cambridge: Harvard University Press.

Parsons, T., and K. Clark, eds., 1966. *The Negro American.* Boston: Houghton Mifflin.

Piore, M., and C. F. Sabel. 1984. *The Second Industrial Divide.* New York: Basic Books.

Ritzer, G. 1993. *The McDonaldization of Society: An Investigation into the Changing Character of Contemporary Social Life.* Thousand Oaks, Calif.: Pine Forge Press.

———. 1995. *Expressing America: A Critique of the Global Credit Card Society.* Thousand Oaks, Calif.: Pine Forge Press.

Smith, R. M. 1997. *Civic Ideals: Conflicting Visions of Citizenship in U.S. History.* New Haven, Conn.: Yale University Press.

Soja, E. 1989. *Postmodern Geographies.* London: Verso.

Spencer, H. 1876. *Principles of Sociology.* New York: Appleton.

Thrift, N. 1999. "The Place of Complexity." *Theory, Culture & Society* 16 (3): 31–70.

Turner, B. S. 1996. *The Body and Society,* 2d ed. London: Sage.

———. 1997. "From Governmentality to Risk: Some Reflections on Foucault's Contribution to Medical Sociology." Pp. ix–xxi in *Foucault, Health and Medicine,* edited by A. Petersen and R. Bunton. London: Routledge.

Urry, J. 1996. "Sociology of Time and Space." Pp. 369–95 in *The Blackwell Companion to Social Theory,* edited by B. S. Turner. Oxford: Blackwell.

Wearne, B. 1989. *The Theory and Scholarship of Talcott Parsons to 1951: A Critical Commentary.* Cambridge: Cambridge University Press.

Wiener, N. 1948. *Cybernetics, or Control and Communication in the Animal and Machine.* Cambridge: MIT.

Zolo, D. 1992. *Democracy and Complexity: A Realist Approach.* University Park: Pennsylvania State University Press.

6

Can Functionalism Be Saved?

Jonathan H. Turner

Systems functionalism is built around two key ideas. First, it is useful to analyze social systems in terms of needs or requisites that must be met if the system is to remain viable in a given environment. Second, subsystems of the more inclusive social whole are to be assessed not only in terms of their interrelations with each other but also with respect to their consequences for meeting survival requisites. All functional schemes reveal these two points of emphasis, but there is considerable variability on other questions, such as the number of basic requisites, the perceived universality of these requisites for all systems, and the nature and number of crucial subsystems. For example, Herbert Spencer (1874–96) postulated three basic requisites for superorganic systems ("operation," "regulation," and "distribution"), whereas Émile Durkheim (1893) and Radcliffe-Brown (1935) postulated only one ("integration"), as did Niklas Luhmann (reduction of "complexity"). Bronislaw Malinowski (1944) viewed the social universe as composed of system levels (i.e., "biological," "structural," and "cultural") with each level having its own distinct requisites, whereas Talcott Parsons et al. (1953) conceptualized similar system levels with each having the same four requisites ("adaptation," "goal attainment," "integration," and "latency"). Thus, there is considerable diversity in functional approaches, but they all emphasize requisites and the functions of subsystems for meeting these requisites.

This mode of analysis has been subject to several damaging lines of criticism. One is that explanations employing notions of functional requisites become tautologies in which a subsystem meets survival needs of a more inclusive system because the system exists and, therefore, must be surviving. Another line of criticism is that functional explanations become illegitimate teleologies in which end states (i.e., meeting the functional requisite) cause the subsystem bringing about this end state. A third line of criticism is that functional explanations can become taxonomic in that classes of functional requisites are correlated with classes of subsystems with the dynamics of the subsystem presumed to be explained by its place in this cross classification.

These problems need not haunt functional analysis but most functionalists have, to some degree, fallen victim to them. But, what about Parsons's scheme? Is it immune to these criticisms? The answer is yes, to varying degrees. With respect to tautology, Parsons postulates, for instance, that adaptive problems at the societal level of organization are met by the economy, and we know this because the economy exists and the system is surviving. In regard to teleology, without invoking a mechanism or historical documentation of how adaptive problems led to actions that forged an economy of a given type, the argument does appear to imply that the end state—adaptation—causes the economy to meet this end state. And, perhaps most damaging, Parsons's entire scheme does look like a taxonomy of four functions, system levels, functional sectors, and subsystems in which finding the place of a subsystem like the economy in this scheme is implicitly viewed as the explanation of this subsystem's existence and dynamic properties. Thus, like many functionalists before him, Parsons fell into the chronic traps of this approach.

The question before us, then, is this: Can functionalism be saved? Can we take what is useful in functional analysis—for example, the view of systems as having to meet certain survival requisites to sustain themselves in an environment—and develop an approach that avoids the logical problems that have plagued functional analysis in general and Parsons's approach in particular? I think that the answer is yes, but we need to go back to basics and build a new functionalism from the ground up. I think that we end up with an approach that resembles Parsons's scheme, but this time around, we have a more solid foundation. I see several paths that we must travel, and these will organize this paper. One path is that we must reconnect the notion of functional requisites to selection processes, just as they are in biology. Another path is that we need a more dynamic view of subsystems as both a product of selection forces and as a generator of selection pressures on other subsystems. Still another path involves reconceptualizing system levels in a way that macro-, meso-, and microlevel processes are given prominence as distinctive domains and, at the same time, integrated into a systemic conceptualization of the social universe. And a final path is to recapture the vision of early functionalists like Spencer and Durkheim that theoretical explanation revolves around the development of elementary principles and laws rather than elaborate taxonomies.

RECONCEPTUALIZING SYSTEM REQUISITES

The most fascinating and problematic part of functional analysis is the articulation of system requisites. System requisites tell us what is necessary for a society or any system to survive and remain viable in an environment, and this is a very interesting question and probably explains why functional approaches continue to persist. If we look outside of sociology, functional approaches can be found everywhere, but they emphasize a mechanism—selection—that gets lost in sociological functionalism, despite the fact that ecological theories first appeared in the functional schemes of Spencer and Durkheim. The notions of requisite and function are, in the end, a shorthand way to make a selectionist argument. For example, the argument that the economy exists to meet the requisite for adaptation is transformed by a selectionist reasoning in the following manner: those populations that could not develop procedures for securing resources, converting them into usable commodities, and distributing them did not survive, whereas those that did were more fit and, hence, more likely to sustain themselves in their environment. Function is thus a shorthand way of making a selectionist argument along these lines: the properties of an organism, including what Spencer termed superorganism (organization of organisms), evolve by natural selection; those structural features and associated processes that facilitated fitness (ability to sustain the organism so that it can reproduce) were retained in the phenotype of the organism and those which could not were selected out as organisms carrying them died. The notion of functional requisite adds further to this argument by implicitly introducing the notion of selection pressure: environments in which a given type of organism seeks to survive exert particular kinds of pressure on organisms of this type—for example, groupings of humans are under constant pressure to gather, convert, and distribute organic resources necessary for the survival of their individual members, and to the extent that groupings cannot respond to this pressure, the members and the groups organizing their activities are less viable and less likely to survive in the environment.

At first glance, this may seem like a long-winded way to talk about functional requisites, but it shifts analysis in important directions. First, we now have a mechanism—selection—to account for the emergence and persistence of structures. If employed properly, we can avoid tautologies and illegitimate teleologies by examining the relation between selection pressures and social structures, or to phrase the matter in more biological terms, we can study the relation between the environment conceptualized as a series of selection pressures working on a given social phenotype or structure. Second, by reintroducing the concept of selection, we reconnect functionalism to its biological origins, but without the simplicity of early organismic analogies (which were formulated before an understanding of selection as a driving force of evolution was appreciated). Third, once we have the concept of selection in our theoretical vocabulary, it can be adopted and expanded to fit the Lamarckian realities of social systems in which "acquired characteristics" are inherited and, indeed, are the key to the viability of sociocultural systems.

Once we abandon the tendency in functional analysis to cross-tabulate requisites and sociocultural structures, and instead focus on selection forces, we can return to the question that always made function sociology intriguing: What forces drive selection? It is one thing to say that selection is a key mechanism for creating, sustaining, or changing sociocultural systems, but we still need to return to the issue of whether or not there are fundamental forces that always push selection. Traditional functionalism conceptualized these forces as "requisites" and then proceeded to short-circuit the analysis of selection processes set in motion by these requisites. A new functionalism must avoid both these tendencies—first, to simply posit a list of requisites and, second, to ignore selection processes.

To reconceptualize the notion of requisites, I propose that we introduce the notion of "force." I have in mind here something equivalent to what this idea means in physics—that is, a property of the universe that drives other processes. For example, a force like "gravity" drives the relations among celestial bodies, or more generally, all matter. It is not the only force; it intersects with other forces. But in viewing the universe as composed of fundamental forces, I believe that we can get at what made the notion of requisites so appealing without bringing along the problematic baggage of functionalism. Thus, I wish to reconceptualize the social universe as driven by fundamental forces. Let me hold off identifying just what these forces might be until I deal further with the nature of the selection processes in sociocultural systems set into motion by forces and with the problems encountered in examining levels of analysis.

In human social systems, we need to distinguish between two types of selection (Turner, 1995): (1) Darwinian and (2) Spencerian. Darwinian selection occurs under conditions of density among units competing for resources in a given resource niche. In deference to Émile Durkheim (1893), who was the most explicit in bringing this Darwinian idea into sociology, I will term this "Durkheimian selection" and, as is obvious, it is the key process in ecological theories. Most functional theories invoke implicitly another type of selection which, in deference to Spencer, who was the first to use functional analysis, I will term "Spencerian selection." This second type of selection occurs when there is the absence of relevant structures to deal with problematic conditions, forcing units to create new phenotypes in an effort to cope with the problem. As I will argue, Spencerian selection is most typically driven by the fundamental forces of the social universe, although Durkheimian selection can also be driven by these forces (yet to be enumerated) as well.

Both Spencerian and Durkheimian selection are Lamarckian. Under conditions of Spencerian selection, new sociocultural phenotypes are constructed (by conscious innovation; by experimentation, luck, or chance; or by borrowing and diffusion) to cope with problems generated by forces, whereas under Durkheimian selection, old phenotypes can be selected out (going extinct) or by modification (again, by forethought, chance, or borrowing) in order to secure resources in a given niche. Thus, unlike biological evolution, selection in sociocultural systems involves the ability to change structures and symbols within one phenotypic "lifetime" and, then, to transmit these changes to the next generation. This is perhaps obvious, but it nonetheless is fundamental to an analysis of sociocultural systems in terms of selection mechanisms. Thus, forces of the social universe generate selection pressures, both Spencerian and Durkheimian, that cause either a search for solutions to the problems posed by these pressures (Spencerian selection) and/or a weeding out or modification of existing structures to better cope with these problems. These forces operate, I believe, at three fundamental levels of reality: macro, meso, and micro.

Distinctions among macro-, meso-, and microlevels of human social organization are generally considered to be analytical because they are seen as partitions imposed by the analyst rather than naturally occurring divisions in the social universe. Is this common assumption true? I am not convinced that the partitioning of reality in this way is entirely analytical; it may also be the way social reality actually orders itself. Whether the conventional wisdom is true can remain an open question; my goal here is to indicate the forces driving social reality at these three levels (whether real or fiction imposed by the analyst). In table 6.1, I summarize my views on the forces operating at these three levels. As the table underscores, I see five forces operating at the whole population-level: population, power, production, reproduction, and distribution (Turner, 1995). That is, selection pressures at the societal level of organization are driven by population, power, production, reproduction, and distribution. The structural units created, sustained, and changed by these pressures are institutional systems and the culture of these systems (e.g., economy, polity, law, religion, kinship, education). These institutional systems are built from two basic

Table 6.1. Definitions of Generic Social Forces

Macrolevel Forces

Population:	Absolute number of individuals and the rate of growth in the size of a population.
Power:	Consolidation of power among its four fundamental bases—coercion, administration, symbols, material incentives—and the centralization of power on any or along all of the four bases.
Production:	Technology, physical and human capital, property systems, and entrepreneurship for the gathering of natural resources and their conversion into commodities as well as the necessary services for such gathering and conversion.
Distribution:	Infrastructures to move people, resources, and information as well as exchange systems to distribute resources and information.
Reproduction:	Replication and replacement of members of a population.

Mesolevel Forces

Differentiation:	Formation of different corporate structures in space and over time and formation of different categoric distinctions among members of a population.
Integration:	Boundary maintenance as well as internal and external ordering of relations within and between corporate and categoric units.

Microlevel Forces

Demographic:	Number and categories of individuals copresent.
Status:	Differentiation of power and authority, prestige and honor, and diffuse status characteristics among individuals copresent as well as the density of individuals copresent.
Symbolic:	Norms, values, and beliefs invoked or created among copresent individuals who normatize encounters with respect to rules of (a) communication, (b) framing, (c) rituals, (d) categories, and (e) feelings.
Transactional:	Need states of individuals in (a) self-confirmation, (b) positive exchange payoffs, (c) predictability and trust, (d) sense of intersubjectivity, and (e) group inclusion.

types of structures—corporate and categoric units—and these are the structures of the mesolevel (Hawley, 1986). Two forces drive the creation, maintenance, or change of categoric and corporate units: differentiation and integration. Thus, forces of differentiation and integration push the selection pressures guiding the formation, maintenance, or change of mesolevel structures and associated cultural symbols. These mesolevel forces are connected to macrolevel forces in reciprocal ways: differentiation and integration forces are guided by how population, power, production, reproduction, and distribution have pushed selection of institutional phenotypes; reciprocally, differentiation and integration forces, once unleashed, create new kinds of selection pressures on how institutional systems are formed (e.g., once formed, the nature of corporate actors in the economy influences the kinds of selection pressures generated by production forces). At the microlevel of reality, demographic, positional, symbolic, and transaction forces drive the formation of encounters. These forces are guided by those forming categoric and corporate units, since encounters are generally lodged in these mesolevel structures, but the dynamics of encounters and the forces driving them also influence differentiation and integration forces as they form categoric and corporate units. Figure 6.1 delineates this mutual embeddedness of the structures of macro-, meso-, and microlevels of reality (or analysis) and the forces driving the formation of these structures and associated culture.

How, then, have we reconceptualized functional requisites? Selection mechanisms guide the formation of structures and attendant culture at macro-, meso-, and microlevels of reality; these selection processes are directed by fundamental forces of the social universe; and distinctive, though interconnected, forces operate at the macro-, meso-, and microlevels of reality. All of the elements of functional requisite analysis are retained but recast in a manner that allows us to conduct a more fine-grained analysis.

SELECTION AND SYSTEM LEVELS

Primacy among System Levels

Much of the appeal of traditional functionalism was the view that functional requisites at the societal system level direct the operation of internal system processes. We should not lose this idea in revising functionalism because it is, I believe, empirically true. I would argue that macrolevel forces of population, production, reproduction, power, and distribution generate selection pressures that constrain mesolevel forces of differentiation and integration of corporate and categoric units more than the reverse and, further, that selection pressures generated by mesolevel forces constrain microlevel forces more than the reverse. Thus, the way that categoric and corporate units are differentiated and integrated is constrained by selection processes generating institutional systems, whereas microencounters are circumscribed by the formation of, and pattern of integration/disintegration among, corporate and categoric units.

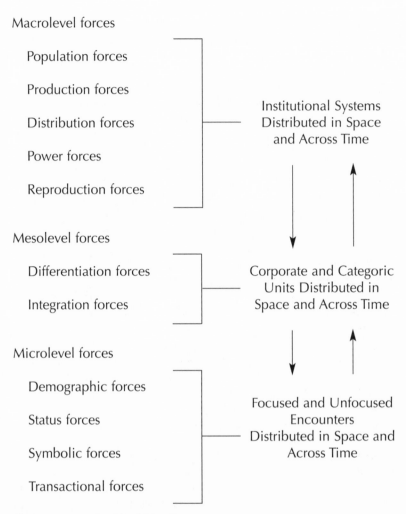

Figure 6.1 Levels of Social Reality

These are, of course, reverse causal effects: encounters either reproduce or change corporate and categoric units, and the latter do the same for institutional systems. But, these effects are not as strong as macro-to-meso-to-microcausal chains, because it takes many repeated encounters among large numbers of individuals in corporate or categoric units to change such units, and similarly, it requires alterations in many categoric and corporate units to change institutional systems. In contrast, a new mode of production immediately generates selection pressures for new kinds of corporate and categoric units as well as encounters. Surprisingly, efforts to theorize across levels have emphasized micro-to-macrochains but these approaches confront the problem of aggregation of microunits in ways that explain meso- and macrolevel dynamics. That is, no one encounter can explain a social category, corporate unit, or institutional system, and so, the problem of how to conceptualize many encounters over longer time frames generally renders theoretical explanations rather vague (e.g., society is constructed from "symbolic interactions" or "interaction rituals").

When we turn the analysis around, however, a macro-to-microanalysis does not encounter this aggregation problem: institutional systems and their associated culture set selection pressures for mesolevel forces of differentiation and integration, and we can trace more precisely how these pressures shape the formation of mesolevel structures and related cultural symbols. The same is true for meso-to-microanalysis.

What I have in mind, then, is a functionalist-inspired vision like that delineated in figure 6.2. Macrolevel forces select for the foundation of institutional systems; and these constrain the forces that drive selection pressures generating corporate and categoric units which, in turn, determine the forces pushing selection pressures for encounters. These are, I believe, the causal connections suggested by functional analysis. The reverse arrows are also important, however. Starting at the microlevel, the viability of encounters affects selection for subsequent encounters, and as these selection pressures operate, they potentially shift the values and configuration of microlevel forces. These microlevel forces, in turn, can reinforce or change the selection pressures on corporate and categoric unit formation that will, if corporate or categoric units change, shape microselection pressures on the forces driving encounters. Similarly, corporate and categoric unit formation generates selection pressures on differentiation and integration forces, and as these change, they can reinforce or change selection pressures shaping institutional systems and the values for various macrolevel forces. These reverse causal processes represent the dynamic side of relations among system levels. These dynamics operate because on the structural side, mesolevel structures are built from encounters, and macrolevel institutional systems are constructed from corporate and categoric units.

Yet, all we have done thus far is summarize the paths of causal forces. We now need to move beyond a conceptual scheme or taxonomy to explanations using this scheme. This requires us to use the scheme to generate propositions about the dynamics of the social universe as suggested by the conceptual framework developed thus far.

Systemic Dynamics within and among System Levels

Institutional Systems

Ultimately, institutional systems are composed of corporate and categoric units, but I wish to emphasize the converse: corporate and categoric units are embedded in institutional systems. Some argue that the notion of institutions is a reification, but a functionalist approach argues that the relations among different types of corporate and categoric units constitute an emergent phenomenon: social institutions. I would go even further than this: corporate and categoric units are created, or selected, under pressures from macrolevel forces and, do not, therefore, have autonomy from the

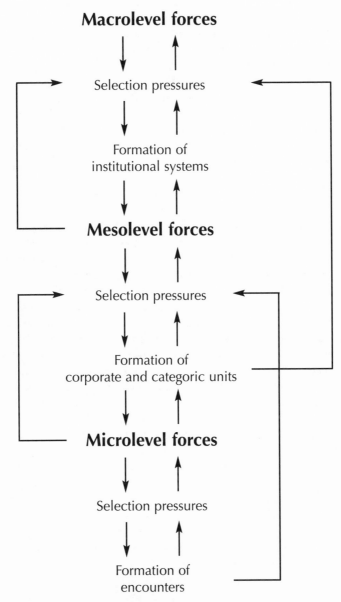

Figure 6.2.   Forces, Selection, and System Levels

macrolevel selection pressures driving their formation. Thus, institutional systems are not just aggregations of mesolevel units; the forces driving their formation constrain the forces guiding the formation of corporate and categoric units. The notion of system requisites is how traditional functionalism made this argument, but as I have emphasized, we need to rehabilitate this idea by recasting it into a conception of fundamental forces and selection pressures that these forces set into motion. Thus varying types and relations among corporate and categoric units are selected under pressures from the forces of population, power, production, reproduction, and distribution.

To appreciate just how selection pushes the differentiation and integration of corporate units, we need to examine in more detail the key properties of institutional systems generated by macrolevel forces. We can best do this, I believe, by first assessing the selection pressures set into motion by each macrolevel force (Turner, 1995). In so doing, we get at the same issues captured—albeit problematically—by the notion of functional requisites.

Population

The number of individuals and the rate of growth (or decline) in this number are forces because they generate selection pressures on corporate units to structure the activities of individuals. Just what kinds of corporate units are selected and just what social categories emerge in a population depend (1) directly upon the absolute number of individuals and their rate of increase and (2), indirectly, on the effects of population on other macrolevel forces (i.e., power, production, reproduction, and distribution). As a general rule, the larger the population, the greater will be the number of corporate units organizing their members and the more population pressures have increased the valences for production, power, reproduction, and distribution, the more diverse will be the corporate units and the greater will be the number of different categoric units. And as the number and diversity of corporate and categoric units increase, the more such differentiation will feed back and exert selection pressures on macrolevel forces for new institutional systems (e.g., law) and associated cultural systems (e.g., values, beliefs, norms, technologies).

Production

Population growth will increase the level of production, per se, but the rate of increase and, ultimately, its level are related to new technologies, levels of physical and human capital formation, nature of property systems, and entrepreneurial mechanisms for coordinating technology, capital, and property (Turner, 1995). Moreover, production is indirectly influenced by how it raises or decreases the levels of power, reproduction, population, or distribution, which, reciprocally, determine the level of technology, physical and human capital, property systems, and entrepreneurial mechanisms. In general, selection for increased production directly increases the number and diversity of corporate and categoric units; and escalating production allows for a larger and a more diverse population to be supported, for consolidation and centralization of power (e.g., the state), for new reproduction systems (e.g., education, medicine), and for new distributive infrastructures (e.g., roads, ports) and distributed exchange systems (e.g., markets). In turn, all of these transformations exert their own effects on differentiation and integration of mesolevel structures, while escalating the level of production forces (as these exert direct effects on corporate and categoric differentiation and integration).

Power

The capacity to regulate is a fundamental force, and, as enumerated in table 6.1, it revolves around four axes or bases: coercive, symbolic, administrative, and manipulation of material incentives. As this force increases in magnitude along any or all of these axes, selection pressures for increased numbers and varieties of corporate and categoric units mount. For as differentiation among these mesolevel units increases, macrolevel institutional power is used to regulate the process of integration. Moreover, increases in selection pressures from the forces of population, production, reproduction, and distribution inevitably escalate selection pressures for the mobilization of power as problems of coordination and control increase. Power also creates distinctive types of corporate units as well as new categories associated with these units but, more fundamentally, the use of power to unequally distribute resources generates new categoric units (e.g., social classes). In general, increasing power proportionately increases the number and diversity of corporate units needed to regulate individuals and other corporate units, but a disproportionate escalation of power increases the number and diversity of categoric units as consolidated and centralized power begins to regulate resource distribution.

Reproduction

Along with production, selection pressures from reproductive forces created the first corporate unit (kin units) and categoric distinctions (age and sex classes) in human populations. Selection pressures beyond these most basic corporate and categoric units from reproductive forces only begin to increase when other forces have created, either directly or indirectly through their effects on institutional systems, new corporate and categoric units that, in turn, exert selection pressures for new reproductive structures. Under these conditions, new corporate units are differentiated (e.g., schools, hospitals) and new social categories (e.g., occupational categories in education and medicine) are generated. In general, then, the more selection pressures from reproductive forces are activated, the more nonfamilial corporate units will emerge, and these units will disproportionately increase the nature and number of categoric units (through their effects on credentialing human capital, later market dynamics, and social class formation).

Distribution

The movement of information, people, and resources among members of a population revolves around (1) transportation and communication infrastructures and (2) exchanges of resources. As selection pressures from population size, production, and power escalate, new kinds of distributive infrastructures and new modes of exchange (in varying types of markets) emerge, creating new types of corporate units and related social categories. Exchange distribution depends upon distributive infrastructures, and vice versa, but once this exchange force reaches high levels it significantly increases the number and diversity of corporate units and social categories directly as well as indirectly through its effects on production and power. In general, exchange distribution and infrastructural distribution mutually escalate each other, and these mutual effects, in turn, place selection pressures on other macrolevel forces and institutional systems and on mesolevel structures.

Key Properties of Institutional Systems

The macrolevel forces discussed above generate selection pressures for institutional systems, but once these systems exist, they have reverse causal effects on the very forces that drive them and, hence, on the formation of new institutional systems. All of these systems have certain key properties: (1) organization of activities in corporate units, (2) evaluative cultural symbols (e.g., values, ideologies), (3) distinctive symbolic media of discourses, (4) sets of generalized and widely understood norms, and (5) distinctive categories associated with incumbency in corporate units. As noted earlier, the forces pushing for the formation of institutional systems also select for distinctive corporate units, and because differentiation of these units is driven by fundamental forces of the human condition, they are imbued with evaluative significance elaborated into value premises, ideologies, symbolic modes of discourses, and generalized norms (in addition to specific rules governing the division of labor). And because of these distinctive cultural components, membership in the division of labor of corporate units generates broad social categories that influence self-definitions of individuals and others' responses to them.

Once established, institutional systems provide "blueprints" for mesolevel structures, and only when the values and valences of the forces driving selection pressures undergo change (as a result of the effects of other forces and other institutional systems, or as a result of reverse causal effects from mesolevel and microlevel forces and structures) does the blueprint also change.

Categoric and Corporate Units

Differentiation of corporate and categoric units is constrained by macrolevel forces as these create selection pressures for institutional systems, but once differentiation of mesolevel units reaches high values, it can drive subsequent formation of corporate and categoric units independently of macrolevel forces. For example, waves of consolidation or mergers among economic units are less driven by production forces than by strategic calculations of corporate units themselves; similarly, the elaboration of ethnic or gender social categories bears little direct relationship to production or power, per se, but to the way corporate actors within the economy, polity, family, and other institutional systems decide in a given historical context to define each other and distribute resources on the bases of these definitions. These mesolevel forces can, of course, feed back and affect macrolevel selection processes, as is the case when conflict over ethnic stratification requires the mobilization of power by polity to manage the conflict.

What is true of differentiation forces is also the case with integrative forces. Just how relations within corporate units are integrated can be generated by processes internal to the corporate units themselves. Moreover, just how relations among corporate units are integrated can also come from strategic decisions of corporate units negotiating patterns of interdependence among themselves. Still, when relations within corporate units become problematic, these integrative problems generate selection pressures on institutional systems. For example, if unions and businesses come into open conflict in capitalist modes of production, selection pressures on polity (and law) increase to the point that institutional-level power is typically used to manage relations between these corporate and categoric units. Thus, macrolevel forces set into motion mesolevel forces of differentiation and integration, but while the latter can reveal considerable dynamic autonomy once in motion, they can also cause changes on selection pressures operating at the macrolevel and, hence, on the macrolevel forces generating these pressures. Indeed, many dramatic changes in society come as a result of these kinds of reverse causal effects from mesolevel to macrolevel, as changes within and between corporate and categoric units begin to exert influence on selection pressures stemming from macrolevel forces. Whether the change be a new religious dogma, a new corporate-generated technology, a sudden proliferation of new types of corporate or categoric units, or a new point of conflict between corporate or categoric units, change is most dramatic when integrative problems at the mesolevel accumulate to the point of escalating selection pressures on the macrolevel.

Just as institutional systems are constructed by corporate and categoric units, so corporate and categoric units are built from encounters. Or, to phrase the matter differently, encounters are embedded in corporate and categoric units, with the latter being embedded in institutional systems. Corporate and categoric units thus have key properties that follow from the institutional system in which they are embedded and which, as we will examine shortly, provide structural blueprints for the dynamics of encounters.

Encounters

Focused encounters are episodes of face-to-face interaction in which participants are oriented to each other, mutually focused on each other's responses (Goffman, 1961, 1967). It is encounters that sustain the division of labor in corporate units and the distinctions defining categoric units, and conversely, it is corporate and categoric units that provide the blueprints for encounters. I see five interrelated properties of corporate units as particularly important as they shape the flow of face-to-face interaction in encounters: (1) size of unit, (2) integrity of its external boundaries and partitions within these boundaries, (3) formality of structure, (4) explicitness of the horizontal division of labor, and (5) explicitness of the vertical division of labor. Corporate units vary along all these dimensions, and they reveal diverse configurations among them. Yet, the first property—size—exerts the most important effects on the others. Large size will generally increase external boundaries and internal partitions, formality of structure, and horizontal as well as vertical divisions of labor. This correlation is not perfect, however, since a large business and a big city (both corporate units) will reveal very different profiles with respect to these properties. In contrast, small size is generally correlated with less pronounced boundaries and partitions, less formality, and less explicit divisions of labor (as is often the case with a group). These are, of course, only rough correlations; and so, we should concentrate on the properties themselves. Depending upon the configuration of properties, the structure of corporate units will vary, and so will the dynamics of encounters that are, to varying degrees, embedded in these structures.

Like corporate units, I see five key properties of categoric units: (1) homogeneity or heterogeneity of the categoric units, (2) discreteness or clarity of the categories that distinguish individuals, (3) inequalities or rank-ordering of categoric distinctions, (4) correlation among, or superimposition of, membership in categoric units, and (5) correlation of categoric units with the structure of corporate units. These properties are less correlated than those of corporate units, and so, let me briefly enumerate each from the perspective of those in encounters that are embedded in categoric units.

An encounter with all members of the same category (e.g., all white males) will have very different dynamics than one where heterogeneity prevails (e.g., males and females); and in general, the greater the heterogeneity, the more individuals will have to work at sustaining the focus and boundaries of the encounter. The clarity of categories is also crucial; categories that fade into each other are easier for participants in an encounter to manage than those which are discrete (e.g., male vs. female or white vs. black). Categories are often rank-ordered, and the greater the rank differences among individuals in an encounter, the more strained is the interaction and the more individuals, especially low-ranking ones, will seek to limit interaction and, if possible, leave the encounter. Membership in categoric units is often correlated (e.g., white, male, rich); and this kind of superimposition magnifies and accelerates the effects of homogeneity/heterogeneity and ranking. Finally, categoric units are, to widely varying degrees, structured by corporate units. When categories reflect positions in corporate units (e.g., managerial executive, or blue-collar worker), the effects of corporate structures on individuals in an encounter are magnified. Conversely, categoric distinctions among individuals in an encounter that are not tied to membership in corporate units will influence the flow of interaction primarily in terms of the other properties of categoric units—homogeneity/heterogeneity, clarity, rank ordering, and superimposition.

These generalizations are only rough and approximate, because they are not tied to the forces operating at the microlevel of analysis. An encounter is constrained by these properties of corporate and categoric units because the latter load the values for microlevel forces—that is, demographic, status, symbolic, and transactional forces enumerated in table 6.1—that drive the flow of face-to-face interaction. Our goal is to develop more refined generalizations, but to do so, it is necessary to examine the microsocial universe in more detail.

Despite this embeddedness within mesolevel structures, encounters evidence their own dynamic forces that set into motion selection pressures that guide the flow of face-to-face interaction and that can potentially change meso- and macrolevel structures. Next I examine the forces listed in table 6.1.

Demographic Forces

The two most critical aspects in the demography of an encounter are (1) the number of individuals copresent and (2) their diversity (Collins, 1975). Large numbers of copresent individuals will reduce the values for many of the key variables defining an encounter: single visual and focus of attention, eye-to-eye ecological huddle, "we" feeling, and ritual punctuations (Noah, 1998). Moreover, as the number of individuals copresent increases, segmentation as well as differentiation of encounters are ever more likely as individuals seek to maintain focus and boundaries by breaking off to form a smaller encounter. At the same time, multiple encounters in a space will often lead to migrations from encounter to encounter (the extreme case being a cocktail party), which reduces the stability of all encounters. The degree to which an encounter, or set of encounters, is embedded in the structure of corporate units is a crucial consideration. This structure can limit fluidity of encounters by providing a common focus for all participants (in line with the culture, structure, and goals of the corporate unit); and this structure can limit both segmentation and differentiation of encounters and migrations across encounters. Conversely, if a growing encounter is not tied to the structure of a corporate unit, then increases in the numbers copresent are more likely to cause segmentation/differentiation and migration, which, in turn, reduce the stability and focus of encounters. In general, the larger, the more formal, clearly bounded and partitioned, and the more explicit the division of labor in a corporate unit, the more likely are encounters to sustain focus even as the size of encounters grows, and to limit migration to encounters related to the work goals of the corporate unit.

The diversity of individuals present in the encounter alters the dynamics of the encounter dramatically. The diversity can follow from the division of labor in a corporate unit or it can be based on membership in broader categoric units, or both. In general the less homogeneous individuals in an encounter, the more the other forces in the encounter—that is, status, symbolic, and transactional—will organize the flow of interaction, and the more individuals will have to work at sustaining the encounter. The more categoric membership is tied to the division of labor in corporate units, however, the less pronounced these tendencies than is the case when categoric membership is disconnected from corporate units. Moreover, the more disconnected from corporate units and the more heterogeneous, discrete, rank-ordered, and correlated are categoric distinctions among members in an encounter, the more activated are status, symbolic, and transactional forces, and the more individuals will need to expend effort in maintaining the focus of the encounter.

J. H. Turner

Status Forces

At the microlevel, structural forces revolve around (1) the distribution of positional power and/or authority, (2) the distribution of positional prestige and honor, (3) the density of connections among positions, and (4) the distribution of diffuse status characteristics (Webster and Foschi, 1988).[1] The more an encounter is embedded in a corporate structure and the more formal/hierarchical is the division of labor in this corporate unit, the more operative are differences in power/authority and prestige/honor and the more salient are diffuse status characteristics. In contrast, the less an encounter is embedded in a corporate unit, the more relevant are categoric distinctions, and, as a consequence, the more salient are diffuse status characteristics in determining the distribution of power and prestige; and the more discrete, clear, rank-ordered, and correlated are categoric distinctions, the greater are these effects of diffuse status characteristics. The greater the density of the encounter—that is, the more all positions in the encounter are connected to each other—the more salient are all other status forces—that is, the distribution of power, prestige, and diffuse status characteristics. Density is, of course, influenced by the number of individuals copresent in the encounter, and the greater the number of individuals copresent, the less dense is the encounter and, hence, the less operative are other status forces. However, this generalization needs to be qualified by the effects on size in differentiating a large encounter into a series of smaller ones; and as encounters become segmented and differentiated through the effects of size, the more salient are the effects of all status forces.

The relationship between embeddedness in corporate and categoric units can become complex. Even within formal and hierarchical corporate units, categoric units exert an influence on the encounter. Age, sex, gender, and ethnicity, for example, still operate but to a lesser extent than the formal distribution of power and prestige. Since membership in categoric units is often a relevant diffuse status characteristic, these categoric distinctions exert their influence on the encounter in terms of the broader cultural evaluation given to these diffuse status characteristics. This influence will be reduced, but rarely eliminated, in highly formal and vertical corporate structures; and the power of diffuse status characteristics increases in less formal and less vertically structured corporate units, and dramatically so when the encounter is not embedded in a corporate unit. Conversely, when encounters are not part of a corporate unit, positions in a corporate unit (e.g., blue-collar worker, executive, professor) can become a diffuse status characteristic for encounters embedded in a categoric unit, or in a different kind of corporate unit with a related division of labor and reduced formality. In general, the higher the evaluation, power, and prestige of positions in corporate units and the higher the evaluation of the corporate unit vis-à-vis other corporate units, the more positions in corporate units become diffuse status characteristics for encounters embedded in categoric units, or other corporate units.

Symbolic Forces

As Goffman (1967) emphasized in his adaptation of Durkheim's sociology to encounters, culture exerts considerable influence on the flow of face-to-face interaction. Status and demographic forces circumscribe which systems of symbols are salient in an encounter; and so, the embeddedness of an encounter in social structures activates which aspects of culture are relevant to the encounter, and which are not. As a general rule, the more formal and explicit the division of labor in the corporate unit, the more the culture of the corporate unit determines the cultural content and dynamics of the interaction; and similarly, the more discrete, clear, rankordered, and correlated membership in categoric units for those in an encounter, the more the cultural symbols associated with social categories determine the cultural content and dynamics of the interaction.

To examine how structural and demographic forces constrain symbolic forces, we need to establish some of the fundamental properties of symbols. Following Parsonian theory, value premises are selected by varying types of institutional systems and codified into beliefs and ideologies (about how value premises are to be realized in a given institutional domain) and then further refined into broad institutional norms or expectations for conduct. At the microlevel, these values, ideologies, and institutional norms are instantiated in the cultural ethos and normative structure of corporate units, while defining membership in categoric units and the evaluations as well as expectations for members of distinguishable categoric units. For example, a general value such as "achievement" might be translated into the institutional domains of a capitalist economy as beliefs and ideologies about capital accumulations, success in jobs, careers, or businesses, and institutional norms about work. In turn, these ideologies and institutional norms are further focused into the "cultural climate" and work rules of specific corporate units and into broad economic categories (workers, managers, owners) and expectations for, and evaluation of, members in these categories. Thus, when an encounter occurs, much of the sorting of relevant cultural content has already been accomplished by simple incumbency in an institutional domain and the corporate and categoric units comprising this domain. For any new encounter, then, vast portions of individuals' inventories of norms have been presorted, greatly reducing the range of symbolic content that must be evoked. To see how this sorting occurs, we require a more detailed analysis of how normatizing operates.

Sociologists often conceptualize norms as a noun, as a set of expectations associated with a position within a social structure. This emphasis is not entirely misplaced, since humans do carry vast inventories of norms in their brains but the process of selecting and applying norms is more active (Turner, 1988, 1989, 1996, 1997). It is a process of norm*atizing* in which rules that will guide the flow of interaction in an encounter are selected, generally implicitly, and used to formulate expectations for self and others. At times, this process can involve the creation of new norms, but more typically, relevant rules can be found in individuals' stocks of knowledge, to use Alfred Schütz's ([1932] 1967) phrase, and adopted to new contingencies.

Individuals first draw from their stocks of knowledge relevant cultural contents of a particular institutional domain (e.g., economy, family) that, in turn, determines the selection of relevant cultural symbols of corporate and categoric units operating in an institutional domain. As the culture of an institutional domain is selected, the value premises and beliefs/ideologies associated with the domain are also invoked, as are the generalized rules of behavior for individuals acting and interacting in this domain. These cultural contents are further specified by the expectations of specific corporate and categoric units in a domain. For corporate units, individuals select expectations for appropriate responses toward positional authority and prestige, toward the density of others copresent, and toward diffuse status characteristics associated with categoric units. For categoric units, individuals first select the relevant categoric distinctions and, then, the expectations toward members of different categoric units and, especially, toward categoric distinctions generated by corporate units.

This initial phase in the process of normatizing narrows the range of options for subsequent phases, and in so doing, embeds normatizing in a structural context that continuously circumscribes the normatizing process. After this initial phase, normatizing selects for the rules of communication, framing, ritualizing, categorizing, and feeling in an encounter. Each of these is briefly discussed below.

Rules of Communication

For embedded encounters, there are always rules of communication with respect to (a) the forms of talk, (b) the forms of reciprocal talk or discourse, and (c) the forms of talk for negotiating over resources. These rules of communication, in conjunction with expectations from social structures (i.e., institutional domains, corporate units, and categoric units), circumscribe other normatizing processes: framing, ritualizing, categorizing, and feeling.

Framing

Norms of communication, coupled with norms from social structure, facilitate the selection of appropriate rules for framing a situation (Goffman, 1974; Turner, 1988). Following the basic contours of Goffman's (1974) argument, framing defines what is to be excluded and included in a sequence of interaction, just as a picture frame includes a subject matter and marks the subject matter off from its environment. But unlike Goffman, I do not see frames as always lodged in a primary frame, nor do I see keying as an image of a primary frame (Turner, 1988). Rather, frames are cognitively imposed boundaries that define what is to be included and excluded, per se; and frames can be rekeyed (or shifted) in many ways (e.g., expanded, contracted, and laminated on each other). These rules of framing select (a) the appropriate frames for an encounter, (b) the appropriate way to key and rekey (i.e., establish and change) frames, and (c) the appropriate procedures for laminating frames (i.e., building up several layers of frames within frames).

Ritualizing

Again, following Goffman (1967), I see rituals as stereotyped sequences of talk and nonverbal gestures that structure the opening, flow, closing, and repairing of episodes of interaction in encounters. Frames help establish the rules of framing with respect to (a) the appropriate repertoire of rituals to be used in an encounter, (b) the appropriate gestural sequences and forms of these sequences to be employed, and (c) the appropriate gestures for opening, closing, forming, and repairing the flow of interaction.

Categorizing

In all interactions there are rules that define the situation, others, and self as being of a certain type. Categorizing involves invoking rules along several dimensions: (a) expectations associated with basic types of situations [e.g., following Goffman (1967) and Collins (1975), social, work-practical, and ceremonial], (b) expectations for level of intimacy with others [e.g., following Turner (1988) seeing others as intimates, persons, or representatives of a category], and (c) expectations for combinations between types of situations and levels of intimacy (e.g., intimacy in a work-practical situation, or representatives of a social category in a ceremonial situation). Structural and demographic forces greatly circumscribe categorizing by establishing who is present in what kind of situation with what obligations and expectations. Still, additional efforts to communicate the relevant categories must often be undertaken in an encounter. Framing and ritualizing help this process by creating a boundary between what and who is inside and outside the encounter and what topics are included and excluded. Conversely, without categorizing, it is difficult to select forms of talk, discourse, and negotiation, to key and rekey frames, or to select rituals.

Feeling

There are always what Hochschild (1979) has termed "feeling rules" in an encounter. These rules reflect a broader "emotion culture" and, in various institutional domains, are translated into "emotional ideologies." Feeling rules indicate (a) the amount of appropriate emotion to be felt in a situation, (b) the direction, whether positive or negative, as well as the duration of the emotions to be experienced, and (c) the nature, intensity, and style of expressive behavior to be displayed. Frames and categories facilitate this process by translating emotional ideologies into more specific and delimited definitions of the situation for invoking the appropriate feeling rules. Reciprocally, use of feeling rules helps sustain categories, forms of talk, and discourse, frames, and rituals.

Normatizing the encounter thus provides guidance for individuals, above and beyond the broader expectations contained in norms associated with institutional, corporate, and categoric structures. Let me offer some tentative generalizations on normatizing and embeddedness. The more an encounter is lodged in identifiable corporate and categoric units within a distinguishable institutional domain, the more the culture associated with these structures will dictate and constrain the process of normatizing. The more readily individuals in an encounter can agree on norms for communication, framing, ritualizing, categorizing, and feeling, the more smoothly will the interaction among those in an encounter proceed. The more norms of communication are established in an encounter, the more likely is mutual framing to be achieved, and as an outcome, the more rituals will be used to structure the flow of interaction and to key and rekey the frames. The more ritualizing and framing of the interaction proceed, the more readily will individuals in the encounter be able to communicate. The more categorizing is unambiguous, the more communication is facilitated and, by extension, framing and ritualizing as well; and conversely, the more there is agreement on rules of communication, framing, and ritualizing, the less likely is categorizing to be ambiguous or problematic. The more rules of communication, framing, ritualizing, and categorizing are in place, the more clear-cut are feeling rules; and reciprocally, the more individuals in an encounter conform to feeling rules, the more categorization, communication, framing, and ritualizing can be sustained.

Transactional Dynamics

Behavior is always motivated, or energized toward the fulfillment of need states that drive individuals to behave in certain ways. Similarly, *inter*action is always guided by the needs of individuals; and while many of these are idiosyncratic to the individuals involved or the unique features of the interaction, there are, I believe (Turner, 1987), more fundamental, generic, and pan-situation needs that always drive the flow of face-to-face interaction. I term these "transactional needs" because they are activated by copresence and interaction in an encounter. At least five of these transactional needs are always present in an encounter: (1) needs for self-confirmation, (2) needs for profitable exchange payoffs, (3) needs for predictability and trust, (4) needs for a sense of intersubjectivity, and (5) needs for group inclusion.

Just how these need states manifest themselves is constrained by demographic, status, and symbolic forces, but there is also a reciprocal causal effect in that these need states (a) influence individuals' willingness to be copresent and their migrations to and from encounters, (b) shape the flow of status-organizing processes, and (c) mobilize individuals to normatize an encounter and, thereby, agree on appropriate forms of communication, frames, rituals, categories, and feelings that are crucial to the reproduction of structure and culture.

When need states cannot be met, the encounter will be strained, causing it to break up or causing individuals to renormatize the encounter, perhaps in ways that loosen its embeddedness in structural units and associated culture, or in ways that change the more inclusive structure and culture. If such disembedding of encounters is frequent and widespread across many different encounters, then microlevel forces begin to alter mesolevel structures and, if the latter are changed, macrolevel institutional systems as well. We can best see how these processes operate by examining each transactional need in more detail.

Self-Confirmation

Individuals have a conception of themselves in all situations. There is considerable debate as to whether these selves or identities are arrayed in hierarchies of salience

(Stryker, 1980) or prominence (McCall and Simmons, 1978), and whether selves are only situational or transsituational. We need not enter these debates to make the general point that people visualize themselves as an object in all encounters and that this perception of self involves both cognitive and emotional meanings toward self.

These meanings carry expectations for persons along two fronts: (1) how they should behave, given the demographic and sociocultural constraints on the encounter and (2) how they should be treated by others in varying positions. These expectations are needs in that individuals seek to confirm their perceptions of themselves through their own actions and through the responses of others. When these expectations are met, self is confirmed; and individuals feel a sense of pleasure. When these expectations are exceeded, this sense of pleasure becomes more intense. Conversely, when self is not confirmed, more negative emotions will be aroused, but the nature and intensity of these emotions vary with attribution processes and cultural contexts (Turner, n.d.).

Exchange Payoffs

As all exchange theories emphasize, individuals seek to realize rewards that exceed their costs in seeking rewards. Most calculations about profits (rewards less cost) are typically implicit, and especially so as the rewards move from extrinsic (e.g., money) to intrinsic (e.g., social approval). One of the most valuable rewards in an encounter is, of course, confirmation of self; and so, individuals are particularly attuned to extrinsic and intrinsic reinforcers that confirm self. Just what these reinforcers are, or can be, is determined by the structures and associated culture in which an encounter is embedded. The distribution of positional authority and prestige, as well as relevant diffuse status characteristics, coupled with density and other demographic features of the encounter, will constrain the kinds of amounts of resources available to individuals in social structures. Similarly, the cultural values, beliefs, and norms of structural units, coupled with the way the encounter is normatized, will further constrain the resources that individuals can expect to receive, not just for confirmation of self but also for other payoffs as well.

In general, the more clearly an encounter is normatized, the more realistic are expectations for resources and, as a consequence, the more likely are individuals to adjust their costs and investments in proportion to available resources. When forms of talk are accepted, frames are more likely to define relevant resources and expectations for payoffs; rituals will pace the flow of negotiations and payoffs; categories will define the nature of payoffs (as related to work-practical, social, or ceremonial rewards, and as tied to intrinsic or extrinsic reinforcers for varying degrees of intimacy); and feeling rules will constrain the nature, direction, and intensity of affect that can be used to reward or punish others or that can be received from others. But as Homans (1961) emphasized long ago, people must perceive that they are getting a profit on encounters; and if they do not, they become angry and will engage in disruptive behaviors that can denormatize the situation. Such is particularly likely to be the case if individuals evaluate their payoffs in relation to what they expected and to what is defined as fair and just (Blau, 1964). There is, of course, a large literature on "justice" and related ideas, and we need not enter this literature beyond the simple recognization that social structures and associated values and beliefs typically imply norms of what is fair and just in relation to what individuals should expect as they normatize a situation and what they should get in light of their position and their expenditure of resources in an encounter. When payoffs meet expectations and correspond to expenditures of resources (e.g., energy, time, investment of self), individuals experience positive emotions; and when payoffs do not meet these expectations or compensate individuals for their expenditures, they become angry;[2] and the greater this sense of injustice, the more feeling rules will be abridged and the more the encounter will be breached and break apart, or alternatively, the more individuals will seek to renormatize the encounter. As anger exceeds the limits of feeling rules, talk shifts to more emotional forms, frames become difficult to maintain, rituals are increasingly devoted to repairs, and categories lose their hold to define the nature and involvement of parties to the encounter. If large numbers of individuals across many diverse encounters experience anger as a consequence of perceived injustices, the more breaches and/or renormatizing the encounter will fail to reproduce the structures and associated culture in which these encounters are embedded, and, hence, the greater the probability of changes in the more inclusive structure.

Predictability and Trust

One valuable resource in an encounter is the predictability of others' actions. When others cannot be relied upon to behave as expected, confirmation of self and, more generally, exchange payoffs become problematic. When predictability is problematic, individuals must incur additional costs to self (e.g., vulnerability to nonconfirmation), costs in expenditures of effort (e.g., heightened monitoring of others' responses), and costs associated with increased risks (e.g., investing resources with uncertain returns); and as a result, the probability of rewards exceeding costs declines, which, in turn, will cause anger and other disassociative responses. Thus, individuals have powerful needs for predictability, because the more predictable the responses of others, the less their costs.

But, more than just greater certainty of exchange payoffs is involved. There is, I believe, a more fundamental need for what Anthony Giddens (1984) termed "ontological security," in which individuals perceive the social universe as more secure when the actions of others can be anticipated in all relevant ways, not just in terms of exchange payoffs. Individuals are risk aversive because they find the anxiety associated with ontological insecurity highly unpleasant. Related to Giddens's notion of ontological security is Erik Erikson's (1950) concept of "trust," which I translate to mean that others can be relied upon to meet their obligations in an encounter. All encounters are steeped in expectations about what self and others are to do, and these become defined as obligations for what others should and must do. When others cannot be trusted to meet their obligations, anxiety and ontological insecurity will increase, while at the same time, anxiety will impose high costs and, as a consequence, decrease profitability in exchanges. Lack of trust thus strains an encounter, making it less viable and encouraging individuals to leave the encounter and/or to denormatize the encounter. Without trust and predictability, forms of talk and discourse become uncertain, frames lose their clarity, rituals prepare for breaches, categories are difficult to sustain, and negative emotions like anxiety and anger place pressure on feeling rules. And so, the less individuals' actions can be predicted or trusted, the less viable is normatization of the encounter and, by extension, the less will the encounters reproduce the culture and structure of the more inclusive system in which the encounter is embedded. And the greater the number of encounters revealing this character, the more likely are broader structures and associated cultural systems to change.

Intersubjectivity

Alfred Schütz (1932) was the first to recognize that individuals need to sense that they are perceiving and experiencing a situation in a similar way, or if differently, in a manner that is explainable. The famous breaching experiments of early ethnomethodology (e.g., Garfinkel, 1967) almost always resulted in either anxiety or anger because individuals' respective sense, even if this sense was only illusionary, that they are experiencing the situation in similar ways was destroyed. Without this sense of intersubjectivity, normatizing an interaction is problematic. Communication becomes stalled in renegotiations over the proper form of talk, frames are broken or remain unclear, rituals are devoted to repairs of breaches rather than the structuring of interaction, categories are subject to renegotiation, and feeling rules are strained as anxiety and anger are aroused to the point of further breaches in the interaction (which, in turn, makes talk and framing difficult and biases rituals toward repairs). Conversely, normatizing greatly facilitates achieving intersubjectivity; for as forms of talk, frames, rituals, categories, and feeling rules are accepted, it is easier for individuals to sustain a sense that they experience the encounter in similar ways. Furthermore, status forces also operate to generate intersubjectivity, in several ways. First, the distribution of positional authority and prestige, as well as diffuse status characteristics, provides ways to make "understandable" perceived or potential differences in perceptions and experiences of the encounter (e.g., as the result of incumbency in different positions). Second, the culture associated with the structures in which the encounter is embedded provides further symbolic guidelines for how to perceive and experience the situation, regardless of positional and status differences. And so, if an encounter is deeply embedded in clear corporate or categoric structures, intersubjectivity is easier to achieve and even more so as the structure and culture of these units constrain normatization.

Group Inclusion

Individuals need to feel involved in the ongoing flow of interaction in an encounter. This sense of inclusion need not represent emersion or engrossment in the encounter or imply high solidarity with others; rather, individuals simply need to sense that others will respond to them and that they can initiate talk without fear of negative sanctions. To the extent that this sense of group inclusion does not exist, individuals experience anxiety and varying intensities of anger (depending upon such variables as the degree to which exclusion is deliberate and explicit[3]). When individuals feel excluded, they become not only anxious and potentially angry, they also will exhibit a variety of disassociate responses, such as leaving the encounter, refusing to be part of subsequent encounters, or engaging in retaliation against others in the present or future encounters, or even different encounters involving some of the parties where a person had been previously excluded.

Thus, for encounters to sustain themselves and to reproduce more inclusive structures and associated culture in which they are embedded, they must generate a sense of group inclusion among their participants. Without this sense, individuals are not committed to forms of talk and discourse, to framing, to ritual practices, to categories, or to feeling rules. Conversely, the more normatization of talk, frames, rituals, categories, and feelings has occurred, the more likely are individuals to know how to respond to others and, thereby, feel included. Moreover, the very structure of encounters—eye-to-eye ecological huddle and common focus of attention, for example—increase the prospects for inclusion, above and beyond normatizing processes. Thus, a lack of group inclusion is often more likely in the space between focused encounters[4] and in the distribution of individuals in liminal space of corporate and categoric units. Often individuals do not enter encounters, or are actively excluded from them, as a result of their personalities or position; and unless the numbers of individuals so excluded is large, exclusion does not threaten the more exclusive structure. But if categories of individuals are excluded, and their numbers are large, then their disaffection from, or anger towards, those who have excluded them increase the level of conflict, while decreasing the viability of encounters and the ability of encounters to reproduce social structures and attendant culture.

As encounters become less viable, they have reverse causal effects on these selection processes that form corporate and categoric units. But these effects are dramatically noticeable in small corporate units, since it takes many iterations of strained encounters involving many individuals to change mesolevel structures. Structural inertia is, therefore, a reflection of how many iterated encounters it takes to generate effects on selection pressures and the mesolevel forces driving these pressures.

CONCLUSION

I have devoted considerably more attention to microforces than either macro- and mesoforces. The reason for this emphasis is my desire to underscore that these forces are constrained by macro- and mesolevel forces and that these forces are not *the only* reality. Too much theorizing has emphasized micro-to-macrocausal processes, including Parsons in *The Social System* (1951) when, in fact, it is the macro-to-micro connections that are more significant in terms of understanding the social universe. Indeed, most micro-to-macroconceptual schemes end up with the following vague assertion: macrostructures are ultimately composed of microsocial processes, and therefore, the micro should be given theoretical priority. But these kinds of assertions do not adequately recognize the embeddedness of encounters and what this embeddedness suggests for how to go about theorizing.

Because the macro and meso are, ultimately, composed of microencounters, there are many more encounters to analyze if we wish to engage in bottom-up theorizing. In contrast, we can perform top-down analysis on just one encounter and generate far more explanatory power than if we do the reverse by analyzing the encounter to explain the dynamics of corporate or categoric units. Encounters are embedded in macro- and microstructures and culture, whereas institutions, categories, and corporate units are not embedded in any one encounter. As a result, we must always engage in conceptual aggregation when trying to explain how the dynamics of mesostructures are influenced by their constituent encounters. And since encounters are short-term, we must also aggregate many encounters over time. The end result is that micro-to-meso- or micro-to-macrogeneralizations will be highly probabilistic and, as a result, often appear vague. To assert, for example, that structure is action, interaction rituals, or symbolic interaction, as others have done, only highlights the problem, emphasizing that micro-up analysis is vague and metaphorical.

Traditional functionalism gave us the critical insight into how to overcome this vagueness: view system requisites as demanding the creation of social structures that constrain action and interaction. What was missing in this earlier functional analysis was the selection processes that connect requisites to structures. My goal has been to reconceptualize requisites in a manner that, first of all, gets us around the problems of tautology and illegitimate teleology and that, secondly, enables us to see the social universe as structured at different levels of reality that are driven by different, though interconnected, forces. By converting functionalism (back) into a more ecological perspective, we may be able to save it.

NOTES

1. This section delves into a large literature on status generalization and expectation states. The generalizations below are, I believe, consistent with findings in this literature, but my focus is sufficiently at variance with most studies in this area that I cannot be sure. A recent series of articles appears, to me at least, to be consistent with my generalizations (see Ridgeway, et al., 1998; Webster and Hysom, 1998; Berger, et al., 1998; see also Wagner and Turner, 1998).

2. Attribution processes may also be important in just how angry an individual becomes and whether this anger is directed at self, others, or the situation.

3. Again, attribution processes may operate here, depending on whether self or others are blamed for noninclusion.

4. In this space, individuals may well be involved in unfocused encounters.

REFERENCES

Berger, J. C., L. Ridgeway, M. Hamit Fisek, and R. Z. Norman. 1998. "The Legitimation and Delegitimation of Power and Prestige Orders." *American Sociological Review* 63: 379–405.

Blau, P. M. 1964. *Exchange and Power in Social Life.* New York: Wiley.

———. 1994. *Structural Context of Opportunities.* Chicago: University of Chicago Press.

Collins, R. 1975. *Conflict Sociology: Toward An Explanatory Science.* New York: Academic Press.

Durkheim, É. [1893] 1933. *The Division of Labor in Society.* New York: Macmillan.

Erikson, E. 1950. *Childhood and Society.* New York: Norton.

Garfinkel, H. 1967. *Studies in Ethnomethodology.* Englewood Cliffs, N.J.: Prentice-Hall.

Giddens, A. 1984. *The Constitution of Society.* Berkeley: University of California Press.

Goffman, E. 1961. *Encounters: Two Studies in the Sociology of Interaction.* Indianapolis: Bobbs-Merrill.

———. 1967. *Interaction Ritual.* Garden City, N.Y.: Doubleday.

———. 1974. *Frame Analysis: An Essay on the Organization of Experience.* New York: Harper and Row.

———. 1983. "The Interaction Order." *American Sociological Review* 48: 1–17.

Hawley, A. 1986. *Human Ecology: A Theoretical Essay.* Chicago: University of Chicago Press.

Hochschild, A. 1979. "Emotion Work, Feeling Rules, and Social Structure." *American Journal of Sociology* 85: 551–75.

Homans, G. C. 1961. *Social Behavior: Its Elementary Forms.* New York: Harcourt Brace Jovanovich.

Malinowski, B. 1944. *A Scientific Theory of Culture.* Chapel Hill: University of North Carolina Press.

McCall, G. P., and J. L. Simmons. 1978. *Identities and Interactions.* 2d ed. New York: Basic Books.

Noah, M. 1998. "Beyond Individual Differences: Social Differentiation from First Principles." *American Sociological Review* 63: 309–30.

Parsons, T. 1951. *The Social System.* New York: Free Press.

Parsons, T., R. F. Bales, and E. A. Shils. 1953. *Working Papers in the Theory of Action.* Glencoe, Ill.: Free Press.

Radcliffe-Brown, A. R. 1935. "Structure and Function in Primitive Society." *American Anthropologist* 37: 58–72.

Ridgeway, C., E. H. Boyle, K. J. Kuipers, and D. T. Robinson. 1998. "How Do Status Differences Develop? The Role of Resources and Interactional Experiences." *American Sociological Review* 63: 331–50.

Scheff, T. 1988. "Shame and Conformity: The Deference-Emotion System." *American Sociological Review* 53: 395–406.

Schutz, A. [1932] 1967. *The Phenomenology of the Social World.* Evanston, Ill.: Northwestern University Press.

Spencer, H. 1874–96. *The Principles of Sociology.* New York: Appleton.

Stryker, S. 1980. *Symbolic Interactionism: A Structural Version.* Menlo Park, Calif.: Benjamin/Cummings.

Turner, J. H. 1987. "Toward a Sociological Theory of Motivation." *American Sociological Review* 52: 15–27.

———. 1988. *A Theory of Social Interaction.* Stanford, Calif.: Stanford University Press.

———. 1989. "A Theory of Microdynamics." *Advances in Group Processes* 6: 1–26.

———. 1994. "A General Theory of Motivation and Emotion in Human Interaction." *Osterreichische Zeitschrift fur Soziologie* 8: 20–35.

———. 1995. *Macrodynamics: Toward a Theory on the Organization of Human Populations.* New Brunswick, N.J.: Rutgers University Press.

———. 1996. "Cognition, Emotion and Interaction in the Big-brained Primate." Pp. 295–315 in *Social Processes and Human Relations*, edited by K. M. Kwan. Greenwich, Conn.: JAI Press.

———. 1997. "The Nature of Dynamics of 'The Social' among Humans." Pp. 105–32 in *The Mark of the Social*, edited by J. D. Greenwood. New York: Rowman & Littlefield.

———. n.d. "Toward a General Sociological Theory of Emotions."

Wagner, D., and J. H. Turner. 1998. "Expectation States Theories." Pp. 452–65 in *The Structure of Sociological Theory*, edited by J. H. Turner. Belmont, Calif.: Wadsworth.

Webster, M. A., and M. Foschi, eds. 1988. *Status Generalization: New Theory and Research.* Stanford, Calif.: Stanford University Press.

Webster, M., and S. J. Hysom. 1998. "Creating Status Characteristics." *American Sociological Review* 63: 351–78.

7

Networks and Systems

Stephan Fuchs

The argument to follow is built on the premise that there is only one theory of so-cial systems, that of Niklas Luhmann, which can legitimately claim to continue the Parsonian heritage in sociology. This heritage is the ambition to construct a general and universal theory of social systems, with a special emphasis on modern society. In a period stretching over thirty years, Luhmann has developed a theory of society, as well as studies of individual social systems, such as the economy, religion, education, love, art, and science (Luhmann 1986; 1989; 1990; 1992; 1995; 1997). At present, there is no sociological theory of comparable range, depth, and consistency. The clos-est anyone else's work comes to this level of universality is Bourdieu's (1984; 1993) theory of fields.

While Parsons's and Luhmann's theories share generalist ambitions and a grand conceptual architecture, Luhmann's theorizing has gradually moved away from its anchoring in Parsons. Beginning in the mid-1980s or so, a recognizable shift occurs in Luhmann's writings, away from the themes of complexity reduction and man-agement and toward a constructivist and reflexive theory of social observers. What remains of the Parsonian influence is the concept of symbolically generalized com-munication media and codes (Luhmann, 1976). But the differences begin to out-weigh the similarities between the two theories of society and social systems. In fact, Habermas's (1984–87) theorizing is much closer to Parsons's than Luhmann's, even though American commentators continue to interpret Luhmann in Parsonian terms.

First, I shall briefly discuss some differences between Parsons and Luhmann, and then show how the architecture of Luhmann's theory resembles that of net-work models. This latter comparison is driven by the conviction that a fusion of systems and network theories offers a promising perspective for renewing and re-energizing the drive toward a comprehensive theory of modern society (Fuchs, 2001).

LUHMANN AFTER PARSONS

In contrast to Parsons, Luhmann stresses the improbability of order and communication. While both theorists recognize the fundamental problem of double contingency, Parsons has much more confidence in social integration and normative consensus as stable solutions to double contingency. In the Parsonian hierarchy of control, universally shared cultural values are translated into more concrete norms, which are then internalized as motivations by means of socialization. Social order ultimately rests on shared general values; "action" is the realization of these values in combination with empirical drives and desires. Values and drives come together in institutions, which are clusters of more or less consensually accepted norms. These norms provide action with its cultural orientations. Order emerges to the degree that these orientations are shared and reciprocal.

Luhmann, in contrast, emphasizes entropy, disorder, and communicative failure. There is nothing in modern society that guarantees integration and consensus. Much less can the consensus that does emerge be grounded in rational argument and discourse. Values and norms have become sources of contest and division rather than normative agreement. Modernity lacks an overall center or apex, from which societal integration could be secured and directed. There is no privileged observer or transcendental foundation anymore. The problem of double contingency cannot really be "solved" at all; instead, it remains a perpetual presence, and can be handled only locally, one step at a time, but never globally and permanently.

The subsystems of modern society are not held together by a system above all systems, such as culture; rather, they form and proceed independently from each other. Each of them does what it does according to its own structural specifications. The subsystems can react to each other, observe each other, maybe even "cooperate," but they remain internally closed. No system can perform another system's operation, and each system will construct its own internal world, according to its specific media and codes, such as true/false (science) or legal/illegal (law). There is no fatherly prince, no all-knowing bureaucracy, and no God to oversee all this, and see to it that a good or reasonable order will eventually ensue.

Society is not really integrated at all, since there is no separate system, such as the Parsonian "societal community," that specialized in such integration. Modern society is radically pluralistic and decentered. It is also characterized by massive parallel processing; think of all the encounters and conversations going on at the same time, with no mega-encounter coordinating or planning how this happens, or with what results. Modern society does not "go" anywhere but "drifts," without anyone at the helm.

This makes social order local and temporary. When it comes to interaction, Luhmann is much closer to Garfinkel than Parsons. That is, any order that does come about is locally accomplished, maintained, and repaired. This is true for organizations as well, insofar as they contain or house interaction systems. Organizations are loosely coupled anarchies with bounded rationality and contested goals or purposes.

Order comes about only if it actually does, and if it does, it does so for empirical and contingent reasons. But there is no special force pushing toward order instead of disorder. An order remains an order only until further notice, or until it becomes apparent, for example, that a consensus was based on generalizations and exaggerations rather than factual or empirical agreement.

Consensus is frequently overstated for the purposes of front-stage political rhetoric, for example. Front stages are also where "values" surface prominently, in an attempt to garner broad popular support. However, the interactants cannot rely on a preestablished cultural value consensus, since "values" are either too abstract and vague, or else they divide rather than unite.

Double contingency makes communication improbable and problematic. "Shared meaning" is an exception, not the rule. This is true even in intimate relations, with their unusually high degree of experiential and existential coupling. More likely is misunderstanding, talking past each other, mutual indifference, or attributing more agreement to the other than could actually be cashed in when agreement is urgently needed as a resource. In this, consensus behaves like money—it inflates.

Different observers construct their own formats and versions of the world. That which does not resonate with these formats and versions cannot be observed or registered by that observer. Think of an immune system unable to recognize and combat a mutated invader. Most of what happens in the world makes little or no difference to any particular observer, for observing is highly selective. That which an observer can observe is a tiny fraction of all observable events. No observer sees the world "as such," only that part of it that the observer is equipped to observe. Observers may learn, but learning occurs within a given spectrum of learning possibilities, defined by what has already been learned thus far.

The mass media, for example, do not simply "report the news," but first select that which they report, and then format an event or story according to their internal blueprints, categories, classifications, and such. Observing is, first, a matter of ignoring and selecting, and then of simplifying, abbreviating, and condensing information according to certain observational devices, tools, and measurements. What observers see, and do not see, tells as much about these observers as about the referents of their observations.

Since modern society contains very many observers, the likelihood of co-constructions, or even compatible construction, is very small to begin with. New observers emerge all the time, and conflicts erupt over who is, and who is not, an observer, what the status of that observer is, how that observer relates to other observers, or for whom or what an observer can plausibly claim to speak. There is no longer a unified and binding worldview, cosmology, or metaphysics on which all reasonable minds can be expected to agree. This is true for science as well, since science is but one observer among others, and also contains many different observers within itself, such as different specialties and disciplines. Science is also a very restless and nervous observer, pushing itself into making more and more new discoveries. At its frontiers, a science increases uncertainty and controversy, rather than dispensing official and binding truths.

AFTER ACTION

Luhmann replaces "action" with "communication" as sociology's core concept. Communication is the unity of constructing, transmitting, and reconstructing information. More radically even than Parsons, who decomposes action into its analytical components, Luhmann dethrones persons with their beliefs, doings, and intentions. Persons are no longer seen as the essential sources of agency and meaning. What something means cannot be decided by individual persons, for example, by means of their intentional acts. Rather, meaning relates to other meanings and emerges from this difference and positional location in an overall structure of meaning.

Society does not consist of persons, much less of complete and undivided "individuals." Society is not the sum or aggregate of individual actions. There are about six billion persons alive now, and presumably they each have certain mental states, experiences, plans, and intentions. Presumably, they all do this or that, possibly even for a reason. But this is as far as agency theorizing goes. For, with whom among these six billion persons, and with which of their actions, should a sociology of action begin?

Rather, society consists of communications, which might be attributed to persons, but which do not really emanate or originate from them. Communication is emergent and autopoietic—communication uses previous communication to keep communication going in the future. Nothing communicates like communication. Persons do not communicate; rather, communication "seizes" persons and their minds to continue itself. Recent "memetics" proposes a similar idea (Blackmore, 1999). To be sure, there would be no society without persons, but it does not follow that society results from what persons think, say, or do. For the same reason, the fact that matter is composed of particles does not explain the rise and fall of large empires.

Take conversational encounters. These have an emergent flow and rhythm that cannot really be controlled or regulated by persons. Persons might say something in a conversation, but what happens later on and down the line of the encounter cannot even be anticipated by them, unless the encounter is highly constrained and formalized. How something that persons utter matters or not in the encounter, and how this is being understood, follows from the encounter itself, not from personal intentions and decisions, and also not from the likes of subjective meanings, emotional states, qualia, or propositional attitudes. Persons can try to steer an encounter in a direction they prefer, but as soon as this attempt is itself being noticed, it might *thereby* already be thwarted.

Communication can *attribute* intentions to persons, however, as in "authorship" or "creativity." In certain situations and relations, communication is more or less likely to take an "intentional stance" (Dennett, 1987) to explain to itself why and how it occurs, and who should be credited or discredited for it. By means of intentional interpretations, attributions to persons might eventually crystallize into "character" and "reputation." As cultural formats and devices for making sense of society, or as Durkheimian institutions, persons may be credited with certain ownership and property rights, but how this is done follows from communication, not individual intentionality and decisiveness. You might privately think of yourself as a genius, for example, but if that status is not warranted by the networks of communication within which someone is usually recognized as a genius, your private convictions hold little social force.

As another example, take reputation. Common sense sees reputation as something persons "have," and that they get for their contributions to, say, a professional specialty. But contributions that no one recognizes much do not make much of a difference; in fact, they are not really "contributions" at all. Next, one might think reputation comes from acknowledgments by other persons, but to build a reputation, especially in a specialized field of cultural production, not just any person will do. Rather, it is other persons' *reputations* that make someone else's reputation, and so we can say that reputation makes reputation, and then attributes it to persons. It is this attribution that is crucial. It is performed by networks of communication within which reputations matter, not by persons, actors, or individuals taken by themselves.

SYSTEMS AND NETWORKS

Luhmann's systems theory is much closer to network models than to Parsons. The most important commonality in systems and network theories is an antihumanism that drops the agency framework in its various versions, such as intentionality, free will, the unit act, and rational choice (White, 1992). Agency turns into a variable attribution and outcome of social structure and communication. It is not the original source of action, meaning, and society. Antihumanism drives toward getting rid of "person," "individual," and "actor"—as the foundational constructs of a sociological science. It is not that persons and actors were somehow "unreal" or "dead," as some postmodernism thinks (Rosenau, 1992: 42–52). Far from it, since persons and actors remain prominent common-sense devices for making sense of social outcomes, as in blaming the responsible parties, distributing rewards, hiring and firing leaders, or acknowledging intellectual property.

However, neither systems nor network theories use, or should use, the agency paradigm to do their own explaining. If they did, they would be redundantly repeating that which common sense already knows—that society consists of persons who act according to their wills and representations. Instead, systems and network theories start with social emergence, and explain persons and actors as *constructs* that some, but not different, social structures employ to do certain kinds of cultural work. This conceptual move turns persons into dependent variables and outcomes, not sources or origins, of society. What is gained by this move is replacement of agency metaphysics by an empirical science of variations in observers.

Agency and intentionality are first-order constructs, used to account for outcomes and distributing responsibility in some common-sense situations, when stories about persons are told to teach or preserve a moral lesson, for example. Agency happens, or is made to happen, in the natural attitude, the life world, and everyday experience. On this level, there can really be no question that persons exist, since personhood is an institution, with its characteristic blind spots and invisibilities. On a second level, the sociological observer observes these first-order observers as dependent variables and contingent outcomes of social structure. "Person" is a variable construct of variable observers, not a natural kind, not an essence, not a constant, and not an origin or source of all things social.

Luhmann's theory, in its later versions, assumes the form of second-order observation. The second-order observer observes how, not what, first-order observers construct their worlds, or niches in the world. In this way, the second-order observer can see what the first-order cannot see, that is, that which remains latent or unsaid when any observer makes the distinctions he or she makes. A sociology of art, for example, is not art, and has nothing to contribute to art qua art. It cannot be understood and evaluated as art, but remains a science, and as such is bound to the standard scientific checks, tests, and battles. As a second-order observer, the sociology of art observes that which art itself cannot observe, at least not as and when it is producing or appreciating art. The blind spots in an art's vision include the dependence of that art on social structure.

Compared with network theories, system theory's constructivism is much more explicit, elaborate, and "radical"—in the original sense of going back to its own roots. Network theory does not occur in its own theory of networks, while systems theory does. In this lies its constructivist radicalness. Systems theory contains an account of itself as part of a social system, science (Luhmann, 1997: 1128–42). As part of science, systems theory is a certain kind of observer, empirically located in time and society. Systems theory is not a "privileged" observer, as if capable of discerning the "objective truth" about its referents from a position outside of society and history.

Rather, "truth" is something that either happens or not, and if it does happen, it happens within a certain system, network, or part thereof. "Truth" is coherence within a cultural system, but this truth is and remains homemade, until it expands into other cultures by means of network (Latour, 1987). But the truth of a science is its own truth. That truth also changes together with a science's advances.

Network theory is less reflexive, not including itself in itself as a construct of certain intellectual and organizational networks. Incidentally, absence of reflexive reentry is also a mark of Bourdieu's theory of fields, which shares with network theory its explicit relationalism. Would it perform reflexive self-observation, network theory appeared as an event, or chain of events, within a social network, housed in a specialty, anchored in organizations, and extending through time and space through generational network (Collins, 1998).

Anti-Essentialism

A second commonality to systems and networks is anti-essentialism, or relationalism. In systems theory, the central relational concept is communication; in network theory, it is links or connections between nodes. Both communication and links are constructed as emergent social realities; they are not further reducible, at least not in, or by, the observer that is sociology. In systems theory, communication is the unity of sending, transmitting, and interpreting information by more than one observer. Nothing becomes socially real or consequential unless it is being observed and communicated by any of the many social observers. In fact, who is an observer in society, as well as his or her status, is an outcome of communication as well.

Insofar as communications use similar distinctions to process thematically related information, a "system" emerges, with its own inside/outside distinctions. These distinctions are variable, and change together with the operations of a system; they cannot be fixed in advance, from above, or once and for all. As soon as a system of communications gets going, these communications are being coupled through recursive *networks*, such as a scientific specialty or an interaction episode. In this way, systems build up their own internal reality and complexity. It is communications, not persons, that make communications fit into the network of related communications, where they are expected to make a difference to subsequent communications. Most of them don't make much of a difference. When they do, coupling occurs, and recursiveness.

A recursive or self-referential network of communications is internally closed, since it cannot step outside its own operations, and do something completely different instead. A science has no equipment to prove moral choices, and the law has no laboratories where scientific truth-claims might be settled. A system or network that is closed in this way must renormalize that which enters it from the outside. It cannot handle raw and unstructured complexity, or indeed complexity structured in a code and semantics foreign to its own. Common sense, for example, might respond to some scientific fact or other, but it will likely restructure this information according to how common sense makes sense, not the science in which that fact is embedded.

Likewise, communication cannot see, smell, or taste anything; for this, it depends on bodies and brains. Bodies and brains are observers in their own right; they register internal and external states in their immediate vicinity. Bodies are stuck in the here and now, wherever this may be at the moment. But that which bodies and brains perceive and experience cannot directly, "as is," enter communication, either. If this does happen, for example, when someone in an encounter among strangers belches or farts loudly, communication gets irritated. Think of saying in a conversation exactly what you feel or think at all times, uncensored, as it were. Or think of writing down your stream of consciousness as it flows this and that way.

Instead of perception and experience directing communication, reverse the arrow, and consider that communication directs perception and experience. Communication "seizes," focuses, and formats the perceptions it needs as it unfolds and continues. To be sure, this sometimes fails, and the conversation loses its focus altogether, possibly soon falling apart. But by far the most possible perceptions and sensations that bodies and brains may experience are discarded outright in this way, as possible themes, topics, or referents for communication. What remains is a more or less focused and communicatively structured attention space, limiting itself to the observations that matter, right now and right here, to the network within which they occur.

If communication occurs "between" several conscious minds, these minds remain closed to each other; they do not merge into a mega-mind, or collective consciousness. A consciousess remains on its own. It cannot step outside itself to experience the experiences of another consciousness. The closest one gets to minds "merging" is music or dance, and maybe poetry. For a time, a very limited number of copresent minds might focus on a common object of attention, but even then, each mind continues to have its own experiences as well. Such foci of attention are also not sustainable for a very long time; the consciousnesses involved in an interaction or encounter get tired, or go their separate ways again, once the encounter is over.

To be sure, minds can reveal bits and pieces of themselves through communication, and hope or expect that someone else will care enough to withhold his or her own mental states for the time being. But while communication still deals with this or that mental state, the minds of the persons involved do not stop having their own experiences. Consciousness and communication flow side by side; they sometimes get tangled up with each other, but never completely so, and never without rest, as if merging into a single mental-communicative delta.

In much the same spirit, relationalism in network theory treats the nodes in the network as more or less derivative from their connectivity. What a node is and does does not follow from any intrinsic properties or categorical characteristics but from their location, position, and history of tenure in the network. This position can change over time, and with it the "meaning" that a node has. In the network of a theory, for example, a term can either be a definition or hypothesis, depending on how it is being wired into the overall structure (Quine, 1964). In the course of a theory's history, hypotheses might turn into definitions, or vice versa. A node that travels to another network becomes reformatted there into a node of a different sort. It assumes a new identity. Think of a cult initiating and transubstantiating its new recruits, or a common household object being transformed into a piece of art by becoming linked to the art that is already secure in its status as art.

The best analogy to network emergence is an electric circuit. Here, the electricity is not "in" any component of the circuit, much as the behavior of a network is not "in" any of its nodes, say the actions of persons. Think of "power," for example, in the same way—as a property of networks, not persons who are "full" of power, as something that they "have." Power is just the ability of a network to get something done, and then this outcome is being attributed to a source of power, usually a powerful person or leader. By means of this commonsensical or folk-psychological attribution, a network explains to itself how it got to where it is. A science, for example, has "genius" and "creativity" to explain to itself, in terms of extraordinary persons and their awesome faculties, how it makes major breakthroughs and advances.

Nodes are selectively activated by their connections, much as the selective activation of a cell's DNA into a neuron or blood cell. What neurons do, for example, depends, among other things, on which other neurons they are connected to, which includes *their* connections, and so on. Nodes are not connected in their entirety or "totality;" rather, the connection constructs a specific *version* of a node, and it does this according to its own, not the node's, specifications. In the special case of the nodes happening to be persons, these are not connected in their full and unique biographical wholeness, but selectively, according to what matters to the relationships in which persons find themselves. Relations among friends are different from relations among colleagues and, consequently, it is these differences that matter to how each set of relationships constructs its own version of "person."

A node that travels to another network will be activated by its new surroundings in ways different from before. A node completely on its own, without any constraints at all, has infinite degrees of freedom, but no robust identity (Krieger, 1992). Such a node free-floats and rambles, if it manages to survive at all, which is doubtful. Outside of a brain, a neuron accomplishes nothing. Outside of the networks of a science, a scientific proposition means little or nothing. As soon as such a node begins to be embedded in relations, these relations will gradually reconfigure a node to make it fit into the webs that are already there.

The new relations will rearrange a node's degrees of freedom. It will not be the exact same node as before. The criteria for similarity and dissimilarity are network-dependent, too, so that no two things are similar or dissimilar in and of themselves, or in all possible worlds, for all possible observers. It is observers in recursive networks, not the world, that make things similar or dissimilar. This can be done in many different ways. To a hunter, the forest appears different from what it appears to an eco-warrior. Problems with commensurability and relativism ensue.

As opposed to systems theory, network theory can point to an impressive array of empirical corroborations and applications (Wellman and Berkowitz, 1988). The basic framework has proven useful in predicting mobility paths and promotions, political participation, state formations and breakdowns, or the distribution of market opportunities. There are networks of kinship and scientific reputations. Networks are where tribal kinship and the modern metropolis come together. Fleck ([1935] 1979) and Latour (1987) use networks to explain the emergence of stable facts. Networks are the building blocks of social structure; they link not only people in local cliques and clusters of intimate relationships, but also organizations and firms in "embedded" social markets (Granovetter, 1985). Networks link groups within and between organizations and states. States themselves are the intersections where multiple networks among organizations overlap to become observed as "politics" (Laumann and Knoke, 1987: 380–81).

Networks are good where systems are weak, that is, explanatory generalizations with empirical content. Systems theory tends to get bogged down in dialectical subtleties, which might stem from its formal, though not material, family resemblance to the *Subjektphilosphie* of Fichte. Systems theory transforms everything into dependent variables for an observer, including "action" and "structure," but network theory is better at actually explaining variations among them.

To be sure, network theory is not without its own problems. One problem is not realizing its power. The main reason for this failure appears to be that networks are frequently equated with social networks among persons. However, this is only one special case, and never are persons, in their full biographical totality, linked to other such persons. It would be more accurate to say that networks link *encounters* between

Fuchs

persons; Collins's (1988: chapter 6) theory of interaction ritual chains moves in this direction. Relationally speaking, networks do not "consist" of persons, and the actions of persons do not aggregate to produce the network's outcomes.

Even worse than person is the essentialist assumption, made in much network exchange theory (Cook, 1987), that the persons in networks act "rationally." Network models should start not with persons and their rational agency, but with the emergent behavior of a network, and then approach "rationality" as an occasioned mode of network sense-making and operation. The challenge in network analysis is to discover some fundamental properties and regularities of networks, regardless of whether they occur in natural or social life, whether they are small or large, or whether they consist of cells, people, statements, instruments, or organizations.

CONCLUSION

What are the similarities between Luhmannian systems theory, network sociology, and Parsons's structural functionalism? It seems to me one common point is critical, and this is the decomposition or deconstruction of "agency," understood as a faculty that human persons have qua persons. In Parsons, "action" is no longer something that persons "do"; rather, action is understood as the synthesis or combination of various forces, including motivational and cultural forces. With Luhmann, communication replaces action altogether as the core concept of sociology. Network analysis, although sometimes still indebted to models of rational exchange and choice, is more compatible with the notion that "action" is a residue of "structure."

Bidding farewell to the agency paradigm has the advantage of avoiding the metaphysical mysteries surrounding persons and agency, such as free will, intentionality, or subjective meaning. These now turn into attributions that certain observers make under certain conditions, but not others. Allowing for variation is critical; what is needed is a theory of observers that explains when the cultural device of "action" is used to make sense of social outcomes, and when an observer manages to observe without the semantics of personhood and action.

REFERENCES

Blackmore, S. 1999. *The Meme Machine.* Oxford: Oxford University Press.
Bourdieu, P. 1984. *Distinction.* Cambridge, Mass.: Harvard University Press.
———. 1993. *The Field of Cultural Production: Essays on Art and Literature.* New York: Columbia University Press.
Collins, R. 1988. *Theoretical Sociology.* San Diego, Calif.: Harcourt Brace Jovanovich.
———. 1998. *The Sociology of Philosophies: A Global Theory of Intellectual Change.* Cambridge: Belknap/Harvard University Press.
Cook, K. S., ed. 1987. *Social Exchange Theory.* Newbury Park, Calif.: Sage.
Dennett, D. 1987. *The Intentional Stance.* Cambridge: MIT Press.

Fleck, L. [1935] 1979. *Genesis and Development of a Scientific Fact.* Chicago: University of Chicago Press.

Fuchs, S. 2001. *Against Essentialism: A Theory of Culture and Society.* Cambridge: Harvard University Press.

Granovetter, M. 1985. "Economic Action and Social Structure: The Problem of Embeddedness." *American Journal of Sociology* 91: 481–510.

Habermas, J. 1984–87. *The Theory of Communicative Action.* 2 vols. Boston: Beacon Press.

Krieger, M. 1992. *Doing Physics: How Physicists Take Hold of the World.* Bloomington: Indiana University Press.

Latour, B. 1987. *Science in Action.* Cambridge, Mass.: Harvard University Press.

Laumann, E. O., and D. Knoke. 1987. *The Organizational State.* Madison: University of Wisconsin Press.

Luhmann, N. 1976. "Generalized Media and the Problem of Contingency." Pp. 507–32 in *Explorations in General Theory in Social Science,* edited by J. J. Loubser et al. New York: Free Press.

———. 1986. *Love as Passion.* Cambridge, Mass.: Harvard University Press.

———. 1989. *Ecological Communication.* Chicago: University of Chicago Press.

———. 1990. *Essays on Self-Reference.* New York: Columbia University Press.

———. 1992. *Die Wissenschaft der Gesellschaft.* Frankfurt: Suhrkamp.

———. 1995. *Social Systems.* Stanford, Calif.: Stanford University Press.

———. 1997. *Die Gesellschaft der Gesellschaft.* Frankfurt: Suhrkamp.

Quine, W. van O. 1964. "Two Dogmas of Empiricism." Pp. 20–46 in *From a Logical Point of View,* edited by W. van O. Quine. Cambridge, Mass.: Harvard University Press.

Rosenau, P. M. 1992. *Postmodernism and the Social Sciences.* Princeton, N.J.: Princeton University Press.

Wellman, B., and S. D. Berkowitz, eds. 1988. *Social Structures: A Network Approach.* Cambridge: Cambridge University Press.

White, H. C. 1992. *Identity and Control: A Structural Theory of Social Action.* Princeton, N.J.: Princeton University Press.

8

Language and the "Family" of Generalized Symbolic Media

Victor Lidz

Language is the most general and elementary mechanism of communication. . . .
[It] constitutes the most important single matrix from which other generalized
mechanisms have been differentiated.

—Talcott Parsons in discussing "Language as a Groundwork of Culture."[1]

With the four-function paradigm and the cybernetic hierarchy of control, the concept of generalized symbolic media of interchange is one of the major theoretical innovations in the later work of Talcott Parsons. The generalized symbolic media figure integrally in Parsons's functional theory and its treatment of social process and
change, but have received comparatively little attention in the secondary literature.
As a result, one of Parsons's most original ideas about the nature of social action has
nearly been dropped from the conceptual repertoire of sociology. The goals of this
chapter are to help revive interest in the generalized symbolic media and to highlight
a new aspect of their importance for the understanding of social dynamics.

There are several reasons for the relative neglect of media theory. First, Parsons's
ideas on the media are technical and difficult. To understand them in detail requires
considerable knowledge of his overall theory of social structure and process. Second,
Parsons over time extended the insights of media theory to a diverse set of problems.
A command of a wide range of materials in cognitive-, personality-, and social psychology, anthropology, economics, and political science as well as sociology is needed
to follow technical media theory with its later extensions (see Parsons, 1969: chapters
14–16; Parsons, 1977: chapter 10; Parsons and Platt, 1973). Third, after a systematic
first paper, "On the Concept of Political Power" (1969: chapter 14), Parsons's writings
on other generalized symbolic media contain obvious theoretical gaps, and many of
their formulations seem provisional. As the basic idea of the media was extended into
new empirical domains, yet key issues not squarely addressed, critics often gained
mixed impressions: were the media truly technical concepts or were they simply suggestive metaphors (Cartwright and Warner, 1976)? Fourth, media theory is closely

tied to summary conceptions of the resources exchanged across the boundaries of coordinate subsystems of action, concepts that Parsons called "interchange categories." While a theory of generalized symbolic media requires clear conceptions of the resources that media help to circulate, Parsons's schemes of interchange categories strike many readers as based too heavily on abstract theorizing and too little on empirical study (see Alexander, 1983).

In the present chapter, we move beyond many of the issues pertaining to the interchange categories to focus on another aspect of media theory. Media theory started with Parsons's insight that money, as measure of value and as symbolic mediator of economic exchange, is not a unique phenomenon, but a particularly clear-cut instance of an entire "family" of media. Money then became his primary model for identifying the features of generalized symbolic media centered in subsystems of social action other than the economy. Critics have been troubled, however, by some obvious ways in which other media (power, influence, commitments, intelligence, affect, definition of the situation, and collective representations) do not possess important characteristics of money. The present chapter, following up two previous articles (Lidz, 1976, 1981), responds by proposing that language is a better model than money for understanding certain key features of the media.

THE CONCEPT OF GENERALIZED MEDIA

Parsons developed the idea of generalized symbolic media in the early 1960s when he was at the peak of his creativity. Several years before he had, with Neil J. Smelser, written *Economy and Society* (1956), a study of the relationships between economic and other social institutions. He had since written a series of innovative essays on formal organization, economic development, social change, and the world political order (Parsons, 1960; 1969). With colleagues, he had edited the massive textbook *Theories of Society* (Parsons, Shils, Naegele, and Pitts, 1961), recodifying relationships between the major traditions of social thought and contemporary sociological theory. His own lengthy introductory essays in *Theories of Society* blended strong statements of established social scientific principles with bold proposals for recasting sociological theory in dynamic terms (Parsons, 1961a, 1961b).

Parsons believed that he was on the verge of breakthroughs in dynamic analysis. This belief came to rest on two interrelated ideas: application of the four-function paradigm to analysis of subsystems of society, and the concept of generalized symbolic media. The four-function paradigm first emerged in 1953 as a set of parsimonious generalizations about how members of small task-oriented groups interact (Parsons, Bales, and Shils, 1953: chapter 3). However, it was presented as possibly having broader application, and soon Parsons proposed that it might be used to define major subsystems of society. This possibility was explored further in his Marshall Lectures later in 1953 (Parsons, 1986). In 1956, *Economy and Society* used the four function schema to treat the economy as one of four primary, coordinate subsystems of society and to distinguish subsystems and sub-subsystems of the economy itself.

Economy and Society also outlined a schema of input and output relations between the economy and the three other primary subsystems of society. This schema built on classic economic analyses of the factors of production, but added the important insight that each of the factors (labor, capital, organization, and land) has its source in noneconomic institutions. In this analysis, the productivity of the economy depends importantly on factor-inputs from the other three subsystems of society. As Parsons developed his idea of interchanges by generalization from the treatment of factors of economic production, he emphasized the dynamic interdependence among subsystems of society. Each of the four subsystems of society was portrayed as depending for its capacity to function on inputs from the other three subsystems. In his "General Introduction" to *Theories of Society*, Parsons suggested that, important as markets are to industrial economies, modern societies have a series of other dynamic mechanisms based in noneconomic institutions.

Parsons's model of double interchanges was developed principally by generalizing from Keynes's treatment of the "circular flow" market exchanges between business firms and households (Keynes, 1936). A similar treatment is given in Frank Knight's discussion of the "wheel of wealth" (Knight, 1965). Business firms hire labor to be performed by members of households and pay wages or salary for the labor. In Parsons's terms, the promise to perform labor on the part of an employee is an input from the pattern maintenance or fiduciary system, and the business firm controls the inputs to manage processes of economic production. The wages received by employee households are monetary payments that households use for purchases of goods and services in support of their consumption needs. However, there is also a second exchange between business firms and households. The firms commit themselves to producing consumer goods and services for sale to households in exchange for consumer spending. Parsons called the full set of exchanges between firms and households a "double interchange," emphasizing that there are two sets of equilibrium or disequilibrium processes affecting both the economy and the fiduciary system (Parsons and Smelser, 1956). Keynes's analysis of the importance of change in aggregate circular flow between firms and households to overall economic conditions suggested to Parsons that generalizing the double interchange model to the six pairwise relationships among the four societal subsystems was an approach to analysis of the general equilibrium of society.

In a series of essays in the 1950s, Parsons developed a conception of the polity as a primary subsystem of society analytically parallel to the economy. These essays include an analysis of the political phenomenon of McCarthyism in the early 1950s, a critique of C. Wright Mills's analysis of the American power structure in *The Power Elite*, and an interpretation of *Voting* by Berelson, Lazarsfeld, and McPhee, a study of the 1948 presidential election (Parsons, 1969: chapters 7–9). The article on *Voting* sought to understand how political processes involve making adjustments to a series of broader societal processes. Discussion focused on the electoral process, where positions of leadership are filled through competitive efforts to gain support from the citizenry in the form of votes. Parsons suggested a formal analogy between the process of appealing for votes to gain election and the process by which business firms market products to consuming households. Just as businesses can remain operational only if selling their products for consumer spending covers costs of production, so political leaders remain in office only by attracting a majority of votes in exchange for the policies they develop. On the basis of this insight, Parsons proposed a functional analysis of the electoral process as a double interchange of resources between political leaders and constituents in the community parallel to the double interchange between business firms and households.

The idea of treating the polity as a subsystem of society with an analytical status formally analogous to the economy also capitalized on proposals in political science, notably David Easton's *The Political System* (1953) and *A Systems Analysis of Political Life* (1965). However, Parsons advanced a bolder and more specific conception. He differentiated three other subsystems of society as environments of independent significance for political functioning. He proposed that different resource interchanges could be identified for each of the boundaries shared with other societal subsystems. His analysis of the double interchange between leaders and constituents, focusing on the input of political support from the community, required complementary analyses of two other interchanges, later treated as focusing on inputs of control of productivity from the economy and legitimation of authority from the pattern maintenance subsystem of society (Parsons, 1969: chapters 14, 13, 17).

Since *The Social System* (1951), Parsons had consistently emphasized identifying mechanisms that enable social systems to adjust flexibly to changes in their environments and enable their various components to adjust to one another's changes. Dynamic analysis in *The Social System* concentrated on role-structures that lead actors to develop normatively grounded, but differentiated expectations of one another; the tactical give and take between actors in adjusting their expectations to one another; the motivational forces that come into play during this process of reciprocal adjustment; and the rewards and punishments (sanctions) that actors exercise to gain performances from one another that are in compliance with their respective expectations (Parsons, 1951: chapters 5–7). In *Economy and Society*, Parsons and Smelser argued that in economic markets, whether for labor, capital, consumer products, capital goods, or whatever, the mechanisms of supply and demand are special cases of the performance and sanction model developed in *The Social System*. The familiar processes of economic market dynamics were essentially special cases of processes of interaction as analyzed by sociologists.

The key breakthrough in dynamic analysis was achieved in 1963, when Parsons introduced his conception of generalized symbolic media of interchange in the article "On the Concept of Political Power" (reprinted as Parsons, 1969: chapter 14). The essay is one of Parsons's most thorough and methodical presentations of a novel idea. It begins with a critical review of shortcomings in previous conceptions of power. Parsons argued that assumptions about the nature of power that dated from Machiavelli and Hobbes, yet were still accepted by such figures as Harold D. Lasswell, Robert Dahl, Edward C. Banfield, and Carl J. Friedrich, are empirically faulty. Among such premises were the ideas that power is always hierarchical, always exercised on a basis of self-interest, intrinsically involving zero-sum relationships, and necessarily based on force. In line with an effort to treat political theory as a direct analogue of economic theory, with each focusing on the operations of a functionally defined sub-system of society, Parsons suggested that power should be viewed as a "generalized symbolic medium of interchange" facilitating political process similar to money's role in facilitating economic exchange.

Allowing for differences between economic and political relationships, Parsons argued that power is a *collective* resource for making binding decisions and a circulating medium that enables individuals in roles of authority to establish policies for adjusting to shifting conditions in the environment, including other societies as well as other subsystems of the same society. With this conception, Parsons showed that systems of power are often not based on zero-sum relations, but enable individual and collective actors in differentiated, even competing, roles to share in the growth of a power system. He demonstrated that political systems typically include important forms of power that are not hierarchical, for example, the citizen's power of the vote and collegial powers of boards, commissions, and appeals courts. He argued that uses of generalized power to promulgate public policies rest on the acceptability to constituents of legitimate binding decisions. He thus proposed that true power is a symbolic matter (a capacity to command others, coordinate the actions of organizations, or promulgate regulations) that force alone cannot create. Yet, power relations can be preserved by appropriate tactical uses of force to sanction challenges to authority. Used indiscriminately, however, force is more likely to undermine public relationships of trust on which power rests than to build power. Parsons thus demonstrated that conceptualizing power as a generalized symbolic medium resolves a number of long-standing problems and confusions about the nature of political power.

For Parsons, the idea of power as symbolic medium was tied to the conception of the polity or political subsystem of society that he had, as we have seen, been developing for several years. In this conception, the aggregate of a society's political institutions should be treated as a dynamically integrated system analogous to the economy. Like the economy, the polity is open to a variety of inputs from other institutional complexes in three other subsystems of society. The polity also feeds outputs back to these other institutional complexes, and problems of equilibrium between inputs and outputs arise both for the polity and for the coordinate subsystems of society. The conception of power as medium thus opens to analysis dynamic properties of political institutions that had largely escaped systematic study in prior political science.

Parsons's treatment of power as a generalized symbolic medium of political process explicitly followed a model of money as a generalized medium developed from conventional economics. Parsons's leading themes can be found in classic sources, including Smith ([1776] 1937), Marx (1973, 1976), and Marshall (1925), although Keynes's (1936) and conventional contemporary economics (Samuelson, 1973) were more immediate sources. In Parsons's account, the critical point is that money has no (or only trivial) intrinsic value as itself a means of want satisfaction or implement of production. Money has importance as a symbol or representation of economic value. It serves as a measure of economic value when objects are given prices in terms of money, when accounts are prepared to summarize the consequences of many exchanges and productive processes for business firms, or when budgets are created to forecast the effects on organizations of transactions over given periods. Money stores economic value, as in bank accounts, to extend purchasing power into the future. Money can be freely exchanged for an immense variety of objects of economic value. Monetary funds enable firms, households, and other organizations to have access to, in principle, all of the goods and services available in a given market system. Modern economies depend utterly on the capacity of monetary mechanisms to mediate exchange, as demonstrated by instances when the mechanisms have been disrupted, as in the German hyperinflation between the world wars or in the collapse of the Nationalist currency in China in the late 1940s (when rice was often substituted as a medium of exchange). Without money, including checks and bank accounts as well as currency and coinage, the market structure of a modern economy is not feasible. Nor are the processes of savings and capital investment so crucial to economic growth and development. With his proposal that power is a generalized symbolic medium, Parsons worked out the senses in which power is a symbolic political resource rather than a "real" factor of political effectiveness. Power thus serves as a measure of value for political institutions, stores capacities to issue binding decisions, and is expended in the making of binding decisions. Moreover, power credits can be created through an organization's history of using power effectively to attain goals on behalf of constituents (Parsons, 1969: chapter 14).

By 1967, Parsons had followed his essay on power with articles on influence and commitments (also called value-commitments) as generalized symbolic media comparable in importance to money and power for overall societal functioning (Parsons, 1969: chapters 15 and 16). Influence is the medium that represents, in Parsons's original formulation, capacity to persuade others, whether through leadership, status of prestige, or specialized (e.g., professional or scientific) expertise, that certain decisions or policies should be followed regarding potential courses of action. More recently, this author has argued that influence is better defined as a symbolic representation of solidarity in social relationships (Lidz, 1991). Influence is thus a means for one actor to propose to others that "our solidary relationship should be borne in mind as you reach a decision" about a course of conduct under consideration. The relationship may be one of doctor to patient, lawyer to client, neighbor to neighbor, classmates in college, kin, members of a voluntary association, or fellowcitizens. Influence as generalized medium facilitates processes in the subsystem of society concerned with social integration. Although Parsons was less specific in delineating institutions that make up the integrative subsystem of society than in outlining the organization of the economy and polity, he emphasized that law and the processes of social control, institutions of social stratification, and relationships of community solidarity are all central to social integration (see Parsons, 1969: chapter 15; Parsons, 1971; Parsons and Platt, 1973). He anticipated that the concept of influence as a generalized medium would guide future analysis of social integration.

Commitments represent a capacity to give direction to a course of action through the social values that imbue it with importance. When an individual or collective actor gives a commitment to others, a generalized promise is made to act in valued ways in the future (Parsons, 1969: chapter 16). Typically, the commitment is fulfilled only after other actors have readied the situation through their contributions. Commitments in this sense are generalized promises and are essential to extending coordination of complicated projects among multiple actors into the future. A marriage ceremony is an example of an exchange of highly generalized commitments— generalized in the sense that the commitments to share life chances are made with little specification of conditions that might limit them, as symbolized in the phrase "for richer, for poorer, in sickness as in health." Through their connection to values— valuation of marriage and shared family life, for example—commitments also relate planned action to institutionalized principles of continuity and the function of pattern maintenance. Parsons expected his conception of commitments as generalized medium to facilitate the development of an overall theory of the pattern maintenance (or fiduciary) subsystem of society from the initial sketch he was able to provide in his essay.

Parsons viewed the output of labor from households to business firms as a form of commitment. For both firms and households, investment in human capital is a way of upgrading the quality and economic value of commitments entailed in labor. The theme of upgrading commitments through higher education later figured prominently in *The American University* (Parsons and Platt, 1973), which provides Parsons's most detailed analysis of fiduciary institutions and processes.

Parsons understood that not all of social process occurs directly in interchanges between subsystems of society. Although units of any subsystem of society obtain basic resources directly or indirectly through interchanges, many of their routine activities are concerned with the creation of things of value to exchange for those resources. In the example of business firms, most of economic production involves the creation of goods and services within the economy as a system. Some firms specialize in supplying goods and services to other producers, while others create objects for sale directly to consuming households. A goal of economic production in the aggregate, however, is to obtain monetary income through the sale of consumer goods and services. Similarly, on the part of households, a great deal of interactive process contributes to the ability to sell the labor of household members to business firms for wages or salary. Members of a household must, through long-term processes of socialization and education, gain the ability to perform labor under the standards of the workplace. In the short term, household members need food, clothing, sleep, social support, and other help in order to be prepared to carry out routine work duties for employing business firms.

In Parsons's understanding, the productive processes of business firms and the commitment-generating processes of households share the characteristic that he called value-addition. The processes are designed to add value as measured in terms of the function-specific predominant medium, that is, monetary value for the business firm, commitment value for the household. A successful business produces goods and services that accountings show to be worth more in monetary terms than the cost of the resources consumed in production. A successful household similarly combines its various resources to create greater value as measured in terms of its members' abilities to make and fulfill commitments to other units of the society, including performance of labor for employers. More generally, Parsons viewed the creation of value-added, as measured in terms of a functionally appropriate generalized medium, as a feature of all rational social action, regardless of the subsystem of society in which it occurs.

Although Pareto had introduced the idea of a general societal equilibrium more than a generation earlier, Parsons's conception of six separate but dynamically interrelated double interchanges was the first substantive suggestion about how to approach its analysis. A common feature of Parsons's essays on power, influence, and commitments was his attention to dynamic analysis of double interchanges between pairs of subsystems. The essays all outlined double interchange relationships and suggested ways in which their aggregate equilibria might be analyzed. Parsons also identified specific empirical processes in the noneconomic subsystems of society that are analogous to saving, investment, and growth or disinvestment, contraction, and depression in economies. The widespread political distrust engendered by McCarthyism in the 1950s was a political process analogous to disinvestment, and the blockage in development of new policy in the latter years of the Eisenhower administration was a mild political depression (Parsons, 1969: chapter 7). By contrast, the early years of the Johnson administration (before the political crisis over the Vietnam War), with the skillful development of support for new civil rights and antipoverty measures, amounted to a brief period of new political investment and growth. In his discussions of social integration, Parsons suggested that the open status order of American society more effectively encouraged growth in social trust, solidarity, and overall social integration than the more rigid class systems of Europe (Parsons, 1971; also Parsons, 1954: chapter 19). Such growth is indexed by the vast nineteenth- and twentieth-century expansion in the proportions of American population accorded the respectability of membership in the middle class (see Lidz, 1989). A comparable (and related) expansion in the system of education and in the proportions of the population receiving, first, secondary, and, later, higher education played a major role in the growth of the fiduciary or pattern maintenance subsystem of American society (Parsons and Platt, 1973). One measure of the resulting fiduciary growth is the capacity to provide economic institutions with large numbers of educated persons capable of commitments to fill technical, professional, and managerial roles in production. The same educated capacity for sophisticated commitment enhances the quality of human resources available to political and civic institutions as well.

In 1968, Parsons proposed that his earlier classification of culture, social system, and personality as the primary subsystems of human social action be replaced by a new formulation applying the four-function paradigm (see Parsons, 1977: chapter 10). He identified culture, social system, personality, and behavioral organism as the four primary systems that organize the operations of systems of human action. Later, the conception of behavioral organism was determined to violate the basic definition of systems of action and was replaced by a concept of behavioral system comprised, in Jean Piaget's sense, of cognitive schemata that are resources for planning and implementing action (Lidz and Lidz, 1976). More recently, I have used the term "mind," broadly in George Herbert Mead's sense, as a clearer designation for the system of cognitive schemata.

In the 1968 essay, Parsons also proposed that each of the newly defined primary subsystems of action provides a base of operations for another generalized symbolic medium. The theory of media was thus extended to a second level in the organization of action systems. Media were no longer mechanisms associated specifically with the functioning of societal subsystems, but rather mechanisms grounded in the complexity of all action systems (Parsons, 1977, chapter 10). Culture, personality, and mind also have media. Social systems were also hypothesized to have a unifying medium that circulates more comprehensively than money, power, influence, and commitments in the interchanges of the general action system. However, Parsons did not specify how this medium relates to the media of money, power, influence, and commitments. This has been an obvious lacuna with major consequences for the coherence of the theory of generalized symbolic media. Parsons also suggested that the *subsystems* of culture, personality, and mind must have generalized symbolic media of their own (Parsons, 1977: chapter 10; Parsons and Platt, 1973), analogous in the overall organization of action systems to money, power, influence, and commitments, but he never developed an authoritative or even persuasive classification of such media.

The 1968 transformation of media theory was not as sudden as it may have appeared. Parsons had been preparing the new concepts of media for nearly a decade in discussions with colleagues and students. Some of the new concepts had roots in the formulations of Freud, Durkheim, W. I. Thomas, and others. Despite the lengthy preparation, the new formulations were far from fully worked out. At the time of their publication, many problems were still unresolved about the general action system media, in particular their relations with the societal media. While the idea of general action media was bold and potentially fruitful, terms for and underlying conceptions of certain of the media seemed provisional, as did some of the interchange categories. Parsons was soon at work on a revision, which appeared in *The American University* (Parsons and Platt, 1973), a major study employing the concept of a general action system.

While *The American University* was in preparation and again after it was published, Parsons and the present author taught seminars on media theory together at the University of Chicago and then at the University of Pennsylvania. Further revisions of the scheme of general action media grew out of our collaborative teaching, with an agreement on basic concepts reached in the last seminar in 1975. In this version, "collective representations" is the designation for the medium anchored in culture, "collective sentiment" for the social system medium, "affect" for the medium of personality, and "intelligence" for the medium of mind (Lidz, 1981: 1982). This formulation will be used in the following discussion with one change: use of the term "definition of the situation" for the social system medium. The earlier formulation emphasized the shared sentiment with which actors invest the normative understandings that guide situated interaction. The present formulation emphasizes the situation-specific normative understandings themselves, mindful that individual actors also invest these understandings with personal effect.

PROBLEMS OF THE MONEY MODEL

As we have seen, money was the central model for Parsons's conception of a "family" of generalized symbolic media, and his discussions of power, influence, and commitments highlighted parallels between the newly identified media and money. However, critics have noted a difference in quantitative form between money and the other media. To be sure, we can speak of a president as having greater power than a cabinet secretary or the governor of a state, of a leader of a prominent voluntary association giving expert testimony at a congressional hearing as having greater influence on proposed legislation than most other citizens, or of one researcher or university making a larger commitment than another researcher or university to conduct research in a specific field. Power, influence, and commitments thus have quantitative aspects that can be conceptualized in quite specific terms. Yet, there is a difference in calculations of quantity between power, influence, or commitments and money. We can learn what it costs to purchase a given model of computer or automobile and we can measure our current monetary resources with quantitative precision. Our ability to make these calculations is due to the social fact that money, as an institution, has the form of a continuous measure of economic value. To be sure, the relationship between money as measure and the economic value of goods and services is subject to change over time. Inflation, deflation, and changes in the real costs of goods and services, due to changes in production technology, supply (scarcity), and demand, all affect prices. However, the use of money in any setting, whether for purchases or for accounting purposes, involves calculation with a continuous measure. The same is not true for power, influence, or commitments. Although they are institutionalized in ways that enable us to think in terms of relative quantities, they are not continuous measures. We cannot calculate quantities of power, influence, and commitments with precision comparable to monetary calculations. The modern businessperson is dependent on financial calculators, computer spreadsheets, and other tools for refining monetary calculations, but the modern politician has no such precise means for forecasting his or her power position, nor does the modern influential or a person trying to assess the quantity and value of commitments given or received.

How significant is this difference between money and other media? Parsons thought it not of critical importance to media theory, but acknowledged that it renders calculations of equilibrium points in analyses of political, integrative, or pattern maintenance processes less precise than analyses of economic equilibria. There are no analogues for the other subsystems of society of such measures as National Income, Gross Domestic Product, Balance of Trade, Aggregate Savings, Aggregate Debt, and so forth. The climates for political, integrative, or fiduciary investment and growth are not indexed by such precise measures as the prime interest rate, federal funds rate, and thirty-year treasury bond rate. Yet, quantitative imprecision did not prevent Parsons from putting forward empirical analyses of the analogues of investment and growth, disinvestment and contraction, in his essays on power, influence, and commitments.

Cartwright and Warner (1976) argued, however, that the concept of generalized symbolic media is entirely vitiated by the inability to measure power and influence in the continuous terms used for money. Habermas (1987) called attention to the same difficulty, but did not draw such radically negative conclusions. Baum (1976) proposed that the differences between money and the other media may be due to differences in phases of development among subsystems of society. He foresaw that future institutional developments might create circulating markers for quantities of power and influence denominated in the same way as dollars.

Parsons was not persuaded by Baum's proposal. In his view, the model of interchanges requires that the principal subsystems of a society function on comparable levels of institutional development, including broadly similar levels of generalization of the symbolic media. For example, the labor market matches wages or salaries to judgments regarding the quantities and qualities of commitments to perform labor purchased by employers. In assigning wage and salary levels, employers are making quantitative judgments about the value of the commitments they obtain.

However, Parsons (personal communication, circa 1965) did consider an idea regarding differences in forms of measurement among the media suggested to him in discussion by Edward Laumann. Laumann's proposal was that, while money is denominated on a continuous scale, power is possibly quantifiable on a ratio scale, influence on an interval scale, and commitments on a nominal scale. The differences in scales are presumably adaptations of the media to the different institutional environments in their respective subsystems of society. In this conjecture, power in a given polity is allocated in ratios among positions of authority—for example, the differences in power between a president and the various cabinet secretaries might be formulated as ratios. The power ratios are presumably linked to structural features of the political system, so they remain comparatively stable over time and circumstance. They might prove constant even when overall quantities of power increase or decrease with growth or contraction of sectors of the power system, for example, the executive or legislative branches of government or federal, state, and local levels of government.

Parsons never reached a final judgment on the value of Laumann's idea. It is possible that with further specification of how the ratios, intervals, and nominal values are to be measured, it will prove to be an insightful proposal. However, power seems to provide the clearest test of the conjecture, and it does not appear that power in working political systems is allocated in ratios. The quantitative dimension of power derives its broad structure from the rights, duties, and responsibilities that are prescribed for specific offices in various constitutional, legislative, and regulatory documents. As Parsons demonstrated in compelling analyses, actual circulating quantities of power are also affected by officeholders' skills or lack of skills in using legally prescribed powers to attract returns of support from their constituents. As any political system has many holders and seekers of power, success in cultivating power also depends on the skills of competitors, as, for example, the president's power is interdependent with the powers developed by leaders of the Senate and House of Representatives. Moreover, as Parsons also showed, the workings of power are not zero-sum.

A contentious stalemate in politics may cause both the president and the leadership of Congress to lose power. Alternatively, successful development of policies may bring greater power to both branches of government. Such flux in power relations cannot be captured by any set of constant ratios. It appears likely that no political system could limit its allocations of power to stable ratios without loss of capacity to adjust its functioning to changing circumstances.

Cartwright and Warner (1976; see also Alexander, 1983) also emphasized an issue of the concreteness of media. Money is concrete. We carry bills and coins in our pockets. We can know how much money is in our wallets, how much we have in bank accounts, and the worth of our properties and investments. Do we know how much power, influence, or commitments we have? Even if we claim to know how powerful or influential we are, where is the power and influence? Where are the power, influence, or commitment "chits"? Who can carry them in his or her pocket or write checks on them? How can power, influence, and commitments be "measures of value" if there are not any concrete entities to serve as the measures? Cartwright and Warner suggested that Parsons's writings on the media had too hastily elevated a metaphor to a theoretical category.

The criticisms that media other than money lack clear quantification and concrete substance follow from an expectation that authentic media must share the properties of money. This expectation follows Parsons's own emphasis on money as the prototype for all of the media. However, the effort to conceptualize all characteristics of the media on the model of money may be too inflexible. It may have placed undue emphasis on certain formulations, the double interchanges and circular flow for Parsons, quantification and concrete substance for Baum and for Cartwright and Warner, while failing to highlight other properties of generalized media. The following discussion of language as a central medium proposes a different model for identifying and assessing properties of generalized symbolic media.

LANGUAGE AS MEDIUM AND SOCIAL ACTION

Insight into the nature of the media and their parts in processes of social action may be developed by examining the part of language in social action. Language, too, is representational and may be regarded as a generalized medium that permits information to circulate throughout an action system. It consists of semantic, syntactic, and phonological rules that make it possible for linguistically presented information to be conveyed effectively across the boundaries of cultural, societal, personality, and mental systems. The significant representation made possible by the rules of grammar constitutes a symbolic common denominator among the primary subsystems of action. Linguistically expressed information also circulates among actors and across social situations and cultural settings. Actors who command the finite content of a language's rule structure are able, as Noam Chomsky (1957, 1965, 1966, 1968, 1980) elegantly demonstrated, to speak or write indefinitely numerous meaningful statements with an expectation of their being understandable to indefinitely many other speakers of the language. No less importantly, they also gain interpretive access to an indefinite number and variety of meaningful statements formulated by other speakers or writers. The flexibility that language imparts to expression enables it to facilitate the circulation of information in and among minds, personalities, social systems, and cultural systems. A common language is a key marker of the integration and unity of a system of action, while the absence of a common language limits the closeness of integration of social action (Greenberg, 1963).

The special role of language in systems of human social action is deeply embedded in the evolutionary origins of homo sapiens as a species. To the best of contemporary knowledge, all societies since the origin of homo sapiens have had use of languages with essential similar formal properties. Certainly all societies that have been examined linguistically, either by direct observation and analysis or by historical reconstruction, have organized interpersonal communication with formally comparable languages. The field of "linguistic universals" is informed by knowledge of a few thousand more or less independent cultures and their languages, not to mention thousands of dialects of major languages.

Language provides the formal capability for a human social actor to objectify ideas, thoughts, feelings, expectations, and beliefs so that they can be reconstituted in the understanding of another actor or actors. To be sure, uses of language are not infallible processes of communication. Just as actors are fallible in their use of grammatical rules, they often disagree about the meaning of what has been said or written. Some expressively and rhetorically complicated speeches and writings (the radio addresses of Franklin D. Roosevelt, the poetry of Emily Dickinson, the plays of Shakespeare, the novels of Thomas Mann or James Joyce, the political pamphlets of Alexander Pope or Thomas Addison, the Constitution of the United States of America) are so dense with meanings that efforts to interpret or explicate them are never exhaustive. However, human society also relies heavily on the objectivity of meaning of a wide variety of spoken and written statements, ranging from the expressive formulae of religious rituals to legal contracts to scientific articles. In many everyday communicative acts as well, including greetings, directives, statements of feeling, and interpretations of norms, whether in the intimate setting of the home, business transactions, or the world of public affairs, we expect statements that are properly formulated in terms of shared language and grammar to convey our intended meanings reliably and with reasonable accuracy. Uses of language as well as the interpretative efforts of others typically entail errors in application of grammatical and semantic operations, yet are sufficiently rule-abiding that meaning can be effectively communicated.

Jean Piaget (1955, 1962, 1970; also, Lidz, 1976; Lidz and Lidz, 1976) emphasized the importance of *signification* to the human capability for sharing information among the minds of different individuals who each have their own personal histories of thought and experience. In his usage, signification is distinguished from other modes of symbolization by employing established or conventional codes of meaning. Particular expressions of ideas can thus be interpreted and understood by reference to a shared code. Language is the most widely used means of signification in all human societies, but certainly others meet Piaget's criteria of significance, for example, mathematical notation, musical notation, signing, standard and commonly understood gestures, and facial expressions. However, only so-called sign language even approximates the scope of meaningful expression and communication embodied in everyday uses of ordinary language.

In relation to Parsons's conception of generalized symbolic media, it is important to note that language stores as well as transmits thoughts and ideas. Once an idea has been fashioned in terms of the formal properties of a grammar, it becomes more durable. Even within the mind of a given individual, a linguistically formulated thought is more readily recalled in new situations and capable of being used in new sequences of action. Moreover, if communicated to other persons, the thought can then be used by them in a wider range of situations. Writing, of course, immensely expands the capacity of language to store valuable thoughts and ideas (see Parsons, 1966: chapter 4). The storing of thought no longer depends on the limited capacities of human memory, with its susceptibility to distortion. Written records can store thought and information with minimal distortion over long periods of time— lifetimes, centuries, millennia—although changes in culture may make the task of recovering the originally significant meanings a formidable task for expert scholars. Despite the complications of interpretation, however, there is little doubt that the commercial records of ancient Babylonia, the religious rituals of Pharaonic Egypt, the poetry of Homer, and the philosophies of Plato and Aristotle can be meaningfully understood today (see Voegelin, 1956–87). Indeed, ancient Greek poetry, dramas, histories, and philosophies remain important resources for contemporary Western or Western-influenced cultures more than two millenia after they were written (Dilthey, 1996; Gadamer, 1975).

Noam Chomsky's insight into the *generativity* of language has reconstructed contemporary linguistic scholarship and recast the understanding of the role of language in human thought and action. Chomsky's key idea is that the grammar of a language consists of a finite body of rules that enable speakers of the language to produce and interpret indefinite numbers of well-formed expressions. A speaker of a language can produce new sentences never spoken or written by another person before and yet expect other speakers of the language to understand the sentences accurately. Command of a language is thus not based on familiarity with a vast set of grammatically correct sentences or even structural forms of sentences. Rather, it consists of command of a set of rules, which in the sociologist's usage are specialized norms, that enable a speaker to take an elementary set of grammatical relationships and transform them through a series of recursive operations into the intended syntactical structure of a spoken or written sentence or sequence of sentences (Chomsky, 1957, 1965, 1968). Reciprocally, the hearer or reader of the sentence or passage can use the same transformational rules to reduce the sequence of expressions to the underlying elementary grammatical relationships that can be directly interpreted. In more technically detailed formulations, Chomsky and colleagues have added accounts, on the one hand, of the phonological rules for speaking and hearing the syntactical arrays of fully formed sentences and, on the other hand, though less completely, the semantic rules for capturing the intended meanings of the underlying grammatical kernels of sentences (Fodor and Katz, 1964; Katz, 1966). However, the overall emphasis of Chomsky's work has been on the universal human command of generativity, the ability formally to create and to interpret new sentences and sequences of them.

The scholarship on the universals of language has also emphasized that the grammars of all known languages parse sentences into some common categories. Although grammars of various language families differ in important ways, all languages appear to employ subjects, verbs, objects, and modifiers of subjects, verbs, and objects (Greenberg, 1963; Lidz, 1976). These categories correspond to essential terms in the framework of Cartesian logic and the adaptation of that framework that figures such as Émile Durkheim (1950, 1995), G. H. Mead (1934), and Parsons (1951; Parsons and Shils, 1951b) himself used to establish frameworks for social-psychological analysis. Parsons suggested, without ever elaborating on the point, that such terms may constitute a core of a phenomenology of social action (Parsons and Shils, 1951b). In the present context, it is important that the basic grammatical categories of all human languages reflect or, indeed, *represent* phenomenological essences of social relationships. Like all sentences, all action involves a subject of the action and a manner of being or acting, corresponding to the verb-element. Like many sentences, most action involves an object of the action and various qualities or modalities of the subject, verb, or object elements that must be considered to comprehend the significance of the action. Every social relationship, as Mead (1934) and later Parsons (1951) emphasized, involves a double relationship between two or more actors: each actor is a subject and each takes the other(s) as well as self as object(s) of action (Lidz, 1976). All parties must perceive that the other is a subject as well as object of action (see Dilthey, 1954, 1989, 1996). This perceptual operation is, at least in grammatical terms, a formal prerequisite for interpreting a sentence spoken by another in the first person.

Basic grammatical categories thus project essences of social being and relating into our elementary modes of signification. They may be said reflexively to socialize our thinking and communicating. Similarly, transformational rules at the linguistic level set forth permissible operations for varying relationships among grammatical elements. In many respects, the transformations also reflect the socialized essences of language. Transformation of a sentence from active to passive voice (or from passive to active) projects basic types of difference in being and acting into the sentence structure. The creation of syntactically complex sentences through transformational linkages among clauses, including the specification of dominant and dependent clauses, also reflects modes of action and, indeed, creation or modification of social relationships. Performative transformations through which subjects proclaim that they are definitively taking action—"I hereby leave all my possessions to . . ."; "I declare the previous orders of the court null and void . . ."; "I offer $50 per share for 1,000 shares of . . ."—all intrinsically change relationships with some set or sets of objects, including perhaps material possessions, objects to be purchased, and classes of social others, in the above examples, family members, parties to some litigation, or sellers of stock on a formal market. It is notable that grammatically, performatives are produced by transformation of simple declarative sentences, but their pragmatic significance depends on reference to particular social relationships and institutions (see Habermas, 1979: chapter 1).

LANGUAGE AND DEFINITION OF THE SITUATION

Although Chomsky has highlighted the psychological underpinnings of generativity in his bold yet empirically precise claims about the respects in which the human species is characterized by inborn abilities to learn and use language, his theory of language has equally important sociological implications. Foremost among these are two points that frame much of the present argument. First, Chomsky's demonstration of the transformational workings of the rules of grammar applies to other normative structures as well. As we will see, aspects of this point have been discussed by a number of authors, with varying degrees of acknowledgement of Chomsky as a source. Second, the coordination of a complex series of transformations in contexts of human social interaction is tied to signification. Objective markers, indicators, or signifiers of the meanings undergoing complex transformation are needed for actors to maintain common orientation to the meanings through the flux of events. Such signifiers may in some situations be implicit and understood through processes of socialization and acculturation that are broadly shared by all participants. Where important interests—emotional, material, cultural, or whatever—are affected by the ways in which normative standards are transformed in sequences of action, however, there are pragmatic advantages to the use of coded and therefore objective signifiers to clarify what is happening and the consequences. This second point will lead us back to consideration of generalized symbolic media.

A leading discussion of the sociological significance of transformations is Erving Goffman's *Frame Analysis* (1974). Goffman, using the term "keyings" instead of transformations, showed that events in many everyday social situations are understandable only as transformations of events in other settings. Court testimony is a special transformation of other forms of narrative and has a specific, if problematic and often contested, relationship to the meaningful events it recounts. Stage, movie, or television dramas about a court case further transform such narration, each in somewhat different traditions of dramatization. A news article or television news report about the court scene or the primary events recounted in the testimony are other keyings, regulated by different normative traditions than drama. Gossip, moral critique, psychotherapy, political discourse, and history writing are other forms of keying or transformation of either the original events (e.g., an accident or alleged homicide) or the court testimony or both. By detailed examination of a wide variety of keyings and their formal relationships with one another, Goffman showed that all settings in which human individuals interact are framed by sequences of underlying transformations. Moreover, the understanding of the situation, whether commonsensical by parties to the interaction, through the professional reasoning of lawyers, physicians, or engineers, or sociological through interpretation by an "objective" professional observer, requires implicit or explicit recapitulation of the underlying transformations.

In an essay on the phenomenology and sociology of law, the present author (Lidz, 1979a) argued that the law must be understood as a body of transformational rules. At many points, the law is generative in Chomsky's sense. Contract law, for example, consists at its core of a set of understandings that permit the drafting of formally new and different contracts to regulate innovative business relationships. A lawyer does not simply choose one contract from a set of legitimate contracts and apply it mechanically to the anticipated business dealings of a client. Rather, the lawyer selects and chooses from standard terms and elements, but then elaborates and transforms them into a contract that is often an authentically new entity. Yet, the lawyer must accomplish this generative work in a way that his or her client, as a party to the contract, can have confidence will prove to be enforceable in court if a dispute arises. For this reason, the lawyer relies on standard terms and is careful to follow the guidance of tried and true rules, previously enforced by courts, in generating the new design for a contractual relationship. Similar analyses can be made of the generativity involved in the legal work of drafting wills, planning the procedures to be used in complex litigation, or deciding cases and writing opinions from the bench.

Sacks, Schegloff, and others (Schegloff and Sacks, 1973; Sacks, Schegloff, and Jefferson, 1974; Schegloff, 1968, 1987) have studied the norms of turn-taking in conversation, demonstrating both the complexity of the rules observed in this everyday sort of cooperation and the close relationship between rules of grammar and rules of interpersonal etiquette. To act on a right of quick reply to the statement of another, for example, one must be able to recognize the impending end of his or her statement by noting the parts of speech that are spoken and the changes in inflection and tone that indicate an approaching end of the remark. One may then initiate one's own remarks with intonations that transform the sounds used in one's first sentences to indicate the urgency with which one wants their content to be considered. Other examples can be given, but the key point is that rules of grammar and norms of interaction are connected in our everyday relationships. Norms of interaction are another level of transformation underlying rules of grammar, and both our ability to make our conduct interpretable to others and our ability to interpret the conduct of others require that we have facility in using transformational rules at a number of levels in the organization of social action.

From the foregoing considerations we can see that the social actor, when framing a statement in a particular social situation, uses a number of levels of normative transformation. A series of transformations of normative rules is needed to define the situation or clarify, in a way that can be shared with other parties, the rule-guided significance of the action to take place. A sequence of action may involve playing a game of cards, presumably regulated by the game's rules and tactics. But is it high stakes gambling or a "friendly" game? Is it played with unknown members of the public, with friends who are also serious rivals, or with family members? Are all players formal equals or are some novices who are being taught the game while playing it? Are some players children who may be allowed flexibility in applying rules that might harm their chances of winning? Is the game also an occasion for exchange of gossip and small talk—or would such conversation be rejected as distracting? Might it be an occasion to conduct business, if, for example, the game is part of socializing with or entertaining a business partner or customer? Finally, is it actually a game or might it be a dramatization of a game on stage or television? As these questions suggest, social situations are typically complex events with multiple normatively significant dimensions. Actors must clarify the nature of the situation by signifying their understandings about what they expect to happen. Often there is explicit discussion to clarify the emerging situation, for example, stating the stakes ("A dime each point.") or clarifying the application of rules ("Jacks and deuces wild.") before starting a game of cards. Comments may be made during the course of interaction to correct another person's definition of the situation, for example, commenting that the rivalry is too serious for anyone to engage in gossip. Arguments may erupt over terms in the definition of the situation, such as, whether bets were twenty-five cents per point or per ten points. If agreement on the definition of the situation cannot be reached and maintained, disruption in the interaction is likely. Such was W. I. Thomas's (1967) point in stating that defining the situation is a preliminary phase of interaction.

In the present terminology, "definition of the situation" is a mode of signification. Definitions of the situation are produced, as indicated in the example of the card game, through a series of transformations that construct the nature of the interaction that is expected to occur. The essential normative information for defining the situation is typically abstracted from a series of conversations or linguistic exchanges (formal situations typically include written exchanges, such as contracts, as well) that take place to clarify the expected course of events. In familiar settings, some elements of a definition of the situation may be carried over from previous occasions with little or no overt discussion. In general, it is the ability to hold conversations in linguistic form or to exchange written documents that enables the participants in a situation to objectify the definition of the situation—that is, to establish it at the level of signification. Uses of language are thus fundamental conditions of the possibility of significantly defining social situations. The effort to define situations involves only a small portion of the linguistic exchanges in our lives, but for that small portion, the meaning of the speech or writing can only be understood by reference to the normative transformations involved in the effort to define the situation. The normative transformations become semantic factors underlying—and giving meaning to—the spoken or written expressions.

LANGUAGE AND OTHER GENERALIZED MEDIA

If, as Parsons suggested in the passage quoted at the beginning of this chapter, language is the common matrix of the media, it should also provide, at least in certain respects, a model for understanding other media. A key idea is that all of the other generalized symbolic media are modalities of providing functionally specialized *significance* to uses of language. The other media provide actors with ways of formally commenting on and adding significance to meanings communicated through language in particular settings. They enable actors to objectify consequences of linguistically communicated actions. Other participants in a given situation gain clarity about what has happened and can plan their own courses of action with greater certainty. At the same time, invoking the other media places a situated course of action in contexts of broader systems. When linked into more extensive systems, a planned course of action engages a range of additional factors, including the allocation of scarce resources and possible consequences of the action for distant actors and situations.

We have already seen that definitions of the situation are forms of signification conditioned by and related to social uses of language. We now add that they constitute a medium that circulates among the parties to a situation, including individuals who may not play roles in the immediate interaction, but have stakes in its outcomes. Viewed in more analytic terms, definitions of the situation circulate in the general action system and establish significant features of the expected interaction. In doing so, definitions of the situation indicate the kinds of intelligent operations of mind, affective or motivational states of personalities, and collective representations of culture that are salient to the interaction, and thus serve to integrate the general action system resources needed for the planned sequence of social action to go forward.

Consider, for example, a person who writes his will in interaction with his attorney-at-law. The definition of the situation as one of will-writing selects as salient to the interaction the attorney's professionally trained intelligence and mental judgment, affectively neutral professional motivation, and orientation to the legal culture that regulates wills, estate planning, and related matters. The client also brings to the situation intelligent memories and understanding of personal and family history, affective attachments to and motivations toward members of his or her family and perhaps other intended beneficiaries (church, college, community associations, etc.), and cultural traditions that affect his or her sense of duty in planning a personal estate. The resulting will is created through interaction to which all of these factors are inputs. Typically, the attorney will take several steps to ensure that the interaction meets formal criteria of will-writing. For example, the attorney may take specific measures to document that an elderly testator was of sound mind at the time of will-writing. If the testator intends to disinherit a "natural object of his or her affections," for example, a child, a specific statement of that intent will be included in the will. The testator's signature is witnessed, the document is dated, the attorney ensures that language in the will revokes any prior will, and the document is carefully stored, typically in the law office safe.

The definition of the situation as one of will-writing and its outcome, the will, if deemed to have been produced by a valid will-writing process, have effects outside the situation in which the will was produced. After the testator's death, the will is used as a guide, along with applicable law and custom, for administration of the estate by the executor and his or her attorney. Although heirs typically have no direct part in the situation of will-writing itself, their interests are objectively affected if a court agrees to probate the will as valid. The court acts on evidence that formal procedures of will-writing were properly observed in the production of the will, not on the substantive effects of the will for potential heirs. The law thus treats situations that have met the formal criteria for will-writing differently from all other discussions that a wealthy person may have held with family, friends, business associates, or charitable associations about his or her intentions to leave them property. The differences between will-writing and other situations become particularly evident when after the testator's death, the will regulates who inherits what property (and who receives none), while other discussions or even written instructions have no authority. The definition of a situation as having been one of will-writing then circulates through a variety of other situations involved in the administration of the estate, such as sales of real estate and personal property and transfers of stocks, bonds, and bank accounts.

Definitions of the situation control the scarce social resource of normative governance of expectations for the conduct of participants in planned interaction. The scarcity of this resource gives rise to competition among actors over opportunities to alter definitions of the situation. Particular definitions of the situation tend to be limited to stable circumstances, and they become subject to alteration whenever pragmatic conditions and/or participants in the situation change. For any given definition of the situation, there are, implicitly or explicitly, alternative definitions that might supplant them. Their control over the nature of the developing sequences of interaction may be challenged by definitions proposed by actors who believe their values, outlooks, or practical interests would be better served if the situation were defined differently.

In principle, definitions of the situation are always formulated in contrast with other possible definitions. How situations are defined, however, is not arbitrary. They are typically defined by actors who, as participants, have vested interests or stakes in the outcome of the planned interaction. The actors enter situations with established interests and expectations. As they engage one another, they start to communicate their respective expectations and try to create shared definitions of the situation. As they communicate, they rely upon means of signifying to one another their respective stakes in the expected courses of action. The social system media of money, power, influence, and commitments are exactly such means of signification. These media enable actors to use the control of resources that they have gained from other situations in the past as means of objectifying the consequences of their spoken or written contributions to defining new or altered situations. Moreover, uses of the social system media to define situations are often, perhaps generally, reflected in the language of participants.

Consider, for example, the use of power. Uses of power are typically directives from a figure of authority to a class of other actors—perhaps subordinate officials, perhaps members of the public—who are formally bound by the directives in their own future conduct. The directives are typically promulgated in terms of the common language of the community. Secret or unexpressed regulations are intrinsically unjust, and promulgation in a language unfamiliar to members of the affected community would be little different. However, uses of power are something other than the casual linguistic expressions of personal desires by figures of authority. In being officially promulgated, as in the president's signing of an Act of Congress or a judge's issuing a court order, formal properties are added to (or embedded within) the linguistic expression. Typically, there are references to the status of the promulgator, the status or statuses of persons affected by the regulation or order, and a specific performative, such as, "It is so ordered" at the end of a court decision. When used by a person with the proper authority, in an appropriate situation, and in a formally correct manner, the performative transforms the language of the regulation or directive into an actual command or binding regulation. If issued in a formally correct manner and by an authorized actor, the performative is the use of power, the act that binds other parties (see Habermas, 1979: Chapter 1 on illocutionary expressions as acts).

A similar performative or illocutionary quality characterizes uses of money as a medium. It is the signing of a contract and handing over of cash, writing a check, or authorizing charges against credit that enables the uses of language entailed in negotiating a purchase to take effect. An individual can enter an antique store and speak admiringly of a chair, table, or sideboard. Such remarks may express aesthetic appreciation of the object and even a desire to own it. However, only the tendering of money in a quantity equal to the object's price (possibly a price reached after a negotiation initiated by the expression of appreciation) is an effective offer to purchase. Actual purchase involves a transfer through money of a definite quantity of purchasing power from the buyer to the seller. A condition of the purchase is that the seller have sufficient confidence in the capacity of money to represent and store economic value or purchasing power that it is acceptable as an alternative to ownership of the good or service being sold. A long developmental history through which money gained general acceptability as a formal code to represent purchasing power stands in the background of every mundane purchase and sale in modern economies.

As a specialized code, money is akin to a specialized language constrained by its own set of grammatical rules. Parsons often emphasized in his lectures on media that writing a check is essentially sending a form letter to one's bank instructing its officers to transfer funds from one's own account to the order of the recipient of the check (or a third party to whom the recipient has endorsed the check, often the recipient's financial institution). Currency, too, is a sort of form letter or note: it has been prepared with care by the issuing agency, such as the U.S. Department of the Treasury, to certify that it represents a specific quantity of economic value and can be used for legitimate purchases at the order of the bearer. In modern economies, the issuing of currency is typically monopolized by the state to protect against debasing currency, as often occurred in the past when private banks issued currency. Circulating currency is now generally backed by the credit of national treasuries, and its issue involves acts of power. Money is a specialized economic medium, but its acceptability as a medium of exchange rests on the powers of the state.

Influence, too, consists in a specialized type of performative capacity. As we have seen, it involves an actor's capacity to invoke relationships of solidarity with other actors as means of affecting their decisions regarding present or future courses of action. The types of solidarity are numerous, and in communities with complex networks of intersecting group affiliations, their salience as sources of influence varies by the types of relationships and courses of action in question. An actor's influence with others may rest on a common *Gemeinschaft*-type solidarity, for example, shared family, kinship network, home community, ethnic group, and so on, or it may rest on status in broader *Gesellschaft*-type relationships, for example, professional expertise and reputation, public leadership, or role of spokesperson for cultural, style of life, or status groups. Typically, influence is exercised in conjunction with substantive argumentation, linguistically developed and rhetorically delivered, that is designed to affect judgments or decisions of a category of persons. The argument may concern sustaining the way of life of an ethnic or regional community, the political interests of a particular status group, or opinion on a matter of public policy, for example, gun control. Influence invokes solidary relationships with which the objects of appeal are presumed to identify. The actor exercising influence may share the invoked relationship or may simply highlight respect for a group in which membership is not claimed, perhaps reinforced by status in another group with overlapping membership or convergent interests. Candidates for public office often appeal to constituents of a different ethnicity, region of the country, or economic status by emphasizing respect for, shared loyalties with, and/or convergent interests with them. In all efforts to invoke influence, solidarity is invoked in the expectation of being able to affect the outlook and judgment of the objects of appeal. The performative act of influence occurs when an actor claims a social likeness (or solidary relation) between himself or herself as subject of action and another actor (or actors) as social object(s) to invoke ties and loyalties as a context for considering the issues under discussion.

Uses of influence create issues of legitimacy, authenticity, and trust similar to the ones created by uses of money and power. Just as money and power have undergone lengthy historical development to reach modern levels of generalization and formal codification, so the generalization and codification of legitimate influence has involved the historical processes characterized by Durkheim (1984) as the growth of organic solidarity and by Tönnies as the creation of *Gesellschaft*. Forms of solidarity that permit communities to encompass racially, ethnically, economically, and religiously diverse populations sharing impersonal loyalties have emerged only under special historical circumstances. The capacity of the sciences, professions, and occupational groups to operate with effective ties of solidarity across lines of particularistic groups has also been comparatively recent in the histories of most societies. Yet, all solidary groups—families, local communities, racial or ethnic groups, professional societies, political movements, churches, sects, or denominations, or entire societies—have their own historically evolving codes for authenticating appeals to solidarity. Actors claiming influence must be able to invoke the symbols of the solidary groups or communities in conformity with the current codes, or their claims to be similar to the objects of their appeals will be ineffective. Often the codes combine a number of formally discrete elements, for example, appeal to the shared solidarity itself, to chief periods of trial or challenge in the history of the group or community, to its current public symbols, to responsibilities it ascribes to leadership, and to duties of common members. These formal elements may be seen as analogues of the formal properties of a check or circulating currency and of duly promulgated uses of power.

THE MEDIA AND THE DIFFERENTIATION OF SOCIAL ACTION

Human social action is based to a large degree on differentiation of mechanisms of signification. In every setting of social action, with the exception of situations involving only infants or persons with profound intellectual disabilities, actors command the generative mechanisms of language (or equivalents such as sign languages) and the primary media of the general action system as means of adding specialized commentary to uses of language. All actors are capable of applying methodical thought organized by the schemas of mind to shape what is spoken or written with intelligence. They are capable in greater or lesser measure of conveying the intelligence of their conduct to others. All actors use the motivational patterns of their personalities to invest their conduct with emotional meaning and, indeed, shape their conduct in terms of its potential to provide emotional satisfaction. They also communicate the affective significance of projected courses of action to others engaged in the situation. As we have seen, all actors are invested in normative features of a social situation and often take part in processes of defining the situations in which they anticipate interacting. All actors also have connection with cultural traditions and are capable of indicating with significant collective representations the specific elements of culture that provide orientation for their anticipated endeavors. Actors who collaborate in an endeavor may exchange collective representations at many points in order to clarify shared cultural beliefs for orienting their activities.

Beyond the elementary differentiation of primary subsystems of action and their generalized symbolic media, the subsystems are themselves differentiated into further subsystems. Parsons devoted much effort over twenty-five years to clarifying the lines of differentiation among subsystems of society and their subsystems. He also outlined the primary patterns of differentiation in cultural systems, some aspects of which are discussed further in a study by the present author (Lidz, 1976). Parsons's essays on personality systems (Parsons, 1964) also address the issue of differentiation into subsystems, as do key writings of the psychoanalyst Marshall Edelson (1975), which also discuss issues of representation and signification in processes of the personality. The present author's essay on mind and circulation of intelligence within the general action system (Lidz and Lidz, 1976, with technical appendix by V. Lidz) brings elements of Piaget's research findings to bear on the problem of analyzing the differentiation of mind into subsystems. However, currently available discussions do not present persuasive arguments about more specific symbolic media associated with subsystems of culture, personality, and mind. It is possible that discussion of these subsystem media has been hindered by an expectation that the model of money should apply. Future analyses may therefore be aided by application of the language model. At present, it is only for social systems that we have a differentiated view of the media associated with the operations of subsystems, and our understanding of social system media is best developed for the cases of advanced societies and civilizations.

In comparative perspective, it is quite clear that societies vary widely in the degree to which they command differentiated generalized symbolic media. Anthropological evidence suggests that many societies have flexible means for defining social situations, but lack differentiated mechanisms for signifying control of economic resources, political power, influence, and value-commitments separately from one another. Mauss's writings on the gift relation (Mauss, 1954) as a "total social phenomenon" suggest that relations of prestation in elementary societies become enmeshed in economic, political, community, and fiduciary aspects of institutions without the possibility of selectively activating only one or more of these dimensions of social organization. Gift exchanges permit circulation of resources among units of the society (individuals, households, kin groups, villages) in a manner that may have important consequences for economic and ecological adaptation, but tie control of the resources to relations of power, influence, and commitments.

Studies (Suttles, 1960) of the potlatch institutions of the American Northwest are particularly pertinent. They have shown that exchanges of food and labor for blankets and then large numbers of blankets for ceremonial coppers gave the local groups of a regional economy considerable flexibility in adjusting to better and worse times across a range of ecological conditions. In times of plenty, local groups enjoying surpluses might present other local groups with food and/or perform labor for them. In return, the group making gifts of food and labor received blankets. The blankets represented an obligation of another group to return food and/or labor. A group holding a store of blankets had the ability to present the blankets to another group and thereby compel the other group to return food and perhaps labor. The blankets thus stored economic value and ensured that a local group could obtain means of survival in lean years. But the blankets also stored political power. They represented not only value in exchange, but also the ability to *compel* others to make return gifts.

The competition among local groups to be generous in making gifts of food and labor involved efforts to gain power over gift-recipients as well as material security. Groups that accepted food and returned blankets might be pleased to be able to eat or, in better times, to enjoy a feast, but they also knew, ambivalently, that they were vulnerable to return of the blankets and an obligation to make gifts of food and/or labor. Over time, some groups accumulated large stores of blankets and the ceremonial coppers that represented many blankets in worth. The resulting differences among local groups in wealth and power threatened the pragmatic equalities among communities on which the regional social order was traditionally based. When inequality in control of means threatened solidarity, the ritual potlatches became means of redressing the imbalance. The advantaged groups publicly threw blankets and coppers in ritual fires, thereby destroying their tokens of economic value and power, releasing others from future obligations to return food and labor. By destroying means of compelling others to make gifts of food and labor, a clan leader gained acclaim for generosity and, with it, influence in the broader community. Regional solidarity was strengthened along with a renewal of commitment to association among local groups of the region. The sacred quality of the coppers, venerated in the rituals of the potlatch, gave the entire system of exchange relations a grounding in basic value-commitments, making failure to fulfill obligations to return appropriate gifts of food and labor virtually unthinkable. In turn, the inviolability of the sacred obligations to return food or labor for blankets, and blankets for coppers, was essential to the entire system of exchange and its economic and ecological advantages.

Between the diffuse mediating mechanisms of elementary societies and their highly differentiated and functionally specific counterparts in contemporary "developed" societies, long and complicated historical processes of the symbolic generalization of media have taken place. Each of the primary media of societal subsystems has its own tortuous history of development, mixing times of fascinating innovation with other times of regression or retrenchment. In the present context, it is possible only to note some of the major changes in institutional development that have affected differentiation and generalization of the societal media.

For money, a key landmark was the creation, in the early Renaissance, of the Florentine florin with its strictly standardized metallic content (Weber, 1950). The standardized florin freed money as currency from the underlying value of precious metals to the degree that the quantity and purity of the metal did not have to be assessed as part of every exchange. At another phase of history, the monopolization of currency by states was a landmark, reducing the risk that private interests would debase its value by issuing excessive quantities of notes. Of course, states also have succumbed to the temptation to balance budgets, for example, in times of war, by running the printing presses in an inflationary manner. In American history, the democratization of banking institutions, such that individuals other than respected members of the upper class became legally eligible to establish banks and extend loans, vastly broadened the process of credit creation and access to credit by common citizens (Hacker, 1970). Modern entrepreneurship was facilitated when business people of various backgrounds outside the upper class could borrow capital to implement enterprising plans.

In Western history, the process of rendering power impersonal has been essential to the development of political institutions at a number of stages. The replacement of feudal ties based on personal relationships between lords and vassals (often in tangled hierarchies of relationships) with territorial authority of king over subjects was a key development. It rarely occurred simply. In most areas of Europe, it was embedded in other changes, was confused by ideas of the personal and divinely ordained powers of royalty, and was qualified by claims of national aristocracies to privileges. Yet, when kings came to rule as heads of objectively institutionalized states with policy developed through consultation with advisors, parliaments, and courts, the personal quality of royal powers was diminished (see Bendix, 1978; Weber, 1968). The emergence of public and private bureaucracies as means of impersonal administration furthered the objectification of power. Constitutional regulation of the powers of office, procedures for orderly replacement of officials, who could then no longer "own" their offices, and public and democratic election of chief officials further extended the objectification of impersonal power. The capacity of officials to wield power through routinely issued and observed directives grew vastly through these changes.

Influence has been generalized through a few separate but independent processes. One has been growth in the scale of community relationships. Communal feeling was in the past limited to small local communities of individuals who personally knew one another. In many contemporary societies, communal identification extends to large metropolises, ethnic groups of many millions, and entire nations of tens or hundreds of millions. Leadership forms of influence may draw upon solidarity embedded in a large number of community identities. A second process has been the impersonalization of influence, such that it attaches less to personal status than the reputations of institutions, and is exercised less through personal relationships than functionally specific social organization. A person may gain political influence by virtue of being the nominee of a major political party, professional influence by virtue of being a graduate of specific universities and training programs, or civic influence through membership in particular voluntary associations. A third process has been the differentiation of settings and associations through which influence circulates. In his time, Newton achieved influence as a natural philosopher, but today scientists typically gain influence in more narrowly defined sciences or scientific specialties. Similarly, the influence of businesspeople tends to be based in specific industries, such as automobile manufacturing, or even lines of work within them, such as automobile engineering or marketing.

The main historical watershed in the development of commitments was the formation of the world religions and their characteristic ethical outlooks (Weber, 1968). The world religions all established transcendental ethical principles for the evaluation of human life and action. These principles have provided fundamental references for individuals and collectivities as they generate their commitments. As Weber (1968) showed, commitments were vastly changed by the transcendental frameworks of belief. Tradition was no longer an unchallenged basis of commitment, and actors sought out deeper principles than attachment to traditional relationships as grounds of their commitments. Another wave of change started with the emergence of inner-worldly orientations among the transcendental religions, starting with the Protestant Reformation (Weber, 1930), but today encompassing movements in nearly all of the world religions. The inner-worldly orientations have given a new dignity to the everyday world of practical affairs, starting, as Weber argued, with economic entrepreneurship, but now extending to nearly every sphere of life. The ideological processes initiated by the Enlightenment can be interpreted as a third major phase of innovation affecting the processes of commitment (Lidz, 1979b; Durkheim, 1977; Cassirer, 1951; Gay, 1966, 1969). The Enlightenment promoted the principles of Reason and rationality as grounds of action and commitment. Rationality was established as a critical standard for evaluating all previous commitments and challenging commitments that failed to legitimate themselves in the light of Reason. Critique of salient social institutions and methodical effort to improve them became a ground of commitments in practically every sphere of social life.

Media theory can help us to understand social action in every stage from the diffuse relationships of elementary societies to the highly differentiated mechanisms of signification in "modern" and "postmodern" institutions. However, analysis must address the degree of diffuse entanglement or differentiation that exists among the media of a society at a given epoch. The feudal society of the European Middle Ages, for example, had greater differentiation among media than, for example, the nineteenth century Kwakiutl who engaged in potlatching. Yet, power relations in feudal Europe were personalized and tied to *Gemeinschaft* forms of influence and traditionalistic forms of commitment (Bloch, 1962). Monetary mediation of economic exchange was typically limited by needs to weigh and test the quality of the silver or gold, and exchange generally followed traditional and/or personal channels of trust in relationships.

THE GENERALIZED SYMBOLIC MEDIA AND THE IMPLEMENTATION OF ACTION

As we have seen, when Parsons began the task of generalizing from money as symbolic medium to a larger set of symbolic media, he quickly focused, in analyzing social processes, on double interchanges between coordinate subsystems. This approach was rooted in the importance of exchanges between households and business firms for the economic theory he followed. One of his first steps in developing the broader theory of media was to outline a "circular flow" of political life involving a double interchange between political leadership and constituencies in the integrative subsystem of society. By the time he had completed an overview of the primary societal media, he had discussed, in greater or lesser detail, six double interchanges, each involving a pair of societal subsystems (see Gould, 1976, 1987 for another critique). Later, he proposed a parallel set of six double interchanges involving pairs of the primary subsystems of action, that is, culture, social system, personality, and mind.

For all twelve interchanges, Parsons followed a model of analysis based on Keynes's treatment of circular flow between particular types of system units (e.g., business firms and households) and aggregate equilibria between large subsystems (e.g., economy and fiduciary subsystems). Although he also noted that the subsystems of society have a variety of internal processes that develop resources for the interchanges between subsystems, Parsons suggested that aggregate analyses of the six societal interchanges could provide at least an approximate analysis of a society's general equilibrium. His analysis of the general action system and its subsystems treated processes internal to subsystems and the interchanges in a conceptually parallel manner. Again, there was an implication that analysis of the general action interchanges, properly conceptualized, would permit analysis of overall equilibria (or disequilibria) of the general action system. Parsons never specified the scope of what might be involved in general action disequilibria, although some discussions in *The American University* are certainly pertinent. We may suggest that aspects of diffuse phenomena such as anomie might be analyzed as incapacities of an action system to generate definitions of the situation with sufficient clarity, specificity, and flexibility to integrate intelligent mental abilities, affective and motivational states, and salient cultural representations into coordinated processes of action (see Lidz, 1991; Baum, 1975).

Parsons consistently noted that his hypotheses concerning relationships between specific processes and abstractly defined system functions are entirely analytic in character. They do not apply to concrete action processes, but to analytically defined aspects of them. In stating this qualification, Parsons had in mind that concrete processes of action typically involve a variety of aspects with different functional alignments. To discern the complex functional organization of whole systems, it is necessary to abstract each functional dimension separately from the diffuser connections of every process of action. A shared foundation of four function analysis of subsystems, media theory, and interchange analysis is the conceptual operation of abstracting specific functionally defined aspects from diffuse processes.

An example may clarify the point. Consider a dean of a university who is deciding which of two departments will be permitted to add a faculty position in the next fiscal year. The budgetary decision is obviously economic and monetary, involving judgments about incomes and expenses of two departments. A decision to permit a new appointment becomes an expenditure of funds, typically one extending over a number of years. But the decision also involves a use of power, for it is the dean who binds the university in authorizing the hiring of an additional faculty member and in denying the application of the second department for a new position. The dean likely has to justify the decision to both departments and perhaps to other members of the university faculty and administration, perhaps a provost, president, and trustees. Such justification involves the use of influence as a spokesperson for the local academic community. Decisions and efforts to justify them in university life are often challenged by other persons of influence, for example, leaders of the department that has been denied a new position and possibly members of other departments who have been their allies in other controversies. The dean must advocate his decision in ways that do not leave him vulnerable to challenge, a matter often requiring tactful yet firm use of influence. Finally, decisions about where a university expends its resources may also involve reconsideration (or even redefinition) of the institution's basic academic commitments. Does the new position go to classics because of the university's commitment to the liberal arts? Or to engineering because of its commitment to train productive professionals for the regional economy? Or to computer science to demonstrate that the university is on the "cutting edge" of new technology? Authorizing a new appointment, combined with refusing a new appointment to another department, entails a fresh statement of the university's ongoing commitments. With these considerations, we see that an action such as a dean's creation of a new faculty position may combine specific uses of all four societal media.

Parsons's approach to working out functional connections and interchange processes requires abstracting the monetary and economic, power and political, influence and integrative, and commitments and fiduciary processes separately from the diffuse process of the dean's decision making. Each of the four sets of relationships must be abstracted from the whole individually and then aggregated with other processes similar in functional type to describe subsystems. Then the analyses of subsystems can be aggregated to create an analysis of a system, in this case the university as system. This approach makes it possible to trace out different systemic pressures on decision making, whether on the dean's choices about a new appointment, on subsequent work of department chairs, or on student plans to study in one field or another.

However, Parsons's approach does not address a different problem: how particular processes of action, drawing on analytically diverse elements, are composed or made coherent. With respect to the dean's decision as process, how does he or she bring economic, political, integrative, and fiduciary elements together into an integrated course of action? It is this problem that the language model of generalized symbolic media helps us to address. The language model highlights the multiple transformations that a process of action, starting with an initial purpose or plan, goes through as uses of the various generalized media add adjustment to a series of other factors. When an action is expressed in a setting of interaction, typically in speech or writing, it can be richly understood only by interpreting a series of transformations that have entered into its composition. The linguistic transformations occur at the surface of a series of transformations brought about by other media. Interpretation of the linguistic form of the expression typically enables other actors to apprehend the underlying transformations introduced by other symbolic media.

Processes of action thus have structures similar in form to an inverted tree. Uses of language, hence the medium of linguistic representation, occur at the surface or primary level of social interaction. At a second level, the media of the four primary subsystems of action are engaged, that is, intelligence, affect, definition of the situation, and collective representations. At a third level, the sixteen secondary subsystems of action are engaged, that is, the four subsystems of each of the four primary systems of action. In the social system, this level of process involves money, power, influence, and commitments. At a fourth level down, differentiated structures within each of the sixteen secondary systems are involved. In societies with highly differentiated institutional structures, and with compatibly developed cultural, personal, and mental resources, the sources of particular actions may be located even further down in the inverted tree structure.

The present use of media theory to outline the transformational composition of social action is as thoroughly analytic as the interchange model, but governed by a different set of abstractions. In the interchange model of the media, the controlling abstractions follow from the definition of subsystems as presented in the four function paradigm. In our model, the controlling abstraction, derived largely from linguistic theory, is a conception of the multidimensional composition and multistaged transformation of processes of action. The four-function paradigm and media theory are used to map out the principal dimensions of the composition of an action process. The transformational-generative complexity (or depth) of any given action process must be determined pragmatically. Some processes of action require longer sequences of transformations to attain coherent resolutions than others. Interpreters implicitly trace back longer sequences of transformations to understand and find meaning in some sequences of action than in others. Moreover, as we have suggested, there is cultural and historical relativity to the depth and complexity of the transformation. Some societies have more highly differentiated mechanisms of signification and mediation than others. Where the generalized symbolic media are more highly developed, actors command greater resources for elaborating the transformational processes.

The transformational perspective emphasizes signification and reduction in ambiguity concerning the practical consequences of action. Each medium that becomes engaged in the transformation of a process of action serves to signify intentions and reduce ambiguity regarding consequences with regard to a specific domain of action. Language is the primordial matrix of signification for meaningful human action and the broadest mechanism of significant expression. It serves as the medium through which practically any intention and any anticipated set of consequences can be expressed significantly. For this reason, we treat it as the central generalized symbolic medium and the one that transforms the outputs of other media into coherent expression. Other media are then treated as mechanisms that have gradually differentiated from one another in the course of human history as mechanisms for establishing specialized significant or objective meanings before linguistic transformation of the planned action into specific expression.

We can readily see this relationship of other media to language for the cases of the social system media. An offer of money transforms a wish to obtain a desirable good or service to an effective demand for it. The offer of money is typically accompanied, as we have seen, by particular uses of language to express and/or clarify the particular purpose of the offer. Yet, in a purchase, money itself must be offered in addition to the related linguistic expressions. Similarly, a use of power transforms a statement addressed to a class of others into a directive or command. We have seen that the issuing of directives is typically perceptible in the accompanying language, especially in the use of performatives. However, again, power is expended in parallel to the use of language: other persons might use the language with which General Eisenhower ordered the start of the D-Day invasion of Normandy, but do not have his power to start the invasion. At the general action level, intelligence characterizes an idea for solving a problem as one supported by methodical and capable thinking. Intelligent action has its characteristic linguistic signs that others can interpret, but the allocation of intelligence to solving a problem or communicating a solution to another person is separate from the use of intelligent language itself. Affect indicates the motivational meaning of social objects and courses of action for the individual or individuals involved. We are accustomed to interpreting the affect with which a person engages in a course of action through close attention to his or her expressions. Yet, the emotional state that a person invests in a course of action is independent of the expression itself. In these ways, we can see the close relationship between uses of generalized symbolic media and the multistaged transformation of linguistic expressions for a course of action. The actual linguistic expressions enable us to interpret how various media have entered into the shaping of the course of action. But the actual invoking and use of the media cannot be reduced simply to linguistic expression. The other media are independent ways of giving specialized significance to uses of language.

In Parsons's treatment of interchanges, the relationship between the social system and general action sets of interchanges was not closely specified. Parsons never presented an unambiguous model for linking the two levels of process, although he suggested that the general action system involves a wider range of variables and, in some way, it should be possible to entail the societal interchanges within the social system operations of the general action system. However, the present author has also noted that the general action system appears as the "particular action system"—that is, the general action variables enter action when, in social system terms, particular situated sequences are being formed (Lidz, 1976, 1981, 1991). The general action media circulate into and across the myriads of particular sequences of action that make up the everyday experiences of the members of society. Although there are aggregate flows of general action media, aggregate limits to their availability as resources, and aggregate equilibria, the general action media become observable only as they enter particular sequences of situated action.

With this background, we can discuss one form of linkage between the social system and general action media. The social system media—money, power, influence, and commitments—are modalities of significantly constraining definitions of the situation at the general action system. The significant acts of spending money to make a purchase, issuing directives with power, exerting influence over others, or making commitments to others establish parameters of "what is happening here" that constrain the process of defining the situation at the next level of transformation closer to the "surface" of action. In cybernetic terms, significant acts taken with the societal media control the processes of defining situations. As we have seen in our example of a faculty dean, it is often the case that, in creating concrete courses of action, actors need to invoke more than one of the societal media. Each use of a societal medium then sets up additional requirements that must be resolved at the level of definition of the situation. The process of defining situations therefore addresses the particular combinations of needs created by the uses of various societal media in the given setting. Definition of the situation also serves to establish immediate normative terms for reconciling uses of the societal media with the engagement of intelligent, emotional-affectual, and cultural resources available for synthesis into the concrete sequence of action.

This abstract discussion can perhaps be clarified by returning to the example of the university dean. As we saw, the dean's decision to authorize a new faculty position for one department while refusing a position for another department is a complex matter involving uses of all of the societal media. As the dean proceeds to act, he or she invokes terms from the university's normative order, including academic traditions, its own policies and procedures, specific precedents, and the status of his or her own office, to establish a definition of the situation that opens up opportunities for his efficacious use of each of the media. Other members of the university, faculty members, students, board members, and so on, may challenge this definition of the situation with alternatives designed to open up opportunities for their uses of influence or restating of university commitments. If disagreements persist, action may in effect be halted in the preliminary phase of definition of the situation for some period of time as the university community strives to clarify how the situation should be defined. When a viable definition of the situation emerges, it serves to integrate into the process of action (i.e., the dean's decision and its reception by others) significant resources supplied by the media of the other general action subsystems. Collective representations of the university's particular academic traditions and their background in the broader culture provide legitimacy for the dean's decision and/or challenges to it. Whether the local version of academic culture gives priority to practical technology or humanistic scholarship may be, for example, an important factor in shaping the institution's academic appointments. The dean's (and others') affective relations to particular fields of study, departments, department chairs, the scholarship of prospective faculty members, the prestige that a particular new appointment may bring to the university, and so forth may also shape the decision and its reception. So, too, may the intelligence that the dean brings to planning a way through the dilemmas of allocating scarce resources among university programs. Perhaps the dean discerns that one of the two departments can be offered some other resource, for example, authorization to start a new degree program, to assuage its disappointment at not receiving a new position. As the general action resources are integrated into the process of action, it moves to its "surface" for expression through uses of language, surely in this case amply fortified by rhetoric.

To sum up, the present perspective on processes of action emphasizes the differentiated capacities for signification represented by each of the generalized symbolic media, the complex transformational processes in the genesis of action, the inverted treelike structure of action in which cybernetic control is exercised at a point of origin at the lower levels of action, and the multidimensional composition of action related to its functional organization. It becomes clear in considering these several characteristics that processes of action ("unit acts" in the terminology of *The Structure of Social Action*) proximal to one another in time, place, and significance may also be intricately connected in the elements through which they are generated. Where one draws lines to distinguish one act from another follows from analytic purpose, not compositions intrinsic to the acts. When the dean plans his or her decision in anticipation of certain reactions, and accordingly strives to define the situation with normative terms designed to place critical responses at a disadvantage, what are the boundaries of the action? Is the dean's act separate from or part of the university's overall deliberations or even the angry responses of critics, whose overt conduct is oriented to many of the same underlying factors as the dean's?

CONCLUSION

The present argument has arisen from an effort to respond to long-standing criticisms of Parsons's conception of the media. I have suggested that Parsons's emphasis on money as a model for understanding the entire "family" of media resulted in a reductive understanding of the media. In this understanding, the reality of the other media tends to be reduced because they do not have the same concrete qualities or provide the same forms of measuring value that are readily found in money. By emphasizing language-related characteristics of media, however, we have found another way of pointing to realities embodied in other generalized symbolic media. In turn, this approach emphasizes other qualities of the media: signification, transformation, generativity, and hierarchical relationships. At the same time, it suggests the importance of examining the complex composition of particular sequences of action, a perspective with a different analytical status than Parsons's emphasis on double interchanges. The present perspective on the role of generalized symbolic media in the composition of concrete processes of social action is independent of and orthogonal to Parsons's own focus on double interchanges between adjacent subsystems of action. In the "compositional" perspective, analysis focuses on the simultaneous use of multiple media, on relations between media at different levels of analysis, and perhaps on tactical planning in the use of media. In the "interchange" perspective, analysis focuses on aggregation of uses of media and eventually on system equilibria. The two perspectives are basically complementary elements of a larger theory and seem not to contradict each other. Integrating the two perspectives should improve our understanding of the generalized symbolic media and, more broadly, of processes of social action. Further clarification of the relationships between the two perspectives may be the next step in study of the generalized symbolic media.

NOTE

1. Talcott Parsons, "Introduction" to Part Four, "Culture and the Social System," in Parsons, Shils, Naegele, and Pitts (1961: 971).

REFERENCES

Alexander, J. C. 1983. *Theoretical Logic in Sociology*, Vol. 4: *The Modern Reconstruction of Classical Thought: Talcott Parsons*. Berkeley: University of California Press.

Baum, R. C. 1975. "The System of Solidarities: A Working Paper in General Action Analysis." *Indian Journal of Social Research* 16: (1–2): 306–53.

———. 1976. "Communication and Media." Pp. 533–56 in *Explorations in General Theory in Social Science*, Vol. 2, edited by J. J. Loubser, R. C. Baum, A. Effrat, and V. Lidz. New York: Free Press.

Bendix, R. 1978. *Kings or People*. Berkeley: University of California Press.

Bloch, M. 1962. *Feudal Society*. Chicago: University of Chicago Press.

Cartwright, B. C., and R. S. Warner. 1976. "The Medium Is Not the Message." Pp. 639–60 in *Explorations in General Theory in Social Science*, Vol. 2, edited by J. J. Loubser, R. C. Baum, A. Effrat, and V. Lidz. New York: Free Press.

Cassirer, E. 1951. *The Philosophy of the Enlightenment*. Princeton, N.J.: Princeton University Press. First published in German, 1932.

Chomsky, N. 1957. *Syntactic Structures*. The Hague: Mouton.

———. 1965. *Aspects of the Theory of Syntax*. Cambridge: MIT Press.

———. 1966. *Cartesian Linguistics: A Chapter in the History of Rationalist Thought*. New York: Harper and Row.

———. 1968. *Language and Mind*. New York: Harcourt Brace Jovanovich.

———. 1980. *Rules and Representations*. New York: Columbia University Press.

Dilthey, W. 1954. *The Essence of Philosophy*. Chapel Hill: University of North Carolina Press. First published in German in 1904.

————. 1989. *Selected Works*, Vol. 1: *Introduction to the Human Sciences*, edited by R. A. Makkreel and F. Rodi. Princeton, N.J.: Princeton University Press. First published in German as *Einleitung in die Geisteswissenschaften* in 1883.

————. 1996. *Selected Works*, Vol. 4: *Hermeneutics and the Study of History*, edited by R. A. Makkreel and F. Rodi. Princeton, N.J.: Princeton University Press.

Durkheim, É. 1950. *The Rules of Sociological Method*. New York: Free Press.

————. 1977. *The Evolution of Educational Thought: Lectures on the Formation and Development of Secondary Education in France*. London: Routledge and Kegan Paul. First published in French in 1938.

————. [1933] 1984. *The Division of Labor in Society*. New York: Free Press. First published in French in 1893.

————. [1915] 1995. *The Elementary Forms of Religious Life*. New York: Free Press. First published in French in 1912.

Easton, D. 1953. *The Political System: An Inquiry into the State of Political Science*. New York: Knopf.

————. 1965. *A Systems Analysis of Political Life*. New York: Wiley.

Edelson, M. 1975. *Language and Interpretation in Psychoanalysis*. New Haven, Conn.: Yale University Press.

Fodor, J. A., and J. J. Katz. 1964. *The Structure of Language: Readings in the Philosophy of Language*. Englewood Cliffs, N.J.: Prentice-Hall.

Gadamer, H.-G. 1975. *Truth and Method*. New York: Continuum. First published in German in 1960.

Gay, P. 1966. *The Enlightenment: An Interpretation*, Vol. 1: *The Rise of Modern Paganism*. New York: Vintage.

————. 1969. *The Enlightenment: An Interpretation*, Vol. 2: *The Science of Freedom*. New York: Norton.

Goffman, E. 1974. *Frame Analysis: An Essay on the Organization of Experience*. New York: Harper and Row.

Gould, M. 1976. "Systems Analysis, Macrosociology, and the Generalized Media of Social Action." Pp. 470–506 in *Explorations in General Theory in Social Science*, Vol. 2, edited by J. J. Loubser, R. C. Baum, A. Effrat, and V. Lidz. New York: Free Press.

————. 1987. *Revolution in the Development of Capitalism: The Coming of the English Revolution*. Berkeley: University of California Press.

Greenberg, J. H. 1963. *Universals of Language*. Cambridge: MIT Press.

Habermas, J. 1979. *Communication and the Evolution of Society*. Boston: Beacon Press.

————. 1987. *The Theory of Communicative Action*, Vol. 2: *Lifeworld and System: A Critique of Functionalist Reason*. Boston: Beacon Press. First published in German in 1981.

Hacker, L. M. 1970. *The Course of American Economic Growth and Development*. New York: Wiley.

Katz, J. J. 1966. *The Philosophy of Language*. New York: Harper and Row.

Keynes, J. M. 1936. *The General Theory of Employment, Interest, and Money*. London: Macmillan.

Knight, F. 1965. *The Economic Organization*. New York: Harper and Row.

Lidz, V. 1976. "Introduction to Part II: General Action Analysis." Pp. 124–50 in *Explorations in General Theory in Social Science*, Vol. 1, edited by J. J. Loubser, R. C. Baum, A. Effrat, and V. Lidz. New York: Free Press.

————. 1979a. "The Law as Index, Phenomenon, and Element—Conceptual Steps Toward a General Sociology of Law." *Sociological Inquiry* 49 (1): 5–25.

———. 1979b. "Secularization, Ethical Life, and Religion in Modern Societies." Pp. 191–217 in *Religious Change and Continuity*, edited by H. M. Johnson. San Francisco, Calif.: Jossey-Bass.

———. 1981. "Transformational Theory and the Internal Environment of Action Systems." Pp. 205–33 in *Advances in Social Theory and Methodology: Toward an Integration of Micro- and Macro-Sociologies*, edited by K. Knorr-Cetina and A. V. Cicourel. Boston: Routledge and Kegan Paul.

———. 1982. "Religion and Cybernetic Concepts in the Theory of Action." *Sociological Analysis* 43 (4): 287–305.

———. 1989. "Founding Fathers and Party Leaders: America's Transition to the Democratic Social Condition." Pp. 231–75 in *Social Class and Democratic Leadership: Essays in Honor of E. Digby Baltzell*, edited by H. J. Bershady. Philadelphia: University of Pennsylvania Press.

———. 1991. "Influence and Solidarity: Defining a Conceptual Core for Sociology." Pp. 108–36 in *Talcott Parsons: Sociologist of Modernity*, edited by B. S. Turner and R. Robertson. London: Sage.

Lidz, C. W., and V. Lidz. 1976. "Piaget's Psychology of Intelligence and the Theory of Action." Pp. 195–239 in *Explorations in General Theory in Social Science*, Vol. 1, edited by J. J. Loubser, R. C. Baum, A. Effrat, and V. Lidz. New York: Free Press.

Marshall, A. 1925. *The Principles of Economics*. London: Macmillan.

Marx, K. 1973. *Grundrisse: Introduction to the Critique of Political Economy*, trans. with a foreword by M. Nicolaus. New York: Vintage Books. Translation of manuscripts written in German in 1857–58.

———. 1976. *Capital*, Vol. 1, introduced by E. Mandel, trans. B. Fowkes. New York: Penguin Books. First published in German in 1867.

Mauss, M. 1954. *The Gift: Forms and Functions of Exchange in Archaic Societies*. London: Cohen and West.

Mead, G. H. 1934. *Mind, Self and Society*. Chicago: University of Chicago Press.

Parsons, T. 1937. *The Structure of Social Action*. New York: McGraw-Hill.

———. 1951. *The Social System*. New York: Free Press.

———. 1954. *Essays in Sociological Theory*, rev. ed. New York: Free Press.

———. 1960. *Structure and Process in Modern Societies*. New York: Free Press.

———. 1961a. "General Introduction." In *Theories of Society: Foundations of Modern Sociological Theory*, Vols. 1 and 2, edited by T. Parsons, E. A. Shils, K. D. Naegele, and J. R. Pitts. New York: Free Press.

———. 1961b. "An Outline of the Social System." Pp. 30–79 in *Theories of Society: Foundations of Modern Sociological Theory*, Vols. 1 and 2, edited by T. Parsons, E. A. Shils, K. D. Naegele, and J. R. Pitts. New York: Free Press.

———. 1964. *Social Structure and Personality*. New York: Free Press.

———. 1966. *Societies: Evolutionary and Comparative Perspectives*. Englewood Cliffs, N.J.: Prentice-Hall.

———. 1969. *Politics and Social Structure*. New York: Free Press.

———. 1971. *The System of Modern Societies*. Englewood Cliffs, N.J.: Prentice Hall.

———. 1977. *Social Systems and the Evolution of Action Theory*. New York: Free Press.

———. 1986. "The Integration of Economic and Sociological Theory: The Marshall Lectures, University of Cambridge, 1953." Research Reports From the Department of Sociology, Uppsala University, Vol. 1866: 4. Introduction by R. Swedberg.

Parsons, T., R. F. Bales, and E. A. Shils. 1953. *Working Papers in the Theory of Action*. New York: Free Press.

Parsons, T., and G. M. Platt. 1973. *The American University*. Cambridge: Harvard University Press.

Parsons, T., and E. A. Shils, eds. 1951a. *Toward a General Theory of Action.* Cambridge, Mass.: Harvard University Press.

Parsons, T., and E. A. Shils. 1951b. "Values, Motives, and the Theory of Action." Pp. 47–275 in *Toward A General Theory of Action,* edited by T. Parsons and E. A. Shils. Cambridge, Mass.: Harvard University Press.

Parsons, T., E. A. Shils, K. D. Naegele, and J. R. Pitts, eds. 1961. *Theories of Society: Foundations of Modern Sociological Theory,* Vols. 1 and 2. New York: Free Press.

Parsons, T., and N. J. Smelser. 1956. *Economy and Society.* New York: Free Press.

Piaget, J. 1955. *The Language and Thought of the Child.* Cleveland, Ohio: Meridian Books.

———. 1962. *Play, Dreams and Imitation in Childhood.* New York: Norton.

———. 1970. *Genetic Epistemology.* New York: Columbia University Press.

Sacks, H., E. Schegloff, and G. Jefferson. 1974. "A Simplest Systematics for the Analysis of Turn-Taking in Conversations." *Language* (50): 696–735.

Samuelson, P. A. [1948] 1973. *Economics,* 9th ed. New York: McGraw-Hill.

Schegloff, E. A. 1968. "Sequencing in Conversational Openings." *American Anthropologist* 70: 1075–95.

———. 1987. "Between Macro and Micro: Contexts and Other Connections." Pp. 207–34 in *The Micro-Macro Link,* edited by J. Alexander, B. Giesen, R. Münch, and N. J. Smelser. Berkeley: University of California Press.

Schegloff, E. A., and H. Sacks. 1973. "Opening Up Closings." *Semiotica* 7: 289–327.

Smith, A. [1776] 1937. *The Wealth of Nations.* New York: Modern Library.

Suttles, W. 1960. "Affinal Ties, Subsistence, and Prestige among the Coast Salish." *American Anthropologist:* 296–305.

Thomas, W. I. [1923] 1967. *The Unadjusted Girl.* New York: Harper and Row.

Voegelin, E. 1956–87. *Order and History,* Vol. 1: *Israel and Revelation* (1956); Vol. 2: *The World of the Polis* (1957); Vol. 3: *Plato and Aristotle* (1957); Vol. 4: *The Ecumenic Age* (1974); Vol. 5: *In Search of Order* (1987). Baton Rouge: University of Louisiana Press.

Weber, M. 1930. *The Protestant Ethic and the Spirit of Capitalism,* trans. T. Parsons. New York: Charles Scribner's Sons. Originally published in German in 1903–4.

———. [1927] 1950. *General Economic History,* trans. F. H. Knight. New York: Free Press. First published in German as *Wirtschaftsgeshichte* in 1923.

———. 1968. *Economy and Society,* 3 vols., edited by G. Roth and C. Wittich. New York: Bedminster Press. First published in German in 1925 as *Wirtschaft und Gesellschaft,* edited by M. Weber.

9

Parsons's Analysis of the Societal Community

Uta Gerhardt

Parsons came to world fame in the 1950s when his *The Social System,* which was a seminal achievement despite the fact that the book reviews castigated its style and abstractness, was a milestone of post-World War II sociology.[1] Subsequently in the 1950s, Parsons's systems theory became an icon of systematic thinking. At the end of the decade, however, this same theory began to be turned into a bête noir of sociological thought through ambitious critics such as Ralf Dahrendorf (1958) and C. Wright Mills (1959). They rejected "grand theory" and charged Parsons with propagating the wrong kind of utopianism which, to them, signified complicity with nondemocratic forces in society. In contradistinction, they meant to promote humanism when they pleaded for political partisanship of sociology in the name of either laissez-faire liberalism or socialism.

In an atmosphere of anti-Parsonianism growing during the 1960s, Parsons's revision of his systems theory went nearly unnoticed. When he recapitulated, in 1976, in his "Afterword" to the reissue of Max Black's collection entitled *The Social Theories of Talcott Parsons,* that his original "The Point of View of the Author" had been written in the early 1960s at a time when "a major line of development was barely beginning," he announced to his readers that "a major development of the theory" had taken place since (Parsons, 1976: 367). As it happened, however, this major development, his theory of societal community, became less well known than his earlier attempts at understanding modern society. Whereas *The Social System* was still acknowledged as a classic throughout the 1960s before it was attacked in Alvin Gouldner's anti-Harvard polemic *The Coming Crisis of Western Sociology* (1970), Parsons's theory as rewritten in the 1960s failed to gain the fame of his earlier work. Indeed, his reformulation of his systems theory on the basis of cybernetics, finding a first culmination in his *Politics and Social Structure* (1969a), was often not even recognized, let alone adopted, by the devoted, if dwindling, group of Parsonians in the 1970s and after Parsons's death.

Ironically, among the many scholarly accounts which have stated and restated Parsons's intellectual biography and achievements in the last decade and a half, surprisingly few have appreciated the novelty and salience of his theory of societal community. The very first attempt at reappraisal other than critical reconstruction, Robert Holton and Bryan S. Turner's *Talcott Parsons on Economy and Society* (1986), interestingly, came nearer appreciation than many other later accounts although they did not apprehend the whole story of Parsons's achievement of the 1960s. Holton and Turner realized that Parsons had new things to say on the integration of Blacks in American society, although they overlooked the serendipity of his theory of citizenship. They rightly credited Parsons with transcending both utopian optimism centering on the nineteenth-century ideal of *Gemeinschaft* and cultural pessimism centering on twentieth-century skepticism against presumably individualistic *Gesellschaft* (Holton and Turner, 1986: 232), but failed to comment on the fact that Parsons had welded together the twin concepts of *Gemeinschaft* and *Gesellschaft* into one groundbreakingly innovative notion—namely, societal community. Prior to Holton and Turner, an earlier reconstructive work originally published in Parsons's lifetime, Francois Bourricaud's *The Sociology of Talcott Parsons*, which first appeared in French in 1977, had acknowledged Parsons's use of cybernetics in the works of his later life and understood the importance of the analysis of interaction media and polity, but failed to recognize the serendipity of Parsons's findings about societal community. In recent years, two authors have recognized that societal community became a central concept for Parsons in his later life. One is Jeffrey Alexander (1998) in his reformulation of the notion of civil society in the terms of so-called Neo-Functionalism, and the other is Richard Münch (1999) who analyzes the problem of order in present-day, globalized society, in his contribution to the volume edited by Bernard Barber and myself, celebrating the achievement of *The Structure of Social Action*.

In this chapter I wish to delineate Parsons's theory of societal community and prove its viability by applying it to the themes of globalization and civil society as they were analyzed in the 1990s—with an eye on the future. First, in a short work biography (Part I) I recapitulate how Parsons's revised theory of social systems evolved mainly during the 1960s. Subsequently, his theory of societal community is reconstructed in two parts. Part II deals with interaction media as they are the substrate of social differentiation in developed industrial societies. Part III deals with moral consensus and security in the social order as foci of the concept of societal community as it evolved until around 1970. Part IV, finally, takes up the topics of globalization and civil society showing that these two themes in the sociology of the post–Cold War world may be welded together using Parsons's conception of societal community.

Only today, in the "One World" of globalized aspirations toward ubiquitous democratic systems, does Parsons's notion of societal community reveal its true value. During Parsons's lifetime, some seemingly unnecessarily complicated tenets in his conceptualization of societal community might have appeared overly "academic." Today, however, Parsons's analysis of societal community provides an answer to the question of integration in pluralist, multicultural society, an answer involving theory that fits the contemporary world. To be sure, social integration is an issue whose urgency has newly arisen in Europe that aims to unify sixteen nations, and worldwide in the wake of peace missions of the United Nations, developmental policies of the I.M.F. or World Bank, and similar contemporary endeavors. It is obvious that the dramatic changes spurred between 1989 and 1991 have created a world situation requiring new theoretical answers in sociology. In this situation, Parsons's theory of societal community is a step in the right direction. The theory focuses on pluralist multiplicity, integrated through societal community. This long underestimated theory fits the triad of capitalism, political freedom, and ethnic identity that is the hallmark of today's transitions in world society.

A SHORT HISTORY OF PARSONS'S "LATE" THEORY OF SOCIETY

In 1959, at the General Assembly of the United Nations, Soviet General Secretary of the Communist Party and Prime Minister, Nikita Krushtshev, staged an éclat. He demanded that the Western Allies abandon Berlin to exclusively Soviet-Russian control, causing a crisis that led to the construction of the Berlin Wall starting on August 13, 1961, and eventually the Cuban missile showdown mastered by the Kennedy Administration in October, 1962 (Snell, 1959; Speier, 1960; Kennedy, 1969). Against the background of this world situation, Parsons (1959b, 1961a, 1961b, 1962a) turned to the topics of community as well as polarization between the Western hemisphere and the Eastern bloc along the axis of the capitalism-communism divide. In a parallel endeavor, in the beginning of the 1960s, he investigated social change in the terms of modernization, analyzing progress as the fusion or fission of systems producing ever-increasing differentiation in industrial societies. His first venture into the latter topic was an article analyzing how the rural world of the family farm had been drawn into the urbanized arena of industrial production, leaving a "residual" family with apparent loss of function vis-à-vis an apparently dominant economic-occupational sector of employment (Parsons, 1961c). At that point, therefore, the agenda was set by Parsons discussing two preliminary topics anticipating his conception of societal community, namely community and social differentiation.

A breakthrough was his contribution to the annual conference of the American Philosophical Society in 1962. When he explored the notion of power, he made a serendipitous discovery.[2] He realized that power, in terms of social theory including political science, was not a "zero-sum" phenomenon where one agent was being given what had been taken from another. Power was a resource for effectiveness, in principle limitless, which could extend to every single member of an entire community (Parsons, 1963b). Two insights preceded or accompanied this finding. One was that the concept of influence had to be understood as distinct from that of power, and the other that the concept of force should be clearly distinguished from, although in the last resort was related to, that of power (Parsons, 1963a, 1964a). In this vein the dynamics of interaction through exchange using symbolic media such as money, power, and influence became visible.

These clarifications facilitated a first formulation of the problem of the evolution and nature of societies in general. At the request of Alex Inkeles, series editor of *Foundations of Modern Sociology* and longtime colleague and collaborator, Parsons wrote the slim volume *Societies: Evolutionary and Comparative Perspectives* (1966a). In the second chapter, the core of the book, he used the notion of societal community for the first time. He ventured what were the integrative forces that held a society together to the effect that social relations would not disintegrate in the face of institutional differentiation in the course of the history of modernization. His answer contained the concept of societal community, explained tentatively as that forum for moral commitment which rendered more or less diverse populations identifiable members united in their identification with their cultural and/or national common heritage.

To arrive at this, two lines of thought appear to have inspired Parsons. One was that, first in 1958, on the occasion of the one-hundredth anniversary of the birth of Émile Durkheim (Parsons, 1959a), and again when he contributed to the new edition of the *International Encyclopedia of the Social Sciences*, Parsons reread Durkheim and rediscovered the latter's concern for integration as opposed to anomie.[3] When he recapitulated his personal history of the discovery of systems theory, toward the end of the 1960s, he accounted to this rereading of Durkheim his renewed awareness of the importance of forces of integration as it had become an incentive to conceptualize societal community (Parsons, 1970a).

The other trigger was more political. In 1964, just as the first Civil Rights Act passed Congress, Parsons, together with Kenneth Clarke, who was African American, organized a conference at the American Academy of Arts and Sciences on Race and Poverty in the United States. To be sure, the topic of poverty had concerned the American public in the wake of Michael Harrington's bestselling book, *The Other America*, published in 1962, ushering in the Vietnam War corollary in domestic activism, the War on Poverty. The topic of race had occupied the American public since the 1950s when the Supreme Court had ordered desegregation of schools and Martin Luther King Jr. had initiated a campaign of nonviolent defiance against discrimination of Blacks who, among other things, demanded their constitutional voting rights, culminating in the famous "I have a dream" speech in August 1963, in Washington, D.C. As it happened, from the late 1950s on, violent clashes between white supremacists and Black peace marchers in the Southern states were being publicized to a nationwide television audience, many of whom were shocked by police violence against unarmed protesters. Only in 1962, for the first time, were legitimate demonstrators, who in the event supported entry into a university of a Black student, protected against local whites by the National Guard (such protection being fully granted only two years subsequent to President Kennedy's assassination). Parsons, in this situation, wrote "Full Citizenship for the Negro American?," an investigation into the conditions of equality as a prerequisite for democracy. He used T. H. Marshall's triple conception of citizenship to postulate full participation of Blacks in American society, presupposing not negation but ascertainment of race as a differentiating but not discriminatory quality of U.S. citizenship. This thought, which Parsons explored in a number of unpublished papers as well,[4] became one of the stepping-stones for his conceptualization, in *Societies* (1966a), of societal community as a pivotal perspective for sociological analysis.

As this occupied him, Parsons also realized that his understanding of symbolization processes in interaction was still incomplete. Power and influence, he had come to understand, were linked to the system functions of goal attainment (ensuring effectiveness of endeavors in a group or society) and integration (securing social order, presupposing voluntary commitment in the community); a third medium, money, symbolized adaptation (through economic production as well as, more generally, monetary means utilization). The idea was that exchange media distinct from but functionally similar to money were resources traded in social interaction. A fourth "symbolic medium" of interactive reciprocity, however, Parsons felt in 1968, needed attention urgently. When the system of university goals and governance came apart in the "hot summer" of 1968, producing deliberate disavowal of values indispensable for the democratic social fabric, he undertook to analyze value-commitments. His idea was that commitment to the values of civilized community could decrease to a point where anomie prevailed, and that, in situations of this type, even dictatorship could grasp the imagination of a population who might then vote for a leader misusing their trust.

Subsequently, from this vantage point, having dealt with a range of four symbolic exchange media (only money, he admitted, had not been the focus of a separate analytical essay of his but, of course, had been at the center of the function schema in *Economy and Society* coauthored with Neil Smelser in 1956), Parsons revisited the notion of societal community in the introductory chapter of *The System of Modern Societies*, published in 1971 (the book's second chapter was prepublished as Parsons, 1969b). He made an attempt to reconcile the thought of social integration with that of action space and civil liberties for the actor in democratic societies, in his collection of essays published in 1969, *Politics and Social Structure* (Parsons, 1969a). Mainly using contributions of his systems theory already published earlier in the 1960s, partly supplementing them with postscripts and additional footnotes and crowning them with a new concluding chapter on the polity, he drew together theoretical and empirical texts, ranging from the two introductory plus the concluding chapters conceptualizing societal community to analyses of contemporary society explaining, among other issues, McCarthyism or the prospects of reconciling polarization in the international order.

Politics and Social Structure is important for two reasons. For one, it documented the range of theory of politics and social structure which Parsons had developed between the early 1940s and late 1960s, thus ostentatiously spanning the topics of German fascism and American democracy. Furthermore, the book went beyond the twenty-year achievement in Parsons's systems theory, which had reached from *The Structure of Social Action* (1937) to *The Social System* (1951) and beyond, drawing new conclusions from his reconceptualizing the nature of power beyond the "zero-sum" formula. Starting with some of his essays on National Socialism, which he had published between 1942 and 1945, proceeding to the topic of democratic society and politics, which he had tackled throughout the 1950s and 1960s, he added four pieces dealing with his immediate present and what was the then expectable future. For the future beyond the 1960s, he focused on the analytical perspective of interaction media in their relationship with the societal community, supplemented by what he addressed as polity.

In the same year, besides reviewing his intellectual biography to take stock of when and in which context his theoretical insights had originated and where they had led to, he also undertook to revisit a problem that had occupied him since at least 1940. In a major manuscript published in 1970, he analyzed social stratification as related to equality as much as inequality. His idea was to apply the new concept of societal community to the age-old problem of social class and division of labor, attempting to put to rest the specter of a deficit of social equality in the world of today that had haunted sociological theory ever since Karl Marx and Durkheim had aimed to remedy classical political economy (Parsons, 1970b).

All these endeavors, to be sure, came together in another attempt at taking stock of the state of the art of systems theory, opening up, at the same time, a broader dimension of the analytical perspective. In a forty-page contribution to John McKinney and Edward Tiryakian's *Theoretical Sociology: Perspectives and Developments* (1970), Parsons (1970c) pulled together the new systems theory stressing its strong origins in cybernetics and emphasizing that communication media were generally relevant for action systems theory though they concerned primarily the theory of *social* systems. Now he came to broaden the range of relevance of societal community, in that he saw in it not only a nucleus of social systems but also the main topic of generalized action theory. The latter, he found, suggested an integrative function of action systems intelligence that structured any kind of "definition of the situation." This broadening of the range of the societal community idea, in turn, opened up a new perspective on the viability of occidental culture as it had been institutionalized in the modern Western world, above many others in one pivotal institution, in *The American University* (Parsons and Platt, 1973).

During the following years, Parsons explored in a number of essays the analytical outline that he had elaborated more or less fully by the time of the turn between the 1960s and 1970s. Most noteworthy, apart from various investigations in medical sociology, was his exploration on the basis of the societal community conception of the race issue in the 1970s, now suitably renamed ethnicity, in a paper first prepared for a conference on ethnicity convened by Daniel Patrick Moynihan and Nathan Glazer in 1972 (Parsons, 1975a). Eventually, in 1974, in a plenary speech on the occasion of the Ninth World Congress of Sociology in Toronto, he focused on the interaction media, elaborating their ubiquity and importance for the democratic type of society in yet another clarifying endeavor, marking his last major public appearance (Parsons, 1975b).

At the end of his life stood a heroic effort to put together the various contributions of his "latest" systems theory in two major volumes that he planned together. The first was *The Evolution of Societies,* published in 1977, and the second was *Action Theory and the Human Condition,* published in 1978. Only now was it obvious that, in the early 1970s, Parsons had crowned his sequential reformulations of his theoretical approach by yet another revision of his approach. Introducing the theory of societal community, it was now obvious, he had added yet another turn to the spiral of fifty years' effort to understand the nature of society. In another last achievement, now adopting the construct of *teleonomy* introduced in 1970 by Harvard biologist Ernest Mayr, and also building on the much earlier nonmechanistic conceptions of science, nature, and system elaborated by Alfred N. Whitehead and Lawrence J. Henderson, Parsons finally reconciled the levels of action and system, through his focus on symbolization in structures. His "The Human Condition," closing arch in the edifice of his oeuvre, was his final statement on societal community, among other topics, little understood as it has remained until today (Parsons, 1978b).

Not even during the last decade of his life was Parsons a theoretician who confined himself to the ivory tower of Harvard University. In the first half of the 1970s, while he was engaged in rethinking yet again his systems theory, the Watergate scandal and its parallel, an apparent defeat of the U.S. in the Vietnam War, occupied the public mind. Parsons, to be sure, did not shy away from engaging in the political themes of this troubled era. In 1972, he actively campaigned for Nixon's adversary as presidential candidate, George McGovern. Two years later, together with Dean Gerstein, he started a document-based inquiry into the Nixon case, analyzing the obsessive, indeed fascist, power craving of president Richard Nixon that had prompted as it did the country's moral crisis in the wake of this president's resignation to avoid impeachment and sure removal from office. Parsons's interest in this, it appears, was how an amoral individual could threaten the fabric of an entire society's value community (Parsons and Gerstein, 1977).

After his death, an unfinished manuscript was discovered of a book partly consisting of essays written in the 1970s, entitled *American Societal Community*. This manuscript that is being preserved in the Harvard University Archives assembled essays such as the one on social inequality first published in 1970 and ethnicity first published in 1975, together with a newly written piece on the American value system that has been published separately since then (Parsons, 1989).

My reconstruction focuses on the original period when the thought of societal community evolved in the 1960s. Parsons first created this idea to deal with the modern world that had progressed beyond the post–World War II constellation. (I leave it to a future paper to deal with the still unpublished book on American societal community whose analytic accomplishment remains open.)

My topics, in the next two parts of this chapter, are the two main foci of Parsons's theory elaborated predominantly in the 1960s, namely, for one, interaction media as related to the processes of social differentiation and, second, societal community as related to moral consensus and its precondition, security of the normative order.

COMMUNICATION AND INTERACTION MEDIA

In the early 1960s, Parsons acknowledged linguist Roman Jakobson's insight that "language consists of a variety of mechanisms for controlling, by means of codes, the regular emission of messages."[5] This involved that a code was "a fixed transformation, usually term by term, by means of which a set of information units is converted into a sequence of phonemes and vice versa."[6] Parsons, at the outset of his essay on the

concept of influence introducing the topic of "General Mechanisms of Social Interaction: The Case of Money," adopted Jakobson's thought thus:

> In the well-known formulation of Jacobsen [sic] and Halle, a language must be under-
> stood to involve two aspects: on the one hand, the use of language is a process of emitting
> and transmitting messages, combinations of linguistic components that have specific ref-
> erence to particular situations; on the other hand, language is a *code* in terms of which the
> particular symbols constituting any particular message "have meaning." In these terms, a
> message can be meaningful and hence understood only by those who "know the lan-
> guage," that is, the code, and accept its "conventions." (Parsons, 1963a/1969a: 406)

In this adoption of the linguistic understanding of communication, Parsons found
a way to incorporate the broad knowledge on material and immaterial media of social exchange into a comprehensive conceptualization of communication as interaction. Exchange, to be sure, had been a topic in then-recent publications by George
Homans (e.g., 1961), who had focused on utilitarian principles of actor motivation
in social behavior (as discussed in Parsons, 1964b). Parsons wished to stress a factor
disregarded by Homans. Money, he clarified, was not so much a plainly material as a
symbolic entity of valuation, that is, "a symbolic 'embodiment' of economic *value*, of
what economists in a technical sense call 'utility'. . . . Money introduces altogether
new degrees of freedom. . . . Only mutual acceptability can make money a functioning medium rather than simply a way of getting something for nothing" (Parsons,
1963a/1969a: 407–09). In this vein, money represented a normatively institutionalized medium of exchange in social interactions, he explained, establishing a comprehensive reciprocity system that involved four dimensions, namely "(1) a category of
value . . . , (2) a category of *interest* . . . . (3) a *definition of the situation* . . . , and (4) a
normative framework of rules discriminating between legitimate and illegitimate
modes of action in pursuit of the interest in question" (Parsons, 1963a/1969: 409).
On this note, he stated, applying Jakobson's conception of language as communication medium to the interaction that involved money as the medium of exchange, that
money had to be treated as one generalized medium of societal interchange. More
precisely, what Parsons did in the introductory part of his essay on the concept of influence was to liken both money and influence to language, recognizing that both
were a "generalized medium of communication."

> For my purposes, I would like to say not merely that money resembles language, but that
> it *is* a very specialized language, i.e. a generalized medium of communication through
> the use of symbols given meaning within a code. I shall therefore treat influence as a gen-
> eralized medium which in turn I interpret to mean a specialized language. (Parsons,
> 1963a/1969a: 407)

Influence

As a distinguishable mediator between actors exchanging influence in a framework of
normative rules, influence had to be distinct from power. Parsons proposed that influ-

ence equaled prestige, that is the "capacity to bring about desired decisions on the part of other social units without directly offering them a valued *quid pro quo* as an inducement or threatening them with deleterious consequences" (Parsons, 1969b: 43).

In this vein, influence was lodged with mutual orientations other than those derived from ego-based considerations of utility, and institutional relationships other than those of authority, as in the state. Its hierarchical organization in society was centered on inducement other than Weber's classic chance of an actor to find obedience of another in the framework of a legitimate relationship of superordination/subordination. Influence, Parsons clarified, was "the symbolic medium of persuasion," concretizing: "Influence . . . is bringing about a decision on alter's part to act in a certain way because it is felt to be a 'good thing' *for him*, on the one hand independently of contingent or otherwise imposed changes in his situation, on the other hand for positive reasons, not because of the obligations he would violate through noncompliance" (Parsons, 1963a/1969a: 415). Influence, in these terms which derived from the idea of prestige as it had inspired research about social stratification since the early 1940s, marking a noneconomic and nonpolitical dimension of equality/inequality, was a truly democratic force in society.[7] On the level of societies as entire systems, influence found its institutional order in the realm of public opinion, an institution vastly relevant for democratic societies.[8]

Influence, as a means of communication, had an egalitarianizing quality that, on principle, made it available for anyone vis-à-vis anyone. Prestige and its realization in the guise of influence were available in quantities that were expandable to ever-larger proportions of the population in ever more contexts of communication, far exceeding the extent to which is prevailed in present-day society. Such chance for extension and expansion meant that social relationships anchored in influence as a medium of exchange could multiply when they were conducive to universalistic achievement as their main value orientation. In contradistinction, particularistic ascription apparently was less suitable to value orientation that denoted influence/prestige in modern status hierarchies.

"Is influence a fixed quantity in a social system?" asked Parsons at the end of his essay "On the Concept of Influence," and gave an answer truly revolutionary in conceptual terms. His answer first introduced a consideration on how money was a medium involving credit through banking. He then proceeded, making the observation that this meant a potential increase of the overall amount of money circulating at any point in time (including "book money" of various degrees of "solidity"). From this vantage point, he ventured that a similar phenomenon could be observed for power where an increase of the overall quantity of political authority exerted in a given society meant two things. One was extension of the allocation of resources, and the other the inclusion of ever-growing proportions of the population in active power relationships. This explained power (as a communication medium) through banking, as an analogy. As his third related point, Parsons added, "[i]n the field of influence, the analogy with banking and credit seems most obvious in connection with the allocation of loyalties. . . . My suggestion is that the principal way in which this is done in a society like the American is through voluntary associations. . . . Such associations may thus be considered to be a kind of 'influence bank' " (Parsons, 1963a/1969a: 428). As if to warn his reader that much remained to be done until this thought could stand as an un-controversial element of consistent social theory, he added, "It should go without say-ing that this essay has been very tentative indeed" (1963a/1969a: 429).

As an addendum, Parsons exemplified in a footnote what the analogy with eco-nomic processes could yield when he interpreted McCarthyism in terms of the in-fluence/prestige theme. McCarthyism, he remarked, appeared as a "deflationary episode entering in the influence field, which at its culmination approached panic proportions: the demand for 'absolute loyalty' was analogous to the demand for a re-turn to the gold standard in the financial area" (Parsons, 1963a/1969a: 429)—thus spoke, to be sure, the convinced defender of Keynesianism.

Power

In the twin essay of this, apparently written in close connection with "On the Con-cept of Influence," Parsons focused on the similar perspective applied to power.[9] "On the Concept of Political Power" undertook to explicate power from three perspec-tives. One was a reformulation of political theory inasmuch as the latter, from Thomas Hobbes in the 1600s to Robert Dahl in the 1960s, conceptualized power not as a relational quality in interpersonal exchanges but an achievement of persons in office wielding authority over others who succumbed to their more or less coercively enforced orders or wishes. The second was a suggestion that power was lodged in consensus between equals as much as it might characterize conflict or hierarchy in-volving coercion or force. The third perspective concerned a shift from a "zero-sum" model conceptualization of power systems to one of expanding marketlike networks of resource production and allocation, modeled on the idea of money market as ex-change arena involving credit regulation and level of productivity.

Power in this vein, though frequently lodged with office, was not necessarily iden-tical with authority. Using an analogy with the economy, Parsons ventured that "the type case (though not the only one) being an employing organization in which the role-incumbent commits himself to performance of an occupational role, a job, as a contribution to the effective functioning of the collectivity" provided a "service . . . [that was] in the economic sense the 'real' counterpart of interest as monetary in-come from the use of funds" (Parsons, 1963b/1969a: 357). On this baseline, he sug-gested a likeness between economy and the polity. The gist of the matter was that both were organized as collectivities whose members contributed to their continued efficiency. Power, the medium of exchange in the collectivity affecting citizens in their roles of political participation, was

> generalized capacity to secure the performance of binding obligations by units in a sys-tem of collective organization when the obligations are legitimized with reference to their bearing on collective goals and where in case of recalcitrance there is a presump-tion of enforcement by negative situational sanctions—whatever the actual agency of that enforcement. (Parsons, 1963b/1969a: 361)

The thrill of the thought was that power, so to speak, was limitless in the sense that everybody could have it without a "War of All Against All" necessarily resulting from equal distribution. Such democratic potential had two sources. One was that power was a "symbolic" medium inasmuch as it constituted only a "capacity to secure compliance" from others in a network of mutual relationships institutionalized in the community as a collective (Parsons, 1963b/1969a: 361). This made power a holistic characteristic of entire collectivities distributed as interactional empowerment among its members. Parsons recognized this "symbolic" quality, and went on to emphasize that the "symbolically" guaranteed rights to the services of others as embodied in power were not arbitrary but depended on legitimation. Deviating somewhat from Weber's classic view on legitimation, he stated, again using an analogy with money: "Legitimation is . . . in power systems, the factor that is parallel to confidence in mutual acceptability and stability of the monetary unit in monetary systems" (Parsons, 1963b/1969a: 362). A thought similar to what he had remarked on McCarthyism in the context of influence could clarify this further. Crediting his colleague Karl Deutsch with the insight, Parsons ventured:

I spoke above of the "grounding" of the value of money in the commodity value of the monetary metal, and suggested that there is a corresponding relation of the "value," i.e. the effectiveness of power, to the intrinsic effectiveness of physical force as a means of coercion and, in the limiting case, compulsion. (Parsons, 1963b/1969a: 365)

In this way, he likened confidence in the services of others in a political system to currency stability facilitating trust in market exchanges. Legitimation of power allowed for a much wider distribution of empowerment to voter-citizens in democracies. But in less legitimated, and consequently more coercive, regimes the power system could entail disenfranchisement of large parts of the population. Therefore, pluralism separating the legislative, executive, and judicative branches of government as well as establishing a political system distinct from a legal system in a society emulated the conditions favorable to a stable high-productivity economy in the Keynesian model. But dictatorship meant that power was concentrated in few positions entrusted with coercive force whose basis was not the confidence of the masses, depriving large parts of the population of any measure of power to determine and control their government. Lacking legitimation, the dictatorial type of system yielded considerably less effectiveness than the democratic type. Legitimation that established trust, Parsons was convinced, explained the long-term stability and high effectiveness of modern democracies such as the United States and accounted for the low level of consensus and considerable deficit of effectiveness of less democratic regimes such as the then contemporary Soviet Union or, previously, Nazi Germany.

Value-Commitments

The third, or rather fourth, medium of interactional exchange, value-commitments, underwent close study only five years later. Indeed, Parsons had already completed his first analysis of societal community by two years when he eventually turned to the companion article supplementing the earlier two, "On the Concept of Value-Commitments." He clarified in advance two specifics, thus guarding against misunderstandings that could derive from two established contemporary approaches. The latter were "the 'Chicago' approach" in sociology, which suggested external forces of normative control through labeling,[10] and "the 'Chicago' tradition" in political science, notably David Easton, whose then recent "new political economy" subsequently merged into the rational-choice model of action explanation[11] (Parsons, 1968e/1969a: 440). These views, Parsons felt, went wrong because normative orientations (in a democratic society) derived from commitment of the actor rather than coercion, and values (in a democratic society) represented not solely goods and services attained or craved by actors but, rather, their images of reciprocal social relations defining an ideal-type society.

Two clarifications were that Parsons, first, defined values and, second, concretized what he meant by commitment. Values, he stated, were "conceptions of the desirable" (not necessarily identical with, he warned, that which is empirically desired by the majority of the population) in the sense concretized by anthropologist Clyde Kluckhohn. These were "'patterns' at the cultural level" that were relevant for actors as "conceptions of the desirable *type of society* held by the members of the society of reference and applied to the particular society of which they are members." He clarified further, "A value-pattern . . . defines a *direction* of choice, and consequent commitment to action" (Parsons, 1968e/1969a: 441).

In value-commitments, a linkage between institutionalization and internationalization was crucial. Parsons's presupposition was that a society's conceptions of the positively valued, including normative and moral ideas, images, conditions, or patterns of action were, while built into powerful institutions, necessarily also firmly ingrained in individuals' personalities. Only this double grounding made values, honored through commitment, effective forces in motivation to action. His object of study, then, was clear:

> Our master conception under that of value-pattern here is that of *commitment*. Regardless of what other value-commitments an acting unit may have, our concern is with his or its commitment to implement value-patterns in his capacity as a member of one or more social systems. (Parsons, 1968e/1969a: 442)

To be sure, the issue was not whether or not values existed that characterized the desirable in a society. But, rather, the question was whether individuals as members in their society were sufficiently committed to the values of a prevailing conception of, say, pluralist egalitarianism through rule of law. Was that commitment established in a group of actors to an extent that would make them resist pressures from deviant agents? Could particularistic specific groups demand from a group of actors to adhere to alternative values such that, for instance, they would feel loyalty to a proletariat avant-garde presumably symbolizing a world revolution? Parsons, to be sure, acknowledged moral leadership but recognized how it related to the religious sect character of certain political groups, arguing that commitment to values did not necessarily mean following a leader defining for his followers what values to believe in:

In the ideal-type case, generally, commitment to a highly general value-pattern is shared by all units of the social system in which it is institutionalized. . . . A *stratification of responsibility* in the direction of segmentation focuses about the phenomenon often called "moral leadership." . . . The predestined "Saints" of early Calvinism and the Communist Party have in some respects been similar elites of moral leadership, both treating political power as on the whole an *instrument* for implementing their moral commitments. . . . Weber, among many others, emphasized the tension between moral leadership and political power. (Parsons, 1968e/1969a: 451–52)

The "symbolic" quality ingrained in value-commitments was moral not in an egocentric but in an interpersonal sense. The idea was that ego and alter, any two actors in an exchange relationship, might define each other's situation as one of moral communality demanding respect for each other, as distinct from one of moral superiority/inferiority of one vis-à-vis the other. In this vein, Parsons knew that "when we speak of *an ego activating an alter's commitments,* we mean that, through symbolic communication, ego helps alter 'define the situation' for alter's exercise of his moral freedom" (Parsons 1968e/1969a:456) in the sense of "the freedom to make its own decisions of legitimacy" (Parsons 1968e/1969a 455). Such use of the symbolic medium of moral dignity, to be sure, could vary in " 'intensity' of commitment" (Parsons 1968e/1969a: 454). Depending on a person's relative standing in any hierarchy of "moral leadership," "persons in the requisite statuses are *more or less* intensively committed, as personality systems, to the implementation of the value patterns institutionalized in their respective statuses" (Parsons, 1968e/1969a: 456). In this, Parsons acknowledged that there were differences in degree and intensity of value-commitment, but a democracy required that persons in leadership positions, more than others although in the same way, needed to have internalized the values of reciprocity and respect characteristic of humane social order.

Finally, Parsons returned to his analogy with money to epitomize two further aspects of commitment in interaction. He conceptualized variations in degree and intensity of value-commitments using the inflation-deflation image borrowed from Keynes's theory of the monetary system. Another aspect, again modeled on banking, which he rendered in quotation marks, was that he visualized commitment processes either as characteristic of charismatic or genuinely democratic regimes.

On the inflation-deflation analogy, he had this to say: "The inflationary case involves what is frequently called *over-commitment,*" he began; "it occurs when a unit has made so many, so diverse, and such 'serious' commitments that its capacity to implement them effectively must reasonably be called into question" (Parsons, 1968e/1969a: 463). Although he found this precarious though not necessarily dangerous to the stability of a system, he was aware of the danger that overcommitment could mean loss of credibility of promises made, or loss of bindingness of commitments thus acquired. In the latter case, deflationlike loss of normative security loomed large. "The deflationary tendency is a disposition toward unwillingness to 'honor' the commitments that units are willing to make," he found. Instead of allowing individuals the freedom to choose their own commitments, in a situation of "deflationary tendency" "some outside agency, e.g., the 'law'" would acquire the function to impose on citizens what were their binding commitments. This, Parsons added, could lead to a vicious circle of potentially diminishing returns in terms of lesser and lesser norm compliance. "Major movements in this direction . . . have the familiar consequence of purchasing 'security' at the expense of benefits which may accrue from greater freedom for autonomous responsibility," he concluded (Parsons, 1968e/ 1969a: 463).

Using the metaphor of banking for his analysis of value-commitments, he had this to say: "Commitment 'banking,'" he ventured, could be likened to entrusting commitments to 'purpose-built' institutions, with the proviso that commitment could be withdrawn when trust in the institution disappeared. The test case, he felt, was that a charismatic leader might boast with his capacity to change an entire system of values in a society, thereby rendering to citizens opportunities for commitment to an entirely "new" moral order. But, he warned, in case of "failure of success" of the "new" order, deflationary tendencies in citizens' trust in the system might result inevitably; these tendencies could lead to eventual mass "withdrawal" of citizens' willingness to put their commitment assets in the "bank" of state authority as such (Parsons, 1968e/1969a: 469). He stressed what were the links with social change but cautioned that there were two types of value innovation, one potentially disastrous for the stability of the social order, the other potentially beneficial:

> Probably the most generalized formulation of the role of the "commitment banker" in sociological thought is Weber's concept of charismatic leadership. The charismatic leader imposes compliance with his "demands" as a *moral duty*, not as enhancement of self-interest. . . . One of the more difficult problems in interpreting Weber's conception of charismatic "breakthrough" concerns the degree of "totality" of the break. . . . If breaks were as drastically radical as ideologists often hold them to be, it is difficult to see how their movements could avoid occasioning, almost immediate "runs" on the "commitment banking" system, so that commitment-creation through the charismatic type of process would be impossible. . . . If the first flashes of a charismatic movement immediately polarized the attitudes of individuals at the commitment level, the result would almost certainly be quick suppression of the movement. The answer lies, I think, in the conception of the *institutionalization* of value innovations. A charismatic commitment-expansion will be noninflationary insofar as it represents a first step in a process of institutionalization. (Parsons, 1968e/1969a: 467–69)

A PERSPECTIVE ON DIFFERENTIATION AND DEDIFFERENTIATION

The question may arise why Parsons, after having completed *The Social System* in the early 1950s, would have returned to the topic of systems theory in the 1960s at all, elaborating on the four communication media. Why did he engage in the theoretical delineation of four interaction media as means of exchange in social life? What was the general question that besieged him when he engaged in the exploration and explication of symbolic media, welding together Jakobson's understanding of language and Keynes's analysis of monetary systems into a paradigm of communication through symbolic codes?

My answer refers to Lewis Coser's *The Functions of Social Conflict* (1956), a book that had been a Ph.D. dissertation supervised by Parsons's erstwhile student and longtime collaborator, Robert K. Merton. Coser's criticism against Parsons's systems theory, voiced clearly if indirectly, was that conflict, diversified in multiple levels or spheres throughout a society establishing cross-cutting antagonistic tendencies, failed to have dysfunctional effects; in the guise of intersecting loyalties taking a multitude of directions, Coser argued, social conflict was far from dangerous to social cohesion. On the contrary, as he showed in ten propositions adapted from Georg Simmel, conflict distinguishing ethnic groups, social classes, religious denominations, political organizations, or cultural associations could even be a source for effective reconciliation within a society between, on the one hand, individual freedom and, on the other, system integration.

From the beginning of his concern for differentiation as a phenomenon characteristic of modern societies, Parsons coupled the topic of conflict with that of social change. Already in 1961, on the first occasion that he explicitly addressed the problem of differentiation of social spheres, he concerned himself with social change as contrasted with social process. The latter, he clarified, belonged to the duality of structure and process; in effect, social process signified time-related realization of social structures and had no impact on differentiation. Social change, however, was related to differentiation, which, in turn, meant modernization. Differentiation of social worlds resulted in diversification that created separate realms, thus transforming through social change what originally had been a unified sphere. In the course of differentiation, a societal realm securing functions such as, for example, economic production or political authority, disintegrated into two or more separate spheres now forming independent system-type units. Through social change involving differentiation, he knew, modernization occurred. In this, three contexts were affected. They were, first, "a process by which facilities, previously ascribed to less differentiated units, are freed from this ascription and are made available through suitable adaptive mechanisms for the utilization of the higher-order new class of units that are emerging"; second, "structural reorganization . . . [,] the way in which the two new and differentiated classes of units are related to each other in the wider system, in the first instance from the point of view of the structure of collectivities"; and, third, "normative components of structure . . . [,] reorganized as part of a process of differentiation. . . . The prototype here for large-scale and highly differentiated social systems is the system of legal norms . . . Standards of performance or achievement, of technical adequacy, and the like are also involved" (Parsons, 1961c: 235–36).

Differentiation into more diversified and, at the same time, more universalistically oriented, separate system-collectivities, therefore, was at the heart of modernization of societies in general. Parsons, in *Societies*, explored this thesis by contrasting, for instance, the Egyptian and the Mesopotamian cultures among archaic societies. His hypothesis was that the stability of ancient Egyptian society, but also its inability to develop, were due to the fact that the political and the religious in this society were literally fused into one and the same institutional structure; this institutional unity rendered the pharaoh a veritable god, which meant that no legal system existed as guarantor of individual rights. In contradistinction, in Mesopotamia, religious and political authority had been differentiated to a certain extent, and a legal system of degrees had developed concomitantly; nevertheless, further differentiation and consolidation of institutional spheres had been hindered by the fact that "a unified conception of the grounding of the meanings of the obligations" did not develop such as it did in Ancient Greece, creating the idea of *polis*.

Eventually, in 1968, after he had elaborated successively on the four communication media, in the closing part of "On the Concept of Value-Commitments," Parsons laid open the mechanics of differentiation and dedifferentiation in their complicated relationship with the four communication media. To be sure, as he had remarked on various occasions, the four communication media explicated what was the specific nature and main direction involving action orientation of the four main societal institutional realms. The latter, he clarified, were economy, polity, "society," lodged with, as its two main foci, the legal system or medicine, and culture concretized, among other spheres, in learning—particularly, in Western-type societies, higher learning. Culture, he ventured, was guarantor of maintenance of normative patterns although he acknowledged that the university, as epitome of professionalism, also had connotations of integration as lodged with the "society" realm. The communication media helped understand what characterized the ever-growing diversity of institutions and institutional orders in modern society. In due course, an ever-growing number of subsystems developed within the main four functional systems, each diversifying along the lines of the fourfold scheme of interaction mediation. Diversification within each of the four sectors established secondary institutions. For instance, in the money realm arenas were created for, in a financial context, the media of power, influence, and value-commitments; or, within the realm of power, ones emerged that, within the polity, were arenas for money, influence, and value-commitments. Parsons established a complicated scenario. He conceptualized differentiation as explaining multiplication cum interpenetration between the various functional realms and their subrealms in modern pluralist societies.[12]

But this was not enough. If differentiation could be envisaged through the four communication media, its obverse, namely dedifferentiation, had to be pictured in the same framework. This Parsons did at the end of the essay "On the Concept of Value-Commitments," discussing "Some Sources and Consequences of Dedifferentiation." Resuming, from the previous part of the paper, the topic of charisma, redefining it in terms of value-commitments as a "loan" by citizens to an entrepreneurlike charismatic figure, of "commitment-capacity," which, in due course, required legitimation, he saw in charismatic authority a "focus of a process of *dedifferentiation* relative to the historical background" (1968e/1969: 470). He ventured for a historical situation when a charismatic leader and movement repudiated some higher developmental phase of differentiation, instigating regression to a lower level of more "fundamentalist" commitments:

Responsibilities focusing in other "normally" obligatory areas may be neglected or, if the tension rises sufficiently, explicitly repudiated to the point of being declared specifically illegitimate. Thus a very large sector of common Western liberal socio-political values were repudiated by the Communist movement, especially in its Stalinist phase. The values of free speech, orderly procedure in reaching collective decisions, and many other aspects of "civil liberties" have been downgraded. . . . [T]he fundamentalist implication [was] that those who share the values, but insist on retaining a broader pattern for allocating rights, are "enemies" of the innovative movement. (Parsons, 1968e/1969a: 470)

Parsons found four scenarios in which such dedifferentiation could occur. In varying degree, they implied a return to, or increase in, in Weber's terms, *Gesinnungsethik* as an alternative to *Verantwortungsethik*.[13] They were (1) more or less "exotic" sectarian movements that had little impact on societies as a whole; (2) "mildly revolutionary" movements such as derived from, for instance, modern physical science when the reference was to their "progressive," utterly revolutionary explanations of the world and nature that had temporarily caused some anomie allowing for dedifferentiation but eventually led to subsequent societal (re-)differentiation; (3) major schisms in modern society that would split a world or even *the* world into blocs of apparently irreconcilable regimes along the axes of religion, politics, ideology, or whatever. "The Communist movement has also divided on an East-West axis," Parsons observed here, "broadly between the more fully 'industrialized' societies and those to the East of the European center, which are in 'need' of more basic economic development." And he added, "The more 'revolutionary' alternative may now make the 'road back' to reintegration exceedingly difficult" (Parsons, 1968e/1969a: 471). Finally, (4) reformations were a way out of the dilemma between innovation and regression in charismatic movements, thus proving that pluralism was an answer to the question of reconciliation between tradition and progress.

In the last paragraph of the essay, Parsons stressed his view that not so much the depth of value-commitments but rather their capacity to combine intensity of attachment with tolerance for plurality was the answer to the question of differentiation, a hallmark of modern democratization. In the situation of the "hot summer" of 1968 when students revolted against the institutional structures of higher learning in the presumed interest of power-free communication, he had this to say as a warning against facile credos:

We must ask which is most important: (1) fundamentalist regression to more primitive levels, (2) schismatic revolutionary outcomes, which will tend to maximize conflict, or (3) institutionalization of new levels of generality in value systems? Sociology has a grave responsibility to help clarify the understanding of what is going on and of what lies at stake in the balance among these possibilities. (Parsons, 1968e/1969a: 472)

VALUES OF MORAL CONSENSUS AND THE SECURITY-STRAIN DIMENSION OF THE SOCIETAL COMMUNITY

Modernization qua differentiation meant two distinguishable processes. One was that institutional pluralism developed. The other was that every citizen in the community, irrespective of ethnicity, religion, class origin, or gender, would become a full member, entitled to participate in the social life of differentiated institutional structures. In an unpublished memorandum dealing with "The Problem of Polarization on the Axis of Color," Parsons envisaged a two-stage course of modernization qua differentiation. The initial stage, representing conditions to be overcome, was a division between first-class and second-class citizen status. In such vein, for instance, as in the United States in the early 1960s, whites were separated from nonwhites, or, as in seventeenth-century England but also, to a lesser degree, the United States until the early 1960s, Protestants were separated from Catholics in terms of social rights.[14] Parsons explained:

> Very generally, relations between polarized components include a dimension of superiority-inferiority, which in certain circumstances became dominant over other dimensions. I am particularly interested in the case in which the superior component—as judged by some relevant institutional criterion—comes eventually to include the inferior component in an integrated societal (or other forms of social) community on grounds of fundamental equality in some basic sense.[15]

The second stage of modernization meant to overcome such cleavage. The idea was that full membership in the society came to include both or any previously polarized groups, integrating them into a community of shared mission, or duty, or dignity of men. In this vein, in the Reformation, laity had become full-fledged members of the divine community of "God's children" equal to their pastors; in post civil-war England Catholics, through *Habeas Corpus,* had become subjects protected under the crown equal to all groups of Protestants; or, in the American case, Parsons emphasized, the "Puritan" modifications of Protestantism meant that "the 'invisible' church ceased to be a 'two-class' system and became an association of presumptive equals, in principle open to all who would join." To be sure, political processes followed the same rationale. The American and also the French Revolutions established a principle of citizenship including "all who would join" under the banner of freedom and nation. Thus was constituted a realm regulating the rights and duties of legitimate lawful citizens established in their solemnly instituted Constitution. The pluralization process thus accompanied the development of a community of citizens, Parsons clarified. Such union between pluralization (institutional differentiation) and community of citizens (universalistic value integration) had a condition and a consequence.

The condition was legitimation. That is, within the community thus established, incorporating as members previously separated categories of persons, a spiritual or moral principle of their common duties, mission, or dignity had to prevail. In order to render a previous out-group equal members, legitimation had to secure their being the same as previous in-group personnel on account of both groups' representing one and the same quality of humanness or achievement. Parsons delineated two types of historical society where such pluralization had occurred, along the line of differentiation qua integration. One transformed a diversity of political privileges and prerogatives of one religious group over another into secular rule, with all denominations becoming equal and "private," and, on a secular level, the other was transformation from an aristocracy-commonness hierarchical stratification to a society where "all com-moners came to be fully integrated in the societal community." Thus evolved, Parsons knew, a structure incorporating "a variety of qualitatively different types of compo-nents each of which performed different functions in the larger system."

The consequence of pluralization, however, was that the differences between social units—previously separating first-class from second-class citizen status—now be-came equal individual variations. In this vein, after religion had been eliminated as an ascriptive category defining access to the higher echelons of social status, it became one among a number of "privatized" forms of denominational identity. In a similar vein, in Parsons's lifetime, race in the wake of the Civil Rights legislation of the mid-dle 1960s was in the process of changing its societal relevance from major condition for participation in achievement systems to "privatized" personal characteristic.[16]

Pluralization, as it became legitimate (through the disappearance of prejudice, and the incorporation into full-citizen status of previous out-groups) and engendered differentiated private identities supplementing equal social rights of citizens, neces-sitated a centripetal force. The counterpart of pluralization, which ensured a society's integration into a societal community, was moral consensus. In a short text on the nature of American pluralism, Parsons clarified:

> Pluralization . . . has a double implication. One aspect concerns . . . the principles of tol-eration. . . . The other aspect is that the community itself must be grounded in a moral consensus. Groups within a community who differ on the explicit religious level not only are to be "permitted" to go their varying ways but must be held to have a *moral right* to do so—the difference is crucial. (Parsons, 1967: 253)

To concretize, Parsons explicated the equal rights doctrine as the legal basis of modern democracy. The American Constitution had established a right of the citi-zen to religious practice irrespective of denomination (which had eventually bene-fited millions of Catholics and Jews who had immigrated after 1890) and had insti-tuted a right to protection under the law from disenfranchisement or discrimination (which had only begun to benefit in increasing proportion nonwhites and women in the 1960s). Parsons stated in 1968:

> I regard the constitutional doctrine that has been so prominent in recent Supreme Court decisions, that every citizen is entitled to equal protection of the laws, as a fundamental statement of values about the desirable type of society in which we live. (Parsons, 1968a: 376)

Values made understandable what were the generalized principles setting the frame of reference for citizenship in the societal community. "What do I mean by values?" he posed the rhetorical question, answering, "Commitments to a conception of a good type of society," and clarified that this related to Kluckhohn's conception of the *desirable* as opposed to the merely desired (Parsons, 1968a: 376).

In a short text discussing conceptual mistakes in the approach of Homans, Par-sons charged that the latter had defined value not as belonging to the sphere of "the 'desirable'" but "Homans' concept of value being clearly confined to the desired" (Parsons, 1964b: 217). In his seemingly plausible adaptation of economics to the analysis of social behavior, cultivating the principles of utility and social justice, Parsons charged, Homans had misjudged the mode of functioning of the interaction media. Recurring to seemingly universal utilitarianism, thereby taking too literally the money analogy of symbolization processes, Homans implicitly negated the importance, if not existence, of the societal community rooted in moral values. Homans had confused money and its similes in social interaction with valuation in general, thus confounding payment equivalents or analogies with social approval, which represented an entirely different medium of social exchange, Parsons clarified. Justifying his own conception that the four interaction media functioned as *symbolic* rather than merely material rewards, Parsons referred to James Olds's research. Olds had proved in psychological experiments involving animals whose motives presumably emulated humans, that a capacity to appreciate symbolic rather than merely food rewards could be found even in laboratory rats. In this vein, Parsons condemned Homans for his revival of utilitarianism thus:

> In my terminology, money and social approval are generalized symbolic media of interaction, whereas technical help and food objects are not. The distinction has become important even at the level of behavior psychology in the way in which Olds and others have shown that learning processes in rats can be rewarded by electrical stimulation of what Olds calls the pleasure mechanism of the brain instead of by intrinsic "satisfiers" such as those of the classical Hullian learning theory. (Parsons, 1964b: 213)[17]

Against Homans, representative of utilitarianism in the 1960s, Parsons stressed that interaction media were the backbone of exchange in social life, and that institutionalization prevailed, which was based on internalization of moral principles responsible for the establishment of social order. In this vein, he stressed the cultural definition of the situation presupposed by the actor in the modern society, which made for a moral quality of the equality of human beings in the modern pluralist social order:

> I believe with Homans that there are elementary principles that govern the behavior of organisms in general, and that govern the behavior of "men as men," if one understands by that formula creatures which are not only organically human but which live in systems of complex social relationships organized in relation to *cultural* symbolic codes and norms. I do not believe that the two are the same, because [of] the *cultural* level of organization of living systems. (Parsons, 1964b: 215–16)[18]

The two dimensions of societal community requiring further elucidation were moral consensus (as criterion defining social order) and the security-strain balance (as phenomenon allowing for historical dynamics).

Moral Consensus

Values, Parsons held, on an orientation level of culturally mediated conceptions of the desirable as opposed to only the desired, needed understanding on a level of so-

cial collectivity. If values were nothing but what "interacting units" desired empirically, utilitarianism would prevail, which meant that—implicitly if not explicitly—a
"War of All Against All" could become unavoidable.[19] Therefore, moral consensus,
establishing values defining a conception of the type of society aimed at by citizens
who were its committed members, became irrefutably crucial.

Against this background, Parsons undertook to clarify the notion of societal community twice. In 1966, introducing his book on premodern societies, *Societies*, he
highlighted societal community as a sui generis entity on a collectivity level, with
three accomplishments: It distinguished between members and nonmembers, constituted solidarity between citizens allowing them to develop a common identity, and
represented a society's self-sufficiency, territorial as well as political.

> A society must constitute a societal *community* that has an adequate level of integration
> or solidarity and a distinctive membership status. . . . This community must be the
> "bearer" of a cultural system sufficiently generalized and integrated to legitimize nor-
> mative order. Such legitimation requires a system of constitutive symbolism which
> grounds the identity and solidarity of the community, as well as beliefs, rituals, and other
> cultural components which embody such symbolism. . . . Self-sufficiency implies ade-
> quate control over the economic-technological complex so that the physical environ-
> ment can be utilized as a resource base in a purposeful and balanced way. This control is
> intertwined with political control of territory and with control of membership in rela-
> tion to the residence-kinship complex. (Parsons, 1966b/1969a: 19–20)

These functions of the societal community, in the context of *Societies*, which discussed partly undifferentiated societies such as ancient Egypt or Greece, were important inasmuch as they signaled what were basic integrative forces usually invested
in moral beliefs, or religious rituals. Rituals and other cultural institutions, no doubt,
oriented action through guidance of internalized motivational forces in personalities. In archaic and premodern societies, religion frequently was identical with moral
normative order (often also incorporating the political and even what there was in
terms of a legal order). Irrespective of the degree of structural-institutional differentiation of a society, Parsons stressed, the cybernetic function of societal community
had to be one of opening up, through common-culture normative codes, motivations to societally adequate and agreeable social actions. Whatever type of desirable
society prevailed in a culture, social action as a matter of course (and, of course, a
matter of virtue) would aim at achievements, thereby unleashing energies of economic, political, and religious fulfillment in the service of a sacred or secular ideal.
This steering or control function of the cultural, he knew, was the key to understanding orientation as well as motivation in the society's members' interaction. The
perspective of societal community, therefore, allowed to see how contributions from
the collectivity of members in a society were bound together by solidarity and guided
by values of moral consensus.

In *The System of Modern Societies*, written in 1969, Parsons presented a more sophisticated view of societal community—as befitted occidental democracies. The latter, to
be sure, meant full-fledged differentiation of the legislative, executive, and judicative

functions of government, supplementing the four functional subsystems of economy, polity, "society," and culture (involving cultural patterns across generations) as they, in turn, split into further sub-subsystems. For instance, banking in the monetary sector had grown into an independent sub-subsystem, developing further ramifications; or government in the power system had become different from political parties. In the realm of "society," three developments were noteworthy. One was the emergence within education of an independent institution of higher learning, another was the establishment of a legal system differentiated into a network of institutions of jurisdiction, such as law enforcement, and a third was the growth of medicine into a noncharity, nonstate institution of professional practice. He stated:

> [Our core category] is the component centering about the definition of obligations of *loyalty* to the societal collectivity, both in the capacity of membership as such and in various categories of differentiated status and role within the society. . . . Loyalty is a readiness to respond to properly "justified" appeals to the collective or "public" interest or need. The normative problem concerns the definition of occasions when such a response constitutes an obligation. . . . Particularly important are the relations between subgroups' and individuals' loyalties to the societal collectivity and their loyalties to other collectivities of which they are members. (Parsons, 1969b: 41)

In this latter remark, Parsons referred to the fact that conflicting loyalties were a serious threat to the integration of a society. At the same time, to be sure, pluralist participation of citizens in a multitude of social spheres was a hallmark of modern democracies. Above the level of role pluralism, he knew, integrating forces had to rule such that moral consensus would prevail. Citizens were compelled to different loyalties depending on, for instance, their gender (e.g., when men rather than women were expected to fulfill their national duty in the army), although an increasing proportion of loyalties in modern societies depended not on ascriptive conditions such as gender or age, but on achievement such as professional training that had become increasingly mandatory for incumbency of public office. He remarked:

> On the whole, an increase in role-pluralism is a major feature of the differentiation processes leading toward modern types of society. Therefore, the regulation of the loyalties of members, to the community itself and to various other collectivities, is a major problem for the integration of a societal community. (Parsons, 1969b: 41)

As regarded membership, modern societies, similar to premodern ones, had to distinguish between full-fledged "actual membership in the societal community" and "temporary visitors and long term 'resident aliens' as well as the property holdings of 'foreign' interests'" in order to provide a focus for identification of its proper citizens (Parsons, 1969b: 49). No doubt, the modern citizen status was one of equal legal rights that entitled a person, among other things, to free religious practice, free choice of marriage partner, and free choice of education and occupational career. But national solidarity had to be expected from "actual members" as opposed to "temporary visitors." What was different in modern as compared with premodern societies, for one, was that associational freedom was granted by right to members (and

frequently visitors, though possibly to a limited extent) under the proviso of absten-
tion from criminal acts. Furthermore, such associational organization followed three
crucial principles: They were egalitarianism, voluntariness, and regulation through
procedural institutions.

In the societal community representing the "society" subsystem of modern society, three realms that resulted from institutional differentiation represented morally
binding forces. These morally binding forces ingrained in three institutions in modern American society, and modern society in general, helped sustain moral consensus in the nation and, indeed, the world. They were, first, religion not as a particular
denomination such as Protestantism or Judaism but as a set of moral convictions en-
gendering mutual respect between fellowcitizens in their individual beliefs and human dignity (as explained in, for instance, Bellah 1967). Second, higher education
was a guarantor, grounded as it was in the tradition of academic freedom reinforced
by a moral obligation to trust evidence that resulted from strictly scientific verifica-
tion. Thirdly, the legal system was a strong basis for the incorporation of the totality
of members into a nonparticularistic, nonascriptive system of rules and roles, based
as it was on universal principles of justice. These principles were established in the
law as much as in the Constitution, both representing charters of rules linked with
generalized value-commitments. In his essay on "Polity and Society" crowning his
seminal volume *Politics and Social Structure*, Parsons observed that the law was important in more than one way:

> Some aspects of legality are literally given in constitutionally defined terms. Insofar as
> this is a variable component . . . , the most important agency of variation seems to be ju-
> dicial decision or its equivalent. . . . The Constitution itself . . . is by no means only an as-
> sertion of value-commitments. It states many rather specific *norms* concerning the con-
> duct of government itself and the relations of its various agencies to units in the private
> sector. (Parsons, 1969c: 481)

The law, one major dimension of societal community, was clearly related to the
polity. What about the polity made the law an arena of political process constituting
consensus? In modern society, no doubt, the political aspect of social structure and
process was obvious (Parsons, 1966c). This concerned collective effectiveness of a
group or nation to achieve its goals through efficient acting together. Such effectiveness could be achieved either through a structure of more or less hierarchical authority (e.g., government), or equally through a joint effort of all members working
for the common good on the basis of their shared values denoting moral consensus.[20]

Both types of arrangement, for Parsons, constituted a polity. He gave as a general
definition: "The polity . . . [is] conceived as the 'goal-attainment' subsystem of any social system, but in particularly important ways, of a society," concretizing for the government side on the basis of Max Weber's sociology of the state:

> One source of [the] importance [of the relation between government and the societal
> community] is that in general only government is authorized to use socially organized
> physical force as an instrument of compulsion. Indeed an effective governmental

monopoly of force is a major criterion of integration in a highly differentiated society. Moreover, only government is entitled to act for the societal collectivity as a whole in contexts of collective goal-attainment. Any other agency that directly presumes to do so commits a revolutionary act *ipso facto*. (Parsons, 1969b: 49)

The other type of polity, no doubt, went beyond the governmental realm when it integrated the population on the background of processes ensuring that "modern levels of differentiation . . . have tended to make the power of political leadership contingent on the support of very extensive proportions of the population" (Parsons, 1969b: 46). The moral yardsticks here were contained in rights derived from the American Bill of Rights, and similar codices worldwide. That moral principles ensured equality of protection from disenfranchisement and exploitation in democratic societies meant that the self-sufficiency of each citizen in his/her effort to contribute to the effectiveness of the nation could be a realistic possibility. Parsons knew that the polity in this sense depended on highly generalized cultural value standards. These standards, held together through an image of the "desirable" democratic social order, made citizens agents for the common good in modern differentiated societies.

To be sure, Parsons's idea of the political aspect of structure and process that characterized the societal community grew out of his discovery that the proper notion of power was one beyond the "zero-sum" conception. This new, cybernetically grounded notion of power allowed for an increase of the overall sum of power wielded in a society by the totality of its citizens.

Security and Strain in the Societal Community

A social order, Parsons asserted in 1968, was not "somehow given in 'nature'" but needed explanation in terms of interpersonal dynamics. "So fundamental is the problem of order that the structure of systems of human action . . . consists of internalized and institutional normative patterns," he stated (Parsons, 1968a: 374). Such a union between institutionalization and internalization meant that action orientations of members of a society would, in the type case, be in harmony with the structure and culture of the society of the time (Parsons, 1968a: 375). Explicating that this involved the four levels of values, norms, collectivities, and roles, Parsons proceeded to discuss the intricacies of a voluntaristic social order. In this endeavor, he invoked the scheme of the interaction media, especially money.

Money required a "duality of formula," he maintained, in order to fulfill the function of exchange. One was "what you might call the security base of monetary systems," that is, the grounding of money in circulation in some gold reserve or a certain stock of "metallic" assets. The other was that "productivity of the economy" represented the formula that secured exchange between goods and services in money terms whose value was all but symbolic (Parsons, 1968a: 382).

Undeniably, though there was a relationship between these two levels of monetary exchange value that entered into the "duality of formula," the two sides were two different kinds of security. One the one hand, security meant possibility or chance to transfer money (or another exchange medium) into a baseline, "metallic reserve" type commodity/capacity/entitlement. In this sense, security was the "backdrop" for some kind of "bundling" of communication. Money thus represented or could be referred to a "bottom line" in a functional system such as "gold reserves" in the monetary system. Likewise, such "metallic"-type baseline of "backdrop" quality was "coercion" in the power system (Parsons, 1964a).

On the other hand, security prevailed when a state of integration of a social collectivity was reached. In a highly differentiated system with elements intertwined through a multitude of reciprocity relationships in an integrated functioning whole, Parsons knew, trust was essential. Trust, in turn, meant security inasmuch as an actor could be certain of others' motives and intentions in a system based on apparent absence, through abhorrence, of force and fraud. Mutuality of expectations in a network of concatenated pluralist structures could function only if trust—acted out as counterpart of taken-for-granted trustworthiness—prevailed. "We . . . depend tremendously on the kind of mutuality of expectation and trust that is involved in the operation of the generalized mechanisms," Parsons explained, suggesting that such security could be found in the level and type of expression of interaction media in general (Parsons, 1968a: 387).

Security, in this picture, was crucial inasmuch as it was the obverse of insecurity. Insecurity, to be sure, in the tradition of Harold Lasswell's influential analysis in the 1930s,[21] had come to signify a highly dangerous loss of personal identification with a nation, or an economic or political type of system. In this view, explaining the Bolshevist and Nazi "revolutions," personal insecurity (loss of rootedness in traditional lifeworlds) engendered predisposition or willingness to join revolutionary movements and/or submit to dictatorial regimes.[22] Insecurity threatened the social order itself. The societal community could be weakened or even destroyed through insecurity.

The two types of security, namely, "gold-standard"-type dedifferentiation transforming a communication medium into its basic, solid "metallic"-type representation, on the one hand, and trust-based expansion of a communication medium into the pluralist, differentiated range of moral resources in a peaceful social order, on the other, had vastly different implications for the social structure. The first-type concept of security, no doubt, was a corollary of anomie, as Parsons had analyzed, for one, in *The Structure of Social Action* (1937). Thereby, insecurity that meant lack of security, in the sense of the second-type concept, transfigured into the kind of security addressed in the first-type concept. This transformation, evidently, deserved sociological attention.

How could security signaling well-being of the citizens become security of the "gold-standard" "fundamentalist" type? Parsons mentioned two processes that weakened integration in a societal community. The two processes meant dedifferentiation converting, for example, a democracy into an autocracy. The two could be likened to developments in the monetary system, namely inflation or deflation.

Inflation, in respect to money, meant loss of exchange value of the monetary unit; the consequence was deterioration of important balancing mechanisms in the market system. Deflation, in contradistinction, meant loss of accessibility of money for growing proportions of participants in the economy. One consequence of deflation was citizens' increasing dispossession from chances to work or consume. Another consequence, in due course, was accumulation of means of exchange in fewer and all the more powerful hands. To be sure, inflation and deflation processes concerned all four interaction media. Not only money, but also power, influence, and value-commitments were media whose expression in social structure followed a logic of inflation or deflation. Both these modes of deterioration of social structure were an alternative to stable modes of relations of mutuality. As an example of how inflation and deflation worked, Parsons explained with special reference to the exchange medium of value-commitments:

> The problem of deflation-inflation . . . affects the functioning of all generalized media. The inflationary case involves what is frequently called *over-commitment*. . . . It occurs when a unit has made so many, so diverse, and such "serious" commitments that its capacity to implement them effectively must reasonably be called into question. . . . The deflationary tendency is a disposition toward unwillingness to "honor" the commitments that units are willing to make. (Parsons, 1968e/1969a: 463)

He knew that one point of danger inherent in the deterioration of stability of the social order connected with the inflation-deflation mechanism was "fundamentalism." He hastened to mention how fundamentalism related to some relevant tensions in the world of the late 1960s:

> [T]he focus of fundamentalism may not be on religion in the analytical sense, but on tenets about the organization of society of "personal" morality. . . . From this point of view, the sharp ideological dispute between socialist and capitalist commitments constitutes a "deflationary" movement within the development of Western society and its commitment system. Each side claims the absolute moral legitimacy of its own commitments, thereby justifying, in the extreme case, "war," if only of the "cold" variety, against the other. (Parsons, 1968e/1969a: 465)[23]

Security, therefore, in the sense of a stable social order multiplying mutual services, could be converted into security in the sense of a "fundamental," presumably baseline, valued "good." Processes resembling inflation or deflation characterized such conversion. What triggered such conversion was strain in the original system—strain that loomed large in every type of society in the modern world. Strain was one source of insecurity and, therefore, danger to the stability, if not existence, of the societal community. "I have suggested," Parsons reminded his readers in 1969, "that the primary roots of McCarthyism lay in strains in the societal community, not in the polity" (Parsons, 1969c: 474).

In his article, originally written in 1954 and entitled "McCarthyism and American Social Tension" but later renamed "Social Strains in America," Parsons had analyzed two types of strain as they affected the social structure of the United States in the post–World War II era. One resulted from a discrepancy between, on the one side, the traditional American creed in individualism as directed against government control and, on the other, an uncontroversial accomplishment of the Roosevelt administration rescuing as it did millions of families from economic disaster through New Deal welfare legislation. The resultant strain was between individualism as American ideology, and state governance as realistic modernization. The other discrepancy, beginning with American responsibility for the reconstruction of Europe after 1945 and leading into the new superpower's defense commitments through costly military protection of the free world against Communist dominance, set traditional isolationism against the new role of world moral leadership. Parsons saw repercussions of these two sources of strain in Americans' identity, in the witch-hunt against alleged Communists in the Roosevelt and Truman administrations and resentment against elite universities such as Harvard.

> Our present problem . . . centers on the need to mobilize American society to cope with a dangerous and threatening situation which is also intrinsically difficult. It clearly can only be coped with at the government level. . . . Consequently, there has come to be an enormous increase in pressure to subordinate private interests to the public interest, and this in a society where the presumptions have been more strongly in favor of the private interest than in most. Readiness to make commitments to a collective interest is the focus of what we ordinarily mean by "loyalty." It seems to me that the problem of loyalty at its core is a genuine and realistic one; but attitudes toward it shade all the way from a reasonable concern with getting the necessary degree of loyal cooperation by legitimate appeals, to a grossly irrational set of anxieties about the prevalence of disloyalty, and a readiness to vent the accompanying aggression on innocent scapegoats. (Parsons, 1962b/1969a: 170)

From this vantage point, he went on to explain why Communism was a "realistic" reproach against the liberals and intellectuals who had come to signify the scapegoats. In all, for Parsons, McCarthyism represented a "deflationary" movement in regard to its unreasonably overly selective attribution of loyalty to groups or individual members in the American societal community. In the eyes of McCarthyites, liberalism and intellectualism, apparently culminating in Communism, meant undue extension of rights and entitlements to uncontrollably ever-larger communities of equals on even an international scale. In respect of "deflationary" zest, however, he found that the reactionary John Birch Society, which in the early 1960s preached aggressive anti-Communism, was even worse than McCarthyism. As he stated in 1962 in his addendum to his article of 1954:

> Their influence is even more drastically "deflationary" than the McCarthyite, in the constriction of commitments to the more highly organized sectors of society. This includes the extensive functions of government, but it also goes beyond them. Even the large corporation is in some sense felt to be vaguely "Socialistic," in that it interferes with the complete independence of the small man. (Parsons, 1962b/1969a: 183)

In a similar vein, Parsons compared McCarthyism with Nazism. Nazism, in the early 1930s, had been an ideological reaction to the strains of German society aggravated by the economic and political crises of the years 1929 and 1930. In this scenario, he ventured, to the Nazis the Jew had represented all that was modern in the economy, capitalist as well as communist, thus embodying industrialism. That industrialism could be opposed by a movement such as the Nazis, who proclaimed a "Blood and

Soil" return to a preindustrial type society in a Germany that indeed was far from preindustrial, he hastened to point out, signaled that the industrial-society-type social order had been incompletely developed in the German social structure of the first half of the twentieth century. Parsons concretized, for Germany, that the danger had been industrialism that appeared to do away with the antiquated political cum social structure; and he insinuated, for the United States, that the danger after World War II had been that a new system of political responsibilities appeared to interfere with the antiquated values of laissez-faire liberalism. He clarified, for Germany in the early 1930s:

> [The "intruders"] symbolized . . . rapid development of industrialism to the older preindustrial *Gemeinschaft* of German political romanticism. It was the obverse of the American case—a new economy destroying an old political system, not new political responsibilities interfering with the accustomed ways of economic life. (Parsons, 1962b/1969a: 176)

To summarize what has been said so far: Parsons's analysis of societal community, in the 1960s, yielded an entirely new perspective on social systems. This perspective had two major conceptual axes. One was interaction (i.e., the structure of social action) that could be characterized through four foci of symbolization of means of exchange—money, power, influence, and value-commitments. These interaction media were foci of concretization in social forces of institutionalization (and internalization, respectively), varying between differentiated modern pluralist constellations, and the outcome of dedifferentiation frequently facilitated by, for instance, charismatic movements.

The other axis was social structure, analyzed through detailed understanding of societal community. In his account of societal evolution but also his explanations of the relationship between politics and social structure, he contrasted the centrifugal forces of pluralist democracy with the centripetal forces involved in the emergence and maintenance of societal community. His two main points were the following: First, a societal community based on common values spurring moral consensus developed on the condition that equal rights were granted to different categories of citizens in a pluralist world. Second, social change happened in both directions, modernization as well as regression. Through processes emulating inflation or deflation in the realm of money, in all four realms of symbolization governing interaction, regression could occur—for example, from democracy to autocratic dictatorship; likewise, modernization could upgrade the level of differentiation denoting democracy in all four realms.

There were two dimensions, then, on which parameters varied that defined societal community, as contrasted with its obverse (whose hermetic fundamentalism failed to be given a name). As it were, the societal community could be likened to Durkheim's organic solidarity, whereas its obverse would be akin to mechanical solidarity. The two dimensions along which social change occurred (in both directions, when anomie was the obverse of integration) were: First, social differentiation qua modernization meant pluralism of systems as well as multiplicity of venues of social membership, expanding the realm of institutionalization of the interaction media; second, social integration qua societal community meant moral consensus, facilitated by security of identification with the functioning of the collectivity based on trust and strictly voluntary commitments.

TODAY'S CHALLENGES: GLOBALIZATION AND CIVIL SOCIETY

One test for Parsons's theory appears to be that it may be applied to the world not only of the 1960s but also today, the start of the new millenium. During the last one or two decades, the secondary literature has pointed out that two features characterized the present-day world, namely globalization and the emergence of civil society. I will now endeavor to test Parsons's conjectures on societal community by applying them to these issues of today.

Globalization

Globalization, discussion of which began in the 1980s but came to the forefront of sociological interest in the post–Cold War era of the 1990s, has two separate but related perspectives. One is that a warning against unanticipated consequences of high-technology systems involving unintended and unmasterable risks of pollution and destabilization, or dangers to political and societal democracy resulting from internationalization of markets or political decision making, raises the spectre of mafialike organizations.[24] In *The Global Age*, Martin Albrow deplores the priority of the economy in the contemporary world set-up. Globalization in the wake of the end of the East-West divide means denationalizaton of the economy, Albrow emphasizes, and he deplores the influence of international institutions regulating national economies such as the International Monetary Fund but also that of large companies spanning ever-larger multinational realms far beyond the reach of national taxation systems.

> Economic globalization involves the growth of economic activity which functions beyond national economies and is organized with reference to the world as a whole. . . . The challenge it poses to national governments is a loss of control, a control which governments hitherto thought the international system guaranteed. (Albrow, 1996: 130)

To counteract this, strengthening national or local realms is not an answer. Roland Robertson (1992) concludes that transnational universalism is nothing but camouflaged particularism due to the fact that the global enterprises of the current decade are linked up with local cultural scenarios. In this way, a fragmentized rather than unitary world emerges, characterized as *glocalization*. The message is that democratic control over ongoing processes is being lost, and irresponsible power elites or business moguls come to more or less openly dominate the scene.

A further aspect is highlighted by Saskia Sassen (1988). She pointed out that the world of today requires that capital as well as labor be highly mobile, transgressing national as well as continental boundaries in a constant flow not only of investment but also of immigration. The new centers of gravitation, she suggests, are the "global cities," conurbation areas functioning as locales for central headquarters of multinational mogul firms but also magnets for masses of uprooted populations. In this vein, categories such as undocumented alien workers or nonimmigrant alien workers involve new elements of the labor force in connection with what she addresses as globalization of production. Frequent separation between production taking place in low-wage countries such as China, Singapore, or Mexico, and top management located in Western countries such as the United States, Sassen suggests, means decoupling between a transnational (potentially, tax-evading) economy and the nation-based, taxation-financed welfare state providing for the living standard of the masses. In this vein, negation of national boundaries through globalization makes for new, and potentially unmasterable, inequalities.

The second aspect of globalization relates to nationalism. In the wake of the decline of the nation, argues David McCrone (1998), national identity acquires connotations of the tribe, particularly in countries such as Germany. The quest for national identity, especially if based on ambiguous identifications, may lead to manichaeist nationalism proclaiming division between the haves and the have-nots out of ressentiment.[25] This danger particularly is seen in the newly emerging democracies in former Communist-Bloc countries[26] but also analyzed in countries, such as the United States and South Africa, where racial discrimination of Blacks was overcome only recently.[27] The main warning in this debate, it appears, is that in the wake of the weakening of the nation, whether or not accompanied by an upsurge of reactionary nationalism, occurs a trend favoring a potentially antiegalitarian, hegemonic though unintended *Westernization of the World.*[28]

Parsons addressed amazingly similar issues in his articles and essays written throughout the 1960s. When he analyzed the issue of then-relevant globalization, the world situation was one of communism posed against capitalism, and "people's democracy" opposed to "democracy." At the time, the world's polarization was between a Communist Soviet Union and its allies in the COMECON economic system intertwined with the Warsaw Pact military union, on the one side, and the capitalist United States surrounded by its allies in the free world united in military vigilance through the North Atlantic Treaty Organization, on the other. The question of convergence of the two types of regimes both representing industrial societies was relatively controversial throughout the 1960s, but occasionally voices would be heard considering supersession of polarization.[29] In 1961, about the time when the Berlin Wall was erected, Parsons had this to say on the topic:

> The polarization of the world community between the so-called free world and the Communist bloc is clearly the most immediate source of the danger of general war, the aspects of which have been subjected to the most intensive discussion. . . . I should . . . like to explore the possibility that . . . this . . . situation presents an opportunity . . . to move in the direction of a stabler system of order in the world. . . . It would be my contention that the very fact of polarization itself implies such an element o[f] order. . . . The crucial fact is the place of the *ideological* "battle" in the situation. An ideological conflict presumes that there is a common frame of reference in terms of which the ideological difference makes sense. The frequent references to the "battle for men's minds" seem to constitute a recognition of this aspect of the situation. (Parsons, 1961a: 115)

He then explicated four elements of order that both sides had in common, albeit in different shape, degree, and distinction. The first element was that economic productivity was given a high value on both sides of the Iron Curtain as were, second, the values of personal as well as political autonomy of the individual; third, equality was a principle for justice in both system types and, as a fourth aspect, education was given high regard as a means to achieve these valued objectives. Since these four elements were present in the " 'imperialist' and in the 'people's' democratic 'nations,'" Parsons went on to say, it appeared conceivable that integration was possible between East and West (Parsons, 1961a: 118).

This insight, no doubt, anticipated the globalization that prevails today. Parsons's analysis may even offer a "new" perspective on the positive and to-be-enhanced aspects of globalization, in the interest of, so to speak, developing a worldwide type of societal community. Considering that integration in the institutionalized social order meant, in the same vein, differentiation between autonomous though not autarchic units, Parsons envisaged four realms where rudimentary communality was already visible between the polarized megasystems. One was "a common set of values" that included economic prosperity and political liberty (although these were incorporated with different emphasis on actual practice into the beliefs and worldviews in the oppositional systems). The second were norms, that is, shared orientations of action such as were established in general in international law, and the United Nations in particular: "The central characteristic . . . is the establishment of consensus at the *procedural* level" (Parsons, 1961a: 125)—with special attention paid to the scope of enforceable sanctions against violators of mutual agreements:

> The UN is a forum short of a court of law in which there is an obligation . . . to hearing the opposition's objections to the case as stated. The very fact of participation in it implies, at some level, recognition of the legitimacy of judgment by "world opinion." (Parsons, 1961a: 126)

The third realm concerned expression of interests either through a monolithic control hierarchy or a pluralist multiplicity of (sub)systems; only the latter allowed for cross-cutting loyalties between different parties, organizations, and so on. "What I am calling a pluralist structure of interests is an important ingredient of stability," Parsons said, stressing the eventual advantages of democracy for peaceful development in any kind of society. The fourth realm, namely ideology, could be related to degree of coercive imposition of a "definition of the situation" when "Communist ideology is the semi-ritual symbolic assertion of the values of modernization." However, Parsons felt that in the long run the "direction of desirable change" was "mitigation of ideological stresses," namely:

> One focus is on the standard of living of the masses, obviously a very sensitive point for the communists. Another is on features of social organization as such, notably, the development of differentiation of collectivities and roles. Still another is on common elements at the cultural level, above all science and the arts. (Parsons, 1961a: 131)

In this way, he conceptualized certain positive aspects of a world order that also appears to be aimed at, more or less inadvertently, today's globalization. Following the (for Parsons, on theoretical grounds foreseeable) breakdown of the divide between a Western world and an Eastern bloc around 1990, a world situation has emerged that contains four elements outlined in Parsons's (first) essay of 1961. In the second essay published in the same year, 1961, Parsons dealt again with the topic of what were "the principal elements of normative order which are present in contemporary international relations" (Parsons, 1961b: 121). He wanted to show elements of community in the polarized scenario of apparent Cold-War conflict, which in turn could help identify the relevant aspects of a world order likely to eventually transcend East-West fragmentation. In an earlier manuscript dealing with the concept of community (Parsons, 1959b), he had identified four problems solved by community structures through their particular set-up of role-categories. These were, he explained, first, territoriality that defined membership through locality for households as they provided foci for identification and identity; second, occupation, which in modern society was linked with education and the provision of services in the economy on a universalistic basis; third, jurisdiction that ensured protection of the individual fulfilling his obligations, who was being protected against illegitimate force encroaching upon his integrity; and fourth, communication that meant exchange through media such as money and generally engendered a common culture of value-commitments.

These four basics, Parsons asserted, helped solve the problem of how nations fit into the picture of the modern world order. Nations provided a locale for the territorial, occupational, legal, and cultural constitution of identity of the citizen in the "globalized" world community. He felt that nations could fulfill the function of territorial reference unit when they safeguarded even control of international organization, through their delegates there: National interests were fulfilled in international organizations, and individual delegates there could act as agents of control who might fight corruption or nepotism. Parsons's second observation concerned pluralism in modern social structures that allowed for common interests of professional groups or private persons in different countries. Professional identity, across boundaries of individual countries, created a "nexus of solidary relationships which crosscut the divisions on the basis of 'national' interest" (Parsons, 1961b: 124). The principle of unity qua diversity, he suggested, could apply to nations as to any social structure. In this vein, nations could become units in an interrelated system held together by international contractual commitments. Such networks encompassing, to use a classic expression, a "noncontractual element of contract," established normative values in the sense explained by Durkheim; internally, as a parallel phenomenon, nations could comprise a pluralistic and nevertheless integrated order.

> This means that the most significant nearly "ultimate" units do not function simply as "individual" units, or as a "mass," but are involved in a complex network of solidary associations which, however, are not completely monolithic but cross-cut each other in significant respects. (Parsons, 1961b: 125)

What can Parsons offer to present-day theory? Both aspects of globalization discussed in current sociological literature were being dealt with by Parsons in the 1960s. For one, that an inadvertently mafialike structure would not emerge that might cause irrefutable deterioration of citizens' lifeworlds, due to extension of the economy beyond the boundaries of countries or continents, was a topic Parsons tackled: He pointed out that four dimensions of common culture were visible that signaled a societal-community type structure in the modernized world. As a second aspect, that unquestionable antidemocratic nationalistic tendencies might emerge due to delegation of control function from nations to international organizations, was a topic Parsons refuted: He pointed out that nations suitably integrated into an internationalized order could become a source of morality on a transnational level. In a way, Parsons's theory of the 1960s appears to have been less pessimistic than some current understandings of globalization.

Parsons's two postulates were (1) Internationalization in the then polarized East-West scenario, for which the United Nations was a forum, could promote differentiation of the world into ever more pluralist spheres. (2) At the same time, pluralism, cherishing values such as universal freedom and equality, held in high regard by both Communist and Western regimes, could strengthen normative commitment to human rights in all the nations that joined together worldwide. In this scenario, nations were no threat to the modern world order. On the contrary, nations constituted a basis for pluralism, both on a regional and global scale. They represented multiculturalism internally, in their social structures, but also, internationally, through sending delegates to organizations such as the UN or the IMF. From this vantage point, today's globalization, in Parsonian terms, may lead to the emergence of a societal-community-type structure worldwide.

Regarding Europe, which in the next decade faces incorporating sixteen and eventually twenty-one nations into an ever-more inclusive entity of transnational community, preserving rather than abolishing individual member nations, Parsons's conception of societal community appears to suggest a theoretical perspective explaining current trends.[30] Although the contemporary process of creating a unified community in Europe (and, indeed, potentially the world) is far from complete, Parsons's "evolutionist-cybernetic" perspective may help understand certain contemporary trends. Not only may Parsons's ideas help us envisage implications of the modernization through unification such as occurs in Europe, but Parsons's theory may also help pinpoint dangers of societal regression such as could loom large in plebiscitarianism, spurring charismatic movements.

Civil Society

The second issue discussed today for which Parsons's theory of societal community is relevant is civil society. In their overview of contemporary society connecting the themes of citizenship and democracy, Jean Cohen and Andrew Arato (1992) endorse approaches ranging from Antonio Gramsci to Jürgen Habermas but fail to take adequate notice of Parsons's work.

Cohen and Arato make two assumptions that might be challenged if Parsons's conceptions are honored. One is their idea that power is lodged with government, whose task is to secure equal distribution of legal rights and economic status, and the other is their presumption that citizenship, which denotes cultural heterogeneity can only be attained subsequent to a revolution (or comparatively drastic social change, respectively).

Cohen and Arato endorse universal politicization as they propose to create an extensive public sphere which, in turn, is an arena for expression of individual rights and needs. Their perspective is that the "self-reflective and self-limiting utopia of civil society" (Cohen and Arato, 1992: 451) is not imminent, let alone already an ongoing process of ubiquitous social change. They proclaim an ideal of cultural heterogeneity, securing freedom of self-realization for every social group and category of persons, but they are convinced that hitherto disenfranchised minorities such as women or Blacks have not seen promising changes in their status position already. They suggest that through political self-expression, social groups should be enabled to voice their needs and make themselves felt as powerful groups, but they are convinced that governments are still far too powerful. Govermental power, they think, needs to be overcome through more or less revolutionary movements, if equality and cultural autonomy are to be achieved.

Parsons, to be sure, made different assumptions and arrived at a different prognosis. As regards political power, Parsons, as discussed above, presupposed a network of interacting associations that was not to be conceived as a zero-sum game. When the cybernetic notion of political power was used, he felt, a world of ever-increasing quantity and quality of empowerment in society became visible. Interestingly, this latter idea of Parsons was precisely what Cohen and Arato proposed, though they thought such a future world could be attained only through some kind of revolutionary change:

> Where the polity is sufficiently differentiated so that power has become genuinely a generalized medium we can say that collective units are expected to be successful in the sense that the binding obligations they undertake in order to maintain and create opportunities for effectiveness, is balanced by the input of equally binding commitments to perform service, either within the collectivity in some status of employment, or for the collectivity on a contractual basis. (Cohen and Arato, 1992: 253)

It appears that Parsons delineated precisely the type of egalitarian society that is being envisaged by Cohen and Arato under their label of civil society. The two approaches differed from each other, interestingly, in that Parsons believed that drastic social change was unnecessary since developmental tendencies in present-day society were already in the desired direction, whereas Cohen and Arato, who failed to use cybernetic analytical concepts, missed this perspective.

Another similarity between Cohen and Arato and Parsons was that future society would be beyond crude economic inequalities. In the eyes of Cohen and Arato, superceding"the logics of money and power" was the answer. In Parsons's view, utilitarianism had to be overcome. He pleaded for a society reigned over by the spirit of solidarity replacing utilitarianism. No doubt, what Cohen and Arato demanded was amazingly close to what Parsons aimed to explicate as modern societies' perspective of (further) modernization, in his theory of societal community.[31]

When Cohen and Arato discuss citizenship, they think of cultural, ethnic, religious, and gender heterogeneity, which they wish to preserve when equal rights are granted to all citizens. They presuppose that society is made up of conflicting elements differing in ethnicity, gender, and class status elements. But, nevertheless, equal claims for participation in the economic, political, and cultural worlds should be realized, they demand. Cohen and Arato see in this ideal a "utopia of civil society." "The project of a democratic civil society, its model of differentiation, is obviously one of decolonizing the lifeworld," they explain, borrowing from Habermas the distinction between system and lifeworld and also the metaphor of decolonization (Cohen and Arato, 1992: 455). They propose that governmental control be confined to an "institutional core of civil society itself," thus allowing for the free development of heterogeneity and differentiation among all groups in society (1992: 456).

What Cohen and Arato seem not to realize, and what Habermas equally appears to have missed, is that their proposals resemble Parsons's analytical findings. The phenomenon here labeled decolonization of the lifeworld had been introduced by Parsons. Under the label of "desocialization" of ethnic and other statuses, he diagnosed as a tendency in contemporary American society what Cohen and Arato (and, for that matter, Habermas) desire only for a future world. Ethnicity, as Parsons explained in his essays published in 1965 and 1975, had defined "second-class citizen" status in the United States until the middle 1960s but increasingly came to lose its stigma quality only in the wake of the civil rights movement and legislation. Parsons thought that ethnicity had changed its social significance in the decade following the civil rights legislation of the 1960s, which was an example of "desocialization" transforming previously ascriptive categories into achieved and/or "privatized" characteristics of individuals.

When he described what kind of society he saw emerging, Parsons anticipated in his own time what Habermas and also Cohen and Arato only postulated as a utopia. He concluded that, albeit in statu nascendi, the relentless modernizing effort of the "first new nation," the United States,[32] made this country a model crowning previous democratization with further modernization.

Parsons's "Full Citizenship for the Negro American?," written at the height of the civil rights struggles in the 1960s, on the occasion of an American Academy of Arts and Sciences conference on race and poverty, equated racial justice with citizenship. Blacks had been denied full citizenship in the United States despite their having been Americans since the earliest days of the nation, he realized. Only their achieving equal opportunities in the political sphere through active and passive voting rights, in the economy through equality of educational and occupational achievement, and in the legal system through control of discrimination in the courts, would ensure at last their full participation as American citizens in their own society. Indeed, he insisted, only citizenship as at the time was being granted Black Americans could secure the very interactional mutuality that had been the hallmark of the nation since its beginnings. Only this, he stressed, ensured a full-fledged societal community:

> The concept of citizenship . . . refers to full membership in what I . . . call the *societal community*. This term refers to that aspect of the total society as a system, which forms a *Gemeinschaft*, which is the focus of solidarity or mutual loyalty of its members, and which constitutes the consensual base underlying its political integration. (Parsons, 1965: 1009–10)

The solution, in this vein, was not in the formula "separate but equal," but only in "mutual solidarity":

> Perhaps John Rawls has formulated, in general philosophical terms, more clearly than anyone else the way in which full citizenship implies a fundamental equality of rights— not equality in *all* senses, but in the sense in which we refer to the rights of membership status in the societal community. (Parsons, 1965: 1010)

Ten years later, Parsons recognized "desocialization" of ethnicity: "The development of what we have called ethnic pluralism in American society has involved major changes in the character of ethnic groups themselves. . . . There is a certain sense in which they have been 'desocialized' and transformed into primarily cultural-symbolic groups" (Parsons, 1975a: 66). The crucial aspect of ethnicity losing its discriminatory effect, he argued, meant that, as could be observed with a person whose parents were immigrants from different racial or ethnic backgrounds, ethnicity tended to become a matter of choice rather than fate. Similar to religion, where choice had replaced ascriptive definitiveness, race now could become optional, most visibly for the considerable part of the population whose parents were of different racial backgrounds. This, he asserted, signaled the kind of assimilation which had integrated into U.S. society millions of Jews, Italians, Irish, Greek, Swedes, and others, who had become full-fledged citizens differing in their "private" ethnicity. This opened up a world of cultural pluralism. Political, economic, and human rights should be the same for every citizen.[33]

No doubt, this kind of world matched the one projected unto the better future by Cohen and Arato and also Habermas, devising their presumed utopia. When Parsons argued cybernetically expectable processes of social change in the 1960s and 1970s, he pictured citizenship in a way that left nothing to be desired when compared with Cohen and Arato's idea of civil society.

CONCLUSION

My argument started with Parsons's conceptualizing, as "another category of symbolic systems, . . . the media of interchange"(Parsons, 1968c/1977: 198).[34] He summarized his thought thus:

> Money . . . is in fact a very highly specialized language. Crucial here is the recognition that it operates at the *symbolic* level and that its primary function is communication,

though of a special normative sort. The "monetary system" is a *code*. . . . Second, money is not the only specialized language of this sort operating in a social system. Political power is certainly another. . . . A third generalized symbolic medium is influence. By this I mean, quite technically, the capacity to achieve 'consensus' with other members of an associated group through persuasion. . . . Fourth is the medium of generalized *commit-ments* to the implementation of cultural values, at the level of the social system as such. It is the most difficult to conceptualize, and the least can be said about it. (Parsons, 1968c/1977: 198)

Exchange media, he understood, helped understand social differentiation which, in turn, meant growth in pluralism not only in modern societies, but already in the ancient world. In order to avoid anomie that resulted from disintegration, he knew, processes of integration were vital, the most important of which culminated in the formation of a societal community.

Societal community, as he defined it, was characterized by consensus regarding morally relevant values. If fully developed, societal community gave a sense of security to the citizens. In a functioning societal community, citizens voluntarily fulfilled their legitimate duties and realized their rights to control the world of power through effectiveness, influencing cocitizens through prestige allowing for persuasion. (In regard to value-commitments, citizens had to put into practice what they preached, optimally reciprocity-prone ideals.)

A functioning societal community, however, was not a given but an accomplishment that was relatively precarious. Processes of dedifferentiation, Parsons explained in the context of the interaction media, could threaten a society or its societal community. In this vein, dictatorships or other forms denoting "deflationary tendencies" could threaten the balance of power and participation in a society. He clarified that, for the United States, McCarthyism had been a "deflationary" reaction of the American mind to the tensions, for one, created by the discrepancy between traditional images of individualism and the scope of modern responsible government in the wake of the New Deal. The obverse of this type of imbalance, inflation, was equally dangerous to the societal community (although he analyzed it less thoroughly than deflation).

To summarize, Parsons's analysis of societal community can serve beautifully to understand contemporary issues of globalization and civil society discussed since the 1990s. Indeed, his analysis of societal community spans both globalization and civil society when welding together these two topics into one theory.

In the last part of my contribution, I compared some recent approaches analyzing globalization, and also Cohen and Arato's analysis of civil society, with Parsons's theory of societal community explicated mainly in the 1960s. My conclusion is that Parsons's theory of societal community is precisely the type of social theory that the sociological community has been looking for since about 1990. When, in the wake of the end of the Cold War, a new agenda has come to be called for, with "new" concepts needed for analyzing contemporary transitions in world society, nobody appears to have looked back to Parsons. However, emulating the title of a well-known movie, *Back to the Future*, might prove a worthy motto for sociology in this respect. When theory is the conceptual framework for analysis and research, Parsons's "evolutionist-cybernetic" conception of societal community will prove the prolific for understanding society in the new millenium.

NOTES

This chapter, suitably shortened, was originally presented at the 97th Annual Meetings of the American Sociological Association at Chicago, 1999. For comments and encouragement, I wish to thank Bernard Barber, Victor Lidz, A. Javier Treviño, and Edward Tiryakian.

1. See book reviews, Becker (1952), Faris (1953), and Gerth (1997) but also House (1950), on the second edition of *The Structure of Social Action*, as well as Coser (1950) on the 1949 volume of *Essays in Sociological Theory*. For instance, Faris wrote in his review:

> An author who proposes to introduce a new set of concepts is under obligation to be very precise in his definitions. Parsons has difficulty in achieving clarity and brevity. . . . The lack of clarity resulting from the unfamiliar combinations in this book are not insuperable obstacles to its understanding if the reader will devote sufficient time to the task. . . . It is my belief that the author can produce a far better book than this. If an old man whose work is done can venture to exhort a gifted scholar in the prime of life, I would urge him to continue to be productive in the hope that his views and my own should come more closely to correspond, assuming at the same time that we both wish to approach ever nearer the truth. (Faris, 1953: 504–6).

House, who reviewed the second edition of *Structure of Social Action* as he had the first, complained that it had remained the same as the first edition (except for five-and-a-half pages of a new preface), losing nothing of its "abstruse[ness] in style." Coser reviewing *Essays in Sociological Theory* saw a common interest with *The Structure of Social Action* to transform American sociology "from an approach to a 'science'" but did not find Parsons's view particularly illuminating. Discussing Parsons's essay "Propaganda and Social Control" (reprinted in *Essays*) in some detail, Coser had this to say:

> Parsons, instead of discussing the reasons for this disparity (viz., between the needs, values, and ideologies of large parts of the population, UG), instead of analyzing the causes of disaffectation, simply turns around and counsels decision-makers on how best to maintain the social structure. This is the point, indeed, at which theoretical analysis of functional interrelations which is limited to total systems turns into a defense of total systems, even to the extent of condoning and advocating manipulation and a sort of intellectual rape. (Coser, 1950: 504)

2. Parsons had first mentioned that power was not a zero-sum phenomenon in his criticism of C. W. Mills's *The Power Elite*, analyzing the American power structure (Parsons, 1957). However, it took until November 1962 when the American Philosophical Society required that he present a paper, as a condition of his membership in that Society, that he dealt with the topic directly. He had come to realize how serendipitous was the discovery judging from the enthusiastic reaction he had received earlier in the same year when he presented a closely related paper, on influence, at the annual meeting of the American Society of Public Opinion Research.

3. For *International Encyclopedia of the Social Sciences*, Parsons also wrote the entry "Social Interaction," elaborating on the four media of communication, invoking Weber's theory of social action (Parsons, 1968c).

4. See, for example, "The Negro American as Citizen," draft of an article for the *Washington Post*, written in 1965 but apparently never printed, at Harvard University Archives, call No. HUG(FP)—Talcott Parsons—42.41, Box 4.

5. Bourricaud (1981: 174), citing Parsons (1963a/1969a: 406). The background story is as follows: In 1956, Harvard linguist Roman Jakobson together with Morris Halle, who taught at MIT, had published a book, which appeared, to Parsons, as a perfect demonstration of how spoken language was systematic when it fit amazing flexibly into the contexts of interpersonal relations in everyday venues (Jakobson and Halle, 1956). Indeed, Parsons and Jakobson, between 1960 and 1962, planned to write a book together, which, unfortunately, never materialized.

6. Bourricaud (1981: 175) quoting Jakobson (1963: 90). Bourricaud (erroneously citing p. 91) quotes from the French book on linguistics, translated into English.

7. For a first comprehensive documentation of research and theory on the topic as it had been discussed since the early 1940s, see Bendix and Lipset (1953). The title of their collection suggested what they substantiated, through the contributions to the volume: that class, which stood for money as a medium and suggested an economic dimension of societies, and power, which stood for the political structures, were to be supplemented by a third medium that had come to be used as the preferred dimension on which social status was measured in empirical studies, namely prestige, which presumably was a noneconomic, nonpolitical dimension of social structures. The first to use prestige as one indicator of social status had been W. Lloyd Warner in the series of investigations on the social structure of a "typical" American town termed "Yankeetown," in the so-called Yankeetown series of studies whose first volume appeared in 1941. See Warner, Meeker, and Eells (1949) (based on seven volumes published from 1941 onward), as well as, for instance, Hatt (1950). A comprehensive overview, assembling the important authors, is Reiss (1961).

8. Public opinion was being researched from the 1920s as a topic of theoretical and empirical interest, instigating survey research (for a theoretical view see, for instance, Dewey [1927]). In the 1930s, a journal was founded that dealt with the nature and measurement of public opinion (*Public Opinion Quarterly*). The theoretical issue was whether public opinion was a phenomenon akin to *conscience collective*. The latter idea involved a political aspect. For a first comprehensive treatise on this latter topic, in the 1940s when the United States, as a democracy, fought against Nazi Germany, see Friedrich (1942).

9. In the reprinted versions in *Politics and Social Structure*, Parsons dated the two papers, giving a publication date of "Spring, 1963" for the influence paper, and "June, 1963" for the essay on power; indeed, he first presented the former at a conference in the summer of 1962 and the latter in the fall of that year. Both papers, however, were presented from notes and elaborated only later, thereby making the final version of the paper follow the conceptualization and first draft of the power paper. Behind both papers, to be sure, was an idea originally meant to warrant a major book tentatively titled "American Society," a book never finished, though Parsons together with Winston White were engaged in drafting various chapters between 1960 and 1963.

10. Parsons cited, and guarded himself against, Herbert Blumer's explication of the social theory of George Herbert Mead and partial rejection of W. I. Thomas and Florian Znaniecki's classic *The Polish Peasant in Europe and America* (originally, 1918–20). In a long manuscript published in 1939 and republished in 1946, Blumer had not only defended his invention of the name of symbolic interactionism for G. H. Mead's theory but distanced himself from Thomas and Znaniecki's research, which Parsons cherished. Parsons now disavowed the perspective created by Blumer's presumptively original, anti–Thomas and Znaniecki "Chicago sociology." See Blumer (1946) but also, for a somewhat wider net cast corroborating Parsons's view, Gerhardt (2000). I should mention that Blumer's symbolic interactionism resembled so-called labeling theory in the 1960s.

11. Parsons opposed Harold Lasswell and equally David Easton, two prominent political scientists at the University of Chicago. He objected to their equating the political system with the sum total of politically relevant events in society, whereas he preferred a more theory-prone notion of system—an ideal-type model, so to speak—against which many empirical systems and events figured but as deviations from the conceptually postulated theoretical model. To be sure, only the latter allowed for a cybernetically adequate conceptualization of democracy. See, for the Lasswell and Easton positions, respectively, Lasswell (1950) and Easton (1953). The criticism, to be sure, was none too sweeping. For instance, Parsons (1963b/1969a: 357) acknowledged that he used the term "demand" in a sense elaborated by Easton (1957).

12. See for elucidation of the complicated scenario, the most elaborate diagrams at the end of the article, "On the Concept of Political Power."

13. Weber, in 1917, explained further these two types of individual ethical orientation in modern societies. He saw, on the one hand, *Gesinnungsethik* that might favor syndicalism, a radical worldview involving willingness to resort to state violence (as in Mussolini fascism, which originated in a syndicalist "revolution" in 1922) which, in Weber's lifetime, fascinated his erstwhile student and friend Robert Michels. The other type of ethics was a more moderate view that denied the state violence despite the fact that the modern state held a monopoly on means of force (as in Imperial Germany but also, after 1919, the Weimar Republic). Weber contrasted *Gesinnungsethik* and *Verantwortungsethik* in his essay, "Der Sinn der 'Wertfreiheit' in den ökonomischen und soziologischen Wissenschaften," originally published in 1917 and translated in 1949 by Edward Shils and a collaborator.

14. See Parsons's most insightful and somewhat moving unpublished considerations on the occasion of the assassination of President Kennedy in late 1963. In this short text preserved in the Harvard University Archives, Parsons argued that the fact that memorial services for Kennedy were being celebrated in the Roman Catholic rite and broadcast on television to millions of Americans had an unanticipated consequence. The Catholic religion, which had been discriminated against even in 1960 during Kennedy's election campaign, was being accepted as equal to Protestantism (or, indeed, Judaism), which many until then had considered, so to speak, "more" patriotic. He wrote: "The funeral was unquestionably a crucially important symbolization of the new ecumenical status of the American community in its relation to the religious affiliations of its members. . . . It was taken for granted that he should have a Catholic funeral. . . . For the first time, . . . the implications of the American system of denominational pluralism, and the peculiar balance between the public and private status of religion in our society, came to the sharpest symbolic focus." Memorandum, starting with "We have put our principal emphasis . . .," in Harvard University Archives, call No. HUG(FP)—Talcott Parsons—42.45.1, Box 1.

15. Parsons, Memorandum: "The Problem of Polarization on the Axis of Color," p. 2; Harvard University Archives, stored under the call number, HUG(FP)—Talcott Parsons—42.45.4, Box 4. Quotations in the next three paragraphs are from the same memorandum, pp. 9–10.

16. This change, to be sure, made Parsons speak of the "Negro American" rather than the American Negro. This rendered race a personalized category of ethnic identity among Americans. In the mid-1970s, he explained this change further as "desocialization" of ethnicity (which was the new term replacing that of race), suggesting that ethnicity (race) lost its discriminatory significance in social life. One background of such "desocialization," he realized, was that ethnicity was a matter of pluralistic participation inasmuch as Americans usually had various ethnic backgrounds that they combined in their person (a case in point was Alex Haley, African-American author of the novel *Roots*, whose father had been Irish). See Parsons (1975a).

17. The learning theory of Clark Hull had stated that stimulus-response chains of an apparently mechanistic nature, allowing for the conditioning of various sorts of building se-

quences of association, were the dominant mode of acquisition of knowledge for humans, as exemplified in the learning process observed in laboratory rats. Hull's behavioristic learning theory, which was first developed in the 1930s, dominated American psychology until the 1950s and beyond.

18. It was following the quoted statement that Parsons went on to say that the cultural level of the organization of living systems was in an evolutionary sense quite different from the behavior of rats and pigeons—thus holding against Homans that, taking Olds's findings seriously, one had to oppose even the psychology borrowed from Hull as used by Homans. In this way, Parsons opposed Homans's grounding his conjectures regarding elementary social behavior in psychological knowledge, suggesting that sociology be grounded in its own proven knowledge on an autonomous reality in society, instead of economics-derived psychology of individual actor(s).

19. This point, to be sure, had been Parsons's main theme in his classic, *The Structure of Social Action*. There, he had argued against social Darwinism as it inspired German Nazi "science," in the 1930s, but also against utilitarianism as first expounded by Herbert Spencer, among others. Parsons found utilitarianism a treacherous road to sociological analysis, replacing social Darwinism and its related approaches in positivism and utilitarianism with theories of European origin, predominantly those of Émile Durkheim and Max Weber. See also, discussing the anti-Darwinist thrust in Parsons (1937), Gerhardt (1999a).

20. It was with respect to these two alternatives that Parsons spoke of the "duality of the category, 'political'" (1969c: 474ff.):

> The category "political," I think, shares with that of "economic" and indeed of "social" a certain duality of reference which sometimes leads to ambiguity. Thus we may ask: Was not the Great Depression an "economic" phenomenon? And was not McCarthyism a "political" phenomenon? The whole tenor of the New Deal, however, made coping with the Great Depression and its consequences as much a political as an economic problem. I have suggested, further, that the primary roots of McCarthyism lay in strains in the societal community, not in the polity as that concept has here been defined with analytical strictness. . . . The primary link between the two references of the concept "political" lies, I think, in the conception of collective system goal-attainment. . . . Full "attainment" of a system goal would then constitute an equilibrium point at which striving for such attainment would cease. . . . "[P]roblems" as that of the health of its population, or of the level of their motivation to role performance, may be political problems for a society, as may be the improvement of the level of knowledge through research. (Parsons, 1969c: 474–75)

21. Lasswell (1934) had argued that personal insecurity due to loss of identification with a nation or type of system endangered the democratic world order. Communism established in the Bolshevist revolution, for instance, had replaced the czarist regime in Russia when personal insecurity, in the course of World War I, had reached enormous proportions.

22. Parsons (1942) used Lasswell's thesis to explain the successes of fascist movements in Europe. His sociological explanation of how democratic nations could lapse into fascism, which was his presidential address to the Eastern Sociological Society, was part and parcel of the antifascism, prodemocracy analytic endeavors at Harvard University supporting the American world effort in World War II. See for details on some of the background, Gerhardt (1999b).

23. He added, "Fortunately, from my point of view (but then I am neither a committed capitalist nor a committed socialist), we have been experiencing a certain loosening of these fundamental rigidities, and new degrees of freedom are now beginning to appear" (Parsons, 1968e/1969a: 465).

24. See, for this type of diagnosis, Beck (1992, 1997). Beck's book entitled *Risk Society* (*Risikogesellschaft*) first appeared in 1986 when it became a best-seller during the next decade.

218   *Gerhardt*

His main point is that despite elaborate systems of security in modern society, residual risks such as those from the use of nuclear power for energy production, or contingent risks such as are in the liberation of women for the dissolution of marriage and the family, produce uncontrollable realms of danger to the peace of mind of the average citizen. Such risks and realms of danger, Beck hypothesizes, characterize today's entire world with the increase in globalization of economic production and political governance throughout the 1990s.

25. See, for such type analysis, Billig (1995), James (1996), or McCrone (1998).

26. See for this, Offe (1994).

27. See, for instance, Fredrickson (1997).

28. See, for this theme, Latouche (1996). His sympathy, no doubt, lies with the non-Westernized forces both in developed countries, where they are said to constitute nonconformist social movements, and underdeveloped countries, where they are meant to strengthen indigenous cultural elements.

29. One such voice, to be sure, was Parsons's, who, originally in a paper first written in 1960, discussed the chances of a world system beyond polarization (Parsons 1961a, 1961b, 1962a). One voice seriously doubting convergence, interestingly, was Goldthorpe (1966), who held that convergence between East and West along the line of their shared industrialism was unlikely, and their political systems differed anyhow. This led to the conclusion, Goldthorpe felt, that for the Communist bloc, democratization that presumably was inescapable was a myth.

30. Mathias Boes's analytical view on gradual transgression, combined with relative preservation of multiple boundaries in the piecemeal development of Europe in the sequence of stages of development of the European Union since it was originally established in 1958, offers an interesting arena for applying Parsons's cybernetic notion of societal community. See Boes (2000).

31. One approach looking at issues of today's society in Parsonian terms, conceptualizing potential parameters of civil society on the background of the likelihood of system convergence worldwide, is Inkeles (1999).

32. Using Lipset's (1963) book for reference, in 1975, in his second major contribution to the debate on ethnicity of Black Americans, Parsons argued that the "melting pot" processes making for the "First New Nation" were all but completed only in the present. See Parsons (1975a).

33. Of course, Parsons was aware of the fact that cultural pluralism flanked by equality of economic, political, and legal rights was far from being fully realized in U.S. society. His point was that he wished to delineate the structural tendencies in the present-day system, as an analytically postulated projection based on available empirical evidence. This allowed him to conceptualize contemporary and future facts and developments in terms of whether or not they fitted the modernization trend, or represented tendencies toward regression, or residues of past constellations.

34. The other two he mentioned were "ideas" and " 'expressive symbols' in the arts and in ritual."

REFERENCES

Albrow, M. 1996. *The Global Age: State and Society Beyond Modernity.* Cambridge, Eng.: Polity Press.

Alexander, J. C. 1998. "Citizen and Enemy as Symbolic Classification: On the Polarizing Discourse of Civil Society." Pp. 96–114 in *Real Civil Societies: Dilemmas of Institutionalization,* edited by J. C. Alexander. London: Sage.

Barber, B., and U. Gerhardt, eds. 1999. *Agenda for Sociology: Classic Sources and Current Uses of Talcott Parsons's Work.* Baden-Baden: Nomos.

Beck, U. 1992. *Risk Society*. Cambridge, Eng.: Polity.

———. 1997. *Was ist Globalisierung?* Frankfurt: Suhrkamp.

Becker, H. 1952. "Book Review: Talcott Parsons's *The Social System*." *Social Forces* 30 (4): 463–65.

Bellah, R. N. 1967. "Civil Religion in America." *Daedalus* 96 (1): 1–21.

Bendix, R., and S. M. Lipset, eds. 1953. *Class, Status, and Power*. New York: Free Press.

Billig, M. 1995. *Banal Nationalism*. London: Sage.

Blumer, H. 1946. *An Appraisal of Thomas and Znaniecki's The Polish Peasant in Europe and America*. New York: A Social Science Research Council Monograph.

Boes, M. 2000. "Die Grenzen der europäischen Gesellschaft—Das Spannungsfeld von Territorien, Bevölkerungen und Kulturen in Europa" (Unpublished manuscript).

Bourricaud, F. 1981. *The Sociology of Talcott Parsons*. Trans. A. Goldhammer. Chicago: University of Chicago Press.

Cohen, J., and A. Arato. 1992. *Civil Society and Political Theory*. Cambridge: MIT Press.

Coser, L. 1950. "Book Review: *Essays in Sociological Theory*, by Talcott Parsons." *American Journal of Sociology* 55 (5): 502–4.

———. 1956. *The Functions of Social Conflict*. New York: Free Press.

Dahrendorf, R. 1958. "Out of Utopia: Toward a Reorientation of Sociological Analysis." *American Journal of Sociology* 64 (2): 115–27.

Dewey, J. 1927. *The Public and Its Problems*. New York: Henry Holt.

Easton, D. 1953. *The Political System: An Inquiry Into the State of Political Science*. New York: Knopf.

———. 1957. "An Approach to the Analysis of Political Systems." *World Politics* 9 (3): 383–400.

Faris, E. 1953. "Book Review: Talcott Parsons's *The Social System*." *American Sociological Review* 18 (1): 103–6.

Fredrickson, G. M., ed. 1997. *The Comparative Imagination: On the History of Racism, Nationalism, and Social Movements*. Berkeley: University of California Press.

Friedrich, C. J. 1942. *The New Belief in the Common Man*. Boston: Beacon.

———, ed. 1959. *Community*. New York: Liberal Arts Press.

Gerhardt, U. 1999a. "National Socialism and the Politics of *The Structure of Social Action*." Pp. 87–164 in *Agenda for Sociology: Classic Sources and Current Uses of Talcott Parsons's Work*, edited by B. Barber and U. Gerhardt. Baden-Baden: Nomos.

———. 1999b. "A World from Brave to New: Talcott Parsons and the War Effort at Harvard University." *Journal of the History of Behavioral Sciences* 35(3): 257–90.

———. 2000. "Ambivalent Interactionist: Anselm Strauss and the 'Schools' of Chicago Sociology." *The American Sociologist* 31 (4): 34–64.

Gerth, H. 1997. "On Talcott Parsons' *The Social System*." *International Journal of Politics, Culture, and Society* 10 (4): 673–84.

Goldthorpe, J. 1966. "Social Stratification in Industrial Societies." Pp. 648–59 in *Class, Status, and Power*, 2nd ed., edited by R. Bendix and S. M. Lipset. New York: Free Press.

Gouldner, A. 1970. *The Coming Crisis of Western Sociology*. London: Heinemann.

Harrington, M. 1962. *The Other America: Poverty in the United States*. New York: Macmillan.

Hatt, P. K. 1950. "Occupations and Social Stratification." *American Journal of Sociology* 55 (6): 533–43.

Holton, R., and B. S. Turner. 1986. *Talcott Parsons on Economy and Society*. London: Routledge and Kegan Paul.

Homans, G. 1961. *Social Behavior—Its Elementary Forms*. New York: Harcourt Brace Jovanovich.

House, F. 1950. "Book Review: *The Structure of Social Action*, by Talcott Parsons" (2nd ed., 1949). *American Journal of Sociology* 55 (5): 504–5.

Inkeles, A. 1999. "Parsons and the Theory of Convergence in Societal Systems." Pp. 233–48 in *Agenda for Sociology*, edited by B. Barber and U. Gerhardt. Baden-Baden: Nomos.

Jakobson R. 1963. *Essais de linguistique générale*. Vol. 1. Paris: Editions de Minuit.

Jakobson, R., and M. Halle. 1956. *Fundamentals of Language*. The Hague: Mouton.

James, P. 1996. *Nation Formation: Toward a Theory of Abstract Community*. London: Sage.

Kennedy, R. [1965] 1969. *Thirteen Days: A Memoir of the Cuban Missile Crisis*. With introductions by R. S. McNamara and H. Macmillan. New York: Norton.

Lasswell, H. 1934. *World Politics and Personal Insecurity*. New York: Macmillan.

———. 1950. *A Study of Power*. Glencoe, Ill.: Free Press.

Latouche, S. 1996. *The Westernization of the World: The Significance, Scope and Limits of the Drive toward Global Uniformity*. Cambridge, Eng.: Polity.

Lipset, S. M. 1963. *The First New Nation: The United States in Historical & Comparative Perspective*. New York: Norton.

McCrone, D. 1998. *The Sociology of Nationalism*. London: Routledge.

McKinney, J., and E. Tiryakian. 1970. *Theoretical Sociology: Perspectives and Developments*. New York: Appleton-Century-Crofts.

Mills, C. W. 1959. *The Sociological Imagination*. New York: Oxford University Press.

Moynihan, D. P. 1969. *Maximum Feasible Misunderstanding: Community Action in the War on Poverty*. New York: Free Press.

Münch, R. 1999. "The Problem of Social Order, Sixty Years after *The Structure of Social Action*." Pp. 211–32 in *Agenda for Sociology: Classic Sources and Current Uses of Talcott Parsons's Work*, edited by B. Barber and U. Gerhardt. Baden-Baden: Nomos.

Offe, C. 1994. *Der Tunnel am Ende des Lichts: Erkundungen der politischen Transformation im Neuen Osten*. Frankfurt: Campus.

Parsons, T. 1937. *The Structure of Social Action: A Study in Social Theory with Reference to a Group of Recent European Writers*. New York: McGraw-Hill.

———. 1942. "Some Sociological Aspects of the Fascist Movements." *Social Forces* 21 (2): 137–47.

———. 1951. *The Social System*. New York: Free Press.

———. 1957. "The Distribution of Power in American Society." *World Politics* 10 (1): 123–43.

———. 1959a. "Durkheim's Contribution to the Theory of Integration of Social Systems." Pp. 118–53 in *Essays on Sociology and Philosophy by Emile Durkheim et al. with appraisals of his life and thought*, edited by K. H. Wolff. New York: Harper and Row.

———. 1959b. "The Principle Structures of Community: A Sociological View." Pp. 152–79 in *Community*, edited by C. J. Friedrich. New York: Liberal Arts Press.

———. 1961a. "Polarization and the Problem of International Order." *Berkeley Journal of Sociology* 6 (1): 115–34.

———. 1961b. "Order and Community in the International Social System." Pp. 120–29 in *International Politics and Foreign Policy*, edited by J. N. Rosenau. New York: Free Press of Glencoe.

———. 1961c. "Some Considerations on the Theory of Social Change." *Rural Sociology* 26 (3): 219–39.

———. 1962a. "Polarization of the World and International Order." Pp. 310–31 in *Preventing World War III: Some Proposals*, edited by Q. Wright, W. E. Evan, and M. Deutsch. New York: Simon and Schuster.

———. 1962b. "Social Strains in America: A Postscript." In *The Radical Right*, edited by D. Bell. Garden City, N.Y.: Doubleday 1963 (reprinted pp. 163–84 in *Politics and Social Structure*. New York: Free Press, 1969).

———. 1963a. "On the Concept of Influence." *Public Opinion Quarterly* 27 (1): 37–62 (reprinted pp. 405–429 in *Politics and Social Structure*. New York: Free Press, 1969).

———. 1963b. "On the Concept of Power." *Proceedings of the American Philosophical Society* 107: 232–67 (reprinted pp. 352–404 in *Politics and Social Structure*. New York: Free Press, 1969).

———. 1964a. "Some Reflections on the Place of Force in Social Process." Pp. 33–70 in *Internal War: Basic Problems and Approaches*, edited by H. Eckstein. New York: Free Press of Glencoe.

———. 1964b. "Levels of Organization and the Mediation of Social Interaction." *Sociological Inquiry* 34: 207–20.

———. 1965. "Full Citizenship for the Negro American? A Sociological Problem." *Daedalus* 94 (4): 1009–54.

———. 1966a. *Societies: Evolutionary and Comparative Perspectives.* Englewood Cliffs, N.J.: Prentice-Hall.

———. 1966b. "The Concept of Society: The Components and Their Interrelations." Pp. 5–29 In *Societies: Evolutionary and Comparative Perspectives.* (reprinted pp. 5–33 in *Politics and Social Structure*. New York: Free Press, 1969).

———. 1966c. "The Political Aspect of Social Structure and Process." Pp. 71–112 in *Varieties of Political Theory*, edited by D. Easton. Englewood Cliffs, N.J.: Prentice-Hall (reprinted pp. 317–51 in *Politics and Social Structure*. New York: Free Press, 1969).

———. 1967. "The Nature of American Pluralism." Pp. 249–61 in *Religion and Public Education*, edited by T. R. Sizer. Boston: Houghton Mifflin.

———. 1968a. "Order as a Sociological Problem." Pp. 373–84 in *The Concept of Order*, edited by P. G. Kuntz. Seattle: University of Washington Press.

———. 1968b. "Durkheim, Émile." Pp. 311–20 in *International Encyclopedia of the Social Sciences*, vol. 4, edited by D. Sills. New York: Free Press.

———. 1968c. "Social Interaction." Pp. 424–41 in *International Encyclopedia of the Social Sciences*, vol. 7, edited by D. Sills. New York: Free Press.

———. 1968d. "Social Systems." Pp. 458–73 in *International Encyclopaedia of the Social Sciences*, vol. 15, edited by D. Sills. New York: Free Press (Reprinted pp. 177–203 in *Social Systems and the Evolution of Action Theory*. New York: Free Press, 1977).

———. 1968e. "On the Concept of Value-Commitments." *Sociological Inquiry* 38 (2): 135–60 (reprinted pp. 439–72 in *Politics and Social Structure*. New York: Free Press, 1969).

———. 1969a. *Politics and Social Structure.* New York: Free Press.

———. 1969b. "Theoretical Orientations on Modern Societies." Pp. 34–57 in *Politics and Social Structure*, edited by T. Parsons. New York: Free Press.

———. 1969c. "Polity and Society: Some General Considerations." Pp. 473–522 in *Politics and Social Structure*. New York: Free Press.

———. 1970a. "On Building Social Systems Theory: A Personal History." *Daedalus* 99 (4): 826–81 (reprinted pp. 22–76 in *Social Systems and the Evolution of Action Theory*. New York: Free Press, 1977).

———. 1970b. "Equality and Inequality in Modern Society, or Social Stratification Revisited." *Sociological Inquiry* 40 (Spring): 13–72 (reprinted pp. 321–80 in *Social Systems and the Evolution of Action Theory*. New York: Free Press, 1977).

———. 1970c. "Some Problems of General Theory in Sociology." pp. 28–68 in *Theoretical Sociology: Perspectives and Developments*, edited by J. McKinney and E. A. Tiryakian. New York: Appleton-Century-Crofts (reprinted pp. 229–69 in *Social Systems and the Evolution of Action Theory*. New York: Free Press, 1977).

———. 1971. *The Systems of Modern Societies.* Englewood Cliffs, N.J.: Prentice-Hall.

————. 1975a. "Some Theoretical Considerations on the Nature and Trends of Ethnicity." Pp. 53–83 in *Ethnicity: Theory and Experience*, edited by N. Glazer and D. P. Moynihan. Cambridge: Harvard University Press (reprinted pp. 53–83 in *Social Systems and the Evolution of Action Theory*. New York: Free Press, 1977).

————. 1975b. "Social Structure and the Symbolic Media of Interchange." Pp. 94–120 in *Approaches to the Study of Social Structure*, edited by P. M. Blau. New York: Free Press (reprinted pp. 204–28 in *Social Systems and the Evolution of Action Theory*. New York: Free Press, 1977).

————. 1976. "Afterword." Pp. 364–70 in *The Social Theories of Talcott Parsons*, edited by M. Black (reprint). London/Amsterdam: Feffer and Simons.

————. 1977a. *The Evolution of Societies*. Edited by J. Toby. Englewood Cliffs, N.J.: Prentice-Hall.

————. 1977b. *Social Systems and the Evolution of Action Theory*. New York: Free Press.

————. 1978a. *Action Theory and the Human Condition*. New York: Free Press.

————. 1978b. "The Human Condition." Pp. 325–434 in *Action Theory and the Human Condition*. New York: Free Press.

————. 1989. "A Tentative Outline of American Values." *Theory Culture & Society* 6 (4): 559–76.

Parsons, T., and D. Gerstein. 1977. "Two Cases of Deviance: Addiction to Heroin, Addiction to Power." Pp. 19–57 in *Deviance and Social Change*, edited by E. Sagran. Beverly Hills: Sage.

Parsons, T., and G. M. Platt. 1973. *The American University*. Cambridge, Mass.: Harvard University Press.

Parsons, T., and N. J. Smelser. 1956. *Economy and Society*. London: Routledge and Kegan Paul.

Reiss, A. J., ed. 1961. *Occupations and Social Status*. New York: Free Press of Glencoe (reprint, New York: Arno Press, 1977).

Robertson, R. 1992. "Globalization: Time-Space and Homogeneity-Heterogeneity." Pp. 25–44 in *Globalization: Social Theory and Global Culture*, edited by M. Featherstone, S. Lash, and R. Robertson. London: Sage.

Sassen, S. 1988. *The Mobility of Labor and Capital*. Cambridge: Cambridge University Press.

Snell, J. L. 1959. *Wartime Origins of the East-West Dilemma Over Germany*. New Orleans: Hauser.

Speier, H. 1960. *Divided Berlin: The Anatomy of Soviet Political Blackmail*. New York: Praeger.

Warner, W. L., M. Meeker, and K. Eells. 1949. *Social Class in America: The Evaluation of Status*. New York: Harper.

Weber, M. 1917. "Der Sinn der 'Wertfreiheit' in den ökonomischen und soziologischen Wissenschaften." Translated as "The Meaning of 'Ethical Neutrality' in Sociology and Economics." Pp. 1–49 in *Max Weber on the Methodology of the Social Sciences*, trans. and edited by E. Shils and H. A. Finch. New York: Free Press, 1949.

10

Empirical Sociological Theory and the Resolution of Normative Dilemmas

Mark Gould

In both economic and critical theory, the nature of the relationship between empirical and normative theory is scrutinized continually. In discussions of Parsonian general theory, and more generally in considerations of empirical sociological theory, the nature of this relationship is almost never examined. In this chapter I explore this relationship, concluding that a Parsonian, general, empirical, sociological theory can make a significant contribution to the resolution of important normative questions.

I begin by indicating what is at stake in my discussion. Simply put, contradictory empirical theories may generate contradictory normative results. I illustrate this in a brief contrast of the implications of grounding jurisprudential arguments in a sociological, in contrast to an economic, theory. I conclude this brief discussion with the contention that the selection of a general, empirical theory can make a significant difference in the resolution of important normative questions.

In this chapter I don't argue this point philosophically, nor metatheoretically, but by example. I make an argument about the appropriateness of college and university policies regulating consensual sexual relations between employees and students, an argument that may be generalized into a normative theory of when social relationships should be accepted as valid. I make a few remarks about the theoretical basis for my argument, emphasizing that it is dependent on the theoretical differentiation between procedural justification, consent, and legitimation in terms of moral values. I show how this distinction is inconceivable in economic theory and in law and economics arguments derived from economic theory and how it is embedded in Parsonian general theory. Within this context I briefly contrast my arguments with ones enunciated by Richard A. Posner, as a representative of "law and economics," who concludes that moral argumentation is "spurious." I demonstrate that his contention is dependent on the atomistic, rational-choice, and empiricist viewpoints embedded within neoclassical economic theory, and that when neoclassical theory is reconstructed sociologically to make it more adequate empirically and more coherent logically, it generates the conclusions that I have advocated and manifests the necessity of both the empirical conceptualization of autonomous moral norms and of their consideration in any normatively grounded legal decisions.

I conclude by arguing that the theory I have enunciated grounds a general normative theory specifying when we should accept social relationships as legally and morally valid. I contend that to be valid social relationships must be both justified and legitimate.

EMPIRICAL THEORY AND MORAL ARGUMENT

I have argued for a long time that while imperfect-information models in economics are more tractable empirically than their perfect-information predecessors, they are logically incoherent, and must be sociologically reconstructed to address adequately anomalies that emerge naturally from within such models (Gould, 1990, 1991c, 1992).

Contrary to Parsons's (1937) arguments, a perfect-information, general-equilibrium model, the so-called Arrow-Debreu Model, resolves the problem of order satisfactorily. In equilibrium, such models arrive at a Pareto Optimum, where all actors are in the best possible situation given their original alienable and inalienable endowments. There is no incentive for any rationally maximizing actor to change his or her position within the system. Given the constraints each actor faces, each will be satisfied with the equilibrium outcome.

In contrast, imperfect information models raise the Hobbesian problem of order in its classical form. In part this is because these models do not generally result in a Pareto Optimum (Stiglitz, 1991), but I can illustrate the nature of the problem of order that emerges more readily in a brief examination of one principle-agent problem.

In perfect information models, in equilibrium each actor receives the value of her marginal product as a wage and all economically homogeneous workers receive the same wage. All actors in the system know the value of the marginal product of all actors, including themselves, and all actors can shift positions costlessly. A maximizing actor with a marginal product of lower value than her peers, perhaps because she was working with less-than-average capital, would shift her employment to a more capital-intensive firm, reducing the wage of the actors in that firm and raising the wages of the workers left behind (as the value of the marginal product in the receiving firm would diminish slightly, while the value of the marginal product of the sending firm would rise slightly). This movement halts in equilibrium, where, as I've indicated, each actor receives the value of her marginal product as her wage and all economically homogeneous actors receive the same wage. If, in any firm, one actor shirks, produces a product of lower value, this will be reflected in her wage.

In contrast, in imperfect information models learning the value of a worker's marginal product may be costly (or impossible) (Alchian and Demsetz, 1972). In consequence, the principal-agent problem emerges. Principals must motivate agents to work hard in the principal's interest. They must endeavor to align incentives to accomplish this goal. In the standard economic literature this is done through the manipulation of situational sanctions. Unfortunately, this strategy is incomplete and inadequate. Often epicycles are added to the models in the form of the evocation of nonrational normative orientations such as loyalty, morale, and value commitments (Alchian and Demsetz, 1972: 790–91; Stiglitz, 1985: fn. 10: 135–36).[1] The problem with this strategy is that it is easy to show that the addition of nonrational normative orientations into neoclassical economic models results in intransitive utility functions and, in consequence, in indeterminate predictions. (This contention is discussed below and argued in Gould, 1990, 1991a, 1992.)[2]

This theoretical anomaly, the necessity of introducing nonrational normative orientations into neoclassical, imperfect information models, is inherent in the project of economics, the examination of the incentives that motivate action (Stiglitz, 1998, 1994). To resolve this anomaly, to resolve satisfactorily, for example, principal-agent problems, neoclassical economics must be sociologically reconstructed. Here I will not pursue this argument, but want to indicate instead that my work in jurisprudence originated in the question of what difference this sociological reconstruction made for the normative resolution of legal arguments.

Let me provide one example. Richard Epstein argues for the abolition of laws prohibiting employment discrimination by grounding his argument in neoclassical models of labor-market discrimination. Such models generate the conclusion that labor-market discrimination, an inefficiency, is driven out of competitive labor markets (Becker, 1971). Thus Epstein (1992) can argue that in eliminating laws mandating discrimination we have done all that is necessary to eliminate all but the idiosyncratic and short-lived (disparate treatment) discrimination that may be readily avoided by its potential victim. I have argued that quite different conclusions follow from a more realistic sociological theory. I've contended that discrimination is structural (in a way not conceptualizable within neoclassical models)[3] and embedded in the way firms are organized, that this discrimination is not eliminated in competitive labor markets, and that the law ought to mandate the restructuring of firms that appear to be facially neutral in form, but in fact have adverse consequences for legally protected groups.[4]

All of this is by way of a preface to the task I undertake in this chapter. Arguments like the one I've just outlined lead naturally to the subject I raise in arguing that a general, empirical, sociological theory can make a significant contribution to the resolution of important normative questions. In principle, the differences between the sociological theory I advocate and the now-standard form of imperfect information modeling within neoclassical economic theory can be adjudicated in terms of the logical coherence and empirical warrantability of the two theories. Choosing one of these theories has normative consequences.

In the next section I argue this point through an example. I outline a normative argument about college and university policies regulating consensual sexual relations between employees and students.

COLLEGE AND UNIVERSITY POLICIES REGULATING CONSENSUAL SEXUAL RELATIONS BETWEEN EMPLOYEES AND STUDENTS

Most college and university policies regulating consensual sexual relationships between employees and students focus on consent, often suggesting that if consent were possible in relationships where a power asymmetry exists, sexual relationships between employees and students, including between teachers and their students, would be acceptable. [5]

A second major concern in such policies is with conflicts of interest. Some policies begin with an ethical statement disparaging sexual relationships between faculty and students, only to conclude that when such relationships are present, the superordinates must recuse themselves from any evaluation of their sexual partners. In principle sexual relationships between teachers and their students are deemed acceptable if conflicts of interest are avoided.

Neither of these concerns raises what I believe to be the central issue that must be discussed in determining which, if any, consensual sexual relationships between college and university employees and students should be prohibited. The focal point of my argument is that while consent is a necessary condition for morally valid sexual relationships, and while the avoidance of conflicts of interest is imperative, they are insufficient conditions for the acceptability of those relationships. Within the context of certain social relationships, sexual contact is morally impermissible, even when the consent of the subordinate cannot be questioned and even when no conflicts of interest are involved. I contend that the relationship between a teacher and his or her student is such a relationship, but that attempts to ban consensual sexual relationships between all faculty and all students, or worse, between all college and university employees and students, are not justifiable.

The basis of this set of contentions is that the identity of colleges and universities is constituted by the goal of fostering the cognitive maturation of students (for a broader, but compatible, characterization see Parsons and Platt, 1973). This often occurs within relationships analogous to the transference relationship in psychotherapy. The redirection of this affective/erotic tie in a genital-sexual direction reduces its capacity to motivate the kind of learning, cognitive maturation, that is, or should be, at the center of a college education. For this reason, consensual sexual relationships between teachers and their students undermine the educational relationship that is constitutive of a college's or university's mission. They violate the social values that make up the identity of the educational organization and thus undermine its moral foundation.

Consent

Two images of consent dominate the literature: The first describes the performances and/or subjective will of an autonomous actor consenting. The second implicates a normative judgment about the nature of consent.[6] In the latter consent is said to be effective only when the consented-to action is viewed as morally legitimate.

In contrast, I argue that a viable notion of consent must focus on the justification provided by the procedures that regulate autonomous action in sexual relationships and on the moral legitimacy of those procedures. It is a separate issue whether the consented-to actions are themselves morally legitimate in terms of the appropriate moral, social values.

Valid social relationships, including sexual relationships, are both procedurally justified, consensual, and morally legitimate. An autonomous focus on moral values, which is implicated in the way that I have characterized validity, raises a crucial question: To which values should we appeal in determining the moral legitimacy of consensual sexual relationship within colleges and universities? To answer this question I have to discuss the nature of the teacher-student relationship, the core relationship in colleges and universities, which will enable me to specify the values constitutive of the mission of colleges and universities, the values that must be defended if these organizations are to preserve their identities.

Transference

Most relationships between teachers and students entail a fairly simple transfer of information. Nonetheless, the exemplar of this relationship is the cognitive development of students. Teaching relationships that foster this cognitive maturation are often erotically charged, where the strong motivational force necessary to enable the student to mature and develop intellectually stems from a relationship analogous to the transference Freud saw manifest in the emotional maturation fostered within therapy.

Freud drew a distinction between suggestion and analysis. Suggestion imposes something on the patient, while analysis brings something from within the patient. Analysis removes a resistance to emotional maturation.

Transference is the most powerful mechanism facilitating a patient's growth. It is constituted through an erotic attachment, a love, for the analyst. It differs from "love" due to the situation within which it emerges. The love the patient feels for the analyst is excessive in both character and degree. It is induced by the therapeutic situation and not by the attributes possessed by the analyst as an individual. Even so, it may provide the patient with the strength to overcome resistances. Thus a premature loosening of transference may inhibit a patient's emotional growth, while the failure to loosen the transference may result in a loss of the patient's autonomy.

Transference is constituted through a tension. The love the patient feels for the analyst is unfulfilled, unconsummated. It is the anomalous situation of identification and loss that motivates the patient's capacity to overcome resistances. Sexual consummation abrogates the tension; and while it may not preclude learning, it will, in all probability, reduce analysis to suggestion. In addition, it may put the patient in control in a way that reinforces resistances. The genital satisfaction of the patient's love was, for Freud, both immoral and inefficacious. The consummation of transference precludes an *analytic* relationship.

Transference in Teaching

Cognitive maturation requires, as I often tell my students, "restructuring their brains," which requires a high level of motivation that is often erotic, that is often manifest in a transference relationship.

This transference is both genuine and inappropriate—genuine as a true manifestation of love and inappropriate in focusing on the role and not the individual. Nonetheless, the strength of the transference, the tensions it promotes, may motivate and facilitate the mastery of a discipline, the overcoming of old modes of thinking. As such, transference is integral to learning within college and it, like the structure within which it emerges, is morally legitimate and deserves protection from forces that undermine it.

The sexual consummation of a transference relationship between a student and his or her teacher undermines the constitutive goal of the teacher-student relationship, the cognitive maturation of the student. In consequence, the sexual consummation of a transference relationship between a teacher and his or her student abrogates the moral standards that constitute the identity of the teaching relationship within which the transference emerges. This is so even when the relationship is fully consensual and even when it is initiated by the student.

Moral Values and the Regulation of Social Relationships

We are now in a position to ask which moral values are appropriately called on to regulate consensual sexual relationships between employees and students in colleges and universities. The answer is that the appropriate values are those that maintain the integrity of the relationships under examination. Other values, for example, those prohibiting sexual relationships between unmarried persons, relate neither to the identity of the community within which the relationships are occurring, a college or university, nor to the identity of the larger societal community. While it is appropriate for individuals to regulate their own actions in terms of such values, it isn't appropriate for them to impose such values on persons who chose not to join *their* community. In contrast, actions in violation of the values supportive or constitutive of a community's identity, in which the actors are members, might legitimately be banned.[7]

If this analysis is reasonable, it implies that it is appropriate to ban consensual sexual relationships between teachers and their students. If the above analysis of the role of transference relationships in teaching relationships is correct, sexual relationships between teachers and their students abrogate the core values of a college or university, retarding or making impossible the implementation of the shared goal of the cognitive maturation of students.

If my analysis is reasonable, it results in a different conclusion about other sexual relationships that have sometimes been banned at colleges and universities. To begin with the easiest case, my analysis provides no grounds to ban relationships between a twenty-one-year-old student and an eighteen-year-old dining center worker. While standards external to the constitutive identity of the college or university might be invoked, the legitimacy of doing so isn't clear. Nor is it clear what in the nature of the employee-student relationship would be protected by such a ban. The dining center worker is not inhibited from fulfilling the responsibility of his or her job; nor is the student inhibited from cognitively maturing owing to their sexual relationship.

Sexual relationships between faculty members and students whom they do not teach and relationships between senior and junior faculty are more problematic. Students can and do learn from professors who are not their teachers. Junior faculty sometimes form collegial relationships with senior faculty that facilitate the intellectual maturation of both parties. In both instances, "subordinates" may be desirous of pursuing such relationships without fear of their intentions being misconstrued as a sexual interest. As one colleague suggested to me, "I don't want to be hit on every time I talk about my work with a senior colleague." No doubt. But what of a junior faculty person desirous of pursuing a sexual relationship with a senior colleague or a student desirous of pursuing a sexual relationship with a faculty member who has no teaching or supervisory responsibility for the student (and who recuses herself from any evaluative judgments about the student)? On what grounds might such a relationship be banned?[8]

The core of such relationships, among faculty and between faculty and students who are not their students, is not the cognitive maturation of the junior colleague nor that of the student. While such maturation may be facilitated by membership in a community of scholars, the purpose of that community is not violated when faculty relationships (even between senior and junior colleagues) are sexual in nature, nor when a faculty member and a student have a sexual relationship. Unlike the teacher-student relationship, where consensual sexual relationships inhibit the realization of the goals inherent in the original relationships, no such consequence is manifest in fraternization among the faculty or in consensual sexual relationships between a faculty member and a student. Unlike the teacher-student relationship, where consensual sexual relationships violate the values constitutive of the mission and identity of colleges and universities, no such consequence is manifest in sexual relationships between junior and senior faculty, between faculty and students whom they do not teach, or more generally, between employees and students at colleges and universities.

Conflicts of Interest

Employees, faculty, and senior colleagues may all be put in situations where a conflict of interest occurs in regard to students or junior colleagues with whom they maintain consensual sexual relations. Here it is easy to enunciate a determinate policy statement: such conflicts must be avoided. When the superordinate in such a relationship is put in a situation allowing for the evaluation of the subordinate, she must recuse herself. If the argument I've made above is accepted, this situation ought not occur in sexual relationships between teachers and their students as such relationships are prohibited on other grounds.

Predators and Lovers

Simplifying greatly, we may suggest that there are two types of consensual sexual relationships between college and university teachers and their students. Some professors are sexual predators; the relationships they form are recurrent, self-serving, and exploitative. They manipulate students's feelings for them, assume little or no responsibility for the students's welfare and well-being, and function in the mode of "all gain, no pain." These are relationships structured for the teacher's convenience, often instrumental, almost always pernicious in their consequences, even though the students consent to their participation within them.

The other type of relationship is manifest when a professor genuinely falls in love with a student. Such relationships may take various trajectories. They are often sustained for long periods of time and they sometimes result in marriage.[9] These faculty are not habitual offenders. They may view their actions as morally wrong, but they are driven by an emotional attachment that gets the better of them (Gould, 2000).

If my analysis is correct, both types of faculty are acting in morally culpable ways, in ways that merit sanction from their colleges and universities. The former have no excuse. The latter are professionals who should be able to put their professional responsibility above their desires, but even professors are human.

I would argue that the sanctions appropriate in the two cases differ. Predators should be punished severely; the punishment appropriate for the professor who falls into a sexual relationship with a student should be individually crafted, and should be, in my opinion, compassionate.

Differentiating between the two types of cases requires crafting a procedure that is equitable, that doesn't simply define a rote path whereby all transgressions of the rules are treated the same. The real problem is figuring out how to implement such a policy, where its executors are likely themselves to be fallible. This is the problem of reconciling the rule of law with equitable justice.[10]

THE LEGITIMATION AND JUSTIFICATION OF CONSENSUAL SEXUAL RELATIONSHIPS

Many discussions of consent conflate legitimation, the subsumption of norms and activities under a set of morally constituted value-commitments, and justification, procedural due process, where a constituted norm or activity is justifiable if it is the calculable outcome of some set of procedural, constitutive norms.[11] Often these discussions treat consent as justification, as if it legitimated sexual activities, forgetting that the procedures that justify must themselves be legitimated and that the sexual activity, even if justified, consensual, must itself be legitimate within a particular social context.

The roots of the confusion between legitimation and justification are found in classical social theory. Weber's analysis of traditional legitimation involves a discussion of the subsumption of norms and activities under traditional-hierarchical values. His discussion of rational-legal legitimation, however, concerns not the activity of subsumption, but instead an analysis of procedural due process. Action is traditionally legitimate if culturally consistent with traditional values; action is rational-legally legitimate if the calculable outcome of activities is regulated by procedural, constitutive norms. Weber confounds a functional discussion of legitimation (invariant across types of society) with a structural analysis of a particular type of (traditional) legitimation, and he confounds a functional discussion of procedural justification with a structural analysis of rational-egalitarian justification. He cannot discriminate between action in response to policies viewed as illegitimate from action in response to policies viewed as unjustifiable.

Durkheim's concept of mechanical solidarity refers to the unification of actors who share a common set of traditional-hierarchical values, the collective conscience. Organic solidarity refers to the integration of actors within a social division of labor; their activities are coordinated through the noncontractual elements of contract, the rationally articulated constitutive norms within which valid contractual relationships are established. He confounds a functional analysis of mechanical solidarity with a structural analysis of that particular type of mechanical solidarity grounded in traditional-hierarchical collective values. Likewise, he confuses a functional analysis of organic solidarity with a particular type of rational-egalitarian contractual relationship. In reading Durkheim it often appears that organic solidarity arises in the place of mechanical solidarity; he tells us that with the emergence of organic solidarity, the collective conscience recedes into the heavens, leaving us with the image of a zero sum game.

Instead of tracing the development of moral value-commitments (the collective conscience) at the same time as the development of the norms of procedural justification, both Weber and Durkheim created social theories that substitute the one for the other. Thus moral obligation appears to give way to procedural rationality, while rational values and non- or irrational procedures take a back place in their analyses. Perhaps even more importantly, the relationship between justification and legitimation is not analyzed, and thus the relationship between commitment and cognition is unclear. Consequently, they fail to recognize that the structure of both legitimizing values and justifying norms alters in the social development of societies, as does their interrelationship. Activities must be both legitimate and justified if they are to be continually reproduced; constitutive, procedural norms must be legitimized, while value-orientations must be justifiable if the system is to function smoothly.[12]

The importance of maintaining the analytical autonomy of legitimation and justification is manifest in the fact that they may be empirically independent. A norm or activity may be viewed as procedurally justified, while at the same time seen to violate institutionalized societal values. Judicial review embodies this principle, recognizing that procedurally valid outcomes may be illegitimate. There is, in other words, a range of activity beyond which procedurally acceptable, constituted norms will not be treated as binding. The clearest manifestation of this is found in acts of civil disobedience, where a moral commitment leads persons into public violations of a law (including procedurally valid laws), even though they expect to suffer a negative sanction for their violation.

Within the context of our discussion, for consensual sexual relations between teachers and their students to be valid they have to be *both justified and legitimate*. When consent is granted in accord with legitimate procedures, sexual relations are justified. When
those relations are consistent with the social values constitutive of the identity of the
community within which they occur, they are legitimate. Less strongly, when those relations are not in violation of the value-commitments constitutive of the identity of the
community within which they occur, they are not illegitimate. Consensual sexual relations must be both consensual (justified) and at least not illegitimate to be acceptable.
When unjustified, nonconsensual, and/or illegitimate, they should be prohibited.

PARSONS'S CONTRIBUTION

The Structure of Social Action may be understood to characterize the relationship between the voluntaristic theory of action, Parsons's position, and Parsons's understanding of positivism and idealism. Positivist theories, according to Parsons, reduce
the determinants of social action to an adaptation to the situation in which that action occurs. All variants of positivist theory posit a single, positively stated normative
orientation, usually the norm of instrumental rationality. The two radical forms of
positivism Parsons discusses derive the ends of action from the situation in which action occurs. Thus ends have no autonomous status and the subjective nature of the
normative orientation may itself be called into question. In such theories there are
two mechanisms that determine action, the situation (which may include the biological organism) and the norm of instrumental rationality, selecting those means
most efficient to attain the actor's goals. Because the normative orientation is univo-
cal we can say that in radical positivism action is situationally determined; it is the
way that the situation is characterized that differentiates among these theories, which
in the contemporary scene include sociobiology and radical behaviorism.

In utilitarian theory, which is for Parsons a form of positivist theory, ends are autonomous, irreducible to the conditions of action. They are exogenous to the theory
and are treated as given within it. Within this theory there are two subjective elements, ends and the single, positively stated normative orientation. Thus there are
three mechanisms determining action: the end, the normative orientation, and the
situation. Neoclassical economists, who are utilitarians in this sense, understand actors to maximize their utility functions, their goals, under situational constraints.[13]

Idealism may be understood as explaining social action in terms of the normative
orientations actors adopt. Often these normative orientations are understood as incommensurable; sometimes they are understood univocally, as characterizing the
essence of a group or individual. Nonetheless, within idealist theories there may be
multiple, positively stated normative orientations. In their extreme forms, however,
idealist theories treat action as emanating from these norms, paying no attention to
the situational constraints actors encounter. They may, for example, ignore situationally restricted actions as not capturing the "essence" of social action. Interestingly, when an idealist theory conceptualizes only one normative orientation, the

norm of instrumental rationality, it may look very much like its apparent opposite, positivist-utilitarianism, which explains why some poststructuralist theories are kindred souls to their rational-choice adversaries.

Readers familiar with *The Structure of Social Action* will realize that this analysis presumes Parsons's characterization of the unit act, the conceptual tool he uses to differentiate between necessarily faulty and potentially viable theories. Parsons argues that positivist theories conceptualize, if not always satisfactorily, only certain of the elements of the unit act, the actor and the situation, and provide only a limited characterization of the normative orientation. In radical positivism, there are no independent ends; instead they emerge within a rational adaptation to the situation. In utilitarianism, ends are autonomous, but they are selected exogenously to the theory. While the normative orientation regulates the selection of means relative to ends, it isn't understood to regulate the selection of ends. Nonetheless, ends have, in utilitarianism, a crucial explanatory role, which largely explains the flexibility of the theory and why it is, ultimately, tautologous: if ends are revealed in action, any action may be explained unless the ends are held constant.

Idealism is even more restrictive. In its extreme form, the ends of action aren't autonomous; they are determined by the relevant normative orientation. Action emanates from norms, and the situation ceases to be relevant. Sometimes the agent loses her autonomy; she is embedded in the relevant normative orientations.

Voluntarism, as conceptualized by Parsons, recognizes the autonomy of all of the elements within the unit act. Voluntarism conceptualizes multiple, positively stated normative orientations, including the norm of instrumental rationality. The ends of action are autonomous from the situation, but their selection may be regulated by social norms. Actors always consider situational sanctions in their actions, but those sanctions do not determine, in conjunction with a single, positively stated normative orientation, how they act. If positivist theories explain action in terms of situations, and idealist theories explain action in terms of normative orientations, voluntarist theories explain action in terms of both situations and normative orientations.

Parsons understands the unit act as a conceptual tool for analyzing *theories* of social action.[14] It can't be used successfully in the analysis of social action for many reasons. One concerns the diffuse conceptualization of normative orientations it provides. There may be multiple, positively stated normative orientations, but the unit act doesn't enable us to differentiate between them.

In his later work Parsons differentiated between cultural norms, which constitute meaningful action, and various types of social norms. From within his functional theory, the so-called AGIL theory, he differentiated between procedural norms and social values. The mechanisms of justification that Parsons associated with Durkheim's characterization of organic solidarity and with his own conception of social integration, the integrative subsystem, must be placed alongside social values, which Parsons associated with Durkheim's collective conscience, mechanical solidarity, and with his own conceptualization of the pattern maintenance subsystem (Parsons, 1960). It was his contention that both justification and legitimation were necessary if social reproduction was to occur smoothly. Thus in any institutional analysis Parsons was forced, by the logic of his theory, to ask about mechanisms of value legitimation and mechanisms of procedural justification.

My discussion of Parsons's characterization of voluntarism suggests that his analysis couldn't be limited to a discussion of normative orientations. He also had to examine the role situational constraints and situational sanctions play in generating social action.

This brief analysis of the logic of Parsonian theory doesn't entail a particular consensual relations policy. It does, however, suggest that such a policy must take into account the social values that legitimate activities within colleges and universities and thus the consensual sexual relations that are legitimate in this institutional context. It must also examine the mechanisms whereby such relationships are justified, focusing on whether or not they are consensual and on the procedures by which that consent may be manifest. In addition, it must ask about the source of goals (here maybe "desires" is more appropriate) the actors bring to these relationships, recognizing that while the selections of ends may be normatively regulated and situationally circumscribed, the selection of ends is autonomous, may be affectually motivated, and should be treated with respect.[15] My reading of Parsons's theory suggests that consensual sexual relationships within colleges and universities, relationships grounded in the mutual desires of the partners, should be prohibited only when they may be argued reasonably to preclude the successful accomplishment of the central mission of colleges and universities, the cognitive maturation of students. Any equitable policy must recognize that while some sexual relationships between faculty and students are predatory, others emerge out of genuine love and affection and manifest another, perhaps competing social value. Finally, any realistic policy must be concerned with the effects of sanctions, as situational deterrents, as mechanisms to reinforce value commitments, and as mechanisms to control actors whose motivations are strategic, ensuring that those committed to the appropriate values are not treated as suckers by those who orient themselves to those values strategically. As we will see in what follows, other empirical theories imply different normative conclusions.

POSNER'S NEOCLASSICAL EMPIRICISM

The great strength of neoclassical theory is that it directs our attention toward incentives, situational sanctions that direct our actions.[16] The great weakness of neoclassical theory is its inability to conceptualize multiple, positively stated normative orientations, and thus its need to reconceptualize moral and other nonrational normative orientations as either individual preferences or the situational sanctions that support the social norms. Both the strengths and the weaknesses are manifest in Richard Posner's work and both are relevant to our discussion.

The Logic of Neoclassical Economics

In neoclassical theory actors are conceptualized atomistically (methodologically individualistically). Atomism involves the restriction of conceptualizations to individual unit acts and to systems of interaction between unit acts. The relationships be-tween actors add no information that is not derivable from the attributes of individ-ual unit acts. Each act is understood to affect others by altering the situation in which the others occur. The relationships between unit acts may be enormously complex (as in general equilibrium theory in economics), but in an atomistic theory they are reducible to the attributes of the unit acts that constitute the system.

In neoclassical theory there is a single, positive conceptualization of the actor's normative orientation. This is usually a form of instrumental rationality, where per-sons are seen as selecting only from among ends attainable within the relevant situ-ation and choosing those means most efficient to attain their ends. This is frequently analyzed as "maximization against (situational) constraints."

Violations of the norm of instrumental rationality are attributed to either error or ignorance (the absence of perfect knowledge, uncertainty). Alternatively, it is possi-ble to suggest that the analyst's attribution of the actor's end was erroneous; the agent may be seen to have been maximizing along a dimension different from the one the theorist previously suggested. This latter possibility, when ends are not held constant, leads to the tautologous nature of much economic theorizing.

Neoclassical theory treats ends as given; they are exogenous to the theory. They are independent of the actor's situation, but the theory says nothing about their selection (except that they must be consistent, transitive, and obtainable within the relevant situation). The only postulated relationships of one end to another are dependent on the consequences of one act, perhaps undertaken by a second actor, helping to con-stitute the environment of other actions. Thus one act may alter the situation within which another occurs, making a particular end attainable or not attainable.

Finally, neoclassical theory is empiricist. In this context empiricism may be briefly characterized as the methodological position that allows the introduction of con-cepts only when they are tied directly to observable "phenomena." Empiricists reject the introduction of "constructs," conceptualizations like the Freudian unconscious, Durkheim's collective conscience, or, more generally, social structures not reducible to the actions of atomistically conceptualized actors.[17]

Neoclassical theory does not allow for the conceptualization of multiple positively stated normative orientations. It necessarily reduces such normative orientations to either individual preferences or desires or to the situational sanctions that support the normative orientation. When they do the former, neoclassical theorists often em-phasize the emotional origins of such desires, reducing moral values (and normative orientations more generally) to emotional needs. When neoclassical theorists do the latter, reduce norms to situational constraints, they eliminate the normative element they were purportedly attempting to analyze.

The logic of neoclassical theory results in a necessary focus on three mechanisms of explanation: on exogenous preferences, situational sanctions, and the norm of in-strumental rationality. This theory is incapable of conceptualizing adequately social norms that are irreducible to preferences or sanctions. While the former gives the il-lusion of retaining a normative orientation other than instrumental rationality within the theory, such orientations are reduced to arguments within actor's utility functions. This becomes problematic when, as is often the case, the reduction of normative expectations to preferences results in preferences that are nontransitively ordered and the predictions of the theory become, in consequence, indeterminate.[18]

Both strategies, reducing moral values to desires and to situational sanctions, are manifest in the work of Richard Posner, and both are relevant to his understanding of the regulation of sexual relationships.

Neoclassical Limitations in Posner's Arguments

In *The Problematics of Moral and Legal Theory* (1998b) Richard Posner argues that the methods of moral philosophy don't work in the law or in any other domain. While he tells us that he doesn't deny "the existence of moral values—only the cogency of moral theory" (1998b: fn. 78: 50), his characterization of moral values reduces them to either emotively or biologically constituted preferences (Posner 1992: 201, 232; Posner, 1998b: 35) or to the sanctions that support the moral values. Such a reduction is mandated by the empiricist nature of his theory. He can't "see" concepts unless they are related directly to observable phenomena; thus a construct like Durkheim's collective conscience, the set of moral values constitutive of the identity of some social order, must remain invisible to him unless reduced to situational sanctions or to the aggregation of individual preferences or desires.

We learn, for example, that "Squeamishness is a big factor in morality" (Posner, 1998b: 56). Moral argument simply rationalizes what makes us comfortable. Moral argument is too feeble to override narrow self-interest or moral intuitions. While the moral emotions, sentiments, are universal, they are object neutral and thus not really moral. Morality, when it is called morality, is "just the gift wrapping of theoretically ungrounded and ungroundable preferences and aversions" (Posner, 1998b: 11).[19]

Sometimes Posner appears to recognize moral values as, for individuals, internalized rules of conduct. For Posner, however, the indignation that an individual feels when an internalized value is violated demonstrates only that the violation of the internalized value triggers an emotional reaction. When he focuses on the psychological sanctions that support moral values, guilt and shame, he recognizes the incompatibility of this discussion with the theory within which the argument is grounded: "Neither guilt nor shame fits comfortably into the implicit psychological assumptions of the rational-choice model of human behavior. We treat them as brute facts, like food preferences, which constrain rather than explain economic theories of behavior" (Posner and Rasmusen, 1999: 371). Ultimately, the internalized moral values are reduced to preferences that, within neoclassical theory, are simply given. It follows for Posner that no one has a reasonable basis to evaluate another's desires.

More generally, Posner's focus is on situational sanctions (Posner, 1998a, 1997, 1998c; Posner and Rasmusen, 1999). He backsteps from the presumption that adherence to moral values is non- or irrational and focuses on the rewards gleaned from conformity to moral values, thus reducing the motivation for conformity to one that fits within "rational-choice theory," focusing on incentives that may not be apparent at first glance. (A helpful example is found in Posner, 1998b: 45.)

Posner's arguments reduce morality to the situational sanctions that support social values[20] and/or reduce the values to individual desires (or, what may sometimes be a more appropriate term, individual "passions"). Action is explained in terms of situational constraints, given ends, and the norm of instrumental-rationality.

The focus on the first, situational constraints and situational incentives, is integral to any analysis of social norms. Unfortunately, the conclusions to be drawn from such analyses are rarely as clear cut as Posner seems to believe. In addition, Posner's understanding of the effects of sanctions is limited by his theoretical perspective.

Situational Sanctions and Consensual Relations Policies

The great strength of Posner's jurisprudential approach is his attempt to assess realistically the consequences of legal decisions. The great weakness is that the theory from within which he makes such assessments is demonstrably problematic (Gould, 1990, 1991c, 1992, 1995b; Gould, Heckscher, and Domurad, 1996). In this section I begin by focusing on the need to assess the consequences of a policy banning sexual relations between faculty and their students. In Posner's terms this entails examining the effects of situational sanctions as motivators of individual action and endeavoring to determine upon whom such incentives will have an effect.

Put very simply, for an economist individuals commit deviant acts when the expected benefits of deviance exceed its costs. Similarly, Posner assumes that sexual behavior is rational and that its regulation is a matter of altering incentives (Posner, 1992: 85). "[T]he decision to engage in a particular sex *act*, that is to act on a preference . . . in light of all pertinent costs and benefits, is a matter of choice" (Posner, 1992: 87). Sanctioning faculty who engage in consensual sexual relationships with their students raises the costs of such relationships for faculty and thus, *ceteris paribus*, should diminish the amount of such activity.

Let us presume that we desire to deter sexual relationships between faculty and their students. A crucial question becomes, Which faculty will be deterred? If we categorize the faculty involved in two groups, the sexual predators and the ones who fall in love with particular students in relationships that appear nonexploitative, which group of faculty is more likely to be deterred?

Ceteris paribus, Posner and I would both predict that those with more alternative choices of sexual partners would be more likely to be deterred. Moving from a preferred partner, the student, to a less preferred partner, if that second partner is readily available, incurs lower costs than giving up the student partner if there is no readily available alternative. Thus the same likelihood of the same sanction ought to better deter the person with more alternatives. Is this person more likely to be the sexual predator? I don't believe that we can answer this question without knowing who becomes a sexual predator on college and university campuses.

Is the sexual predator someone who is attracted to teaching, at least in part, because prey are readily at hand and because outside of his institutional role as a professor he could not attract students? If so he may have few alternatives outside of his students. Alternatively, predators might be concentrated among those successful in attracting sexual partners in a wide variety of situations, while playing a wide variety of roles. If so, consensual relationship policies might lead them to direct their attention away from their students.

The second question concerns the effects of sanctions on those in love in contrast to those acting strategically. We might suggest that, ceteris paribus, those acting strategically are more likely to, consciously or not, adapt their activities to sanctions enforcing a prohibition of certain types of sexual relationships. In contrast, albeit that it is impossible to carry out such an analysis within neoclassical theory, those committed to their partners, in love with them (Gould, 1991b; Luhmann, 1986), should be less responsive to such sanctions. The establishment and perpetuation of such relationships might be analogized to civil disobedience, committed actions undertaken in the face of sanctions, albeit in the instance of a sexual relationship between a faculty member and his student, and unlike in civil disobedience, the activities might remain clandestine.

Posner is able to conceptualize the incentive effect of sanctions on rational maximizers. He may even be able to conceptualize the effects of sanctions on persons committed to a legal or moral value when the imposition of sanctions on deviants not so committed convinces the committed that they are not acting like suckers (for a neoclassical theorist, the commitment would be reconceptualized as a preference). Commitment is undermined when the uncommitted benefit from violating social norms adhered to by the committed. Institutionalized sanctions supporting social norms, institutionalized sanctions that make it costly for rational maximizers to violate social norms, reinforce the commitment to those norms among those who adhere to them out of conviction.

The third function of sanctions makes no sense within a neoclassical theory.[21] Durkheim emphasized that negative sanctions define the boundaries of what is permitted in social orders and reinforce the commitment of the majority to the expectations that codify those boundaries. When ego violates a norm and is punished, that punishment serves as a deterrent to alter, but, as importantly, it may also reinforce alter's commitment to the norm, leading her to adhere to that norm even when the fear of sanction is irrelevant, even when deviance is rational.

A policy prohibiting sexual relationships between faculty and their students, when supported by effective sanctions, should deter the establishment of such relationships. This deterrence effect will be greatest for those who enter into such relationships rationally and for those faculty (and students) who have other alternative partners. It will be less effective in deterring those who fall in love and become committed to their partners. In all instances, however, the social values that an organization wishes to establish to help delineate its identity will be reinforced when a policy that constitutes those values is reinforced and when transgressors of those values are punished.

Consent

From Posner's point of view, the conclusion in the last section begs the question: Should colleges and universities value[22] the absence of sexual relationships between faculty and their students? I believe that his answer must be "no," and I believe that this answer is determined by the neoclassical theory within which he conducts his analyses.[23]

Unlike moral theorists such as Kant and Dworkin, Posner seeks a theory of sexuality not in moral or religious beliefs, but in social interests and practical incentives "as the key to both understanding and judging sexual practices and norms" (Posner, 1992: 4). His theory of sexuality is normatively libertarian; libertarianism, for Posner, "can be summed up in seven words: 'Your rights end where his nose begins.' Government interference with adult consensual activities is unjustified unless it can be shown to be necessary for the protection of the liberty or property of other persons" (Posner, 1992: 3). The crucial term is "consent," and the crucial presumption is that the consent must be voluntary and must be the action of an autonomous actor. Posner emphasizes that force and fraud violate the autonomy of actors and thus vitiate the reality of consent. While, to my knowledge, he doesn't discuss consensual relations policies, we may presume, I believe, that he would be opposed to such policies on the ground that they violate the liberties of the involved adult actors.[24]

While Posner is, sometimes, sensitive to the fact that consent may not be freely given, his image of consent is not restrictive and is never, as far as I can tell, dependent on the social position of the actors. For example, second wives may consent to polygamy, and an actor may buy his or her spouse's consent to a divorce, "in which event the divorce is genuinely consensual" (Posner, 1992: 248).[25] More generally, he suggests, "The title of this chapter ["Coercive Sex"] refers to situations in which one of the participants in a sex act either has not consented to the act or, by reason of being mentally immature or retarded, or deceived, or overawed by adult authority, has not given *effective* consent, that is, consent which society honors" (Posner, 1992: 388). My best guess is that he would argue that colleges and universities should honor the consent college and university students give, absent force and fraud, to sexual relations with their teachers.[26]

If so, if Posner would argue that college and university students are able to consent to sexual relationships with their teachers, he would have no strong grounds for arguing for a prohibition of such relationships, and his normative commitments, preferences, would appear to justify such consensual relationships. The only basis for condemning such practices would appear to be if they evoked wide and deep antipathy and if this antipathy generated consequences deleterious to the functioning of colleges and universities. Given Posner's repeated characterization of the dominant sexual morality in the United States (Posner, 1992, 1999: 14), however, he seems unlikely to make this argument.

In contrast, if my argument that both legitimation in terms of social values and justification in terms of procedures (consent) are both essential for the stable reproduction of social orders is correct, we have a basis for assessing the independent effect of a moral order in regulating social activities, and we have an independent basis for arguing that a particular moral order should regulate social activities.[27]

Durkheim argued that the collective conscience, social values institutionalized in some social order, constituted and reproduced mechanical solidarity, the solidarity that constitutes the identity of a social order, an identity ideally shared by all members of that order. I have argued that the constitutive values of a college or university mandate the cognitive maturation of students.[28] Colleges and universities thus have the right to enact rules and regulations that protect these values, that sanction violations of them, to preclude actions that undermine the capacity of the colleges and universities to function successfully, that is, to implement these values successfully. I have argued that consensual sexual relations between teachers and their students, but not between teachers and other students, nor between senior and junior faculty, undermine the capacity to implement these values, undermine the setting in which the cognitive maturation of students occurs.[29] If this argument is correct,[30] it follows, I believe, that sexual relationships between teachers and their students ought to be prohibited.

Contrary to what Posner might contend (Posner, 1998b: 142), this conclusion is not simply one of personal preference (or emotive revulsion at the thought of such relationships). He is, I think, correct when he suggests the following: "If the only reason that virgins are hurled into volcanoes is to make crops grow, empirical inquiry should dislodge the practice." When he continues, as follows, however, I believe he is mistaken: "But when human sacrificers do not make falsifiable claims for the efficacy of the practice, so that the issue becomes a choice of ends rather than a choice of means to an agreed end (making the crops grow) our critical voice is stilled. Or rather it becomes a voice expressing disgust—a reaction to difference—rather than a voice uttering reasoned criticisms" (Posner, 1998b: 22).

If my argument contending that sexual relationships between faculty and their students undermines the circumstances in which the cognitive maturation of students occurs is false, Posner and I would both agree that this undermines, probably fatally, my moral argument. If my claim is correct, Posner might support my contention on factual grounds, but he might question the moral values that legitimate the policy I advocate, suggesting that all moral values are "just the gift wrapping of theoretically ungrounded and ungroundable preferences and aversions" (Posner, 1998b: 11).[31] For Posner, while questions of fact are, ideally, resolvable scientifically, facts are instrumental to preferences, which are, ultimately, arbitrary. In contrast, I would argue that the moral values I advocate are integral to the nature and mission of colleges and universities. Values that constitute the identity of social orders may, I would suggest, be defended within those social orders. This conviction is, I believe, reinforced when participation within the regulated organization is voluntary and consensual.[32]

CONCLUSION

I have argued that empirical theory is integral in the defense of moral arguments and that the empirical theory we select limits the nature of the moral arguments we can make and defend successfully. I have contended that Richard Posner's neoclassical and libertarian moral theory[33] limits his perspective in a way that determines the nature of the moral argument he makes about the role of consent in validating social relationships. For him, mutual individual consent validates social relationships and moral values that regulate such relationships are violations of his libertarian (moral) theory; they are no more than the imposition of one preference upon another. Parsons, in contrast, provides us with a sociological theory that necessitates a focus on both social values and procedural norms in the constitution of any stably reproducible social order. His theory grounds a moral argument that necessitates our recognition that consent, in light of individual preferences and the rational calculation of sanctions, is insufficient to validate social relationships.

I argue that valid social relationships must be both justified procedurally (consented to) and morally legitimated. The trick is the selection of the values it is appropriate to impose on participants within a social order. I've argued, here with reference to colleges and universities, that the appropriate values are those constitutive of the identity of those organizations. If, in colleges and universities, these values mandate the cognitive maturation of students, and if my analysis of the teaching relationship is correct in contending that sexual relationships between faculty and their students undermine the conditions for the cognitive maturation of students, it is appropriate for colleges and universities to ban consensual sexual relationships between professors and their students, and to ban them even when we do not question the authenticity of the student's consent. It is not appropriate, however, to ban consensual sexual relationships that don't compromise the social values that constitute the college's and university's identities.

NOTES

This is a revised version of a paper delivered at the 1999 Annual Meeting of the American Sociological Association, Chicago, Illinois. There I benefited from perceptive comments by Victor Lidz.

1. Alchian and Demsetz and Stiglitz must argue, if they are to be theoretically consistent, and they do argue that these apparently nonrational commitments are really "rational."

2. For a neoclassical theory to remain consistent, nonrational normative orientations must be reduced either to arguments in a utility function, to preferences, or to the situational sanctions that support the nonrational norm. When the latter strategy is employed, the nonrational normative orientations drop from view; they are reduced to situational sanctions, to constraints. When the former strategy is employed and nonrational normative orientations are introduced, the argument in the text is applicable; nontransitive utility functions may result.

3. See the section "The Logic of Neoclassical Economics," later in this chapter.

4. I criticize economic theories of discrimination, formulate a sociological alternative, and assess the jurisprudential consequences of that alternative (Gould, 1991d, 1992, 1995b, 1999).

5. This discussion derives from my essay, "The Law and Morality of Sexual Relationships: Consent and the Regulation of Sexual Relationships Between Employees and Students in Colleges and Universities" (Gould, 1998). The points made here are argued more completely in that essay.

6. These two images are helpfully manifest, discussed, and contrasted in a number of articles on "Sex and Consent," published in two issues of *Legal Theory* 2 (2–3), 1996.

242   *Gould*

7. Hector Bladuell, in a course paper, "Sex in Academia: A Policy for the Effective Regulation of Student-Teacher Sexual Relationships," argues powerfully that the contention that a college's or university's identity is constituted in terms of the cognitive maturation of students is arbitrary, that some colleges and universities might constitute their identities differently. Such a contention might result in one of two conclusions, that the nature of the sexual relationships prohibited is dependent on the characterization of the college's or university's identity or that no such relationships should be prohibited because the organization's identity is in some sense arbitrary and this collective definition shouldn't be imposed on the members of the organization.

I don't see a commitment to the development of cognitive rationality as arbitrary; rather, it defines the central attribute inherent in the very notion of a college or university, and thus I see the ban on teacher-student relationships as integral to the constitutive identity of any college or university. The question of whether it would be morally acceptable for a college or university related to a fundamentalist religious group to ban other forms of sexual relationships isn't my focus in this chapter. I think, however, that it depends on the voluntary nature of participation in that college or university and the nature of the alternatives available to persons who don't want to conform to a moral code extraneous to the central educational mission of colleges and universities.

8. Remember that I am not discussing relationships that might be regulated by a sexual harassment policy, narrowly defined. I am discussing relationships that are clearly (here, by definition) consensual and free from any tint of harassment or discrimination.

9. See Marcia Bellas's interesting paper "Consensual Relationships Between Professors and Students" for information on this point. I want to thank Professor Bellas for sending me a draft copy of this essay.

10. The distinction between predators and lovers recurs later in the chapter when, in a discussion of Posner's work, I raise the question of the effects of sanctions on different types of actors. Posner makes a similar, but not the same, distinction in his morally neutral assessment of President Clinton's affair with Monica Lewinsky, which is coupled with his condemnation of superordinates who make a practice of having sex with subordinates (see note 26, below).

11. This section derives from two bodies of work. The first formulates the relationship between legitimation and justification, and the second formulates a theory of contractual and consensual relationships that I counterpose to the free contract doctrine (Gould, 1993, 1995a, 1995b, 1996, 1997).

12. I present a theory that argues the importance of both legitimation and justification for the stable reproduction of a social system (Gould, 1987: chapters 2 and 3).

13. A more complete discussion of utilitarianism follows in the section "The Logic of Neoclassical Economics."

14. Sometimes this understanding was incomplete, as in the unpublished essay written after *The Structure of Social Action*, "Action, Situation, and Normative Pattern."

15. Here I can't ground the last claim. (See Gould, 2000; Parsons, 1964.)

16. The "utilitarian" theory Parsons discusses in *The Structure of Social Action* is equivalent in structure to neoclassical economic theory.

17. This characterization of neoclassical theory derives from Parsons's characterization of the utilitarian theory of social action (Parsons, 1937); see also Gould (1981). In other work (Gould, 1990; Gould, 1992), I have emphasized the distinction between perfect- and imperfect-information neoclassical theories.

18. Elster (1989b: 115) gives a wonderful illustration of poorly ordered preferences, which I've discussed in Gould (1991a, 1992: 1540). He is, unfortunately, unaware of the devastating

consequences of this exemplary case for his, and others', attempts to introduce normative orientations other than instrumental rationality into neoclassical, rational-choice theory (Akerlof, 1984; Elster, 1988, 1989a, 1989b, 1989c; Gould, 1991a).

19. Just as Posner is unclear about what counts as "morality," he is unclear about what counts as moral reasoning. Sometimes moral theory dispels errors in moral reasoning (Posner, 1998b: 15); sometimes "Moral reasoning is different from pointing out either logical or factual mistakes in moral argument, the former being a legitimate therapeutic task of philosophy and the latter a task for the social sciences. Only when a moral claim is logically and empirically unassailable does it belong to moral reasoning as I am using the term" (Posner, 1998b: 16–17).

20. I should note explicitly that there is a difference between the contention that moral values are social, collective, and the contention, present in Posner's work, that moral values reduce to material social position (Posner, 1998b: 27–29).

21. The closest Posner comes to the following discussion is in his analysis of the relationship between signals and social norms (Posner, 1998a, 1999: 215).

22. The phrasing is conscious. There are two primary usages of the term "value" in the social sciences. The first refers to what is valued, preferred, "desired." The second refers to what is "desirable." Neoclassical theory must, as I've argued above, reduce what is desirable to what is desired. A viable sociological theory must recognize that what is desired may conflict with what is desirable. It is only from within the sociological theory, where there may be a conflict between what is desired and what is desirable, that it makes sense to prohibit violations of social values.

23. Posner contends, in *The Problematics of Moral and Legal Theory,* that his book falls within the discipline of sociology. If so, this is only because of the subject matter it covers, not because it works within any body of sociological, as distinct from economic, theory.

24. The caveat to this conclusion relates to the difference between private and governmental regulation. Posner might contend that a private college or university may regulate whatever it chooses to regulate.

25. "Rape is a crime usually committed in private, away from eyewitnesses, and all that distinguishes it from ordinary sexual intercourse is lack of consent, which may be difficult to prove in the absence of physical injury, especially if the circumstances make an inference of consensual intercourse plausible" (Posner, 1992: 388).

26. Posner has argued that White House intern Monica Lewinsky's affair with President Clinton was consensual, wronged no one, and was of no concern to anyone other than the participants (Posner, 1999: 9, 13, 17, 39). (When assigned to work in the White House, Lewinsky had been hired into a regular White House job, but the paperwork was not yet completed, so she was technically still an intern.) While he treats this relationship entirely in terms of Lewinsky's personal attributes, which he uses to rebut the charge of exploitation based on age and status, and while he is skeptical of the contention that "sex between a male superior and a female subordinate is sexual harassment per se because of the imbalance of power between them" (Posner, 1999: 137), Posner does maintain that "If Clinton had made a *practice* of having sex with his subordinates, this would certainly be objectionable, as is now pretty universally recognized in American law and morality, even if there was no element of coercion" (Posner, 1992: 138). He appears to believe that this repeated sexual activity would create a hostile environment for other subordinate workers and that it would thus constitute a form of sexual harassment. We can speculate that he might make the same argument with regard to consensual sexual relationships between professors and their students.

I admit to having difficulty understanding why Posner feels that his argument in *The Problematics of Moral and Legal Theory* requires a refusal to take a stand on whether adultery, oral sex, and sex with a subordinate are wrong, when he is comfortable asserting that habitual sex with a subordinate is wrong. If it's because of the effects on other subordinates caused by habitual sex with subordinates, as he appears to suggest, it's not clear why these more widespread effects make the action immoral, while the lesser effects of sex with only a few subordinates means that Posner can't judge those actions morally. It seems to me that his judgment is arbitrary, perhaps reaffirming his conviction that moral judgments are, ultimately, all arbitrary.

27. Posner recognizes that moral norms play an important role in maintaining social control in all societies (Posner, 1998b: 310), but if I am correct in suggesting that he can't conceptualize moral values adequately from within his neoclassical economic theory, this statement is merely rhetorical.

28. More generally, these values regulate activities within colleges and universities in terms of a commitment to cognitive rationality (Parsons and Platt, 1973), a commitment that Posner and I share.

29. If I had more space I would include a discussion of why the nature and effects of transference relationships are inexplicable from within a neoclassical theory.

30. Posner is, in my opinion, correct in suggesting that we may criticize moral codes that aren't instrumentally effective (Posner, 1998b: 21). "We can [and we should] ransack them [moral theories] for their factual implications and then assess the accuracy of those implications, and by that means determine whether these theories provide an adequate positive and normative analysis of our subject" (Posner, 1992: 223).

31. I've quoted out of context. Here he claims this of "many moral claims" (Posner, 1998b: 11).

32. Even so, the disagreement between Posner and me is less stark than I've made it appear. This is so for two reasons. (1) Posner might argue that if a group constitutes itself voluntarily it may enforce whatever values it chooses. (2) Analogously, a critic could question my characterization of the identity of colleges and universities, suggesting that the shared commitment to cognitive rationality is itself immoral. While I might argue successfully that such a commitment is essential to the success and preservation of colleges and universities, my critic might contend that the actions entailed within that commitment are immoral and if that means that colleges and universities must be destroyed, so be it. In this sense there is a fundamental, nonrational commitment inherent in moral values. See, in this context, my criticisms of the work of Jürgen Habermas (Gould, 1996).

33. "The focus will be on the question of what regulations are appropriate under a laissez-faire approach to sex—an approach that, by treating sex as morally indifferent, would limit sexual freedom only to the extent required by economic or other utilitarian considerations. *I grant that economics, when viewed as a guide to social policy, and of course utilitarianism, are themselves moral theories. There is no escaping moral issues in normative analysis.* But there is a difference between thinking of sex as charged with moral significance and thinking of it as just another source of regulatory issues in the libertarian or laissez-faire theory of the state" (Posner, 1992: 181, my italics).

REFERENCES

Akerlof, G. 1984. *An Economic Theorist's Book of Tales.* Cambridge: Cambridge University Press.

Alchian, A., and H. Demsetz. 1972. "Production, Information Costs, and Economic Organization." *American Economic Review* 62: 777–95.

Becker, G. [1957] 1971. *The Economics of Discrimination.* Chicago: University of Chicago Press.

Bellas, M. 2000. "Consensual Relationships Between Professors and Students." Unpublished draft.

Elster, J. 1988. "Economic Order and Social Norms." *Journal of Institutional and Theoretical Economics* 144: 357–66.

———. 1989a. *Cement of Society.* Cambridge: Cambridge University Press.

———. 1989b. *Nuts and Bolts for the Social Sciences.* Cambridge: Cambridge University Press.

———. 1989c. "Social Norms and Economic Theory." *Journal of Economic Perspectives* 3: 99–118.

Epstein, R. A. 1992. *Forbidden Grounds: The Case Against Employment Discrimination Laws.* Cambridge, Mass.: Harvard University Press.

Gould, M. 1981. "Parsons versus Marx: 'An earnest warning...'" *Sociological Inquiry* 51: 197–218.

———. 1987. *Revolution in the Development of Capitalism: The Coming of the English Revolution.* Berkeley: University of California Press.

———. 1990. "The Problem of Order in Perfect and Imperfect Information Theories." Presented at the Annual Meeting of the American Economic Association. Washington, D.C.

———. 1991a. "Book Review. Jan Elster. *Nuts and Bolts for the Social Sciences.*" *American Journal of Sociology* 96: 1546–48.

———. 1991b. "The Generalized Media of Communication and the Logic of Cultural Intelligibility: Macro and Micro Analyses in Luhmann, Habermas and Parsons." Prepared for the Annual Meeting of the American Sociological Association. Cincinnati, Ohio.

———. 1991c. "Parsons' Economic Sociology: A Failure of Will." *Sociological Inquiry* 61: 89–101.

———. 1991d. "The Reproduction of Labour Market Discrimination in Competitive Capitalism." Pp. 102–29 in *Exploitation and Exclusion: Race and Class in Contemporary US Society,* edited by A. Zegeye, L. Harris, and J. Maxted. London: Hans Zell.

———. 1992. "Law and Sociology: Some Consequences for the Law of Employment Discrimination Deriving From the Sociological Reconstruction of Economic Theory." *Cardozo Law Review* 13: 1517–78.

———. 1993. "Legitimation and Justification: The Logic of Moral and Contractual Solidarity in Weber and Durkheim." Pp. 205–25 in *Current Perspectives in Social Theory,* vol. 13, edited by B. Agger. Greenwich, Conn.: JAI Press.

———. 1995a. "Unconscionability in Contract Law: Durkheim, Llewellyn and the Limits of Legal Realism." Proceedings of the 1995 Annual Meeting of the Research Committee on the Sociology of Law, International Sociological Association. Tokyo, Japan.

———. 1995b. "Unconscionability, Free Contract and the Law Against Employment Discrimination: Richard Epstein On and Against the Government's Fiduciary Responsibility for Contract Regulation." Presented at the Annual Meeting of the Law and Society Association. Toronto, Canada.

———. 1996. "Law and Philosophy: Some Consequences for the Law Deriving from the Sociological Reconstruction of Philosophical Theory." *Cardozo Law Review* 17: 3001–124.

———. 1997. "Sexual Consent and Contractual Consent: The Legitimation and Justification of Voluntary Actions." Prepared for the Annual Conference of the Research Committee on the Sociology of Law, International Sociological Association.

———. 1998. "The Law and Morality of Sexual Relationships: Consent and the Regulation of Sexual Relationships Between Employees and Students in Colleges and Universities." Prepared for the Annual Meeting of the American Sociological Association, San Francisco, Calif.

———. 1999. "Race and Theory: The Culture of Poverty and Adaptation to Discrimination in Wilson and Ogbu." *Sociological Theory* 17: 171–200.

———. 2000. "Culture, Personality and Emotion in George Herbert Mead: A Critique of Mindless Empiricism in Cultural Sociology." Prepared for the Annual Meeting of the American Sociological Association, Washington, D.C.

Gould, M., C. Heckscher, and F. Domurad. 1996. "Loyalty, Professionalism, and Rationality in Corporate Downsizing." Presented at the Annual Meeting of the American Sociological Association, New York, New York.

Luhmann, N. 1986. *Love as Passion: The Codification of Intimacy.* Trans. J. Gaines and D. L. Jones. Cambridge, Mass.: Harvard University Press.

Parsons, T. 1937. *The Structure of Social Action.* New York: Free Press.

———. 1960. "Durkheim's Contribution to the Theory of Integration of Social Systems." Pp. 118–53 in *Essays on Sociology and Philosophy,* edited by K. H. Wolff. New York: Harper Torchbooks.

———. 1964. *Social Structure and Personality.* New York: Free Press.

Parsons, T., and G. M. Platt. 1973. *The American University.* Cambridge, Mass.: Harvard University Press.

Posner, R. A. 1992. *Sex and Reason.* Cambridge, Mass.: Harvard University Press.

———. 1997. "Social Norms and the Law: An Economic Approach." *American Economic Review* 87: 365–69.

———. 1998a. "Symbols, Signals, and Social Norms in Politics and the Law." *Journal of Legal Studies* 27: 765–98.

———. 1998b. "The Problematics of Moral and Legal Theory." *Harvard Law Review* 111: 1637–1717.

———. 1998c. "Social Norms, Social Meaning, and Economic Analysis of Law: A Comment." *Journal of Legal Studies* 27: 553–66.

———. 1999. *An Affair of State: The Investigation, Impeachment, and Trial of President Clinton.* Cambridge, Mass.: Harvard University Press.

Posner, R. A., and E. B. Rasmusen. 1999. "Creating and Enforcing Norms, with Special Reference to Sanctions." *International Review of Law and Economics* 19: 369–82.

Stiglitz, J. E. 1985. "Credit Markets and the Control of Capital." *Journal of Money, Credit and Banking* 17: 133–52.

———. 1991. "The Invisible Hand and Modern Welfare Economics." NBER Working Paper 3541.

———. 1994. *Whither Socialism?* Cambridge, Mass.: MIT Press.

———. 1998. "Distinguished Lecture on Economics in Government: The Private Uses of Public Interests: Incentives and Institutions." *Journal of Economic Perspectives* 12: 3–22.

Index

Abbott, Andrew, 3
achievement, xl–xli
Ackerman, Charles, 67
action, 132, 168–70, 172–73, 183; cybernetic theory of, xlviii; frame of reference, xxxiv, xxxvi–xxxvii, xlii; general theory of, xii, xxvii, xxxi, xxxvi, 38, 63, 83, 90, 182; social, xxi, xxviii, xlii, 152–53, 155, 157, 163, 166, 214n2, 232–34, 237, 242n17; systems, xxxv–xxxviii, xliv, xlviii, 90, 149, 152, 159, 163, 182; voluntaristic theory of, xxiv, xxviii, xxxiii–xxxiv, liii, 6, 29, 49, 80, 233–34
"Action, Situation, and Normative Pattern" (Parsons), 242n14
Action Theory and the Human Condition (Parsons), xxxii, 182
adaptation, xxxi–xxxii, li, 101–3, 181. *See also* AGIL scheme (four-function paradigm)
affect, xlviii, lv, 142, 149, 169–72
affective neutrality, xxxix, xl–xli
affectivity, xxxix, xl–xli
affirmative action, xii
Agenda for Sociology: Classical Sources and Current Uses of Talcott Parsons's Work (Barber and Gerhardt), xv, 178
AGIL scheme (four-function paradigm), xxix, xliii–xlv, xlviii, 64, 82–84, 87, 90, 141–42, 148, 168–69, 233. *See also* adaptation; goal-attainment; integration;

pattern-maintenance/tension-management; system requisites
Albrow, Martin, 205
Alchian, Armen, 241n1
Alexander, Jeffrey C., 6–7, 22, 83, 178
Allport, Gordon W., xxxvi
American Societal Community (Parsons), 183
American Sociological Association, xxviii
American University, The (Parsons and Platt), 147, 149, 167, 182
Amherst College, xvii, xix–xx, xxii, 66
analytical elements, xxix, xxxi, xxxiv
analytical realism, xxiii, xxv–xxvi, liv
anthropology, xviii, xix, xxxvi–xxxvii, 93, 141
Antike Judentum (Weber), 53n41
"Approximate Definition of Fact, An" (L. J. Henderson), 76n14
Arato, Andrew, 209–13
ascription, xl–xli
autopoiesis, 132
Ayers, Clarence E., xix–xx, 66

Bales, Robert F., xliii
Banfield, Edward C., 144
Barber, Bernard, xi, xv–xvi, xviii, liv, 76n14, 79–80, 83–84, 84n2, 178, 214
Barnes, Harry Elmer, 36
Baum, Rainer C., 151–52
Beck, Ulrich, 88, 91–94, 217n24
Becker, Howard P., 7, 9, 23n8, 23n11, 37, 52n28, 52n30, 54n52, 214n1

247

About the Contributors

Bernard Barber is professor emeritus of sociology at Columbia University. He has had a long-standing and continuous concern for the clarification and use of Parsons's theory. He is the author of several essays on Parsons and of several books including *Science and the Social Order* (1978), *Constructing the Social System* (1993), and *Intellectual Pursuits: Toward an Understanding of Culture* (1998).

William J. Buxton is a professor in the Department of Communication Studies at Concordia University. He is the author of *Talcott Parsons and the Capitalist Nation-State* (1985) and (with Charles R. Acland) *The Politics of Knowledge and Information* (1998). He is also the coeditor (with Charles R. Acland) of *Harold Innis in the New Century: Reflections and Refractions* (1999). His current research is on the impact of Rockefeller philanthropy on academic and public life, the intellectual practice of Harold Innis, the history of the social sciences in the United States, and the history of the stereoscope.

Stephan Fuchs is an associate professor of sociology at the University of Virginia. He is the author of *The Professional Quest for Truth* (1992) and *Against Essentialism* (2001).

Uta Gerhardt, born 1938, is currently professor of sociology at the University of Heidelberg. Her previous positions include teaching and research at the University of London, Case Western Reserve, and the University of Konstanz. She is affiliated with the Minda de Gunzburg Center for European Studies at Harvard University. She was educated at the University of Frankfurt and Free University Berlin, where she read sociology, philosophy, history, and psychology. Her interest in Parsons dates back to the 1960s, when she first read *The Social System* with gusto. She started to work in the Harvard University Archives, using Parsons's papers there, from the late 1980s onward. Her publications of sixteen books and over 120 articles include *Talcott Parsons on National Socialism* (1993), a collection of Parsons's unpublished and published papers on the topic of national socialism, and *Agenda for Sociology: Classic Sources and Current Uses of Talcott Parsons's Work* (1999), edited together with Bernard Barber. Apart from Parsons, her main fields of interest are the social theory of Georg Simmel, the contribution of American social science to German reeducation after World War II, medical sociology, and the use of ideal types in qualitative research.

Mark Gould teaches sociology at Haverford College. He is author of *Revolution in the Development of Capitalism: The Coming of the English Revolution* (1987) and *Foundations of Internet Governance: Sources of Rules for a Global Network* (2001).

Victor Lidz studied sociological theory with Talcott Parsons as both an undergraduate at Harvard University and as a graduate student in the former interdisciplinary Department of Social Relations at Harvard University. From 1963 to 1968, he was research assistant to Parsons. As a faculty member in sociology at the University of Chicago and then the University of Pennsylvania in the 1970s, he taught courses including graduate seminars on the generalized symbolic media, with Parsons as visiting professor. Since 1989, Lidz has worked in the field of drug abuse research and is currently acting director of the Institute for Addictive Disorders, Department of Psychiatry, MCP Hahnemann University, in Philadelphia.

Lawrence T. Nichols is an associate professor of sociology at West Virginia University and the current editor of *The American Sociologist*. Professor Nichols has done extensive research on the history of sociology in the United States, with emphasis on events at Harvard University and the professional career of P. A. Sorokin. He has also published in several other areas, including white-collar crime, social problems, deviance and social control, sociological theory, corporate social responsibility, and alternate dispute resolution.

David Rehorick is professor of sociology at the University of New Brunswick in Canada. His publications and editorial contributions embrace sociological theory, applied social phenomenology, educational praxis, nursing and the sociology of the body, and the creative arts. He has served on five journal editorial boards, including review editor of *Human Studies*. David was appointed founding faculty member of The Miyazaki International College in Japan, where he also taught in 1996–97. He serves as qualitative methodology research consultant to The Fielding Institute. David is a member of the development team of Renaissance College, the first undergraduate leadership program in Canada.

Neil J. Smelser is director of the Center for Advanced Study in the Behavioral Sciences in Stanford, California, and University Professor Emeritus of Sociology at the University of California, Berkeley. Professor Smelser is a past president of the American Sociological Association. His many books include *Problematics of Sociology: The Georg Simmel Lectures, 1995* (1997) and *The Social Edges of Psycho-*

analysis (1999), and he is coeditor (with Jeffrey C. Alexander) of *Diversity and Its Discontents* (1999).

A. Javier Treviño teaches sociology at Wheaton College in Massachusetts. He has served as book review editor of *Society* magazine and, currently, as book review editor of the *Contemporary Justice Review*. He serves as general editor of the law and society series (Transaction Publishers) and as president of the Justice Studies Association. He is the author of *The Sociology of Law: Classical and Contemporary Perspectives* (1996).

Bryan S. Turner is currently professor of sociology at the University of Cambridge. He has also held professorial positions in Australia, Germany, and the Netherlands. He was the Morris Ginsberg Fellow at the London School of Economics in 1981 and an Alexander von Humbolt Fellow in 1987–88. His research interests have been in sociological theory, medical sociology, and the sociology of religion. He is the cofounding editor (with Mike Featherstone) of *Body & Society* and founding editor of *Citizenship Studies*. He is the editor of *The Talcott Parsons Reader* (1999) and of *Max Weber: Critical Responses* (1999).

Jonathan H. Turner is distinguished professor of sociology at the University of California, Riverside. He is the author of twenty-four books and 150 research papers. Most of his work seeks to develop scientific sociological theory. His current work is on the dynamics of face-to-face interaction and emotion, although he also has longstanding interests in macrolevel theorizing. He is the editor of the journal *Sociological Theory*.

Bruce C. Wearne is an Australian who gained a Ph.D. from La Trobe University, Melbourne, for his work on the theoretical development of Talcott Parsons up until 1951, when *The Social System* was published. This resulted in the book *The Theory and Scholarship of Talcott Parsons to 1951: A Critical Commentary* (1989). Between 1982 and 1998 Professor Wearne was employed in the teaching of sociology at Chisholm Institute of Technology and Monash University. Currently he is an honorary research associate for the School of Political and Social Inquiry at Monash, a member of the editorial board of *The American Sociologist*, general secretary of the Association for Christian Higher Education in Australia, and correspondent for the Center for Public Justice in Washington.